Every

PRAYER

in the Bible

Every

PRAYER

in the Bible

LARRY RICHARDS

Illustrated by
Paul Richards

THOMAS NELSON PUBLISHERS
Nashville

Library of Congress Cataloging-in-Publication Data

Richards, Larry, 1931–
    Every prayer in the Bible / Larry Richards ;
illustrated by Paul Richards.
        p.   cm.
    Includes indexes.
    ISBN 0-7852-4534-0
    1. Bible—Prayers.   I. Title.
BS680.P64R53   1998
242'.5—dc21   98-12171
                                                         CIP

Printed in the United States of America

2 3 4 5 6 7 8—03 02 01

CONTENTS

Every
PRAYER
in the Bible

EVERY PRAYER
AND PETITION

We learn to pray by praying. But we learn about prayer by looking into the Scriptures. In the Bible, we see ordinary people talking with God in natural, conversational speech. Their prayers grow out of all sorts of life situations, emerging as spontaneous cries for help, as laments, and as expressions of joy-filled thanks. In Scripture we also see the people of God at formal prayer as they gather for worship. Here spontaneous prose prayer is replaced by towering poems crafted to express the deepest human emotions to the God who loves and cares for His own.

Along with the many examples of both spontaneous and formal prayer in the Bible, we also find specific teaching on prayer given by Jesus and by the writers of the Epistles. This teaching, along with model prayers offered by Christ and the apostles, guides us into a deeper, warmer relationship with our God.

We learn to pray by praying. But we learn about prayer—and how to take our own first steps into the heart of God—by considering prayer as it is illustrated and modeled in the Word of God.

CHAPTER 1

WHAT'S IT ALL ABOUT?

INSIGHT INTO THE NATURE OF PRAYER

Genesis 1; Isaiah 40

When I think of prayer, the image that comes to mind is that of a small child, reaching up in trust to grasp the hand of a tall adult. The adult smiles, bends down, and gently takes the tiny hand in his own. The image, one of utter intimacy, is one I return to again and again. For I know that I am the child, and the adult is God, my Heavenly Father.

This image is precious to me, but it suggests a great paradox. How can a human being hope to have this kind of relationship with the God revealed by Scripture? Augustine of Hippo expressed his wonder at this idea in one of his prayers, as he cried out:

What are you, my God? What are you, but the LORD God Himself? You are the highest, the most righteous and the most powerful being. You are the most merciful, and yet the most just. You are the most mysterious, and yet the most present.

Augustine's prayer concluded,

What shall I say, O my God, my life, my holy joy? What can any man say when he speaks of you?

The awesome truth is that in prayer we approach One who is far beyond our ability to comprehend. The image of child and adult cannot communicate all the wonderful complexity of prayer, and yet this is basic to a biblical understanding of prayer's essence. In spite of the vast gulf between human beings and the Creator-King of the universe, we are somehow comfortable in His presence.

The prophet Isaiah wrote of the same wonder in one of his most familiar passages:

> Have you not known?
> Have you not heard?
> The everlasting God, the LORD,
> The Creator of the ends of the
>   earth,
> Neither faints nor is weary.
> His understanding is
>   unsearchable.
> He gives power to the weak,
> And to those who have no
>   might He increases strength.
> Even the youths shall faint and
>   be weary,
> And the young men shall
>   utterly fall.
> But those who wait on the
>   LORD

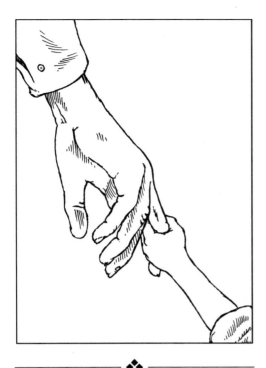

❖

Shall renew their strength;
They shall mount up with
   wings like eagles,
They shall run and not be
   weary,
They shall walk and not faint
   (Isa. 40:28–31).

God is utterly beyond us. And yet God is involved in our lives. God is so vast that the universe cannot contain Him. Yet He does bend down to take our hand. In that personal relationship we have with Him in Christ, the Lord God shares His strength with us when we are weary, and bears us up when we are faint.

The image of trusting child and caring adult is appropriate after all, even though the adult represents the awesome, sovereign, and holy Lord of all.

BIBLE WORDS FOR PRAYER

The Bible describes a God who is all-powerful and yet loving—a God who cares deeply for the human beings whom He created. Thus, we can expect the Bible's vocabulary of prayer to reflect this perception.

HEBREW WORDS FOR PRAYER IN THE OLD TESTAMENT

A number of Hebrew words are used to express the idea of prayer. Thus, the Old Testament's vocabulary of prayer is rich and meaningful.

`*Atar, "to pray, entreat."* Commenting on the use of this Hebrew word, *The Theological Wordbook of the Old Testament* (1980) stated:

> The biblical doctrine of prayer, as Eichrodt attests, is remarkable for the element of freedom from "any trace of hollow pathos or high-flown flattery; rather its marks are a childlike simplicity, sincerity and confidence" toward Yahweh. Further, in contrast to the prayer literature of the ancient Near East, there is not a "disparity between the prayer of the cultus and the prayer of the private individual:" (Eichrodt, *Theology of the Old Testament,* I, p. 175). Biblical prayer is spontaneous, personal, motivated by need, unconditioned by time or place. (Vol. II, p. 708).

Two incidents illustrate the relationship implied by this Hebrew word. Once when the Israelite tribes east of the Jordan were at war, they "cried out to God in the battle." The text tells us that "He heeded their prayer [literally, was entreated for them], because they put their trust in Him" (1 Chron. 5:20).

The other incident involved Manasseh, the most wicked of Judah's kings. Although Manasseh was committed to evil during most of his 55-year reign, near the end he was taken captive by the Babylonians. In Babylon, Manasseh turned to the Lord and humbled himself. The Chronicler tells us that God "received his entreaty, heard his supplication, and brought him back to Jerusalem into his kingdom" (2 Chron. 33:13). Truly converted, Manasseh spent his final years in an effort to reestablish worship of the Lord and to undo the harm he had caused.

In each of these situations, we see human beings looking to God for help in time of need. And in each situation, God responded by bending down to help. The tender care of

God for human beings, even the undeserving, is beautifully reflected in this Hebrew word which portrays prayer as entreaty.

Palal, "to pray." The most common word in the Old Testament for prayer, t^e*pilla*, found 76 times, is derived from this verb, which is itself translated "to pray" in the hithpael, the stem found in 80 of the 84 uses of the verb in the Old Testament.

A number of ideas are expressed by this root word—ranging from invoking God as judge, to calling on God to act as mediator and settle an issue, to seeking God's assessment and thus His intervention. The verb and the noun are both used most often of intercessory prayer. Five of the Psalms are identified as such prayers in their superscriptions (see Pss. 17, 86, 90, 102, 142).

Psalm 17 contains a beautiful section which conveys the awareness of the psalmist that God truly does care and is sensitive to the needs of His own. How clearly we see here the freedom the believer has to appeal to the God of the Bible.

> I have called upon You, for
> You will hear me, O God:
> Incline Your ear to me, and
> hear my speech.
> Show Your marvelous
> lovingkindness by Your right
> hand,
> O You who save those who
> trust in You
> From those who rise up against
> them.
> Keep me as the apple of Your
> eye;
> Hide me under the shadow of
> Your wings,
> From the wicked who oppress
> me,
> From my deadly enemies who
> surround me (Ps. 17:6–9).

In this psalm, we see David as a child of God, looking up for the hand which he is sure will be extended to him by a loving God.

Paga´, "to entreat, intercede." Paga´ is another word in Scripture's prayer vocabulary. The underlying meaning of the root is "to meet" or "to make contact with." In human interpersonal relationships, *paga´* conveys the idea of using one's influence on behalf of another (as in Gen. 23:8). A similar sense is reflected in God's warning to Jeremiah against praying for Judah at a time when He was about to judge the nation. God told the prophet, "Do not pray for this people, nor lift up a cry or prayer for them, nor make intercession to Me" (Jer. 7:16)—something which Jeremiah normally would have done.

Just as a person can contact another person on behalf of a friend, so God's people can come freely to entreat Him for others.

The *Theological Wordbook* notes one other implication: "An intercessor is one who makes 'contact' with God as opposed to the many who dabble in prayer" (Vol. II, p. 715). The intercessor is one who experiences a long-term and close personal relationship with the Lord, pleading for others in this relationship.

Shama´, "to hear, listen to." This common Hebrew word means "to hear" or "to pay attention to." It is sometimes used in the sense of answering prayer. Psalm 94:9 asks a question which has an obvious answer: "He who planted the ear, shall He not hear?" Surely God is fully aware of what His people say and ask.

The Old Testament believer knew God as One who cares. God not only *can* hear—but surely *will* hear—the prayers of His own. Thus, the psalmist can say confidently that "the righteous cry out, and the LORD hears, and delivers them out of all their troubles" (Ps. 34:17).

At the same time, the Old Testament protects our vision of prayer as expressive of a personal relationship with the Lord. Jeremiah was told that the people of Judah, who had refused to hear God's words and who had prayed to pagan deities, need not bother to cry out to Him when calamity comes, for "I will not listen to them" (Jer. 11:11–13). Prayer

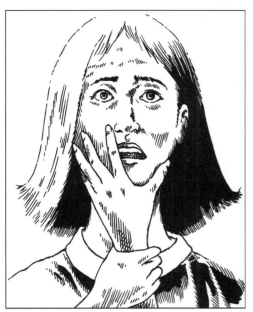

"The righteous cry out, and the LORD hears."

is a trusting act, a reaching out toward God by a person who truly relies on Him.

Sha´al, "to inquire, beg, ask." This verb is found 176 times in the Old Testment, typically with the meaning of asking someone for something. When the request is made by a superior, sha´al means "to demand." But when the request is made by an inferior, the word has the sense of seeking a favor.

The most common use of sha´al is to describe men and women asking or failing to ask God for guidance. David frequently looked to the Lord for guidance, acting on the Word God gave him (see 1 Sam. 23:2; 2 Sam. 2:1; 5:19).

Another typical use of sha´al is to describe requesting something specific from the Lord. The *Theological Wordbook* notes that men and women are seen in the Old Testament "beseeching him through prayer and through a prophet for the needs and the issues of life" (Vol. II, p. 891).

There is also a feminine noun derived from this verb. Sha˓ela means "request" or "petition," and is found 15 times in the Old Testament. This is the word used to describe Hannah's earnest prayer to God for a son (1 Sam. 1:27)—a prayer answered with the birth of Samuel.

Another feminine noun from this root is mish˓ala, which means "to petition" or "to desire." It is found only twice in the Old Testament, but each use is significant. Psalm 20:4 is itself a prayer: "May He grant you according to your heart's desire, and fulfill all your purpose [mish˓ala, petitions]. And Psalm 37:4 is a promise: "Delight yourself also in the Lord, and He shall give you the desires [mish˓ala, petitions] of your heart."

Hanan, "to be gracious." This verb in the hithpael stem means "to beseech," or to ask God to be gracious and kind. This is the word used in Psalm 30:8, in which David recalled that "I cried out to You, O LORD, and to the LORD I made supplication" (Ps. 30:8). God was indeed gracious, and He responded to David's request. The psalm concludes,

> You have turned for me my
> mourning into dancing;
> You have put off my sackcloth
> and clothed me with
> gladness,
> To the end that my glory may
> sing praise to You and not be
> silent.
> O LORD my God, I will give
> thanks to You forever
> (Ps. 30:11, 12).

Two nouns derived from this verb, t˓hinna and tahanun are translated "supplication." T˓hinna is the more formal term, and is found 24 times in the Old Testament. It is found most often in Solomon's prayer at the dedication of the Jerusalem temple, expressing the request that God will respond to His people's appeal for grace and mercy when they approach the Lord at His temple (see 1 Kings 8:30, 38; 2 Chron. 6:29, 35, 39). Tahanun is less formal and more expressive of intense emotion, as in Jeremiah 3:21, "A voice was heard on the desolate heights, weeping and supplications of the children of Israel."

*`Ana, "to answer, respond, speak, shout."* The most common meaning of this word is "to answer" or "to respond." In the imperative, `ana is a cry for God to answer, usually by delivering the petitioner. This sense is clearly displayed in Psalm 4:1, in which David begged,

Hear me when I call, O God
of my righteousness!
You have relieved me in my
distress;
Have mercy on me, and hear
my prayer.

The *Theological Wordbook* observes that "in all instances it is clear that 'to answer' the prayer is equivalent to looking with favor on the petition. The basis for such a petition is the righteousness, mercy, and veracity of God" (Vol. II, p. 679). Psalm 69:13 says it well: "O God, in the multitude of Your mercy, Hear me in the truth of Your salvation."

Na´, "I (we) pray." A final common prayer term is the "particle of entreaty," na´. One special use of this particle is in the Hebrew word *hoshi`ana,* or "hosanna," which means "O save us!" This particle occurs in Moses' heartfelt prayer to God for his sister, Miriam, when she was struck with leprosy (Num. 12:12).

Perhaps the most striking thing about the Old Testament vocabulary of prayer is that it maintains a consistent viewpoint on the relationship between God and human beings. The God worshiped by Old Testament saints is a God of power and glory, who looks kindly on human beings, in spite of His awesome nature. He can be appealed to freely, not because anyone has a right to demand His attention, but because He is rich in mercy, grace, and love. God will respond to believers who appeal to Him, moved by compassion for us in our need and by His heartfelt concern for our welfare.

How powerfully the Old Testament words for prayer and their use in the Scripture reflect the image of a child looking up trustingly, and an adult bending down to take a tiny hand in his own.

GREEK WORDS FOR PRAYER IN THE NEW TESTAMENT

The Greek words used to depict various aspects of prayer were in use long before the

Moses prayed earnestly, asking God to remove his sister's leprosy.

New Testament was written. But we should not attempt to define them by examining how they were used in classical Greek literature or in Hellenistic culture. As with terms found in the New Testament the vocabulary of prayer took on fresh meanings when used in the context of biblical faith. How the words are used in the context of faith defines their meaning.

Three sources help us determine that meaning.

First, we have the foundation for the biblical view of prayer established in early Genesis. All of Scripture derives its understanding of God and of man's relationship with God from this common source. As we have seen, Hebrew words for prayer clearly reflect the relationship defined there, and we would expect no radical change of viewpoint in the New Testament.

Second, we have the way the Greek words for prayer were used in the Septuagint, an early translation of the Hebrew Old Testament into Greek. The faith context of the Greek words was established by the usage of the Hebrew words which they translated.

Third, we can examine specific contexts in which Greek words for prayer are used in the New Testament itself.

Keeping these important points in mind, what words make up the New Testament vocabulary of prayer?

Proseuchomai, "to pray." This is the most common and inclusive Greek word for prayer. In classical Greek, *euchomai* was a technical term for invoking a deity. In the Septuagint—commonly symbolized by the letters LXX—*proseuchomai* normally translates *palal* in the hithpael, the standard Hebrew verb "to pray." The noun form, *proseuche,* "prayer," normally translates *t^epillah* and *tahanun.*

The verb *proseuchomai* occurs 85 times in the New Testament, and the noun *proseuche* occurs 37 times. Prayer is addressed either to God the Father or to Jesus, and the comprehensive nature of prayer is best illustrated in the Lord's Prayer (Matt. 6:9ff and Luke 11:2ff).

In this prayer, Jesus taught us to pray about all things, from our needs, symbolized by daily bread, to the coming of God's kingdom.

How wonderful that the God of Scripture remains concerned with our every need and is eager to be involved in every detail of our lives.

Aiteo, "to ask for." In classical Greek, words in this group had the basic meaning of wanting something. Depending on the situation and the context, *aiteo* would be translated as "to ask for," or even "to demand." The Hebrew equivalent as reflected in the Septuagint is *Sa'al,* "to desire," or "to request."

The verbs *aiteo* and *aiteomai* occur 70 times in the New Testament. Frequently, and wherever the New Testament identifies requests made to God, the text emphasizes that God hears such requests. Thus, Matthew 6:8 says, "Your Father knows the things you have need of before you ask Him," and John 15:7 assures us, "If you abide in Me, and My words abide in you, you will ask what you desire, and it shall be done for you."

And what a basis the New Testament provides in giving such assurances! God answers our prayers because He is our heavenly Father, who cares for us. As Jesus taught in Matthew 7:9–11,

What man is there among you who, if his son asks for bread, will give him a stone? Or if he asks for a fish, will he give him a serpent? If you then, being evil, know how to give good gifts to your children, how much more will your Father who is in heaven give good things to those who ask Him?

Prayer is an expression of our personal relationship with a God whom we know in and through Christ as our Father. We ask, because we rely on His love. And He answers, because He cares so deeply for His own.

Deomai, "to express a request." In the Septuagint, *deomai* is frequently used to render the Hebrew *hanan,* "to ask for grace or favor." The noun form, *deesis,* is also used in the Septuagint to translate many different Hebrew words.

The translation of *deomai* in 2 Corinthians 5:20 captures the warmth of this word, as Paul reminded the Corinthians that "we are ambassadors for Christ, as though God were pleading through us: we implore you on Christ's behalf, be reconciled to God."

In the majority of cases, however, *deomai* is used by individuals who come to Jesus with specific requests growing out of deep personal need, requesting and expecting His help. One incident, which captures both the sense of need and Christ's compassionate response to a request for grace, is reported in Luke 5:12, 13:

And it happened when He was in a certain city, that behold, a man who was full of leprosy saw Jesus; and he fell on his face and implored Him, saying, "LORD, if You are willing, You can make me clean." Then He put out His hand and touched him, saying, "I am willing; be cleansed." Immediately the leprosy left him.

We can confidently come to Jesus for grace to help, for Jesus is able. And Jesus is willing.

***Erotao*, "to ask, request."** In classical Greek, this verb meant to ask a question, or to put a question to an oracle or deity. In the LXX, *erotao* is commonly used to translated the Hebrew verb *sa'al*, "to ask." In the New Testament, *erotao* is used 62 times, with 27 of the usages in John's writings. An intensified form of the verb, *eperotao*, is found 56 times in the New Testament, typically in the Gospels.

When used of prayer rather than of asking a question, *erotao* and *eperotao* imply a close relationship—as between the disciples and Jesus or between Jesus and God the Father. This sense of intimacy is suggested in the story of Jesus' entering Simon Peter's house when Peter's mother-in-law was sick with a fever. The use of this intimate word for prayer seems quite natural in the report that "they made request of Him concerning her" (Luke 4:38). And, as requested by His friends, Jesus healed the sick woman.

***Gonypeteo*, "to fall on one's knees, kneel before."** In the Old Testament, this was an act of submission and homage (Ps. 95:6). In the New Testament, the word for kneeling, when associated with other words for prayer, indicated a sense of urgency growing out of a deep need.

Urgency is also expressed by two other words for prayer, each of which means "to cry out" or "to shout." *Boao* is used to express the cry of a blind man, desperate to attract Jesus' attention and beg for healing (Luke 18:38). The other word, translated "cry," *kraso*, is used in the parallel passage in Matthew 20:30, which described two blind men shouting out their need. *Boao* is also used of Jesus' cry on the cross (Mark 15:31).

How important it is to know that when we are desperate, we may cry out to the Lord, and He will hear and respond.

In addition to these words, *aineo* and *eucharisteo* are used to express praise and thanksgiving, while *entynchano* and *uperentynchano* are used in the sense of making intercession. These last two words are not found in the Septuagint, and are used in the New Testament only to refer to the intercession of Jesus and the Holy Spirit on behalf of God's people.

The deeply personal, intimate relationship of caring and dependence, of helping and gratitude that are reflected in the Bible's prayer vocabulary is summed up in the chart on the following page.

PRAYER AND OUR VIEW OF GOD

In his book *Jewish Prayer* (1986), Earl Klein noted that "in the pagan world, the origins of prayer were magic and incantation; the worshiper attempted to combat evil spirits and powers or influence the deities by spells or conjurations" (p. 1). As Klein rightly pointed out, biblical prayer is free of such influences.

The reason for this is that pagan and biblical concepts of God are diametrically opposed. And every person's approach to prayer will necessarily be shaped by his or her view of God.

PRAYER IN ROMAN RELIGION: A LEGAL TRANSACTION

The deities worshiped by the Romans were portrayed as supernatural but very "hu-

Basic Bible Words for Prayer

Original	Translations	Connotations
HEBREW		
`atar	to pray, entreat	Childlike confidence in and reliance on God.
palal	to pray	Calling on God to evaluate and intervene.
paga`	to entreat, intercede	Coming freely and making contact with God.
shama`	to hear, listen to	Confident expectation of God's response.
sha`al	to inquire, beg, ask	Seeking a favor from God.
sha`la	request, petition	Earnest prayer for something important.
sa`al	to desire, request	To seek from God what one wants or needs.
hanan	to supplicate, beseech	Relying on God's grace and kindness.
t`hinna	supplication	A formal appeal for grace and mercy.
tahanun	supplication	An emotional appeal for grace and mercy.
`ana	to answer, respond	A cry to God for deliverance.
na`	I pray	A particle indicating a phrase is a prayer.
GREEK		
proseuchomai	to pray	The basic word for prayer of any kind.
aiteo	to ask for	To seek from God because He cares for us as a Father.
deomai	to request	To ask, confident of God's grace and favor.
erotao	to ask, request	To seek guidance or response from a close Friend.
gonypeteo	to kneel	To urgently request help.
aineo	to praise, thank	To express gratitude to God.
eucharisteo	to praise, thank	To express gratitude to God.

man" beings. The gods and goddesses were ruled by the same passions that moved ordinary people, and they followed similar human customs. Ritual and prayer were largely designed to placate or please these powerful personalities and to ensure their benevolent attitude toward the people and the government.

In offering sacrifices and in ritual, the Romans assumed they were doing something for the gods and that the gods should do something for them in return. The practice of Roman religion was essentially public; priests and priestesses were charged with performing the correct rites and ceremonies. In time the rituals became so formalized that the slightest error in speech would invalidate a ceremony, and the presiding priest would have to do it all over again.

The prayers of individuals reflected the assumptions of these public ceremonies. The gods expected respect. When respect was shown, they would return the favor.

For example, in Cato's book on agriculture, *De AgriCultura,* he recommended that a farmer wishing to cut down trees should first sacrifice a pig to the deity of the grove. With the sacrifice of the pig, the farmer was "buying" the god's permission to cut down the trees. Cato even included the specific prayer which should be used on this occasion:

Whether you are a god or goddess to whom this grove is dedicated, as it is your right to receive a sacrifice of a pig for the thinning of this sacred grove, and to this intent, I or one at my bidding do it, may it be rightly done. To this end, in offering this pig to you I humbly beg that you will be gracious and merciful to me, to my house and household, and to my children. Will you deign to receive this pig which I offer you to this end?

The legal tone, and the careful wording of the prayer to cover all eventualities, are characteristic of Roman prayer. They reflect Roman assumptions about the basis of any relationship between humans and the gods.

PRAYER IN SUMERIAN RELIGION: BARGAINING WITH THE GODS

In the Atrahasis Story, a Sumerian document later translated into the Assyrian and

A sacrifice of a pig was intended to keep the god of the forest happy.

Babylonian languages, human beings are viewed as workers for the gods, created to take over chores which the younger gods did not want to do. As Part I, line 195 of the creation account records, the divine midwife Mami was told to

> Deliver Aborigines to labor for the
>   gods!
> Let them bear the yoke.
> Let them work of Enlil.
> Let them labor for the gods.

As the story continues, in less than 1,200 years earth became overpopulated with humans. The human hive was so noisy that the sleep of the gods was disturbed. After a bitter debate, one of the gods plotted to destroy the human race by means of a great flood. Another god warned the human hero Atrahasis, who prepared an ark for himself and his family.

When the flood came, even the gods were terrified. Even worse, after earth's population was wiped out and its temples flooded, the gods realized that there would be no sacrifices for them to eat or drink. Section III.iii of the story records the gods' complaints:

> Where is Anu, Our Leader, now?
>   Where are the humans to carry
>   out his commands?
> Where is he who so thoughtlessly
>   decreed a flood?
> . . . who condemned his own people
>   to destruction?

But after some seven days and nights, the floodwaters subsided, and the survivor, Atrahasis, prepared a sacrificial meal for the gods. Section III.v. of the story relates what happened.

> The gods smelled the aroma.
> They swarmed like flies around his sacrifice.

In the story, then, we see reflected the belief that while the gods had powers beyond those of humans, the gods were still dependent on human beings for sacrifices and offerings. And this gave humans a certain leverage for bargaining with the gods, as reflected in the following letter to a god found among documents dating from some 1,800 to 1,500 years before Christ.

Speak to Ida (the river-god) my lord: Thus Zimri-Lim your servant. I herewith send a gold cup to my lord. At an earlier date I wrote my report to my lord; my lord revealed a sign. May my lord make the sign which he revealed come true for me. Moreover, may my lord not neglect to protect my life, may my lord not turn his face elsewhere, besides me may my lord have need of no one else.

Prayer in pagan religions took on the nature of an exchange of benefits. In prayer, the worshiper bargained with a god, providing the god with something of value in exchange for the protection of the deity or other benefits.

PRAYER IN EGYPTIAN RELIGION: MANIPULATION OF THE GODS

The pantheon of Egypt was populated by a myriad of gods and goddesses, whose attributes and names were often confused. The Egyptians saw their gods as responsible for maintaining the harmony and balance of nature. The gods were also the guardians of the next world, which the Egyptians conceived of as a place where every happy activity of this life was to be continued.

The gods and goddesses of Egypt had little concern with individuals. Gaining their aid or gaining access to blessing in the afterlife was more a matter of manipulating the gods by magic than anything else. Joseph Kaster, in

The Wisdom of Ancient Egypt (1968), noted that the "necessary qualifications for eternal felicity are acquired with relative ease, by the method of magic ritual. If the various ceremonies attendant upon the preparation of the mummy of the deceased are observed, if the complicated funerary rituals are scrupulously performed, and extremely important, if the deceased takes along the book of efficacious magic spells and declarations that ensure his passing safely through the various perils on the way to the Other World . . . he will be justified before Osirus" (p. 38).

It is not surprising that a religion which relied on magic spells for acceptance in the other world should view requests for benefits in this world as matters for magic and incantation as well. Thus, in appealing for relief from a headache, a person might use the following spell.

O Ra, O Atum, O Shu, O Beg, O Nut, O Anubis who is before the Divine Shrine, O Horus, O Set, O Isis, O Nephthys, O Great Ennead, O Little Ennead, come ye and see your father who enters clothed in radiance to see the horn of Sekhmet! Come ye to remove that enemy, dead man or dead woman, male adversary or female adversary who is in the face of So-and-so, born of woman So-and-so!

These words were to be recited over a crocodile formed of clay with grain in its mouth, and having an "eye of patience" set in its head. A drawing on fine linen of the gods described was to be tied to the crocodile, and this was to be placed upon the sufferer's head. The assumption was that this prayer would be answered because of the spell, not out of any divine concern for the individual who prayed.

In another prayer-spell for driving away a headache, the petitioner actually threatened the gods he appealed to. If they did not do what the worshiper demanded . . . well, note the following threats:

As for the head of So-and-so, born of the woman So-and-so, it is the head of Osiris Wen-Nefer, on whose head were placed the three hundred and seventy-seven divine Uraei, and they spew forth flame to make thee quit the head of so-and-so, born of the woman So-and-so, like that of Osiris. If thou dost not quit the temple of so-and-so, born of the woman So-and-so, I will burn thy soul, I will consume thy corpse! I will be deaf to any desire of thine concerning thee. If some other god is with thee, I will overturn thy dwelling place; I will shadow thy tomb, so that thou wilt not be allowed to receive incense, so that thou wilt not be allowed to receive water with the beneficent spirits, and so that thou wilt not be allowed to associate with the followers of Horus.

If thou wilt not hear my words, I will cause the sky to be overturned, and I will cast fire among the Lords of Heliopolis! I will cut off the head of a cow taken from the Forecourt of Hathor! I will cut off the head of a hippopotamus in the Forecourt of Set. I will cause Sebek to sit enshrouded in the skin of a crocodile, and I will cause Anubis to sit enshrouded in the skin of a dog.

Additional threats followed, but the above clearly illustrate the conviction of the Egyptians that their deities could be manipulated and controlled by magic spells. This language also seems to reveal a contempt for the deities, as if the person who prayed had power over *them!*

THE IMPACT OF THE CONCEPT OF GOD IN PAGAN RELIGIONS

The above descriptions of the prayers of pagans are not exhaustive. The literature of each culture mentioned contains poems praising the gods that the people worshiped. Yet the prayers quoted above reveal much about the basic assumptions of the Romans, the Sumerians and other Mesopotamian peoples, and the Egyptians concerning the nature of their gods and humankind's relationship with them.

The Romans maintained a respectful attitude toward their gods, yet they assumed that something like a legal contract could be negotiated with them. By presenting something of value to the gods, the Romans expected the gods to behave appropriately, returning an equivalent benefit. The gods and human beings were viewed as parties who entered into formal contracts to the benefit of each.

The Sumerians and other Mesopotamian peoples assumed that the gods were in some sense dependent on human beings. The gods

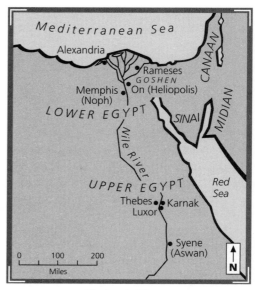

The Land of Egypt

fed on the sacrifices offered by humankind, and they were pleased by gifts such as the gold cup which Zimri-Lim offered to Ida, the river god.

While the Romans tended to assume a quasi-legal mutual obligation might exist between men and the gods, the Mesopotamian peoples hoped that by appeasing their gods the gods might favor them. The fact that the gods wanted what human beings could provide offered some prospect of bargaining successfully, although the gods of the ancient Near East were capricious and could not be counted on.

The attitude of the Egyptians, as expressed in their prayer-spells, was far more cynical. The gods were real, but they could be manipulated by magic. In some sense, human beings could gain power over the gods and force them to do man's will. Even access to heaven depended on having at hand the right magic spells by which to pass various tests imposed by the guardian deities of the otherworld.

While manipulation of the gods by means of magic spells was also an element in most

An Egyptian magician casting a spell

other pagan religions, this approach to prayer was most fully expressed in Egyptian religion.

THE IMPACT OF A BIBLICAL CONCEPT OF GOD ON CHRISTIAN PRAYER

Neither in Rome, Sumeria, nor Egypt would the image of a small child reaching out a trusting hand—or of an adult bending down to take the offered hand—bring prayer to mind. And yet for those of us who have a relationship with the God of Scripture, the image is both powerful and authentic.

The authenticity of this image is rooted in the Bible's creation story, which portrays an original relationship between God and human beings that is dramatically different from the relationship pictured in pagan myths.

God is the all-powerful Creator (*Genesis 1*). Genesis portrays a God who alone existed from all eternity. The universe in all its awesome majesty was His conception, and He

brought it into existence. Everything that exists, from the myriads of galaxies flung across apparently endless space, to the most minute detail of the genetic codes that program living creatures, was designed by Him. The vibrant, pulsing power of the stars represents an infinitesimal fraction of the energy God expended in bringing all things into being.

Even without the knowledge we today have of the size and greatness of the material universe, the psalmist David was overcome by creation's testimony to the greatness of God. He wrote,

> The heavens declare the glory
>   of God;
> And the firmament shows
>   his handiwork.
> Day unto day utters speech;
> And night unto night reveals
>   knowledge.
> There is no speech nor
>   language
> Where their voice is not heard.
> Their line has gone out
>   through all the earth.
> And their words to the end of
>   the world (Ps. 19:1–4).

Writing in Romans, the apostle Paul also reflected on the significance of the creation as a witness to God. Paul wrote that

what may be known of God is manifest in them, for God has shown it to them. For since the creation of the world His invisible attributes are clearly seen, being understood by the things that are made, even His eternal power and Godhead (Rom. 1:19, 20).

The very existence of the universe, and its complex design, point to the existence and power of the Creator.

And so the Genesis affirmation that in the beginning there was God, and that all that exists is His workmanship, is a defining statement for us. The God whom we know through the testimony of nature and Scripture is all-powerful and all-wise.

God crafted earth to be man's home (*Isaiah 45:18*). One of the most striking of Scripture's statements about creation is found in Isaiah 45:18:

> For thus says the LORD,
> Who created the heavens,
> Who is God,
> Who formed the earth and
>   made it,
> Who has established it,
> Who did not create it a waste,
> Who formed it to be
>   inhabited;
> I am the LORD, and there is no
>   other.

Note the phrase, "Who did not create it a waste, *who formed it to be inhabited.*" Earth is no sterile planet like Mars, nor is it wrapped in a corrosive atmosphere like Venus. Earth is the one known warm and friendly planet in the universe, carefully and lovingly shaped by God to be a home for human beings. Earth—warmed by the sun, bathed in rains, populated by fascinating and varied forms of life—was designed for one purpose: To be inhabited by the family of man.

God created human beings for fellowship with Him (Genesis 1:27; Genesis 2:7). The early Genesis vision of the origin of human beings and of our relationship to God is vastly different from that seen in pagan religions. Humans are no "aborigines," created as an afterthought to do menial work for deities. Human beings are special to God.

God created human beings in His image (Genesis 1:26, 27). Perhaps the most stunning of the assertions of Genesis is that God made human beings in His own image and likeness. The two critical words, *image* and *likeness,* are linked in the Hebrew text to form a unique term, *image-likeness.* God not only created human beings. In forming men and women, God shared something of Himself with humankind. Those wonderful and special qualities that make God a person—His ability to love, to think, to design, to appreciate beauty, to communicate, to value and to make moral judgments—all this

and more God infused into Adam and Eve, to be transmitted to our race.

Human beings alone of all earthly creatures have the potential of relating to and responding to God. With human beings alone God chose to share His image-likeness.

God gave human beings dominion over our planet (Genesis 1:28). Only human beings, who share God's image-likeness, were capable of caring for life on our planet. The biblical gift of dominion is not a right to exploit earth's resources, as some have thought, but rather it is the privilege of guarding and caring for living creatures. In giving mankind dominion, God trusted His wonderful life-bearing planet into humankind's hand.

God created Adam and Eve personally (Genesis 2:7, 22). While the rest of the universe, including living creatures, was created by God's spoken word, early Genesis describes the creation of man in different terms. God stooped to personally form Adam's body from the dust of the earth, and then gently breathed into Adam the gift of life. Later God removed a rib from Adam and formed Eve from Adam's substance. God's intimate, personal involvement in forming human beings sets humankind apart from all the rest of creation.

Understanding this special relationship of human beings with God, the psalmist expressed awe at God's demonstrated concern for us. He wrote,

> When I consider Your
>   heavens, the work of Your
>   fingers,
> The moon and the stars, which
>   You have ordained,
> What is man that You are
>   mindful of him,
> And the son of man that You
>   visit [care for] him?
> For You have made him a little
>   lower than the angels,
> And You have crowned him
>   with glory and honor
>   (Ps. 8:3–5).

God desired human beings to reach their full potential (Genesis 2). The early Genesis description of God's design of the Garden of Eden emphasizes His concern for human beings. The garden where the first humans were placed was designed to give Adam and Eve the opportunity to use each of the wonderful capacities God gave them.

God made Eden beautiful, that man might appreciate beauty as God Himself does. He permitted man to tend the garden, that Adam and Eve might know the joy of doing significant work.

He set the Tree of Knowledge of Good and Evil in the garden, and commanded Adam and Eve not to eat its fruit, so they might exercise His capacity for making moral choices. The Lord permitted Adam to name living creatures, and so share in God's creative work.

In the process of naming the animals, God taught Adam His need for a companion who shared His nature and who could relate to Him on every level of His personality. Then God made Eve, enabling the two to experience a fellowship modeled on the fellowship God Himself experienced within the Trinity— a fellowship which Adam also experienced at first in conversation with the Lord.

How different this picture of God's loving concern for human beings is from the distorted images of man's relationship with deity reflected in the creation myths of the ancient world!

God acted to restore fallen human beings (Genesis 3:21). Early Genesis tells of the choice Adam and Eve made to disobey God. This disastrous choice warped human nature, distorting all the wonderful gifts God had shared with Adam and Eve in forming them in His image-likeness. The image-likeness persisted (Gen. 9:6; James 3:9). But the Fall warped humankind and set man on a course of wickedness and hostility toward God.

Yet even after the Fall, God loved Adam and Eve, and sought out the first pair. Their choice had terrible consequences, but God's

God furnished Adam and Eve with their first clothing.

love for humankind was unchanged. God Himself provided history's first sacrifice for sin, as the Lord clothed Adam and Eve with a covering of animal skins (Gen. 3:21).

This first indication of God's commitment to restore fallen human beings foreshadows the death of Christ on the Cross. Today Calvary stands as the ultimate proof of God's redeeming love. Yet how impossible then for Adam and Eve to imagine that God would care so much for humankind that He Himself would step into the flow of history to pay the price for sin that justice demands. He provided forgiveness and offered a return to innocence for all who accept His invitation to trust His amazing grace.

The more clearly we understand the implications of the creation story, the more comfortable we become with the image of God as an all-powerful, loving, caring person. And the more comfortable we become with the image of prayer as an expression of child-like trust in Him.

CONCLUSIONS

This brief survey of prayer from both pagan and Christian traditions highlights several vital truths.

First, a people's approach to prayer is rooted in their view of God and of His relationship with human beings.

Second, the Bible's depiction of God and of our relationship with Him is unique, rooted in the Genesis creation account. In that account, God is Creator, and human life is singularly special to Him. The God of the Bible truly cares for human beings. Those who trust the God of Scripture come to Him spontaneously, joyfully, and freely.

The biblical words for prayer are notable for the way in which they picture the relationship between God and those who trust in Him. God is all-powerful, able to act on man's behalf. God is caring, deeply concerned for our welfare. This God can and will answer the prayers addressed to Him.

On the other hand, we human beings are limited, subject to all sorts of trials. We are dependent on God's goodwill and on His grace. The wonderful message of God's Word is that those who trust the Lord are invited to appeal to Him at any time. We can freely and spontaneously express our every need to Him, as well as offer praise and thanksgiving. And we can be sure that God hears our prayers, and will act in our best interest simply because of His compassion, love, and grace.

And so we return to the image of prayer with which we began. We are like little children, reaching our hand up to God, confident that He cares. And as we pray, our wonderful God reaches down to take our hand in His. He enfolds us in His love; and with our hand in His, we rest secure.

CHAPTER 2

"O LORD, REMEMBER ME!"

OLD TESTAMENT PETITION

Selected Old Testament Scriptures

I was just three years old. When my mother tried to teach me to pray, I would shake my head. I didn't know how to pray.

Then one day I was playing Columbus. I "came ashore" by climbing onto the living room sofa. Using a stick as a flag, I claimed the new land for Spain, and then told God "thank You" for my safe journey over the sea.

My mother, who was sewing, looked up and said, "That's praying."

Surprised, I said, "That's praying? Why, that's easy!"

One of the most wonderful truths of the Christian life is that prayer truly is easy. Perhaps the best place to discover this truth is to look at the prose prayers woven throughout the Old Testament. These prayers are different from the beautifully crafted prayer poetry that we find in the Psalms. Nearly 100 prose prayers are imbedded in Old Testament narrative passages. While many were uttered by important persons like kings or prophets, over a third are prayers uttered by ordinary men or women.

Several things are fascinating about these prose prayers.

First, it's clear that Old Testament saints felt free to speak to the Lord at any time and in any place. It wasn't necessary to go to the tabernacle or the temple to speak freely with God.

Second, Old Testament prose prayers grew out of the life-experiences of believers, reflecting the circumstances of their lives. These were not prescribed or formal prayers to be repeated again and again; they were spontaneous expressions tailored to the moment.

Third, Old Testament prose prayers resemble ordinary speech. They are filled with natural expressions that parallel the way people talk with one another. Old Testament saints spoke with God as naturally as they spoke with one another.

Each of these characteristics of prose prayer is implied in saying that prayer is "easy." We can speak to God any time, any place. Whatever our situation, we can share our experience or express our need to the Lord. We can speak to Him naturally and conversationally, just as we would to a human friend.

In this chapter we want to look at one of the four basic types of Old Testament prose prayers: Petition. In the next chapter we will look at other types of prose prayer: Complaint, confession, and blessing. Also in that chapter we will look at specific teachings about prayer found in the Old Testament.

CHARACTERISTICS OF PETITIONARY PROSE PRAYER

In his book *Biblical Prose Prayer* (1983), Moshe Greenberg analyzed elements in three typical prayers of petition. Greenberg's analysis helps us identify characteristics of prayers of petition.

The first prayer, found in Numbers 12:13, is the simplest. The sister of Moses, Miriam, had been stricken with leprosy for challenging Moses' leadership. Moses' prayer consisted of a phrase addressing God and the petition itself.

Address:	O God, I pray
Petition:	Please heal her.

Samson's prayer recorded in Judges 16:28 is as direct, but another element is added: Motivation. Samson gave the reason he wanted the prayer answered; a reason which may also suggest why God should answer the prayer. Blinded by the enemies of God's people, Samson had been led into a Philistine temple to be displayed as a trophy demonstrating the power of their deity. Resting his hands on the pillars that supported the temple roof, Samson begged God to return his lost strength.

Address:	O LORD God
Petition:	Remember me, I pray! Strengthen me, I pray, just this once!
Motivation:	That I may with one blow take vengeance on the Philistines for my two eyes.

An example of an even more complex prayer of petition is found in Genesis 32:9–13. Jacob was returning to Canaan after twenty years of exile. But Jacob was afraid of his brother Esau, who had threatened his life two decades before. In his petition Jacob followed the basic pattern of petitionary prayer, but added considerable detail. Especially significant is Jacob's expression of his fears.

Address:	O God of my father Abraham and God of my father Isaac, the LORD
(Detail:)	Who said to me, "Return to your country and to your family, and I will deal well with you:"
(*Personal:*)	I am not worthy of the least of all the mercies and of all the truth which You have shown Your servant;
(Detail:)	for I crossed over this Jordan with my staff, and now I have become two companies.
Petition:	Deliver me, I pray, from the hand of my brother, from the hand of Esau;
(*Personal:*)	for I fear him, lest he come and attack me and the mother with the children.
Motivation:	For You said, "I will surely treat you well, and make your descendants as the sand of the sea, which cannot be numbered for multitude."

Jacob's extended petition displays themes which form the foundation of this form of biblical prose prayer. Jacob looked to God as the only reliable source of help. He hoped for God's help, not because he was worthy but because God was gracious and faithful. Jacob counted on God to answer for he was aware that he had a personal relationship with the Lord.

The consciousness of a personal relationship rooted in God's grace makes it natural for us to turn to the Lord in time of need.

Fear of his brother prompted Jacob to seek God's help.

EVERY OLD TESTAMENT PROSE PETITION

GENESIS 17:18
"Oh, that Ishmael might live before You."

God had just promised Abraham that Sarah, 90 years old, would bear his child. Abraham asked God to permit his son Ishmael, born of Sarah's slave Hagar, to inherit the covenant promises God had given to him. God did promise to bless Ishmael, but He told Abraham that the covenant promises would be given to the son Sarah would bear, who was to be named Isaac.

God both granted and denied Abraham's petition. He responded to the *intent* of the prayer in promising to bless Ishmael. He denied the specific request, in reserving the covenant for Isaac. Even when God says "no" to what we request, He will often say "yes" and satisfy the desire that moved us to petition Him.

GENESIS 18:22–33
"Would you also destroy the righteous with the wicked? Suppose there were fifty righteous within the city."

Abraham had just been told by the Lord that He intended to destroy Sodom and Gomorrah. As two angels headed toward the rich plains where these cities were located, Abraham entreated God to spare the cities for the sake of fifty righteous people who might live there. In response to Abraham's prayer of intercession, God promised to spare the cities if fifty righteous persons could be found. Hesitantly but boldly, Abraham—aware that he who was "but dust and ashes have taken it upon myself to speak to the LORD"—then asked God to spare the cities for forty, then thirty, then twenty, and finally ten. God granted Abraham's request, and promised to spare the cities for the sake of ten righteous people.

But, as the angels discovered, the only righteous man in the cities was Lot, Abraham's nephew. Rather than slay the righteous with the wicked, the angels helped Lot and his family to escape. Only then were the cities destroyed.

The story is rich in implications for our prayer lives. We should never be afraid to speak to God on behalf of others. Events at Sodom showed that God is far more concerned for individuals than we can ever be!

GENESIS 24:11–14
"O LORD God of my master Abraham, please give me success this day."

Abraham's servant had been sent to select a bride for Isaac from among Abraham's relatives. When the servant reached the town where the relatives lived, he asked God to guide him to the young woman "You have appointed."

The servant's petition is specific and detailed. He described what the chosen woman should say and do that "by this I will know that You have shown kindness to my master" (Gen. 24:14). The prayer was answered immediately, "before he had finished speaking" (Genesis 24:15).

GENESIS 28:3, 4
"May God Almighty bless you."

These words were addressed to Jacob by Isaac, when Jacob was sent to take a wife from the daughters of his mother's brother, Laban. While the words were spoken to Jacob, they were in fact a prayer to the Lord *for* Jacob.

GENESIS 32:9–12
"O God of my father Abraham . . . deliver me, I pray, from the hand of my brother."

(See the analysis of Jacob's request on page 18.)

This prayer is notable for the freedom with which Jacob expressed his sense of unworthiness and his fears to the Lord. Such free expression of emotions is characteristic of many of the psalms. While relatively few prose prayers include this much sharing, it is clear that most prose prayers in Scripture come from the heart. We should never hesitate to tell God our thoughts and feelings, for we can be sure that He cares.

Another special feature of Jacob's prayer is seen in what Greenberg calls its "motivation"—the reasons stated for why God should answer it. Jacob reminded God that He had promised to treat Jacob well and to give him many descendants. Only by protecting Jacob in this situation could the Lord be true to His word.

What confidence we can have when we know that our prayer is definitely in the will of God.

GENESIS 43:14
"May God Almighty give you mercy before the man."

An aged Jacob faced the fact that unless he permitted his sons to return to Egypt for food, the family would starve. The ruler of Egypt—who, unknown to Jacob, was his own son Joseph—had demanded that Jacob's youngest son Benjamin come to Egypt

with the brothers or they would get no food.

Although the words were addressed to Jacob's oldest son, Judah, they constitute a prayer to God. This prayer might be titled "the prayer of the helpless." Whatever the outcome, all Jacob could do was surrender to the demand of Egypt's ruler. His only hope was that God would be merciful.

Often we are also helpless captives of our circumstances. At such times, we can do no more or no less than Jacob did here: act as we must and leave the outcome to God. Yet we can do so with confidence, knowing that our God is both loving and merciful. He may have shaped our circumstances for reasons we cannot imagine, but which we may discover later as Jacob did.

EXODUS 32:11–13
"LORD why does Your wrath burn hot against Your people?"

While Moses was on Mount Sinai receiving the Ten Commandments, the Israelites at the base of the mountain worshiped a golden idol. God expressed a desire to wipe out the Israelites and make a new nation from Moses' offspring. But Moses pleaded with God to relent. His prayer is significant because it consists almost entirely of motivation, giving reason upon reason why God should relent.

Moses argued that God's reputation was at stake. He had shown His power in bringing Israel out of Egypt. It followed that He must successfully complete His purpose for them. God's dependability was also at stake. The Lord had promised to create a nation from the descendants of Abraham, Isaac, and Jacob; and He must keep His promise.

The text tells us, "So the LORD relented." We can be confident in prayer when our request is not to satisfy our desires but to maintain God's reputation and to display His faithfulness to His word.

EXODUS 32:31, 32
"Oh, these people have committed a great sin."

Moses ordered death for those Israelites who worshiped the golden idol (see above).

Time after time, Moses begged God to forgive the children of Israel.

He then turned to God to ask forgiveness for the people.

The request underlines the biblical concept of community guilt. Every member of a community bears some responsibility for the group's moral commitments.

In response to Moses' plea, God promised to send His angel before the Israelites as Moses led them to Canaan. But this blessing should not be misunderstood as divine blindness to sin. God warned, "Whoever has sinned against Me, I will blot him out of My book" (Ex. 32:33) and "I will visit punishment upon them for their sins" (Ex. 32:34).

God is gracious, and He will forgive. But God will not protect individuals or nations from the natural consequences of their sins.

EXODUS 34:9

"Let my Lord, I pray, go among us, even though we are a stiff-necked people; and pardon our iniquity and our sin, and take us as Your inheritance."

Moses had just been given a unique revelation of God, which emphasized His mercy and justice. In response, Moses worshiped and prayed.

God promised to drive out the inhabitants of Canaan before Israel, but in return He commanded the Israelites to expel all the Canaanites and purge the land of pagan worship, lest the Israelites "play the harlot with their gods" (Ex. 34:15).

God will answer our prayers, but He expects us to be as committed to Him as He is to us.

NUMBERS 12:13

"Please heal her, O God, I pray!"

(See the analysis on page 18.) The simple cry of the heart is perhaps the purest form of petition.

NUMBERS 14:19

"Pardon the iniquity of this people, I pray."

God had brought the Israelites to the border of Canaan and told them to attack the Canaanites. In spite of the pleas of Moses, Aaron, Joshua, and Caleb, the Israelites refused to obey God. Their rebellion aroused God's anger, leading Moses to plead with God not to destroy His people.

Moses then pleaded with God not to wipe out the Israelites. This prayer, parallel to

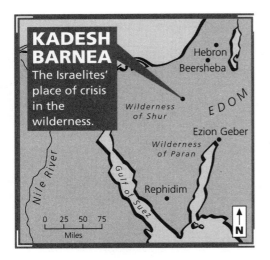

KADESH BARNEA
The Israelites' place of crisis in the wilderness.

the prayer recorded in Exodus 32:11–13 (see page 20), focuses on motivation as Moses lists reasons why God should not destroy the people. In this prayer, Moses appealed again to God's concern for His reputation (Num. 11:13–16). But Moses also based his appeal on the character of God as merciful as well as just (Num. 11:18, 19).

In response to Moses' prayer, God pardoned the people. But they were condemned to wander in the wilderness until all the adults who rebelled had died. God would bless the children of the rebels but not the rebels themselves.

We can ask God for pardon and for mercy. God will be merciful. But when we rebel, we must expect to live with the consequences of our actions, even when God chooses to forgive.

NUMBERS 16:15
"Do not respect their offering."

When Korah, a Levite, challenged Moses' leadership, Moses proposed a test. They and Korah's followers would appear before the Lord with an offering, and the Lord would choose. Moses, angry that people who had recently rebelled against God should now criticize Him and demand leadership, called on God not to respect their offerings.

NUMBERS 16:22
"Oh God . . . shall one man sin and You be angry with all the congregation?"

God was more angry with Korah and his followers (see above) than Moses, and He threatened again to wipe out the Israelites (see above). This time Moses appealed to God to punish only the guilty. Moses warned the people to move away from the tents of the rebels, and God tore open the earth, creating a chasm into which the rebels and all their possessions fell.

NUMBERS 27:16, 17
"Let the LORD . . . set a man over the congregation."

Moses had been told that he would soon die. His prayer was not for himself, but for the people whom he led. The prayer was answered, and God told Moses to ordain Joshua for this role.

DEUTERONOMY 1:11
"May the LORD God of your fathers make you a thousand times more numerous than you are."

These words were addressed to all Israel, but they were a prayer *for* Israel. (See also Gen. 28:3, 4.) Moses was sure God would answer this prayer, for the motivation appealed to God's own promise to bless.

DEUTERONOMY 3:23–25
"O LORD God . . . I pray, let me cross over and see the good land beyond the Jordan."

Moses recalled a prayer in which he entreated God to let him enter the land of Canaan. Moses had witnessed the beginning of the deliverance God promised Israel. He yearned to see the conclusion of what God had begun.

But God told Moses to speak no more of the matter. He had already announced that Moses would not be allowed to cross the Jordan River into Canaan (see Num. 20:8–12).

We are free to bring almost any request to God. But we cannot expect God to be pleased when we beg for something which is against His known will.

DEUTERONOMY 9:25–29

"I prayed to the LORD, and said, O LORD God, do not destroy your people."

This prayer recalls Moses' earlier intercession for Israel when the people refused to enter Canaan. (See the original prayer recorded in Num. 14:13–19, discussed on page 21.)

JOSHUA 10:12

"Then Joshua spoke to the LORD . . . and he said in the sight of Israel, "Sun, stand still."

In spite of a rain of hailstones which killed many enemy soldiers, Joshua desperately wanted the battle to bring total victory. When evening approached, Joshua feared that some of the enemy might escape. He called on God for a miracle. The Lord answered Joshua's prayer, and the sun illuminated the battlefield for an extra 12 hours, during which the enemy force was completely destroyed.

JUDGES 6:36–39

"If you will save Israel by my hand as You have said—look, I shall put a fleece of wool on the threshing floor."

God commissioned Gideon to lead the Israelites against a foreign foe. Gideon had sent out messengers, and thirty-two thousand men had responded. But Gideon was still fearful and uncertain. He begged God for a "sign," an unusual or miraculous event, to reassure him. The familiar passage relates how, in response to Gideon's petition, God made the fleece damp with dew and the ground dry, and then made the fleece dry while the ground was wet.

The significance of this prayer is often misunderstood, as some Christians suggest we "put out the fleece"—ask God for a sign—in order to determine His will. Yet in the Bible's

BIBLE BACKGROUND:

DID THE SUN STAND STILL?

Discussing this miracle, the book *Every Miracle and Wonder in the Bible* (Nelson, 1998) notes:

Commentators who do not simply dismiss this wonder as a fiction have debated the real nature of this miracle. Is the description phenomenological? That is, does the text describe what Joshua and the Israelites *saw?* If so, God may have performed a local miracle, causing the sun's light to shine on Israel while the rest of the world experienced normal day and night. Or does the text make a *scientific* statement? If so, God may have halted the earth's rotation, with all the adjustments that would involve. In either cause, the prolongation of daylight was a miracle.

In commenting on this miracle, the text says "there has been no day like that, before it or after it." But what made the day unique was not extension of daylight. What made the day unique was "that the LORD heeded the voice of a man."

Normally God informed men that a miracle would take place. But here Joshua himself "invented" and asked for the miracle. And God did just as Joshua asked (see above).

Joshua's prayer was special indeed!

account, Gideon already knew the will of God. He had acted on God's command in tearing down his local community's altar to Baal (Judg. 6:24–32). He had also responded to the Holy Spirit's prompting in calling for men to join him to fight the enemy (Judg. 6:33–35). Gideon prayed for reassurance, not knowledge of God's will. And this God graciously provided.

We do not need signs today to determine God's will. Just like Gideon, we have the objective word of Scripture and the presence of God's Spirit. We need to rely on these sources for guidance, not on "signs."

JUDGES 13:8

"O my LORD, please let the Man of God whom You sent come to us again and teach us what we shall do for the child who will be born."

The couple who would become the parents of Samson had been promised a son. Aware of the weight of this responsibility, Manoah and his wife asked God for special guidance on how to rear their child.

The Lord provided the guidance requested. But the life of Samson was notable not so much for Samson's physical strength as for his moral and spiritual weakness! This prayer reminds us that even the most godly parents, who follow the guidance provided in God's Word, cannot guarantee godly children.

Each person makes his or her own choices, and each of us is flawed.

How important it is to continue in prayer for our children. And to remember that Samson was used by the Lord, in spite of his flaws.

JUDGES 16:28

"O LORD God, remember me I pray! Strengthen me, I pray, just this once, O God, that I may with one blow take vengeance on the Philistines for my two eyes!"

(The structure of Samson's prayer is analyzed on page 18.)

Of special note is the motivation expressed. Samson asked God to strengthen him so he could take personal vengeance on the Philistines.

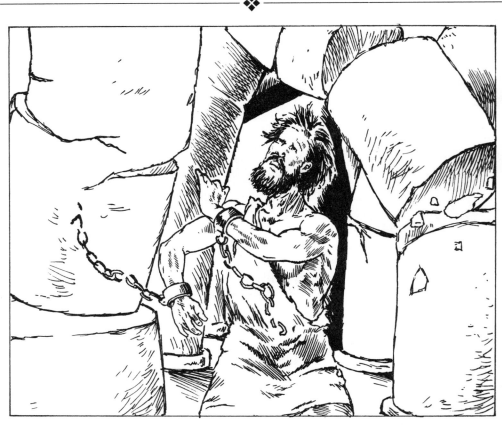

God's answer to Samson's prayer led to a fatal finish for Samson and hundreds of Philistines.

As a judge, Samson was commissioned to lead and to protect God's people. But throughout his life, Samson had been selfish, as reflected in this prayer. He put himself rather than God or God's people first.

Still, Samson's selfish prayer corresponded with God's intent to support the Israelites. The prayer of Samson was answered, and he used his restored strength to topple a Philistine temple. This one act killed more of Israel's enemy than Samson had done during his entire lifetime.

RUTH 1:9
"The LORD grant that you may find rest, each in the house of her husband."

Naomi, planning to return to Judah from Moab after the death of her husband and her two sons, was speaking to her two daughters-in-law. Although addressing the two women, these words were a prayer *for* them, that they might find happiness in second marriages.

1 SAMUEL 1:11
"O LORD of hosts, if You will indeed look on the affliction of Your maidservant . . . but will give Your maidservant a male child, then I will give him to the LORD."

Childless Hannah wept in anguish before the tabernacle as she pleaded with the Lord for a son. This prayer has often been cited as an example of "bargaining with God," and thus something less than "pure" prayer.

It should be noted, however, that the text identifies Hannah's prayer as a "vow." The only Old Testament parallel to the "if . . . then" form of her prayer, found in Genesis 28:20, 21 is also identified as a vow. What is special about the Old Testament vow? The content of a vow was never something that God commanded or required. The vow was also an expression of devotion and thanksgiving.

God did answer Hannah's prayer. And Hannah did fulfill her vow. The child she dedicated to the Lord was Samuel, Israel's last judge, who helped Israel make the transition from a loose coalition of tribes to a united monarchy.

1 SAMUEL 1:17
"Go in peace, and the God of Israel grant your petition which you have asked of Him."

Again we have words addressed to a person in the form of a prayer *for* her. The prayer was offered by Eli, who was high priest at the time, on behalf of Hannah, who had prayed for a son.

2 SAMUEL 7:18–29
"Now, O LORD God, the word which You have spoken concerning Your servant and concerning his house, establish it forever and do as You have said."

David had hoped to build a temple to God in Jerusalem. The prophet Nathan told David not to build the temple. Nathan then stunned the disappointed king by conveying God's promise to establish David's throne "forever."

The words that Nathan spoke are called the Davidic Covenant, and the promise made is fulfilled in Jesus Christ, a descendant of David. Jesus, raised from the dead and exalted in heaven, will one day rule earth as David's rightful successor—and of His kingdom there will be no end.

David's prayer to God in response to the Lord's promise expresses humble wonder that God should choose David (2 Sam. 7:18–20). It also expresses David's awareness that the promise was rooted in God's choice to be gracious (2 Sam. 7:21–24). David then called on the Lord to keep His promise and expressed his confidence that God would do for David everything that He had said (2 Sam. 7:25–28).

The final words of the prayer entreat God to keep His promise: "Now therefore, let it please You to bless the house of Your servant, that it may continue forever before You; for You, O LORD God, have spoken it, and with Your blessing let the house of Your servant be blessed forever" (2 Sam. 7:29).

This extended prayer of David reflects a number of qualities of prose prayer. David's emotions—of wonder, humility, awe, and thanksgiving—come through strongly. The repetition and seemingly jumbled thoughts mark the prayer as spontaneous and unplanned, This prayer is very different from David's many carefully crafted praise poems recorded in Psalms. David simply poured out his heart to God, without worrying about the form of the prayer.

What freedom David felt in speaking to the Lord! And what freedom we have, too.

2 SAMUEL 14:17

"And may the LORD your God be with you."

This expression, addressed to David, was a prayer for David, that he might have the wisdom to make a significant moral decision.

2 SAMUEL 15:31

"O LORD, I pray, turn the counsel of Ahithophel into foolishness."

When David, fleeing from his son Absalom, heard that his old advisor Ahithophel had gone over to the enemy, David uttered this spontaneous prayer. Such brief, spontaneous prayers emphasize how aware we should be of God's presence and of His involvement in our experiences.

2 SAMUEL 24:3

"Now may the LORD your God add to the people a hundred times more than they are, and may the eyes of the lord the king see it. But why does my lord the king desire this thing?"

David had determined to conduct a military census of Israel. His general, Joab, expressed a prayer, speaking to David but at the same time praying *for* him. However, the wording seems stilted and formal, lacking the spontaneity of most Old Testament prose prayers. Joab hesitated to object to his king's plans, and so he prefaced his question with a polite expression of good wishes.

How easy it is for us to replace true prayer to God with phrases intended to impress others.

1 KINGS 1:36

"Amen! May the LORD God of my lord the king say so too."

David had announced his decision to have his son Solomon crowned king. The announcement was greeted with enthusiasm by Benaiah, as seen in this heartfelt, spontaneous prayer that God would confirm David's decision.

1 KINGS 1:47

"May God make the name of Solomon better than your name, and may He make his throne greater than your throne."

This prayer was offered by David's servants (government officials) when David had Solomon crowned king. It was reported to Adonijah, who had tried to lead a coup. This prayer should be understood as a formal expression of submission to David's decision to establish Solomon as his successor.

1 KINGS 3:6–9

"Give to Your servant an understanding heart to judge Your people, that I may discern between good and evil."

Young Solomon was deeply aware of his inexperience. When God appeared in a dream and invited Solomon to ask for a gift, Solomon asked for wisdom to guide God's people. This selfless prayer pleased the Lord. God promised Solomon wisdom, adding promises of long life and wealth as well.

This prayer is significant because of the impact that David's relationship with God had on his son. Solomon knew God because "You have shown great mercy to Your servant David my father, because he walked before You in truth, in righteousness, and in uprightness of heart with You: You have continued this great kindness for him and You have given him a son to sit on his throne, as it is this day" (1 Kings 3:6).

May the testimony of our lives give our children as clear an understanding of God's grace and love!

1 KINGS 8:14–61

Solomon's prayer on the occasion of dedicating the Jerusalem temple is the longest and most complex prose prayer in the Old Testament.

It begins with blessing (1 Kings 8:14–21), moves on to petition (1 Kings 8:23–53), and concludes with blessing and an exhortation to Israel to be faithful to the Lord (1 Kings 8:55–61). Significantly, the root of the verb *palal* and the related noun *t*pilla, which typically refer to intercessory prayer, occurs 30 times in 1 Kings 8 and in its parallel passage (see 2 Chronicles 6).

In offering this prayer of intercession, Solomon acknowledged that God, who fills all of space, cannot be limited to a single place. Yet Solomon asked God to be present in the Jerusalem temple in a special way, so that when Israel sinned they might acknowledge God and signify their return to Him by praying toward the temple.

God signified His answer to Solomon's prayer by filling the temple with His glory. From the temple's dedication in 963 B.C. to Babylon's final defeat of Judah in 586 B.C., God remained responsive to prayers of repentance addressed toward the temple. Then, just before the capture of Jerusalem and the destruction of Solomon's temple, the prophet Ezekiel was given a vision of the glory of God leaving the temple (see Ezek. 8–11). God's people had become so hardened in sin that repentance was impossible, so the Lord removed His presence from the temple that Solomon had built.

1 KINGS 18:36, 37

"LORD God of Abraham, Isaac, and Israel, let it be known this day that You are God in Israel and I am Your servant."

King Ahab and Queen Jezebel had attempted to replace the worship of Yahweh with loyalty to the pagan deity Baal. Elijah, the lone prophet then speaking for the Lord, challenged four hundred prophets of Baal to a contest. All day long the prophets of Baal cried out to their god, begging him to send fire to consume a sacrifice they had laid out. As evening approached, Elijah appealed once to the Lord to reveal clearly that He was the Lord God in order to turn the people of Israel back to Him.

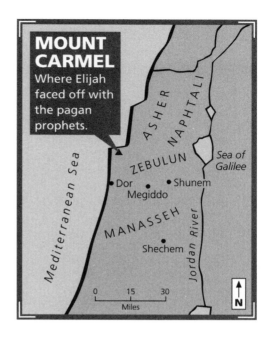

MOUNT CARMEL Where Elijah faced off with the pagan prophets.

Elijah's brief prayer was answered immediately. Fire fell from heaven and consumed Elijah's sacrifice as well as the stone altar, which had been soaked with water.

How clearly this incident illustrates Jesus' reminder that the key to effective prayer is not repetition, but a personal relationship with God (see Matt. 6:7).

2 KINGS 6:17, 18, 20

"LORD, I pray."

Three separate and distinct petitions are recorded in the span of just four verses. The town where Elisha was staying was surrounded by a Syrian raiding force. Discovering the enemy, Elisha's servant was terrified.

Elisha's first prayer was that the servant's eyes should be opened. They were, and the servant saw an army of angels between Elijah and the Syrians.

Elisha's second prayer was that the Syrians might be "blinded." The Hebrew word is better understood to mean that their sight was affected so they saw an illusion rather than reality. Elisha then led the Syrian force into Israel's capital city, Samaria.

Elisha's third prayer was that the Syrians' sight should be restored. It was, and the Syrians realized they were surrounded inside the Israelite capital.

Each of these prayers was brief and specific. Each called on God to confound the ability to perceive a situation accurately.

2 KINGS 19:15–19

"Now, therefore, O LORD our God, I pray, save us from his hand."

Sennacherib of Assyria had demanded the surrender of Jerusalem, ridiculing the notion that Judah's God might save the nation. King Hezekiah brought the Assyrian's demand into the temple and placed the message before the Lord. Hezekiah expressed his confidence in God, asking God to save the nation and so demonstrate His power and authority.

The prophet Isaiah was then sent to tell Hezekiah that not a single enemy arrow would fly over Jerusalem's wall. God later sent an angel, who killed 85,000 Assyrian soldiers in a single night.

The motivational element is the most significant feature of Hezekiah's appeal. The king of Judah knew that God was real, and he asked God to act to protect His own reputation.

God truly is concerned for our welfare. It is appropriate that you and I be concerned for God's reputation and seek to glorify Him.

2 KINGS 20:3

"Remember now, O LORD, I pray, how I have walked before You in truth and with a loyal heart."

King Hezekiah of Judah was sick, and the prophet Isaiah informed the king that he would not recover. Desperately Hezekiah begged God to extend his life.

Note the difference in the motivation offered for answering this prayer and that offered in the prayer in 2 Kings 19:15–19 (see above). In this prayer, Hezekiah appealed to God on the basis of his past loyalty to the Lord and his demonstrated commitment to do what

BIBLE BACKGROUND:
SHOULD WE ASK GOD TO CHANGE HIS MIND?

Hezekiah asked God to extend his life after the Lord announced that he would die. God answered his prayer. But would Hezekiah have prayed as he did if he had understood all the implications of his extended years?

The Bible tells us that Manasseh, Hezekiah's son, was 12 years old when he became king. This suggests that Manasseh was born *after* God extended Hezekiah's life. But Manasseh went on to become Judah's most wicked king, whose hostility toward the Lord turned Judah against God and fixed that nation's ultimate fate. If godly Hezekiah had known that the gift of an extra 15 years of life would affect his nation so terribly, would he have prayed as he did?

We cannot know. But the story should lead us to ask God to answer only prayers of ours that will glorify Him and bless others.

is good in God's sight. In the prayer above, Hezekiah appealed to God to protect His own reputation.

Both the appeal to God to be gracious to a faithful servant and the appeal to God to display His glory are valid. Both of Hezekiah's prayers were answered. God delivered Jerusalem and the Lord graciously added 15 years to Hezekiah's life.

1 CHRONICLES 4:10

"Oh, that You would bless me indeed."

This verse records a prayer offered by one of Judah's descendants, Jabez. It is identified as the prayer of an honorable man. While Jabez sought God's blessing and the enlargement of his territory, he also prayed that "You would keep me from evil, that I may not cause pain."

The Hebrew name *Jabez* means "He will cause pain," and it was given to him because his mother "bore him in pain." Whether the reference is to childbirth itself or to a painful complication arising from Jabez's birth, Jabez clearly became sensitive to man's potential to do things which hurt others. The phrase "so God granted him what he requested" suggests that Jabez's attitude pleased the Lord and he was rewarded.

1 CHRONICLES 17:16–27

(See the discussion of the parallel passage, 2 Samuel 7:18–29, pp. 25, 26.)

1 CHRONICLES 29:16–19

"O LORD God of Abraham, Isaac, and Israel, our fathers, keep this forever in the intent of the thoughts of the heart of Your people, and fix their heart toward You. And give my son Solomon a loyal heart."

This prayer is notable for the bonding of one of David's crafted prayer poems with what seems to be an extemporaneous prose prayer. It is also notable for the content of the request and the priority that David identified. David offered the wealth he had gathered during his lifetime in preparation for building the Jerusalem temple (vv. 16, 17). But David's main concern was that Israel's heart be fixed toward God (v. 18) and that God would give his son Solomon a loyal heart to keep God's testimonies and commandments (v. 19).

2 CHRONICLES 1:8–10

(See the comment on the parallel passage, 1 Kings 3:6–9, p. 26.)

2 CHRONICLES 6:14–42

(See the comment on the parallel passage, 1 Kings 8, pp. 26, 27.)

2 CHRONICLES 14:11

"LORD, it is nothing for You to help, whether with many or with those who have no power; help us, O LORD our God."

The forces of King Asa of Judah were outnumbered by a foreign enemy. Asa cried out to the Lord for help, expressing complete trust in the Lord. God responded by giving Asa a decisive victory.

2 CHRONICLES 20:5–12

"O our God, will You not judge them? For we have no power against this great multitude that is coming against us; nor do we know what to do, but our eyes are upon You."

Another godly king of Judah, Jehoshaphat, appealed to God for help when invaded by the combined forces of Moab, Amon, and Mount Seir. Jehoshaphat asked God to act because (1) the enemy was intent on throwing Judah off the land God gave them, (2) Judah had no power to resist, and (3) God's people were depending on Him.

God responded to this prayer by turning the allies against each other. The enemy armies destroyed each other, and all the men of Judah needed to do was collect the spoil.

2 CHRONICLES 30:18, 19

"May the good LORD provide atonement for everyone who prepares his heart to seek God."

King Hezekiah led a spiritual revival marked by temple worship and festival observances. The response of the people of Judah was so overwhelming that it was impossible to conclude the ritual cleansing of the people required by the Old Testament Law. Hezekiah interceded for the people and asked God to accept the intent of the worshipers' hearts, even though they had not completed the required ritual.

This was a bold innovation. While God agreed to honor Hezekiah's request, it should not be taken as a precedent. In Old Testament times, both worship ritual and a sincere intent to honor God were important.

NEHEMIAH 5:19

"Remember me, my God, for good, according to all that I have done for this people."

To ask God to remember does not suggest that God can or will forget. This was a colloquial expression—a request for God to act in a way appropriate to what is remembered. God might be asked to remember a person's good deeds, as here, or to remember His own covenant promises, as in Exodus 2:24 and Exodus 6:5.

Similarly, God's promise that He will not remember our sins is a promise of forgiveness—a guarantee that God will not punish us as our sins deserve (see Jer. 31:34).

Nehemiah had dedicated his life to rebuilding not only the stone walls of Jerusalem but the moral and spiritual commitment of God's people as well. As Nehemiah recounted his accomplishment, he often repeated this brief request to be rewarded (see Neh. 13:14, 22, 29, 30).

NEHEMIAH 6:9b
"Now therefore, O God, strengthen my hands."

Nehemiah asked for courage and strength when the enemies of the Jews spread rumors intended to weaken their resolve to rebuild Jerusalem's walls.

NEHEMIAH 6:14
"My God, remember Tobiah and Sanballat, according to these their works."

In a prayer that is a mirror image of the prayer in Nehemiah 5:9 (see above), Nehemiah asked God to act against the enemies of Israel who were trying to halt the rebuilding of Jerusalem.

ISAIAH 6:8
"Here am I! Send me."

The prophet Isaiah had been given a vision of the Lord. The vision first stimulated a deep awareness of and confession of sin (see page 47). In response, an angel brought a coal of fire from heaven's altar and cleansed the prophet (6:7). Isaiah then heard the Lord ask who would undertake a mission for Him. Isaiah cried out, "Send me!"

This simple but beautiful spontaneous response of the believer who realizes he has been forgiven should echo in every Christian's heart. God has cleansed us and forgiven our sins. How eager we should be to serve Him!

A big task—restoring the walls of Jerusalem—led Nehemiah to pray for strength.

ISAIAH 37:16–20
(See the comment on the parallel prayer in 2 Kings 19, p. 28.)

ISAIAH 38:3
(See the comment on the parallel prayer in 2 Kings 20:3, p. 28.)

AMOS 7:2
"O LORD God, forgive, I pray! Oh, that Jacob may stand, for he is small!"

Amos had been given a vision of a locust plague intended to punish Israel. Amos was horrified. He spontaneously begged God to forgive rather than judge, pleading the weakness of the Northern Kingdom. God relented, as Amos asked.

AMOS 7:5
"O LORD God, cease, I pray! Oh, that Jacob may stand, for he is small!"

Amos was given another vision of judgment, this time by a fire that raged through the land. Again Amos appealed to God for mercy, and the judgment was withheld. This, however, was the last time God would withhold judgment.

Prayer may delay God's judgment. But only true repentance and a return to the Lord's ways can avoid it.

JONAH 1:14

"We pray, O LORD, please do not let us perish for this man's life, and do not charge us with innocent blood; for You, O LORD, have done as it pleased You."

This desperate prayer of petition was offered by pagan sailors on whose ship Jonah was a passenger. When a terrifying storm threatened the ship, Jonah confessed that God had launched the tempest because he was running from the Lord. The prophet told the sailors to throw him in the sea, promising that the sea would then become calm.

Unwilling to throw Jonah to certain death, the sailors desperately tried to row their boat to shore. Finally, certain they were about to die, the sailors appealed to Jonah's God and did as the prophet had told them.

The prayer is notable because it was offered by pagans, who had no covenant relationship with God. It is important to note, however, that the prayer was addressed to Yahweh, the Lord, and not to pagan deities. There is no suggestion in Scripture that God will hear or answer prayers addressed to false gods.

God did hear the sailors' prayer, and the seas did become calm. Convinced, the sailors

At Jonah's request, the sailors reluctantly threw him overboard into the stormy sea.

offered sacrifices to the Lord and took vows to worship Him.

God may still bring people to Him by answering their prayers.

ZECHARIAH 7:3

"Should I weep in the fifth month and fast as I have done for so many years?"

This brief prayer was a petition for guidance, presented before the Lord by representatives of the Jewish community at Bethel. The question concerned fast days set aside to mourn the fall of Jerusalem and the destruction of the temple. Now that a company of Jews had returned to their homeland, were the fasts still necessary?

God responded to their question with a rebuke. Had the dates been observed as a mark of repentance and sorrow for sins, or were the fasts an expression of self-pity?

When we pray, we need to examine our motives; God will surely do so.

PROSE PETITIONS: A SUMMARY

A survey of Old Testament prose petitions provides many insights into the prayer lives of the men and women of Old Testament times.

The saints of the older covenant clearly felt free to appeal to God in any situation and at any time. Many of the prose petitions are brief, spontaneous expressions that reveal a beautiful and trusting reliance on the Lord. Often longer prose prayers contain descriptive phrases identifying qualities of the Lord or listing His past actions which fill believers with confidence that God can and will respond to their requests.

Longer prose prayers also typically include motivation statements: Statements by the persons who pray which express the grounds of their confidence that God will grant their request. Motivations range from appeals to God to guard His reputation or keep His promises, to appeals to God to show Himself merciful and gracious, to appeals based on the loyalty that the person praying has previously shown to the Lord.

In all these ways, Old Testament prose petitions display a strong sense of personal relationship with God and confidence in His goodwill.

How wonderful that we know personally the God trusted by Old Testament saints. We can also trust Him to hear our prayers and to help us in our needs.

CHAPTER 3

"LORD, WHY HAVE YOU BROUGHT TROUBLE?"

OLD TESTAMENT PRAYERS OF COMPLAINT, CONFESSION, AND BLESSING

Selected Old Testament Scriptures

My father liked to remember something I said when I was three years old. I don't remember it myself, but I heard the story many times. Dad would grin and tell about how I asked for an ice cream cone and, looking up at him, added, "I'll do you a lot of good some day."

Dad didn't mind my asking him for things. Of course, if the only times I ever spoke to him were when I wanted something, he might have. But our home wasn't like that. It was a place where we talked a lot; a place where I wrapped up in a blanket and listened evenings as my mother read to Dad from the *Saturday Evening Post*. I felt comfortable at home. I could run home with my hurts and complaints. I could even come home, sheepish and mud-splattered, to confess that I had skipped school to play in the woods behind our house.

In many ways, the prose prayers of the Old Testament remind me of home. There's the same comfortable awareness that we can speak to God about anything and everything. Old Testament saints felt free to lodge their complaints, to confess their sins, and to share their joys as they thanked God for His bless-

ings. Warmth, spontaneity, and a feeling of "home" in God's presence are all marks of Old Testament prose prayer.

In the last chapter, we saw these qualities displayed in prose prayers of petition. In this chapter, we'll see the same qualities in prayers of complaint, of confession, and in what the Old Testament calls "blessing" God.

CHARACTERISTICS OF PROSE PRAYERS OF COMPLAINT

It seems strange to find prayers of complaint addressed to God. Especially when we read in Numbers 11:1 that "when the people complained, it displeased the LORD; for the LORD heard it, and His anger was aroused." If complaining is so displeasing to God, why do we find so many prose prayers of complaint addressed to Him?

To understand, we need to look at the first occurrences of complaining recorded in the Old Testament. We find them in the story of the Israelites' journey to Mount Sinai after being freed by God from slavery in Egypt. In spite of the miracles God had performed for them, the people murmured and complained.

Three days into the wilderness, the Israelites' water ran out, and the text says, "The people complained against Moses, saying, 'What shall we drink?'" (Ex. 15:24).

God provided the needed water. But about 12 days later "the children of Israel complained against Moses and Aaron in the wilderness" (Ex. 16:2), this time about food. Again God provided what the people wanted. But this time Moses put the Israelites' complaints in perspective. Although the people were complaining about Moses, Moses rightly identified their words as complaints directed against the Lord.

The Israelites had failed to bring their needs to God in prayer. Instead they had criticized and attacked Moses, the leader God had given them. In this, they were complaining to each other *about* God.

This is the key difference between complaint that arouses God's anger and what we may call "godly complaint." Rather than trusting God and bringing their complaints *to* Him, the Israelites complained *about* the situation in which God had placed them.

It is one thing to come to God about circumstances that trouble us. It is another thing entirely to complain to others, for in doing so we criticize the sovereign Lord who orders every circumstance of our lives.

The Old Testament's prose prayers of complaint teach us so much. They teach us that we are free to come directly to God however "negative" our feelings. They teach us that we can be open and honest with the Lord. They teach us to look to the Lord as sovereign and to view every circumstance of our lives as His gift. And Old Testament prose prayers of complaint remind us that God truly does love us. He loves us so much that rather than react to our complaints with anger, He listens, and He shows us that He cares.

EXODUS 5:22
"LORD, why have You brought trouble on this people?"

God had commissioned Moses to deliver the Israelites from slavery in Egypt. Yet when

Moses relayed God's demand to Pharaoh, Egypt's ruler was furious and increased the burden on the Jews. This response dampened the enthusiasm of the Israelites, who had been delighted when Moses reported that God was about to set them free.

Moses was upset too. He immediately complained to God, pointing out that "since I came to Pharaoh to speak in Your name, he has done evil to this people; neither have You delivered Your people at all."

The last phrase seems to move from a simple setting forth of the facts to an accusation. "God, You said You would free Your people. But You haven't done what You promised."

God's response to Moses' prayer is instructive. The Lord was not angry about Moses' complaint. He understood why Moses was upset. What God did was to repeat His promise of deliverance, pointing out some facts that Moses had not considered.

Pharaoh's reaction to Moses revealed the Egyptian ruler's basic attitude toward the Lord and His people. Soon God would act, and with "great judgments" force Pharaoh to free his slaves. God had known all along what it would take to redeem His people. Through the reaction of Pharaoh, Moses and Israel knew what it would take as well.

How often our complaints are rooted in a limited viewpoint. We see only our troubles and reverses. But God sees the end from the beginning. However troubled we may be now, God's ultimate purpose for us is good.

EXODUS 17:4
"What shall I do with this people? They are almost ready to stone me!"

Although God had responded to the Israelites' complaints by providing what they desired, their attitude became worse and worse. Finally the whole people displayed such hostility toward Moses that Moses felt his life was in danger. At this point, Moses again cried out to the Lord.

God responded by telling Moses what to do. The steps God outlined demonstrated that

Angry complaints from the people caused Moses to register a complaint with the Lord.

God was with Moses and that the Israelites' well-being depended on God's chosen leader (see Ex. 17:5–11). God not only accepted Moses' complaint but also showed Moses how to deal with the situation.

NUMBERS 11:11–15
"Why have You afflicted Your servant?"

We need to read this entire prayer to sense the despair expressed by Moses. The people God had called him to lead were impossible. Moses was clearly stretched to the breaking point. He prayed,

I am not able to bear all these people alone, because the burden is too heavy for me. If You treat me like this, please kill me here and now—if I have found favor in your sight—and do not let me see my wretchedness (Num. 11:14, 15).

This is a prayer that helps us when we reach our breaking point and life seems so filled with pain that death would be preferable. If God really cared, we may think, He would let us die rather than face an impossible future.

It's important to note that the Lord did not rebuke Moses for feeling as he did. In this,

He was kinder than many friends, who insist that Christians who feel despair simply lack faith. What God did was lay out a practical plan for Moses to follow that would enable him to share the burden of leadership (Num. 11:16ff).

It is perfectly all right to complain to the Lord when we feel despair. We can trust God enough to be honest with Him about our feelings. But it is important to remember that God does have a practical way for us to deal with our situation and our despair.

JOSHUA 7:6–9
"Alas, LORD God, why have You brought this people over the Jordan at all—to deliver us into the hand of the Amorites, to destroy us?"

After the miracle victory at Jericho, Joshua sent a small force to deal with a minor town nearby. Instead of the expected victory, the Israelites were defeated and 36 Israelites were killed.

Joshua understood the seriousness of the defeat. If word of it reached the other Canaanites, they might take heart and join together to drive the Israelites back across the Jordan

River. Joshua was so upset that he questioned God's motives in bringing Israel to the promised land.

Rather than punish Joshua, God understood the fear that motivated his complaint. God then revealed the reason for the defeat: An Israelite man had taken booty from Jericho in violation of God's command. The defeat was used to teach Israel a vital lesson. Obedience to God would bring victory, but disobedience would bring defeat.

Joshua identified the man who sinned, and he was executed. A second attack on Ai succeeded, and the danger Joshua had feared was past.

At times we also bring the things we complain about on ourselves by our disobedience to the Lord. It is all right to complain to God. But we also need to examine ourselves, to see if God might be using circumstances to alert us to some fault of our own.

JUDGES 15:18
"You have given this great deliverance by the hand of Your servant; and now shall I die of thirst and fall into the hand of the uncircumcised?"

Samson had broken ropes that bound him. Using only the jawbone of a donkey, he had fought and killed a thousand Philistines. The exertion left him dehydrated and exhausted, and he directed this complaint to the Lord.

God responded by providing drinking water for Samson.

JUDGES 21:2, 3
"O LORD God of Israel, why has this come to pass in Israel, that today there should be one tribe missing in Israel?"

The other tribes of Israel went to war against the tribe of Benjamin, which had defended some of their own number who were guilty of rape and murder. In the battle the Benjaminites were nearly wiped out; only six hundred men survived. The problem was that the other tribes had taken a vow not to give their daughters to become wives of any Benjaminite.

Although the Israelites brought their complaint to the Lord, there is no indication that they sought God's guidance. Instead, the Israelites came up with their own solution. If we are sensitive enough to complain directly to the Lord, we should be wise enough to seek His guidance as well.

1 KINGS 17:20, 21
"O LORD my God, have You also brought tragedy on the widow with whom I lodge, by killing her son?"

The prophet Elijah had miraculously provided food for the widow with whom he stayed while a drought devastated Israel. When the woman's son died, she was bitter and heartbroken. Elijah carried the boy into the room where he was staying and brought his complaint to the Lord.

The incident is notable for two reasons. First, the text describes a natural cause of death—a sickness (1 Kings 17:17)—but Elijah viewed the boy's death as an act of God. Second, after lodging his complaint, Elijah prayed that God would restore the child's life.

While God accepts prayers of complaint,

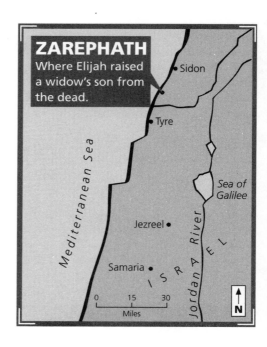

ZAREPHATH
Where Elijah raised a widow's son from the dead.

there is no reason we should limit ourselves to this kind of prayer. With our complaint we can include petition. When we do, we look beyond the immediate situation and remind ourselves that because God is great and good, we do have hope.

1 KINGS 19:4

"It is enough! Now, LORD, take my life, for I am no better than my fathers."

Elijah had just won a great victory over the pagan prophets of Baal on Mount Carmel. God had answered his prayer for fire to fall from heaven, proving His power and presence. As a result, the Israelites recommitted themselves to God and showed their loyalty by killing the prophets of Baal. Yet a day later when Queen Jezebel threatened Elijah's life, the prophet fled in despair.

At the end of the day, exhausted and depressed, Elijah brought his complaint to the Lord and asked God to take his life.

Often there is no rational reason for depression or despair. Certainly Elijah had just seen unmistakable evidence of God's presence and power. He had no reason to be so upset at Jezebel's threat. But human emotions don't always respond to reason. Elijah's complaint to the Lord was totally sincere and heartfelt.

God's responses to Elijah are instructive. God showed support for Elijah by providing food and drink. Days later, when Elijah was ready to hear, God spoke to His prophet (1 Kings 19:15–18). God gave Elijah tasks to perform and a companion to train as his successor. The Lord also reassured Elijah that he was not alone in his commitment to God.

God will not rebuke us if we complain to Him when we're depressed. Instead, God will gently come alongside and lead us out of the darkness into His light.

LAMENTS OF JEREMIAH

Jeremiah is known as the "weeping prophet." During the final 40 years of Judah's existence as a nation, Jeremiah warned of impending judgment, urging God's people to submit to the Babylonians. In return for his faithful ministry of God's word, Jeremiah was ridiculed, condemned, imprisoned, and threatened with death. Compelled to speak out, discouraged by the unresponsiveness of God's people, and burdened by the vision of the suffering that must come upon his nation, Jeremiah's life was filled with pain.

Several passages in Jeremiah fit into our category of prose prayers of complaint. The form of some closely resembles Hebrew poetry, but each of the passages cited below is found in a narrative section of Jeremiah. This, rather than the form, is the critical mark of Old Testament prose prayers. Each is embedded in a narrative passage that provides the specific context of the prayer, describing the situation out of which it arises. By this criterion, Jeremiah 18:19–23, 20:8–12 and 20:14–18 can be classified as prose prayers.

Jeremiah 18:19–23. The people of Jerusalem and Judah became so angry at Jeremiah's pronouncements that they attacked him "with the tongue" and refused to "give heed to any of his words" (Jer. 18:18). Jeremiah felt this rejection deeply and complained to the Lord. Jeremiah had done nothing but to stand before the Lord and "speak good for them, to turn away your wrath from them" (18:20). Hurt and angry, Jeremiah asked God to "provide no atonement for their iniquity, nor blot out their sin from Your sight" (18:23).

Jeremiah 20:7–12. Pashur, the priest in charge of the Jerusalem temple, attacked Jeremiah and put him in stocks. Released a day later, Jeremiah pronounced God's judgment on Pashur but also complained to the Lord. Jeremiah was "in derision daily; everyone mocks me" (20:7). He tried to keep silent, but God was "stronger than I" and Jeremiah simply could not hold back. Jeremiah said:

> For I heard many mocking:
> "Fear on every side!"
> "Report," they say, "and we will
>   report it!"

All my acquaintances watched
    for my stumbling, saying,
"Perhaps he can be induced;
Then we will prevail against
    him,
And we will take our revenge
    on him" (20:10).

In spite of the pressure and his own turbulent emotions, Jeremiah spoke out, aware that his awesome God was with him (20:11, 12).

Jeremiah 20:14–18. Jeremiah was one of the toughest of the Old Testament prophets, both mentally and morally. He remained faithful to God and his mission, in spite of constant and intense opposition. Yet Jeremiah was an emotional person who experienced intense pain. The following verses expressed his feelings as he complained to God:

Cursed be the day in which I
    was born!
Let the day not be blessed in
    which my mother bore me!
Let the man be cursed
Who brought news to my
    father, saying,
"A male child has been born to
    you!"
Making him very glad.
And let that man be like the
    cities
Which the LORD overthrew,
    and do not relent;
Let him hear the cry in the
    morning
And the shouting at noon.
Because he did not kill me from
    the womb,
That my mother might have
    been my grave,
And her womb always
    enlarged with me.
Why did I come forth from the
    womb to see labor and
    sorrow,
That my days should be
    consumed with shame?

Perhaps the most important lesson we learn from Jeremiah is that our emotions need not control our choices. In spite of his inner turmoil and his complaints to the Lord, Jeremiah obeyed the Lord and announced His word. Jeremiah eventually was vindicated. Everything he predicted came to pass, and the people who rebelled against God and ridiculed His prophet were judged by the Lord.

EZEKIEL 11:13
"Ah LORD God! Will You make a complete end of the remnant of Israel?"

While Jeremiah was ministering in Judah, Ezekiel served as God's spokesman to his countrymen who had been carried as captives to Babylon. In a vision, Ezekiel was carried to Jerusalem. He observed a group of false prophets who had contradicted Jeremiah and who predicted prosperity for Judah (Ezek. 11:2, 3). God commanded Ezekiel to prophesy against these men. When Ezekiel did, one of their leaders named Pelatiah dropped dead.

While it was clear that the prophetic word which Ezekiel had uttered had begun its work, why did Ezekiel react as he did? The answer is in the meaning of the name *Pelatiah:* "Yahweh's remnant." Ezekiel took Pelatiah's death as a sign that God would completely wipe out His people.

God responded to Ezekiel's complaint by explaining His intent. Although He would scatter the Jews among the nations, Ezekiel could communicate God's promise, "I will gather you from the peoples . . . and I will give you the land of Israel" (Ezek. 11:17).

JONAH 4:2
"Ah, LORD, was not this what I said when I was still in my country?"

God had sent Jonah to Nineveh to announce the destruction of that city. Instead of going to Nineveh, Jonah took a ship heading south. Thrown overboard in a great storm, Jonah was swallowed by a great fish that God had prepared. Jonah prayed desperately, and

When Nineveh repented, Jonah pouted.

———————— ❖ ————————

was vomited up on the land. Again God told him to go to Nineveh. This time Jonah obeyed. But the people of Nineveh believed his message and repented of their evil ways. God then relented, and did not destroy the city. And this was the heart of Jonah's complaint.

Jonah, a patriot, wanted Nineveh destroyed, for Nineveh was the capital of Assyria—Israel's greatest enemy. How strange to hear Jonah complain that "I know that You are a gracious and merciful God" (Jonah 4:2). Jonah had run in the first place because he was afraid the Ninevites might repent and that the Lord would then be gracious to them!

There are many things about which we may complain and be heard by God. But we have no right to complain about God being gracious and merciful to others, whoever they may be. Rather, we are to praise God for every expression of His mercy. Without divine mercy, where would *we* be?

Old Testament prose prayers of complaint had their roots in a variety of circumstances.

But as long as God's people brought their complaints *to* Him rather than complaining *about* their circumstances to one another, God listened and responded. In bringing their complaints to God, His people found fresh insight and understanding, gained new perspectives, discovered unexpected solutions, and were reassured and healed.

Their experiences encourage us to turn to God when things go wrong or when we are overcome with feelings of hurt or despair. When we do bring our complaints to God, we can be sure that He will listen, and heal.

PROSE PRAYERS OF CONFESSION

The principle of confession is clearly established in Old Testament law as well as New Testament teaching. Leviticus 5:5 specified that when a person was guilty of violating God's law "he shall confess that he has sinned in that thing." While the passage went on to call for a sin offering, it is clear that confession is the first step in becoming reconciled to God.

The Old Testament Law does not give the wording of such a confession. Instead, the command assumes that a person is capable of expressing an appropriate confession in his or her own words.

Significant elements in the prose prayers of confession in the Old Testament support this conclusion. It seems clear that God's people understood that a person must specifically acknowledge his or her fault. While other elements are seen in some prose prayers of confession, a specific acknowledgment of fault is essential.

JUDGES 10:10, 15
"We have sinned against You, because we have both forsaken our God and served the Baals."

God had punished the Israelites by permitting the Philistines to oppress them. Finally, His people turned to Him and confessed their sin. God reminded them that they had sinned before and when they cried out to Him, He had delivered them. He then challenged them to pray to the gods they had chosen.

This challenge from the Lord brought additional confession. "We have sinned! Do to us whatever seems best to You: only deliver us this day, we pray."

The text tells us that the Israelites then "put away the foreign gods from among them and served the LORD" (Judg. 10:16). This demonstrated the sincerity of the Israelites' confession, leading to God's intervention for His people.

It is easy to say "I was wrong" or "I'm sorry." But the sincerity of our words, whether addressed to another person or to God, can only be measured by our subsequent actions.

1 SAMUEL 7:6
"We have sinned against the LORD."

Samuel had told the Israelites, "If you return to the LORD with all your hearts, then put away the foreign gods and the Ashtoreths from among you, and prepare your hearts for the LORD, and serve Him only; and He will deliver you from the hand of the Philistines" (7:3).

The Israelites did as Samuel directed, putting away their idols and serving God only. Then Samuel called the people together to pray for relief. At that great assembly, the people fasted and confessed their sins and Samuel prayed for them.

In this case, confession of sin followed rather than preceded repentance and change. But in this case as in Judges 10, the sincerity of the confession was displayed by a sincere return to the Lord.

1 SAMUEL 12:10, 19

Near the end of Samuel's life, Israel demanded a king. Samuel reminded the Israelites of their history in the land. This had involved repeated cycles of sin and oppression from foreign enemies, followed in turn by confession, repentance, and deliverance by the

When Nathan confronted him, David acknowledged his great sin.

Lord. First Samuel 12:10 summarizes historic prayers of confession.

In his sermon, Samuel pointed out that the motive of the Israelites in asking for a king had been wrong (see 1 Sam. 8:7–19). Moved, the people begged Samuel, "Pray for your servants to the LORD your God, that we may not die; for we have added to all our sins the evil of asking a king for ourselves" (1 Sam. 12:19).

2 SAMUEL 12:13
"I have sinned against the LORD."

David had sinned by committing adultery with Bathsheba, the wife of one of his army officers. When she became pregnant, David attempted to cover up his guilt. He ordered his military commander to send that officer on a mission where he would be killed.

Only when the prophet Nathan confronted David did the king confess his sin.

BIBLE BACKGROUND:

THE DYNAMICS OF CONFESSION OF SIN

Psalm 51	Comment
Have mercy upon me, O God, According to Your lovingkindness;	
According to the multitude of Your tender mercies,	*David's only hope was that God would be merciful. He*
Blot out my transgressions.	*realized that he had no*
Wash me thoroughly from my iniquity,	*other basis on which to appeal for forgiveness.*
And cleanse me from my sin.	
For I acknowledge my transgressions,	*David took full respon-*
And my sin is always before me.	*sibility for his actions. He admitted that he had*
Against You, You only, have I sinned,	*violated God's moral law, and that his sin had been*
And done this evil in Your sight—	*against God first and foremost.*
That You may be found just when You speak,	
And blameless when You judge.	
Behold, I was brought forth in iniquity,	*David's self-examination made him realize that*
And in sin my mother conceived me.	*acts of sin were not the main problem: David was a*
Behold, you desire truth in the inward parts,	*sinner by nature.*
And in the hidden part You will make me to know wisdom.	
Purge me with hyssop, and I shall be clean;	*Only God could cleanse David*
Wash me, and I shall be whiter than snow.	*from guilt, and change him within.*
Make me hear joy and gladness,	
That the bones you have broken may rejoice.	
Hide your face from my sins, and blot out all my iniquities.	
Create in me a clean heart, O God,	*David continued to appeal*
And renew a steadfast spirit within me.	*for a changed heart. Only God's active presence in*
Do not cast me away from Your presence,	*his life could keep David from sinning again and*
And do not take Your Holy Spirit from me.	*again.*
Restore to me the joy of Your salvation,	*Restored by God's grace,*
And uphold me by Your generous Spirit.	*David displayed the joy of salvation, and by*
Then I will teach transgressors Your ways,	*his example showed sinners the way back to God.*
And sinners shall be converted to You.	
Deliver me from the guilt of bloodshed, O God,	*As a sinner, David had to*
The God of my salvation,	*rely on God for salvation*
And my tongue shall sing aloud of Your righteousness.	*and forgiveness. Broken-hearted and humbled, David*
O LORD, open my lips,	*could only plead for a mercy*
And my mouth shall show forth Your praise.	*he did not deserve, but which he would celebrate*
For You do not desire sacrifice, or else I would give it;	*for the rest of his life.*
You do not delight in burnt offering.	*David did not repudiate sacrifice, but realized*
The sacrifices of God are a broken spirit,	*that what God yearns for are hearts fully*
A broken and a contrite heart—	*submitted to Him—a heart now like David's own.*
These, O God, You will not despise.	

Second Samuel quotes only David's admission to Nathan. But David's confession to God, recorded in Psalm 51, reveals true sorrow and repentance.

Even more significantly, the superscription of Psalm 51 tells us that David delivered Psalm 51 to the nation's chief musician, to be used in public worship! David's sin had become public knowledge; his confession must have been public as well.

Psalm 51 is no spontaneous utterance. It is a carefully crafted poem, revealing how shaken David was by his own behavior and how deeply he had thought about his sin. This psalm is Scripture's most penetrating exploration of personal sin and of the restoration available to the believer through confession. While not a prose prayer, Psalm 51 helps to explain the dynamics of confession in our personal relationship with God.

2 SAMUEL 24:10, 17
"I have sinned greatly in what I have done."

King David decided to conduct a census to determine the number of fighting men in Israel. For some reason not explained in the text, this was a sin. After the process had begun, "David's heart condemned him" (2 Sam. 24:10). David confessed his sin and asked for forgiveness. But this time God gave David a choice of one of three punishments that were national rather than personal in nature. David chose a three-day plague.

During the plague, David had a vision of an awesome angel who was striking the people and their livestock, and he appealed to God again. "Surely I have sinned, and I have done wickedly, but these sheep, what have they done? Let Your hand, I pray, be against me and against my father's house."

The prophet Gad instructed David to offer a sacrifice on what would be the site of Solomon's temple. There David prayed for the land, "and the plague was withdrawn from Israel" (2 Sam. 24:25).

It is important in reading this story and its parallel in 1 Chronicles 21 to note 2 Samuel 24:1, which introduces the account. There we read that "the anger of the Lord was aroused against Israel." While David's sin was the occasion for the plague, the people of Israel were not as innocent as David supposed.

Within the story itself, we should notice that David's confession and request for forgiveness were heard. David was forgiven. But forgiveness did not imply freedom from consequences. A person who commits adultery can confess the sin and be forgiven. But God's forgiveness doesn't mean there will be no price to pay. A marriage may be destroyed, a disease may be sexually transmitted, or an unwanted pregnancy may occur.

Those who reason, "I'll do what I want now and confess my sin later," don't understand that every act of ours has consequences. God can and will forgive. But forgiveness does not free us from the burden of the consequences of the choices we make.

1 CHRONICLES 21:8
(See the discussion of the parallel passage in 2 Sam. 24, above.)

EZRA 9:6–15
"O my God, I am too ashamed and humiliated to lift up my face to You, my God; for our iniquities have risen higher than our heads, and our guilt has grown up to the heavens."

Ezra was a man trained in the Old Testament. He came to Judah to teach God's Law to the little Jewish community that had returned there after the Babylonian captivity. On Ezra's arrival, he discovered that God's people had intermarried with pagans in the area and were being pulled back into idolatry (Ezra 9:1, 2).

Ezra's first reaction was not to condemn the guilty but to tear his robe as a sign of deep distress and contrition. Then, weeping and confessing, he uttered the public prayer recorded here. Several aspects of this prayer of confession are especially significant.

Ezra said "we" and "our" *(Ezra 9:6).* It is a temptation when others sin to distinguish between "me" and "them." But throughout this prayer, Ezra identified himself with his people. Ezra understood that he was an integral part of the community of faith. He bore some responsibility for the actions of others, even if he didn't participate in them.

Ezra recalled history *(Ezra 9:7–9).* The faith community of Ezra's day was one with that of past generations. The present has been shaped by God's grace shown toward the fathers, despite the forefathers' sins. The captivity was a consequence of the iniquity of earlier generations. But God showed His mercy in preserving His people and bringing back the group that had resettled the homeland.

Ezra confessed inexcusable iniquities *(Ezra 9:10–14a).* In spite of the lessons of history and in spite of God's mercy, the present gener-

Ezra's public confession of Israel's sin led to a revival.

ation was repeating the same sins which had brought judgment on the nation. In view of God's past judgment and mercy, this was both inexcusable and inexplicable.

Since You our God have punished us less than our iniquities deserve, and have given us such deliverance as this, should we again break Your commandments, and join in marriage with the people committing these abominations? (Ezra 9:13, 14a).

Ezra submitted to God's judgment (Ezra 9:14a, 15). God had every right to be angry, and even to consume the remnant. All Ezra could do was admit guilt and submit to God's justice.

Ezra's public confession of sin moved God's people deeply. Soon he was joined by a "very large assembly" (Ezra 10:1) weeping and confessing with him. They were joined by those who had offended by marrying pagan wives. The entire community joined in a public commitment to stop the practice, while those who had married pagans divorced them.

While personal and private confession of sins to God is important, we need to understand that public confession of sin is called for

at times. David's private sin was confessed publicly, because it had become a matter of common knowledge. In this situation, where sins had infected and corrupted the faith community, public confession was also called for.

The pattern of confession in Ezra 9 has been duplicated often in church history. Many revivals have begun with confession of sins. When God begins a purifying work in the community of faith, this work nearly always involves public confession of sins.

NEHEMIAH 1:4–11

"Remember, I pray, the word that You commanded Your servant Moses, saying, 'If you are unfaithful, I will scatter you among the nations; but if you return to Me, and keep My commandments and do them . . . yet I will gather them from there, and bring them to the place which I have chosen as a dwelling for My name."

Nehemiah, a high Jewish official in the court of the Persian king, was a contemporary of Ezra. Like Ezra, Nehemiah was deeply aware of the sins of his people, and he confessed these sins to the Lord. The prayer recorded here was stimulated by a report that Jerusalem's walls were still in ruins. Nehemiah sensed a strong conviction that he was called by God to restore the honor of his homeland. While Nehemiah confessed Israel's sins, he also quoted God's promise to restore His people when they returned to Him.

Nehemiah's prayer reminds us of the New Testament promise found in 1 John 1:9. If we confess our sins, God is gracious and just to forgive our sin and cleanse us from all unrighteousness.

DANIEL 9:4–19

"O LORD, great and awesome God, who keeps His covenant and mercy with those who love Him, and with those who keep His commandments, we have sinned and committed iniquity."

Daniel had read the promise in the book of Jeremiah that after 70 years

God would permit His people to return to their homeland from their captivity in Babylon. Daniel, a high Jewish official in the administration of the Babylonian and Persian empires, turned to God to "make request by prayer and supplications, with fasting, sackcloth, and ashes" (Dan. 9:3). These three actions—fasting, dressing in sackcloth, and sitting in ashes—were ways in which Old Testament people showed the sincerity of their grief over sin.

Daniel's prayer was a mixture of confession and petition. He was deeply aware that exile from the land was a just punishment for his people's sins. At the same time, Daniel counted on God to keep His promise of a return:

O LORD, hear! O LORD, forgive! O LORD, listen and act! Do not delay for Your own sake, my God, for Your city and Your people are called by Your name" (Dan. 9:19).

PRAYERS OF CONFESSION: A SUMMARY

Genesis portrayed the reaction of Adam and Eve after they ate the forbidden fruit and became aware of their guilt. Genesis 3:8 tells us that when they heard the sound of the Lord God walking in the garden, Adam and Eve "hid themselves." Awareness of sin made them flee from God.

Perhaps the most striking feature of the personal and public prayers of confession in the Old Testament is that when these saints became aware of their guilt, they turned *to* God and *sought Him out.*

What a revelation of the trust that believers can have in the God of Scripture. With David, we know that "You, O LORD, are a God full of compassion and gracious, long-suffering and abundant in mercy and truth" (Ps. 86:15). Without diminishing the seriousness of our sins, we know that if we come to God in repentance, confessing our sins and failures, He will be gracious to us and forgive.

PROSE PRAYERS OF BLESSING

Along with prose prayers of petition, complaint, and confession, the Old Testament records a number of prayers in which believers "bless" God. Scholars have debated how a human being can "bless" God. In biblical times, an inferior was blessed by a superior, thus enhancing or adding to the inferior's reputation. Certainly there is nothing that we can do that will enhance or add to God's greatness.

The best solution is that Old Testament believers used the phrase to express gratitude to God, and that when addressed to the Lord, "bless" (*barak*) is equivalent to "praise" (*hillel*). Note that the two terms are parallel in Psalm 34:2, Psalm 145:2, and Nehemiah 9:5.

The assumption that to bless God is equivalent to praising Him is further supported by the pattern seen in the following quotes. Whether the phrase "Blessed be the LORD" is the whole prayer or an element in a longer prayer, this phrase is generally followed with the reason why God is being blessed or praised. Note how frequently the reason given arises out of the immediate situation, which is the occasion for a spontaneous expression of praise.

GENESIS 14:20
"And blessed be God Most High, who has delivered your enemies into your hand."

Melchizedek blessed Abraham after his victory over raiders who had captured his nephew Lot.

GENESIS 24:27
"Blessed be the LORD God of my master Abraham, who has not forsaken His mercy and His truth toward my master."

Abraham's servant praised God for leading him to a bride for Isaac.

Near the end of his days, David was thrilled to pass the crown to his son, Solomon.

EXODUS 18:10

"Blessed be the LORD, who has delivered you out of the hand of the Egyptians and out of the hand of Pharaoh."

Moses' father-in-law praised God for freeing the Israelites.

RUTH 4:14

Blessed be the LORD, who has not left you this day without a close relative, and may his name be famous in Israel."

Neighbors praised God for giving Naomi a grandson.

1 SAMUEL 25:32

"Then David said to Abigail, 'Blessed is the LORD God of Israel, who sent you this day to meet me.'"

David praised God for sending Abigail, who prevented him from doing a great wrong.

1 SAMUEL 25:39

"Blessed be the LORD, who has pleaded the cause of my reproach from the hand of Nabal, and has kept His servant from evil!"

David praised God for judging Nabal, who had insulted David.

1 KINGS 1:48

[King David said] "Blessed be the LORD God of Israel, who has given one to sit on my throne this day, while my eyes see it!"

David praised God for letting him live to see Solomon established as his successor.

1 KINGS 5:7

"Blessed be the LORD this day, for He has given David a wise son over this great people."

King Hiram praised God for giving Israel a king as wise as Solomon.

1 KINGS 8:56

"Blessed be the LORD, who has given rest to His people Israel, according to all that He promised."

Solomon praised God for giving His nation peace.

1 KINGS 10:9

"Blessed be the LORD your God, who delighted in you, setting you on the throne of Israel! Because the LORD has loved Israel forever, therefore He made you king, to do justice and righteousness."

The queen of Sheba praised God for making Solomon king of Israel.

1 CHRONICLES 16:36

"Blessed be the LORD God of Israel from everlasting to everlasting!"

David praised God on bringing the ark of the covenant to Jerusalem.

2 CHRONICLES 2:12

"Blessed be the LORD God of Israel, who made heaven and earth, for He has given King David a wise son."

King Hiram praised God for giving David a wise successor, Solomon.

2 CHRONICLES 6:4

"Blessed be the LORD God of Israel, who has fulfilled with His hands what He spoke with His mouth to my father David."

Solomon praised God on being confirmed as king of Israel.

EZRA 7:27

"Blessed be the LORD God of our fathers, who has put such a thing as this in the king's heart, to beautify the house of the LORD which is in Jerusalem."

Ezra praised God for moving a pagan ruler to provide resources to restore and beautify the Jerusalem temple.

DANIEL 2:20–23

"Blessed be the name of God forever and ever."

Daniel had asked God to reveal a dream which Nebuchadnezzar had dreamed but forgotten. God answered this prayer, and Daniel's gratitude overflowed in this prayer:

> Blessed be the name of God
>   forever and ever,
> For wisdom and might are His.
> And He changes the times and
>   the seasons;
> He removes kings and raises
>   up kings;
> He gives wisdom to the wise
> And knowledge to those who
>   have understanding.
> He reveals deep and secret
>   things;
> He knows what is in the
>   darkness,
> And light dwells with Him.
>
> I thank You and praise You,
> O God of my fathers;
> You have given me wisdom
>   and might,
> And have now made known to
>   me what we asked of You,
> For You have made known to us
>   the king's demand."

How good it is to lift our hearts to God when He showers us with good things. How good to join the Old Testament's saints in blessing our God.

SINCERITY IN PRAYER

One of the most significant elements of Old Testament prose prayer is that these spontaneous expressions are fervent and sincere. They come from the heart. There is no attempt to manipulate God—no reliance on formal, crafted appeals. Instead, these prayers are characterized by openness and a lack of guile.

Some people have written books on supposed "conditions" that we must meet in order for God to answer our prayers. But the clear teaching of the Old Testament is that having an open heart toward God is vital in any prayer relationship with Him. The words of the prophet Isaiah, represented in a new Jewish translation of the familiar text, make this point clearly. Why does God judge His people rather than answer their prayers? It is . . .

Because that people has approached
  [Me] with its mouth
And honored Me with its lips,
But has kept its heart far from Me,
And its worship of Me has been
A commandment of men, learned by
  rote—
  Tanakh (1988)

How important it is that we reach out spontaneously and openly to God—to share with Him whatever is in our hearts.

❖

CHAPTER 4

THE TRANSFORMING POWER
OF PERSONAL PRAYER

PSALMS 1—72

Some people ask, "What good is praying?" They argue that God is going to do what He has planned anyway. Prayer won't change God's mind. So why pray?

There are at least two good answers to this attitude toward prayer. The first is that God *does* answer prayer. The scriptural evidence is overwhelming.

For instance, Numbers 11:2 says, "When Moses prayed to the LORD, the fire was quenched." Hannah was able to report to Eli the priest, "For this child I prayed, and the LORD has granted me my petition which I asked of Him" (1 Sam. 1:27).

Solomon prayed that God would be present in the temple which the king had constructed for His worship. First Kings 9:3 reports God's response: "I have heard your prayer . . . and My eyes and My heart will be there perpetually." When the Assyrians invaded Judah and threatened Jerusalem, King Hezekiah prayed for God to intervene. God sent the prophet Isaiah to the king with this message: "Because you have prayed to Me against Sennacherib king of Assyria, I have heard" (2 Kings 19:20).

We could multiply these examples again and again. God has acted and does act *because His people pray.* Does this mean that God changes His mind? The question really is irrelevant. All our theological arguments and all our reasoning mean nothing compared to the testimony of Scripture that God does answer prayer. The fact is that God can and does act to change circumstances *because His people pray.* So it truly is important that we pray.

When we come to the personal prayers in the Psalms, we see an additional reason why it's important to pray: We are to pray, *because prayer changes us.*

THE TRANSFORMING POWER OF PRAYER

We see the transforming power of prayer in two of the beautifully crafted poems recorded in the Psalms.

PSALM 3
Prayer Brings Us Peace in Stressful Circumstances

The prayer recorded in Psalm 3 grew out of a specific situation identified in the superscription of this psalm. This was the prayer that King David uttered as he fled from his rebel son, Absalom, whose attempt to seize the throne threatened David's life.

Absalom had laid the foundation of his rebellion by courting the ten northern tribes of Israel. When Absalom at last struck, many of David's most trusted advisers and oldest friends went over to him. How it must have hurt David! A son whom he loved, a people whom he had nurtured and cared for, and trusted members of his court—they all abandoned him! David expressed his pain and his doubts in the first words of his prayer.

> LORD, how they have
>   increased who trouble me!
> Many are they who rise up
>   against me.
> Many are they who say of me,
> "There is no help for him in
>   God." Se'lah (Ps. 3:1, 2).

The wide support for the rebellion made it clear that even David's closest associates had concluded that God had abandoned him. David himself seemed to be filled with doubts—and for good reason. He had sinned with Bathsheba. Although he had confessed his sin and had been forgiven, this shocking flaw in David's character had raised doubts about his commitment to the Lord. Then, as similar sins erupted in the royal family, David had failed to deal with them. Everyone knew that David had been chosen by God to lead Israel. But had David forfeited God's support by his sins?

The rebellion made it clear that the people who rose up against David were sure that God would no longer come to the king's aid. And David himself was not free of doubt. But as David fled, he pondered his relationship with God. He remembered all that God had been to him in the past. And, remembering the Lord, David appealed directly to Him:

> But You, O LORD, are a shield
>   for me,

> My glory and the One who
>   lifts up my head.
> I cried to the LORD with my
>   voice,
> And He heard me from His
>   holy hill. Se'lah (Ps. 3:3–4).

Three descriptive words or phrases sum up David's experience with God. God had been David's shield—the One who had always been his protector. God even now was David's glory. All the pomp associated with royalty meant nothing to David, who valued the Lord more than any worldly honor. And God was also the "One who lifts up my head," an idiom which portrayed the Lord as the source of David's strength.

David, remembering who God was and had been for him, cried out to the Lord. And deep within, David knew that God had heard him.

Suddenly everything changed. The circumstances were still the same. David was still in flight from his son Absalom and from an army intent on taking David's life. The situation, like the night sky, looked just as dark. But within David's heart, peace and confidence had been reborn.

Prayer had made a change *in him:*

> I lay down and slept;
> I awoke, for the LORD sustained
>   me.
> I will not be afraid of ten
>   thousands of people
> Who have set themselves
>   against me all around.

> Arise, O LORD;
> Save me, O my God!
> For You have struck all my
>   enemies on the cheekbone;
> You have broken the teeth of
>   the ungodly.
> Salvation belongs to the LORD.
> Your blessing is upon Your
>   people. Se'lah (Ps. 3:5–8).

"I lay down and slept; . . . the LORD sustained me. I will not be afraid."

PSALM 73
Prayer Provides Perspective That Frees from Doubt

Psalm 73 is not a prayer but the report of the impact of prayer in Asaph's life. Although he was a worship leader, Asaph was wracked by doubts. No sudden event precipitated Asaph's uncertainty about God. But the period of doubt and depression that Asaph experienced seemed about to destroy his faith. Asaph wrote,

> But as for me, my feet had
>   almost stumbled;
> My steps had nearly slipped.
> For I was envious of the
>   boastful,
> When I saw the prosperity of
>   the wicked (Ps. 73:2, 3).

Asaph's doubts have been reflected in believers throughout Old and New Testament eras. If God loves His own, how does it happen that the wicked so often "are not in trouble as other men, nor are they plagued like other men" (Ps. 73:5)? They do violence to others, but "their eyes bulge with abundance"

(Ps. 73:7). They scoff at righteousness and oppress the weak, yet "they have more than heart could wish" (Ps. 73:7). They openly scoff at God, but are "always at ease; they increase in riches" (Ps. 73:12).

Then Asaph looked at his own life. The wicked prospered but he, who had carefully cleansed his heart and "washed my hands in innocence" had "been plagued and chastened every morning" (Ps. 73:13, 14). Although Asaph did not speak of his doubts to anyone, he was eaten up by them, and the pain he felt was almost unbearable (Ps. 73:15, 16).

How could God be so unfair? How could God treat him so shabbily while showering the wicked with health and material blessings?

Most of us can identify with Asaph's feelings. We have struggled to make it, while others who ignored God have prospered. We've fought sickness or loneliness and felt abandoned, while others have seemed to live serene lives. It's no wonder doubt creeps in at times.

But then Asaph took an important step. He went directly to God. He "went into the sanctuary of God" (Ps. 73:17). As he prayed, God gave him a new perspective. In a flash of prayer-inspired insight, Asaph saw the relationship between prosperity and eternal destiny. Suddenly Asaph saw that the success of the wicked was not a blessing, but divine judgment!

> Surely You set them in
> slippery places;
> You cast them down to
> destruction (Ps. 73:18).

In their prosperity, the wicked had never given a thought to God. But in his troubles, Asaph had been forced to rely on the Lord and to turn to Him in prayer. The easy life that Asaph had envied was in fact a "slippery place," for those who enjoy untroubled days are never forced by circumstances to consider their mortality. Prosperity and pleasure are like drugs which induce a euphoria that insulates people from reality.

With this new perspective, Asaph felt ashamed. He had been so foolish. He had, like a "brute beast," acted as if this life was all-important. Suddenly Asaph was filled with praise and joy. Whatever his troubles,

> I am continually
> with You;
> You hold me by my right
> hand.
> You will guide me with Your
> counsel,
> And afterward receive me to
> glory.
>
> Whom have I in heaven but
> You?
> And there is none upon earth
> that I desire besides You.
> My flesh and my heart fail;
> But God is the strength of my
> heart and my portion
> forever.
>
> For indeed, those who are far
> from You shall perish;

> You have destroyed all those
> who desert You for
> harlotry.
> But it is good for me to
> draw near to God;
> I have put my trust in the
> LORD God,
> That I may declare all Your
> works (Ps. 73:23–28).

Each of these psalms illustrates the transforming power of personal prayer. Yes, God can and does answer our prayers. But perhaps as significant, God works through our prayers to *change us*. Meditation on God and turning our stressful circumstances over to Him can fill us with inner peace, just like that which David experienced. Bringing our doubts and uncertainties, our fears and complaints to the Lord can change our perspective and renew our joy in the Lord, as it did for Asaph. And, in the personal prayers recorded for us in the Psalms, we discover that we can bring *everything* to the Lord in prayer.

PERSONAL PRAYER IN THE PSALMS

CLASSIFICATION OF PSALMS

Not all psalms are prayers. In fact, only five psalms state "a prayer" in their superscription (Pss. 17, 86, 90, 102, and 142). A number of psalms are prophetic, speaking of Christ (see Pss. 2, 22, 110, for example). Many of the psalms are addressed not to God but to God's people, and they are instructional in nature (see Pss. 1, 8, 14, 40—42, 95—100, etc.). Many psalms incorporate brief prayers within them, but are not themselves prayers (see Pss. 38, 84, 99, 106, 125, etc.).

Furthermore, not every prayer psalm can be considered a *personal* prayer. Some are corporate prayers, in which the people of God addressed the Lord when they were gathered for worship. Other psalms, although using the singular "I" in speaking to God, are shown by their superscriptions to be intended for public worship. In many cases, such psalms can function both as a model for individual prayer as well as expressions of faith uttered along with others as part of Israel's worship liturgy.

CHARACTERISTICS OF PERSONAL PRAYER PSALMS

The above makes it difficult at times to determine which psalms are "personal," in contrast to "liturgical." Thus, there may be some disagreement over the psalms chosen by the author for this chapter on every personal prayer in the Psalms. The same goes for those included in the following chapter on every public prayer in the Psalms.

What no one will disagree with, however, is that both personal and public prayer psalms are marked by the free expression of human emotions to the Lord. The psalmists remind us that as God's children, we have the freedom to share *everything* with our Heavenly Father.

This wonderful freedom is reflected in more traditional classifications of psalms, as represented by the following list from the *Revell Bible Dictionary* and a paragraph from *Nelson's New Illustrated Bible Dictionary*.

Under a "Topical Guide to the Psalms" (p. 835), the *Revell Bible Dictionary* noted the psalmists express anger (Pss. 4, 17, 18, 36, 109), disappointment (Pss. 16, 92, 102, 130), discouragement (Pss. 12, 42, 55, 86, 107, 142), a sense of insignificance (8, 23, 86, 119, 139), and joy (22, 47, 63, 84, 96, 97, 98, 100, 148). The psalmists cry out against injustice, calling on God to punish the wicked (7, 9, 10, 17, 35, 52, 56, 94, 109). They freely express their loneliness (3, 13, 17, 25, 27, 69, 91) and their grief (6, 31, 71, 77, 94, 123). The whole range of human emotions is expressed in the psalms as believers pour out their hearts to the Lord.

Commenting on this same thing, *Nelson's New Illustrated Bible Dictionary* (p. 1049) notes that while the psalms give us an exalted vision of God, they also portray Him as "One who is close enough to touch and who walks beside us along life's way." In fact,

The psalmist admits he sometimes feels abandoned by God as well as his human friends (88). He ago-

nizes over the lies directed against him by his false accusers (109). He calls upon God to deliver him from his enemies and to wipe them out with His wrath (59). Whatever else we may say about the psalms, we must admit they are realistic about human feelings and the way we sometimes respond to the problems and inequities of life.

This is a significant message for all believers. We can bring all our feelings to God, no matter how negative or complaining they may be. And we can rest assured that He will hear and understand.

When we look at the personal prayers recorded in the psalms, we want to be especially sensitive to the example of openness and honesty with God that they provide. We can express all our every emotion to the Lord, even as we bring Him all our needs. In the process, we can expect God to answer our prayers by changing the situation, when this is best. And, even when God doesn't choose to change our circumstances, we can be sure that as we share all with the Lord, God will certainly change *us*.

IDENTIFYING PERSONAL PRAYER PSALMS

Several criteria can be used to identify a personal prayer psalm. First, the psalm must be addressed to God rather than to other persons. Second, the psalm must express the psalmist's personal concerns in the first person singular, rather than the first person plural. Third, the superscription of the psalm should have minimal reference to any liturgical use of the psalm in corporate worship.

The superscriptions of the psalms reveal that many psalms—although they are personal in nature—had an important role in the worship of the believing community. These psalms will be discussed in the next chapter. Because opinions as to the liturgical use of certain psalms do differ, the author's classification of personal and public psalms should not be taken as authoritative.

However, using the above criteria, we can identify many of the psalms as personal prayers. And we can learn much from them for our own personal prayer lives.

PROFITING FROM PERSONAL PRAYERS IN THE PSALMS

The book of Psalms has been given a variety of names. The rabbis called it the "book of praises." Christian commentators have dubbed it "the Bible's guide to prayer." There is no doubt that personal prayer psalms do provide models of personal prayer intended to lead us into a deeper, closer relationship with the Lord. Specifically, personal prayer psalms:

- reveal the freedom we have to share everything with the Lord;
- frequently shift the focus of our thoughts from ourselves to those qualities of God's which reassure us and meet our deepest needs; and
- often identify specific situations which led to the prayer. When this is the case, the situation is identified in the superscription of the psalm.

To profit most from personal prayer psalms, we need to explore the circumstances under which they were written. Historical roots are frequently identified in a psalm's superscription. We also need to understand and identify with the personal need or emotion that drove the psalmist to prayer. We will also need to focus our attention on the trait or quality of God which is emphasized in the prayer. And we will need to consider how expressing such a prayer to the Lord may change and transform us.

So in considering every personal prayer in the psalms, we will briefly explore the following elements:

- the setting of the psalm;
- needs or emotions expressed in the psalm;
- qualities of God emphasized in the psalm;
- the prayer's transforming power; and personal application of the psalm.

In this chapter, we will examine the personal prayer psalms in the first two collections of these wonderful poems, Book I (Pss. 1—41) and Book II (Pss. 42—72).

In the next chapter, we will look at the personal prayer psalms in the last three collections, Books III-V.

EVERY PERSONAL PRAYER IN THE PSALMS
Books I and II (Pss. 1—72)

PSALM 3
"You are a shield."

The setting. David was fleeing from his son, Absalom, who with the support of the ten northern tribes and many of David's chief officials had attempted a coup (see the discussion on page 49).

David was forced to abandon Jerusalem with only a few loyal followers in a desperate attempt to reach the south, his base of support (2 Sam. 15, 16).

David's emotions and needs. The rebellion had shaken David's confidence, not in God but in himself. He was aware of his own flaws, and was driven to consider whether his enemies were right when they assumed "there is no help for him in God" (Ps. 3:2). Driven from his throne, his life threatened, David's uncertainty about God's attitude toward him made this one of the most stressful events in his life.

Qualities of God. In his distress, David's thoughts turned to the past, and he reviewed all that God had done for him. God had been his shield, protecting David in times of extreme danger. God had been David's glory. The Hebrew word translated "glory" means "weighty," and it stands for all that is important in a person's life. To some people, their wealth or position is their glory. But as David examined his heart, he realized that all he truly valued was God and his relationship with the Lord.

The Lord had also been "the One who holds up my head,"—the One who had always strengthened and supported David. In

Absalom's rebellion forced David to flee for his life.

turning his thoughts to God, David reminded himself that truly "salvation belongs to the LORD," and that God's blessing "is upon your people" (Ps. 3:8).

Prayer's transforming power. David's prayer didn't change his circumstances. But in turning to the Lord, David found God's peace. David was able to lie down and sleep, for his fears were gone (3:5, 6). Yes, David still called on God to act and defeat his enemies (3:7). But until God did act, David would experience an inner peace that cannot be explained by circumstances, but only by a vital, trusting confidence in our loving, powerful Lord.

Personal application. We too are often victims of anxiety. We find ourselves in circumstances beyond our control—perhaps the victims of

enemies we once thought of as friends. How wonderful at such times to remember all that God has done for us in the past, and to refocus our lives on Him. When we do, we will also find God's glorious peace as we wait for Him to act.

PSALM 7
"Rise up for me to the judgment."

The setting. The superscription locates this psalm, like Psalm 3, in the days when David was forced to flee Jerusalem during Absalom's rebellion (2 Sam. 16). The Benjamite whom the Psalm calls "Cush" is identified as Shimei in 2 Samuel. This man, a relative of the late King Saul, cursed the retreating David, throwing stones at his party. Abishai, one of David's loyal men, begged permission to kill Shimei for reviling the king. David refused. Instead, he pondered the possibility that Shimei's accusation that David was a "man of blood" [a murderer] might reflect God's own assessment. David hoped that his restraint might please the Lord, and that God would deal with Shimei (2 Sam. 16:8–12).

David's emotions. David's restraint was notable in view of his surging emotions. He was truly angry at Shimei. But the first thing Shimei's taunts did was to lead David to reaffirm his reliance on the Lord to deliver David from his persecutors (Ps. 7:1, 2).

David next looked within his own heart. Perhaps he deserved what was happening to him. So David prayed,

> O LORD my God, if I have done
>   this:
> If there is iniquity in my
>   hands. . . .
> Let the enemy pursue me and
>   overtake me;
> Yes, let him trample my life to
>   the earth,
> And lay my honor in the dust. Se'lah
>   (Ps. 7:3, 5).

But even as David opened his life to the Lord and invited His scrutiny, David called on God to judge Shimei as well.

> Oh, let the wickedness of the
>   wicked come to an end (Ps.
>   7:9).

Qualities of God. David's anger and his sense of the injustice of his situation led him to consider the nature of God as Judge. God truly is the moral ruler of His universe. God Himself would evaluate David's actions. If David were found guilty, then he would accept God's verdict willingly (Ps. 7:4, 5).

At the same time, David called on God to arise and deal with his enemies (Ps. 7:6). David honored God's commitment to justice, as he reminded himself,

> God is a just judge,
> And God is angry with the
>   wicked every day.
> If he does not turn back,
> He will sharpen His sword (Ps. 7:11,
>   12).

Prayer's transforming power. As we read the description of this event in 2 Samuel, we sense not only David's frustration but also his suppressed anger. But David realized that God is Judge, and so he refused to act against Shimei until God's will concerning the rebellion had been made clear.

Psalm 7, identified as "a meditation," takes us deeper than 2 Samuel does. Psalm 7 shows, step by step, how David dealt with persecution and injustice through prayer.

Step 1: David reaffirmed trust in God   vv. 1, 2
and appealed to Him.

Step 2: David invited the Lord to judge   vv. 3–8
and admitted the possibility that
his troubles might be deserved.

Step 3: David reminded himself that God   vv. 9–16
does judge the wicked. Surely
any violence done by the wicked
will "come down on his own crown."

Step 4: Totally freed from his anger   v. 17
and frustration, David praised
God "according to His righteousness"
and sang praise "to the name of
the LORD most High."

Personal application. We can't help becoming angry at the wicked who do violence to us or our loved ones. Perhaps their actions do merit punishment. But how are we to respond? This meditation leads us to consider the wonderful truth that God is Judge. If what has happened to us is not deserved, God will vindicate us. God too is "angry with the wicked every day." Because of this, the trouble that the wicked make for others "shall return upon his own head."

As we meditate on these truths, something wonderful happens within us. We find ourselves released from the terrible burden of our anger. Rather than being eaten up by hostility toward those who harm us, we turn these negative feelings over to the Lord, confident that He will judge. And what flows into our hearts to replace the anger? Praise. Praise for the Lord, who is righteous and who will right every wrong in His own good time.

PSALM 10
"Why do You stand afar off?"

The setting. No historical setting is provided in the superscription, nor is the author indicated.

The psalmist's emotions and needs. The psalmist was troubled at the persecution of poor by the wicked. We are not told whether the writer was reflecting on personal experience. However, the psalmist's descriptions of the behavior and attitudes of the wicked (vv. 2–11) suggest he was expressing a godly concern for the oppressed in his society.

The psalmist was conscious of sin's expression as injustice, and he was fully aware of the disregard for God which lies at the roots of oppression. Thus, the psalmist prayed, "Let them be caught in the plots which they have devised" (v. 2), and called on God to arise and "lift up Your hand" (that is, *act!*) (v. 12).

Qualities of God. Faced with the existence of injustice and the exploitation of the poor by the wealthy, the psalmist looked to God. He couldn't understand why God seemed to "hide in times of trouble" (v. 1). But the psalmist did know his God:

- God is omniscient. He observes trouble and grief (v. 14a).
- God is just. He will repay the wicked (v. 14b).
- God is the helper of the fatherless [the powerless in society] (v. 14c).
- God is King forever. In spite of His apparent inaction, our God rules (v. 16).
- God, who has heard the desire of the humble, is preparing their hearts for the day when He will act to do away with oppression and establish justice on earth.

Prayer's transforming power. Psalm 10 expresses one of the great paradoxes of our faith.

"The wicked . . . persecutes the poor; let them be caught."

We know that God is good and loving. Yet we see injustice all around us. We know that God cares for the helpless. Yet we see the powerless oppressed and persecuted. The evidence seems to support the wicked, who assume that God can be ignored (v. 4), for if God does observe, surely "You will not require an account" (v. 13).

But the evidence we observe runs counter to everything that we believe! We believe in an omnipotent, omnipresent God of love, who is actively involved in the affairs of this world. We believe in a God who sees trouble and grief, who takes sides with the persecuted against their persecutors, and who as ruler of all is free to act in judgment. It is no wonder that the more familiar we become with sin's impact in society, the more we question, "Why do You hide yourself in times of trouble?"

The psalmist had pondered this question, and he came to the only conclusion that could be reached. Our sovereign God is preparing the hearts of the humble for that day when He will "do justice to the fatherless and the oppressed" (v. 18). We cannot explain why He delays. But we know God. And we trust Him to do what is best.

Personal application. There is always a tension between what *is* in our sinful world and what *ought to be.* We will always have occasion to wonder why God permits institutionalized injustice and the oppression of the poor and the helpless. Yet we must not allow the existence of evil in the world to shake our trust in God. In fact, the existence of wickedness underlines the necessity of faith in God!

We human beings have been blessed with a moral sense: We recognize wickedness and sin and we decry their expression. We feel outrage at the unfeeling way in which the wicked exploit the helpless. Yet we seem powerless to change society or to root out the oppression we see all around us. We know intuitively that wrongs *must be* set right.

This conviction that wrongs must be righted is powerful evidence for the existence of God. Our moral certainty that evil must be repaid and the persecuted restored is an affirmation which requires the existence of the God of the Bible. Only such a God can bring justice to our fallen race and accomplish what we know must be done.

Let us never mistake the presence of injustice in society as an argument against faith in God. In fact, the presence of injustice is evidence that the God of the Bible must exist. Otherwise, there would be no way to set right what we know is wrong.

PSALM 13
"Will you forget me forever?"

The setting. The superscription tells us that this is a psalm of David's, which was set to music. But no details are given about the specific circumstance which moved David to write the psalm.

David's emotions and needs. It is fascinating to compare this psalm with Psalm 10. In Psalm 10, an unknown writer contemplated the plight of the poor and oppressed, pondering why God remained silent while the wicked exploited the helpless. In this psalm, David himself was oppressed by enemies. Suddenly the situation seemed different. This was no mere intellectual inquiry, which could be resolved by reasoning theologically. David was hurting! It was deep, personal pain that caused David to cry out urgently to God, "Will You forget me forever?"

In this situation, David was not looking for answers. With his enemies on the verge of victory (vv. 3, 4), and David broken by the "sorrow in my heart daily (v. 2)," what he was looking for was help. Now!

Qualities of God. In his extremity, David fixed on a quality of God which he had experienced. "I have trusted in your mercy," David declared (v. 5).

This is one of the most endearing of God's many wonderful qualities. In the Old Testament, "mercy" speaks of the response of a person moved by another's need. The word *mercy* not only suggests a deep concern for the needy person, but also the ability and willingness to provide help. Although the needy person has no right to demand aid, he or she can rely on the God who shows mercy to be moved by His feelings to act.

Thus, David reminded himself of previous experiences in which he had been shown mercy by God, and reaffirmed his trust in God as One who truly is merciful. This vision of a merciful God freed David to affirm "My heart shall rejoice in Your salvation" (v. 5). God, who had delivered David in the past, would surely deliver him in this situation.

Prayer's transforming power. As we read David's words in verses 1–4, we can almost sense his panic. David was in grave danger, and God had not acted to put down his enemies. The situation was serious enough that David feared for his life. How bitter it would be if David's enemies should rejoice over his defeat and humiliation!

But verses 5 and 6 reveal a total change in David's attitude. David remembered that God is merciful. And David responded to this truth with trust.

What a difference was wrought by trusting in the Lord. David was filled with renewed confidence: "My heart shall rejoice in Your salvation" (v. 5). And, "I will sing to the LORD, because he has dealt bountifully with me" (v. 6).

David expressed his panic and his fears to God in prayer. God reminded David of His mercy. And David, responding to God with renewed trust, was filled with confidence and hope.

Personal application. Let's be sure we grasp the difference between the concern expressed in Psalm 10 and that expressed in this psalm. In Psalm 10, the psalmist raised a question that troubled him intellectually. It was a serious question—one which has troubled many people. Yet the psalmist's reasoned inquiry led him to a resolution which was intellectually satisfying. As we read this prayer and trace the psalmist's thoughts, we realize that although the dilemma was significant, it was not one that shook the psalmist to the core of his being.

But when we turn to Psalm 13, we meet a deeply shaken and distraught David. Although the question he raised was essentially the same as in Psalm 10—"Why does God seem to hide from the person in trouble?" (cf. 10:1b; 13:1b)—the two psalms are radically different in tone. Here David was shaken to the core of his being. He was in personal danger, desperate for God's intervention. In a voice filled with emotion, David expressed his fears to the Lord.

And, just as the two psalms differ in tone, they differ in the ways the dilemmas were resolved. In Psalm 10, the resolution was reasoned. In Psalm 13, the resolution was emotional, marked by an intense personal response to God's reminder that He is merciful.

In Psalm 10, we learn that the way to resolve our intellectual doubts is to think the issue through. There truly are answers that will satisfy our minds.

In Psalm 13, we learn that the way to quiet our fears is to throw ourselves in trust on the mercy of God. Only trust in the Lord will satisfy our hearts.

PSALM 16
"In Your presence is fullness of joy."

The setting. The superscription of this psalm tells us it was written by David as a "michtam"—as lyrics to be sung. It is possible that this psalm became a popular song in Israel. The words and the tune were probably sung and hummed by David as he meditated on his blessings in the Lord.

David's emotions and needs. It is helpful to remember that prayer is essentially communion with God. The trusting child walks hand in hand with the Lord—with thanks and admiration—filled with a peace and joy that come only from a comfortable relationship with God.

The dominant emotion reflected in Psalm 16 is gratitude, flowing from satisfaction with the blessings David has found in his relationship with the Lord. We see this expressed in a variety of ways in the psalm.

David was satisfied with God's goodness, and he took delight in fellowshiping with God's saints.	verses 2, 3
David was thrilled that God was his true inheritance. He was overjoyed at the role in life God had chosen for him.	verses 5, 6
David blessed [praised] God for His counsel. He knew that keeping the Lord always in mind protected him from wrong choices.	verses 7, 8
David looked beyond this life and rejoiced in the fact of resurrection. Verse 10 is prophetic, referring to Easter.	verses 9, 10
David took delight simply being in God's presence, for he knew that "at Your right hand are pleasures forevermore."	verse 11

Prayer's transforming power. It is so easy to become caught up in the pressures of daily life and to lose our joy. In this prayer psalm,

David pointed the way to true happiness. That way is simply to contemplate the Lord and His goodness, and to tell Him how much our relationship with Him means to us. As we offer the Lord our praise, our hearts are filled with an awareness of His goodness. Then even the most ordinary days sparkle in the light of His presence.

Personal application. If we truly desire to experience God, this michtam of David points the way. Let us take time to affirm God, to express our delight in Him and His goodness. Our life will take on a different hue.

PSALM 17
"Satisfied when I awake in Your likeness"

The setting. The occasion for this prayer is not identified. This is, however, one of just five psalms described in their superscription as "a prayer." This is the most common word for prayer in the Old Testament, occurring most often in the Psalms. One suggestion about the meaning of the word is that it comes from a root meaning "to assess." Thus, in prayer the believer asked God to evaluate and act on His assessment of a situation.

It is striking that in this particular prayer, David seemed to assess his own commitment to God and its consequences, as well as to assess the end of the path chosen by the wicked.

David's emotions and needs. While the psalm speaks of David's enemies, there is no overwhelming sense of urgency or danger as in Psalm 13. Instead, David seemed confident, satisfied that God was with him and that he had chosen the path of blessing.

In this prayer, David looked into his own heart and invited God to examine him too (17:3–5). David was confident that "by the word of Your lips, I have kept away from the paths of the destroyer" (17:4). What's more, David has "called upon You" (17:6)—evidence of David's trust in God to show His lovingkindness (17:7).

Two metaphors express David's sense of God's love: God will keep him as the apple

"Hide me under the shadow of Your wings."

[pupil] of His eye, and God will hide him as a hen shelters her chicks, under the shadow of His wings (17:8).

David's attitude toward God was in sharp contrast with that of those who had closed their "fat (unresponsive) hearts" to God. Such persons were concerned only with this life and with possessions they gathered, only to leave them to their children. How different such persons are from David, who looked beyond this world to find meaning in eternity. David's desire was to see God's face in righteousness, and David knew "I shall be satisfied when I awake in Your likeness" (17:15).

Qualities of God. In this psalm, David drew our attention to several qualities of God. God tests the hearts of men (17:3). He has given us His Word to keep us "away from the paths of the destroyer" (17:4). God hears our prayers, and His answers display His "marvelous lovingkindness" (17:7). God truly is One who will save those who trust in Him (17:7). He will deliver David from the wicked (17:13).

Prayer's transforming power. As David reviewed his commitment to the Lord and the blessings commitment brought, he was able to assess what was truly important in life. The worldly goals men set their hearts upon turn to ashes. But David's thoughts ranged beyond the present to eternity. One day David will see God. Only then will David be satisfied, for he will awake, purified, in God's likeness.

Personal application. Prayer helps us fix our thoughts on God, giving us perspective on life. How blessed we are when we can invite God's scrutiny, confident of our commitment to God and His commitment to us. What a joy to realize that the meaning of our lives rests in God. We can be content in the knowledge that we bear His likeness because we have been created in His image.

PSALM 25
"Let me not be ashamed."

The setting. No specific occasion for this psalm is identified in the superscription.

David's emotions and needs. The repeated phrase, "Let me not be ashamed" (25:2, 20), sums up David's concern. In Hebrew thought, a person was "ashamed" when something or someone he had counted on failed him and his confidence was thus shown to be misplaced. David's appeal, "Let me not be ashamed," was a prayer that God would act, and so reveal to all that David's confidence in God had not been misplaced. David's concern was for God's glory, not his own shame.

It is not until the end of the psalm that we realize David himself was hurting. He cried out to the Lord,

> Turn Yourself to me, and have
>   mercy upon me,
> For I am desolate and
>   afflicted.
> The troubles of my heart have
>   enlarged;
> Bring me out of my distresses!
> Look on my affliction and my

> pain,
> And forgive all my sins.
> Consider my enemies, for they
>   are many;
> And they hate me with cruel
>   hatred.
> Keep my soul, and deliver me;
> Let me not be ashamed, for I
>   put my trust in You (Ps.
>   25:16–20).

Qualities of God. Again and again in this psalm, David looked to God as teacher. He asked God to teach David His paths and to lead him in His truth (25:4, 5). David affirmed God's goodness and uprightness, praising His willingness to "teach sinners in the way" of mercy and truth (25:8, 10). David appealed to God to pardon his iniquity, not because David deserved mercy, but for the glory of God's name (25:11).

David believed with all his heart that the person who fears (reverences, respects) God will be guided into a blessed life (25:12, 13). He was sure that God would watch over the person who looked to Him (25:14, 15).

Prayer's transforming power. David's convictions about God provided the basis for his appeal. David was distressed and desolate. Through this prayer in which David expressed his confidence in the Lord, he found the patience to wait confidently for the Lord.

Personal application. Speaking to the Lord about His faithfulness and expressing our trust in Him is pleasing to God. But it is also enriching for us. This kind of prayer strengthens us to face life's trials with confidence, waiting in patience for God to act.

PSALM 26.
"I have walked in Your truth."

Setting. No historical setting is provided for this psalm of David.

David's emotions and needs. While David called on the Lord to vindicate him, this prayer was not driven by any particular sense of need. Instead, it is a psalm of personal commitment, in which David took great joy in his past faithfulness to the Lord and expressed his intention to remain faithful.

Qualities of God. In this psalm, David was sensitive to God as One who could be trusted and who examined human hearts (26:1, 2). God's "wondrous works" (26:7) referred to His historic interventions [miracles] performed for the benefit of His people. David also may have been thinking of times when God intervened on his behalf.

Prayer's transforming power. To some, this prayer of David's sounds suspiciously like self-righteousness. After all, David again and again reminded the Lord of the godly choices he had made.

- "I have walked in my integrity" (v. 1).
- "I have trusted the LORD" (v. 1).
- "I have walked in Your truth" (v. 3)
- "I have not sat with idolatrous mortals" (v. 4).
- "I have hated the assembly of evildoers" (v. 5).
- "I have loved the habitation of Your house" (v. 8).

How can we square this with the psalms in which David confessed his sins and weaknesses, or those in which David expressed his dependence on God's mercy and His lovingkindness ("grace")? The answer is that David's relationship with God had made the difference in his life, even as it will make a difference in ours. All the good we do flows from God's work within us, so that the glory is His and His alone. None of the credit belongs to us.

As David looked back at what God had done in his life, he also looked ahead. What God had done in the past foreshadowed what God will do in the future. Thus, David was confident that

- "(I) will not go in with hypocrites" (v. 4)
- "I will wash my hands in innocence" (v. 6).

- "I will go about Your altar . . . and tell of all Your wondrous works" (vv. 6, 7).
- "I will walk in my integrity" (v. 11).
- "I will bless the LORD" (v. 12).

The God who had been at work within David would continue to demonstrate the reality of redemption through David's choice of a godly life.

Personal application. We can never come to God and plead for His help on the basis of our own righteousness. But how our confidence is increased when we realize that God has been at work in our lives!

PSALM 27
"The goodness of the LORD in the land of the living."

The setting. No historical setting is provided as the occasion for this psalm of David. While the first stanzas of this psalm are about God, and are thus instructional, the second half is directed to God, and is thus a prayer.

David's emotions and needs. This is a praise psalm, in which David reflected on the wonderful benefits of a personal relationship with God. A striking feature of the psalm is the interaction that took place between David and the Lord. David was sensitive about and responsive to everything that God revealed about Himself.

Because God is "my light and my   (vv. 1–3)
salvation," David did not
fear his enemies, but was confident
"though war should rise against me."

Because the one thing David desired   (vv. 4–6)
was God Himself, David knew God
would hide [protect] him in the
time of trouble.

Because David had responded to God's   (vv. 7–10)
call to seek His face, the God of David's
salvation would never leave or forsake
him. "The LORD will take care of me."

Because David relied on the Lord to   (vv. 11–13)
teach and lead him, David was convinced
that he would see the goodness of the
Lord in the land of the living.

David spoke from personal experience (v. 14) when he urged us to wait on the Lord and to be of good courage. He promised that God will strengthen our hearts.

Qualities of God. David knew from personal experience that God was his salvation and "the strength of my life" (v. 1). David knew that God had mercy on His worshipers and answered their prayers (v. 7). David knew that God wants people to seek Him and that He will never forsake those who do (vv. 8, 9). David knew that God's way leads to blessing in this life, and that He reveals that path to those who look to Him for guidance.

Prayer's transforming power. In prayer, we both speak to and listen to the Lord. In this sense, prayer involves dialogue. Dialogical prayer leads to a more responsive relationship in which we act on what God says to us. How wonderful that we can respond to God as He reveals Himself to us, and that in responding we can see His grace and goodness.

Personal application. Take time to meditate when you pray. Listen for Him to speak to you. Talk your experience over with the Lord, and He will encourage your heart.

PSALM 28
"He has heard the voice of my supplications."

The setting. No historical setting is identified for this psalm of David.

David's emotions and needs. David asked God to listen when he cried out. The psalm presupposes that God had heard David's prayer, and the dominant emotion is one of joy and praise (v. 7).

Qualities of God. In this prayer, David portrayed God as sovereign and all-powerful. God judges the wicked (vv. 3–5), but saves His own people (vv. 6, 7). He is the source of strength to all who trust in Him.

Prayer's transforming power. David blessed God for responding to his prayers and for

strengthening him. Further contemplation of God's grace and goodness moved David to rejoice, and this filled his heart with songs of praise.

Personal application. God does answer prayer. Taking time to thank God when prayers are answered is both right and beneficial. God deserves our thanks. In thanking God "because He has heard the voice of my supplications" (v. 6), we will find that our own hearts will "greatly rejoice."

PSALM 30
"I will give thanks to You forever."

The setting. The superscription tells us that this psalm was written for the dedication of "the house of David." The phrase "house of David" may be taken literally as a reference to the dedication of a building, as in Deuteronomy 20:5. But it may also be taken metaphorically, as a reference to David's family line. There are references to the house (palace) in which David lived (cf. 2 Sam. 20:3; 1 Chron. 17:1), and we can assume it was dedicated when completed. But the phrase "house of David" normally refers to David's descendants and the royal line.

Assuming the most common meaning of "house of David," the psalm reflects David's emotions on being crowned king of the southern tribes of Judah (2 Sam. 2:1–7). After years as a fugitive, fleeing from King Saul and in constant danger of losing his life, David assumed the glory of royalty.

David's emotions and needs. This psalm is an expression of unmixed praise and joy. God had turned David's "mourning into dancing." The man who once cried out to God because his life was in danger had been "healed" and brought "up from the grave" (vv. 2, 3). David sang praises to God, declaring, "will give thanks to You forever" (v. 12).

Qualities of God. David had experienced God's grace. God had kept David alive (v. 3), transforming his poverty into prosperity (v. 6)

After the madness of King Saul's final years, David's coronation was a day for rejoicing.

and his mourning into gladness (v. 11). David was aware that it was God who had worked this wonderful change in his circumstances in answer to prayer.

Prayer's transforming power. Prayer had changed David's circumstances as well as his heart. As we noted on page 48, prayer brings about changes in our lives as God grants our requests. The answer to prayer led to changes in David, as gladness replaced despair.

Personal application. We can expect God to answer prayer. When God does answer prayer, our changed circumstances will glorify and bring praise to Him. And His answers to prayer will make us glad.

PSALM 35
"Let destruction come upon him."

The setting. No specific historical context is identified in the superscription of this lengthy psalm.

David's emotions and needs. In this psalm, David lashed out against his enemies, calling on God to destroy them. David was incensed by the actions of his foes. They had returned David evil for good (v. 12). They had mocked David and rejoiced at his troubles (vv. 15, 16). They had stirred up trouble in Israel and told lies about him (vv. 20, 21).

In his anger, David appealed to God to "let their way be dark and slippery, and let the angel of the LORD pursue them" (v. 6). He appealed to God to "let destruction come upon him unexpectedly, and let his net he has hidden catch himself; into that very destruction let him fall" (v. 8).

It was not enough for David to ask God to rescue him (v. 17). David also prayed against his enemies:

> Let them be ashamed and
>   brought to mutual confusion
> Who rejoice at my hurt;
> Let them be clothed with
>   shame and dishonor
> Who exalt themselves against
>   Me (Ps. 35:26).

Qualities of God. David's appeal to the Lord was rooted in his conviction that God is One who saves the godly from the wicked (vv. 3, 9, 10). Because he was innocent in this case (v.

19), God who is righteous could be expected to judge His enemies (v. 28).

Prayer's transforming power. Some are troubled by the apparent conflict between Jesus' "turn-the-other-cheek" teaching and imprecatory prayers like this one. It is important to make a distinction. Jesus taught that believers are not to take personal vengeance on those who harm them. Jesus never suggested that God would not judge the wicked or avenge the innocent. In fact, in each of the Gospels Jesus spoke clearly of a coming day of judgment when the wicked *would* be punished.

The issue is not whether the wicked should be punished, but *who is to punish them!*

In this psalm, David surrendered the right of judgment to the Lord, asking Him to punish the evil ones. In this, David's action was in harmony with the teachings of Jesus! Rather than taking matters into his own hands, David called on God to vindicate him "according to Your righteousness" (v. 24).

Prayer's transforming power. We need only compare this prayer psalm with an incident recorded in 1 Samuel 25 to sense the transforming power of prayer. David had been insulted by Nabal, a man whose flocks David and his band had protected. Furious, David set out to kill Nabal and all his workers. Only the intervention of Nabal's wise and courageous wife, Abigail, kept David from taking revenge.

But this psalm portrays a wiser David. Rather than channeling his anger into action, David channeled his anger into prayer. As he set his case before the Lord, David called on God to pay back his persecutors—and then he left matters in God's hands.

Seen in this perspective, angry prayers in which we ask God to punish those who have wronged us may be the first step toward a truly godly way of dealing with a destructive emotion. We can share our anger with the Lord, honor Him as the righteous judge of all, and then—our anger expressed and gone—rest quietly in the conviction that He, not we, will repay.

And as a second step, we may then be moved to pray for our enemies, as Jesus taught in Matthew 5:44.

Personal application. It is wrong to hold anger in and let it warp our attitude toward others. It is wrong to channel our anger into hostile acts. Instead, we should bring such feelings to the Lord, express them to Him, and then let them go. Because God will judge, we will then be free to deal with others in love.

PSALM 38
"I will be in anguish over my sin"

The setting. No historical context for this psalm is given in the superscription. The phrase "to bring to remembrance" indicates that the psalm was for regular use by a person bringing this plight to the Lord.

David's emotions and needs. Some interpreters view this as the prayer of a sick man. Phrases such as "no soundness in my flesh" and "nor any health in my bones" (v. 3) are taken literally. However, David's constant references in this psalm to his sin and his "foolishness" (moral evil) make it more likely that such phrases are metaphors (cf. Isa. 1:4–6). Sin had proven as debilitating to David as a serious illness!

The consciousness of his sin was a burden that David couldn't carry (v. 4). He was "troubled" and "bowed down greatly" (v. 6). He felt "feeble and severely broken" (v. 8). David said, "I groan because of the turmoil of my heart" (v. 8). In his consciousness of sin, David felt alienated from his friends and relatives as well as from the Lord (v. 11), and vulnerable to his enemies (v. 12). Paralyzed by guilt, David felt unable to respond (vv. 13, 14).

Two powerful appeals broke into David's recitation of the inner impact of sin. David cried,

> For in You, O LORD, I hope;
> You will hear, O LORD, my
> God.

and,

> Do not forsake me, O LORD;
> O my God, be not far from me!
> Make haste to help me,
> O LORD, my salvation! (Ps. 38:15,
>   20, 21).

Overcome by his guilt, David was desperate for reassurance that the God in whom he still hoped would be his salvation.

Qualities of God. This prayer psalm is introspective. While David begged God not to chasten him and appealed to the Lord to help, he failed to focus on any quality of God that might lift him out of his distress.

Prayer's transforming power. The failure of David to focus on such qualities of God as His mercy or His readiness to forgive perhaps explains the fact that the psalm ends as it begins—with David struggling with guilt and despair. Yet when we link Psalm 38 to two other psalms of David—32 and 51—we see a transforming process.

In Psalm 38, David revealed the impact of sin and cried out to God. In Psalm 51, a teaching psalm, David cried out for mercy. David confessed his sins to the Lord, acknowledged the fact that he was a sinner by nature, and relied on God to cleanse him and "blot out all my iniquities" (Ps. 51:9). God forgave the brokenhearted David. Forgiven and again in fellowship with the Lord, David praised God as he sought to convert other sinners to the Lord (Ps. 51:12, 13).

In Psalm 32, a contemplation, David reflected on his experience. He recalled the paralyzing impact of sin and the pain that gripped him until he confessed his transgressions to the Lord (Ps. 32:3–5). How blessed is "he whose transgression is forgiven, whose sin is covered" (Ps. 32:1). Truly, "blessed is the man to whom the Lord does not impute iniquity" (Ps. 32:2).

But David's thoughts ranged on beyond forgiveness to the fact that God also instructs and teaches the forgiven, and guides the believer in the way he should go (Ps. 32:8, 9). While the lifestyle of the wicked leads to many sorrows, mercy surrounds the person who trusts in the Lord (Ps. 32:10).

Taking these three psalms together, we see the transforming power of prayer. The debilitating impact of sin on the personality leads a person who is sensitive to God to cry out to Him. That cry leads to confession of sin and cleansing. Cleansed and forgiven, the believer not only instructs others but realizes how vital it is always to trust and obey God.

Personal application. Even when our pain is caused by our own sins, we can bring our hurt to the Lord. As we focus on Him, we will be moved to confess our sin and to appeal for His forgiveness. How wonderful that our loving God will forgive, cleanse, and restore.

Don't let sin drive you away from God. The pain caused by sin is intended to drive us *to* Him.

PSALM 43
"Why do I go mourning?"

The setting. No historical setting or author is given for this prayer, which some commentators see as part of Psalm 42 (compare the refrain in 42:11; 43:5). While Psalm 42 is a corporate lament, Psalm 43 is clearly an individual prayer.

The psalmist's emotions and needs. The psalmist was downcast and disquieted (v. 5), for his circumstances suggest that God had cast him off (v. 2). He was confronting the mystery of the silence of God—a mystery that troubles us all when the God we trust fails to act and come to our aid.

Qualities of God. In spite of the mystery of why God had not acted, the psalmist maintained a correct view of the Lord. God was the source of strength (v. 2), and the source of that light and truth (v. 3) which leads mankind aright. God was the source of all joy, the One in whom we can confidently hope (v. 5).

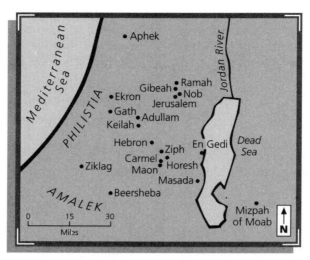

David's flight from Saul—throughout Judah and Philistia

❖

Prayer's transforming power. We will never solve the mystery of God's will. We will never completely understand why He sometimes seems to leave us in the hands of the unjust. But the fact that we do not understand need not shake our trust in God. We do not need to know why He acts as He does; knowing Him is enough.

Personal application. Life holds trials and troubles for each of us. There will be times when we are disquieted and disturbed. At such times, we can pray the psalmist's prayer of faith and cast off our doubts in this affirmation:

> Why are you cast down, O my
>   soul?
> And why are you disquieted
>   within me?
> Hope in God;
> For I shall yet praise Him,
> The help of my countenance
>   and my God (Ps. 43:5).

PSALM 63
"My soul shall be satisfied"

The setting. The superscription tells us that David wrote this psalm during his exile in the wilderness of Judah, described in 1 Samuel 23. King Saul, jealous and fearful of David, was determined to kill him. David fled from Saul's court. Over a period of months, he was joined by about six hundred men. Saul assembled an army to kill David. But David "stayed in strongholds in the wilderness" (1 Sam. 23:14) and avoided his pursuers. It was during this period of his life that he found comfort and joy in the Lord.

David's emotions and needs. The historical setting gives us insight into what David must have been feeling. His life and the lives of his men were in danger. Only by being on the move constantly was David able to avoid being found and killed by Saul. Harried, tired, and hungry, David's little band lived in constant fear. Earlier Samuel had anointed David king of Israel in a private ceremony. How ironic it must have seemed to David that a future king was forced to run for his life from an army that would one day be his own.

Yet these emotions are not reflected in David's psalm. We can only infer them from the historical context. In the psalm itself, we sense only David's desire to know God better and his firm trust in the lovingkindness of the Lord.

Constantly threatened by Saul and his army, David still found comfort in the Lord.

Qualities of God. While David mentioned God's power, glory, and lovingkindness [grace], his thoughts were not focused on any particular quality of God. Rather, David focused on the person of God. In other psalms, David praised God for those things about Himself that He had revealed. In this psalm, David was caught up in the wonder of loving God for Himself, not for His qualities.

We can perhaps understand. We can list things about our spouse that we appreciate and admire. But what we love is the person, not his or her qualities. In this psalm, David showed that he was in love with God.

Prayer's transforming power. When we contrast David's situation with the love he expressed in this psalm, we sense this prayer's transforming power. Love for God—expressed as praise, thanksgiving, and wonder—has the ability to lift us out of ourselves and beyond our circumstances. As we look to the Lord, expressing our love for Him, our troubles seem insignificant. Surely the God whose lovingkindness we know and experience will see

to all our needs, and we will be able to rejoice in Him.

Personal application. In life's darkest moments, we discover that all we really need is God. Let's follow David's example and meditate on Him in the night watches, letting our hearts fill to overflowing with love for the Lord.

PSALM 71
"Be my strong refuge."

The setting. Neither author nor setting is given for this psalm.

The psalmist's emotions and needs. This lengthy prayer psalm is divided into two distinct parts. In verses 1–13, the psalmist cried again and again to God. His appeals, although mixed with expressions of trust, seem almost desperate:

- "Deliver me . . . and cause me to escape" (v. 1).
- "Deliver me . . . out of the hand of the wicked" (v. 4).
- "Do not cast me off" (v. 9).
- "O God, do not be far from me" (v. 12).

Then in verses 14 through 24 the tone changes. The psalmist seems full of confidence.

- "I will hope continually" (v. 14).
- "I will go in the strength of the LORD God" (v. 16).
- "To this day I declare Your wondrous works" (v. 17).
- "You shall increase my greatness" (v. 21).
- "My lips shall greatly rejoice when I sing to You" (v. 23).

Qualities of God. The quality of God mentioned most frequently in this psalm is His righteousness. While mention is also made of God's faithfulness, strength, and power, it is the psalmist's awareness of God's righteousness which seems to serve as an anchor for all his hopes (vv. 2, 15, 16, 19, 24).

The Old Testament, in which God is frequently described as righteous (cf. Pss. 4:1; 7:9; Isa. 45:21) portrays God as displaying this quality in two ways. First, God displays His righteousness in acts of judgment (cf. Pss. 9:8; 96:13; 98:9). But second, God also displays His righteousness in offering salvation to His people. Isaiah 45:21 describes the Lord as "a just ["righteous"] God and a Savior," and the link between God's righteousness and salvation is established in other passages as well (cf. Pss. 31:1; 19:9). Thus, the psalmist was encouraged by the certainty that God would judge the wicked who troubled him and would be his Savior as well.

How wonderful to know that God is righteous and that we can trust ourselves completely to Him as Savior.

Prayer's transforming power. This two-part psalm illustrates a wonderful experience described in 1 John 5:15: "If we know that He hears us, whatever we ask, we know that we have the petitions that we have asked of Him." As the psalmist brought his requests to God at the beginning of this psalm, God's Spirit spoke to his heart. Without hesitation, the tone of the prayer shifted from supplication to thanksgiving. Even while the psalmist was praying, he realized that God had heard and answered his prayer.

Personal application. In petitionary prayer, we turn our problems and needs over to the Lord. How wonderful to sense that God has heard our prayers. Even as we pray, we can experience the transformation of our supplication to thanksgiving and joy.

CHAPTER 5

THE TRANSFORMING POWER OF PERSONAL PRAYER

PSALMS 73—150

Abraham J. Heschel expressed a basic concept underlying contemporary Jewish prayer when he noted, "The Jew does not stand alone before God, it is as a member of the community that he stands before God" (*Man's Quest for God,* 1954, p. 103).

A recurrent emphasis in rabbinic works is that prayer is essentially a congregational rather than an individual exercise. It is striking to read the Bible's great collections of prayer psalms, and to note that in nearly all of these psalms, individuals speak with the Lord. The writers of the psalms were deeply aware that the Lord is "My God," and not simply "Our God." The psalms clearly reflect the fact that believers have an intimate, personal, I-Thou relationship with the God of the universe.

NURTURING OUR PERSONAL RELATIONSHIP WITH GOD

In chapter 4, we noted characteristics of a vital relationship with the Lord, as reflected in personal prayer psalms (see pp. 51–68). We saw that believers have the freedom to express every thought and feeling to the Lord. Even those "negative" emotions which we find diffi-cult to express are freely shared by the psalmists with God.

We also saw that in expressing needs and feelings to the Lord, the psalmists opened their lives to God's transforming power. As our concerns are brought to the Lord and left in His hands, fears are calmed, anger is drained, despair is replaced by hope, and hearts are flooded with peace and joy.

The personal prayers recorded in Psalms serve as models that we can follow in our own prayer lives. These models can guide us into a deeper relationship with God. Thus, while many psalms have been adapted to modern congregational worship by both Jews and Christians, the psalms have great value for us as individuals. Praying along with the psalmists is one of the best ways to nurture an intimate, personal relationship with God.

In this chapter, we continue our look at personal prayer psalms, following the pattern established in the last chapter.

PSALM 73
"That I may declare all your works"

(See the discussion of this psalm on pp. 50–51.)

BIBLE BACKGROUND:

THE FIVE "BOOKS" OF PSALMS

Scholars believe that the "books" of psalms are collections that were compiled and added to the Psalter at different times. Book I (Pss. 1—41) is Davidic, and was probably compiled before David's death. Book II (Pss. 42—72) may have been added during the reign of Solomon. Books III and IV (73—89, 90—100) are collections from the time of the Babylonian captivity, while Book V (101—150) has a liturgical emphasis. It may have been added during the time of Ezra.

While the "book" designation may indicate addition of groups of psalms to the official biblical collection, many psalms in later books were written much earlier. They had probably been used for many years by the Hebrew people in worship and for private contemplation.

PSALM 74
"Remember Your congregation"

The setting. No specific setting for this psalm is identified, although it is clear from the content of Psalm 74 that the nation had been invaded and the temple threatened. This is the second of 11 consecutive psalms designated Asaphite, a reference to temple singers.

The psalmist's emotions and needs. The language of verses 1–11 and 18–23 is that of a communal lament. Some great distress had driven the congregation to the Lord. Because no liturgical instructions are provided in the superscription, we are treating this communal psalm as the prayers of individuals, along with Psalms 79, 90, 101, and 123.

The psalm begins with a puzzling question: Why was God's anger smoking against the sheep of His pasture (vv. 1–11)? An enemy had attacked God's people and even "burned up all the meeting places of God in the land" (v. 8). Shouldn't God direct His anger against His enemies rather than His own people?

The psalm closes with an urgent appeal to God (vv. 18–23) to honor His covenant promises (v. 20) and act, that His oppressed people may again praise His name (v. 21).

Qualities of God. In spite of the state in which God's people found themselves, the psalmist led the congregation to express confidence in God (vv. 12–17). To him, God was "my King from of old, working salvation in the midst of the earth" (v. 12). God's sovereignty is clearly revealed not only in His past actions on Israel's behalf (vv. 13, 14), but also in nature. Although God's silence in the face of his enemies puzzled the psalmist, it did not take away his confidence that the Lord remained in control.

Prayer's transforming power. We might expect the situation described in verses 1–11 to raise doubts about the existence or the power of God. But Asaph led the community to reaffirm the sovereign rule of God (vv. 12–17). Surely in times of national disaster, believers can appeal to the Lord, and trust Him to act (vv. 18–25).

Personal application. We also need to remember always that God is King. He rules not only the nations but our lives as well. We may not understand why He permits the things that trouble us. But no circumstance should deter us from bringing our appeal to Him.

PSALM 79
"Pour out your wrath on the nations"

The setting. No specific historical setting is given in the superscription of this psalm. But it is clear from the content of Asaph's psalm that foreign enemies had invaded Israel.

The psalmist's emotions and needs. This is another communal psalm, in which the psalmist prayed as a member of the faith community. The psalm is a mixture of complaint (vv. 1–7), implied confession (vv. 8, 9), and appeal (vv. 10–13).

The complaint is rooted in the fact that God had poured out His wrath on His own people rather than the kingdoms that "do not call on Your name" (v. 6). The complaint graphically describes the suffering which God's people had experienced (vv. 1–4). Yet Asaph's concern was that the success of Israel's pagan enemies would lead them to scorn God and His power (v. 10). While Asaph acknowledged that Israel's "former iniquities" may have merited punishment, he appealed to the "God of our salvation" to "provide atonement for our sins" (vv. 8, 9).

Asaph believed this would be appropriate, for Israel is "Your people and sheep of Your pasture" (v. 13).

Qualities of God. This petition for God's people acknowledged the fact that Israel's suffering was a divine punishment. But while God was Israel's judge, He was also the judge of the nations. Thus, Asaph called on the Lord to be merciful and exercise His great power to preserve His covenant people, paying back those who had persecuted them (vv. 11, 12).

Prayer's transforming power. The psalmist ended on a note of expectation. God would answer his prayer, and

> So we, Your people and sheep
>   of Your pasture,
> Will give You thanks forever;
> We will show forth Your praise
>   to all generations (Ps. 79:13).

Personal application. Troubles do drive us to God in prayer. Often such prayers express complaints. But the prayer's final verse reminds us of an important truth: Answers to prayer should stimulate us to thank God. And to share the answers with others, in order that God might be praised.

PSALM 83
"That they may know."

The setting. No setting is given for this Asaphite song.

The psalmist's emotions and needs. This is another imprecatory psalm (see Ps. 35, pp. 63–64). Hostile nations had taken "crafty

Biblical writers often described Israel as God's sheep.

counsel" against God's people, intending to "cut them off from being a nation, that the name of Israel may be remembered no more" (vv. 3, 4).

The psalmist rightly viewed this as a conspiracy aimed against God Himself, for Israel was God's covenant people. Looking back, the psalmist called on God to deal with Israel's current enemies as He did with her past enemies (vv. 9–12).

The psalm concludes with a vivid description of the fate which the psalmist desired for Israel's enemies. No punishment seemed too extreme, as the psalmist cried, "Let them be confounded and dismayed forever; Yes, let them be put to shame and perish" (v. 17).

Qualities of God. The only specific description of God is found in the last verse. God is referred to as "the Most High over all the earth." Belief in God's sovereign control of history and His power to act for His people are also reflected in the psalmist's recitation of past victories over Israel's enemies, as recorded in sacred history (vv. 9–12). In his prayer, the psalmist reminded himself and the Lord of what He had already done for Israel, confident that God would intervene in this situation as well.

Prayer's transforming power. We can sense the psalmist's anxiety as he began his prayer with an urgent request:

> Do not keep silent, O God!
> Do not hold Your peace,
> And do not be still, O God!
> For behold, Your enemies
>   make a tumult (Ps. 83:1, 2).

The psalmist saw Israel surrounded by hostile powers intent on the nation's destruction. His prayer's intensity reflects the crisis. Yet as he listed the enemies that threatened Israel in his day, the psalmist's thoughts turned to those who had threatened his people in the past—Midian (Num. 31), Sisera (Judg. 4), Zebah and Zalmunna (Judg. 6–8). God had delivered His people from these past enemies; surely He would deliver from these current enemies as well.

More confident now, the psalmist called on the God who had saved in the past to save today, making Israel's enemies like whirling dust or chaff before the wind. In judging His people's enemies, the Lord will demonstrate that "You, whose name alone is the LORD, are the Most High over all the earth" (v. 18).

Personal application. There is great value in remembering God's past faithfulness. We can see in this psalm a pattern of hostility toward God's ancient people that had been repeated throughout history. But we can also see God's faithfulness in the preservation of Israel as a separate and special people.

We can also reflect on our own personal history and see God's faithfulness. The God who has guarded us from real and imagined dangers will continue to be with us. When we turn to God for help, recalling how He has

"Frighten [Israel's enemies] with Your storm."

been with us in the past can reassure our hearts.

PSALM 86
"You, LORD, have helped and comforted me."

The setting. No historical context is provided for this psalm of David. It is clear from the psalm itself, however, that David had experienced God's goodness on many occasions. No matter how great his present need was, David remained confident that God would hear and answer his prayer.

David's emotions and needs. Perhaps the most impressive feature of this prayer is the interweaving of request, praise, and expressions of total confidence in the Lord. Although David asked God for mercy and said, "I cry out to You all day long" (v. 3), he immediately reflected on the fact that

> You, LORD, are good, and
>   ready to forgive,

And abundant in mercy to all
    those who call upon You (Ps.
    86:5).

This pattern of request followed immediately by expressions of confidence and praise is seen throughout the psalm, in verses 6–10, 11–13, 14–16, and 16–17. While David had needs that he brought to the Lord, he simply could not dwell on them. Each petition reminded him of something special about the Lord.

Qualities of God. David mentioned many qualities of God in this prayer. God was merciful (v. 3, 5, 13). He was good, and ready to forgive (v. 5). God answered prayer (v. 7), and unlike other so-called gods the Lord was great and did wondrous things, for He alone was God (v. 10). Even though a mob of violent men sought his life, David was not afraid, for he knew that God was "full of compassion, and gracious, longsuffering and abundant in mercy and truth" (v. 15). What a wonderful God David had—a God who in harmony with His nature had "helped me and comforted me" (v. 17).

Prayer's transforming power. It is valid for us to cry out to God in our need. Yet we need to be careful lest our prayers simply refocus our attention on our problems. In this psalm, David modeled one way to bring perspective to our petitions. As we bring each request to the Lord, we can pause to direct our thoughts to Him, focusing our attention on His goodness, mercy, compassion, grace, and power. As petitions yield to praise, our hearts will be filled with fresh confidence in the Lord.

Personal application. Consciously pause after each petition, and think about those qualities of God which give you confidence in Him. Use Psalm 83 as your model.

PSALM 89
"Where are your former lovingkindnesses?"

The setting. No specific historical context is indicated for this contemplation of Ethan the Ezrahite. Ethan is mentioned in 1 Kings 4:31 as a noted wise man. But as the two books of Kings date from after the monarchy, we cannot assume that Ethan lived before Solomon. It is clear from the psalm itself that Ethan prayed in a time of serious decline in the Southern Kingdom, Judah, whose rulers were descendants of David.

The psalmist's emotions and needs. The psalm is a contemplation, recording Ethan's thoughts. He began by affirming and praising God (vv. 1–18), especially for God's covenant promises to King David, quoted in verses 3, 4. Ethan had no doubts about God's righteousness or the favor He had shown His people.

In a second major section, Ethan again quoted God's promises to David (vv. 19–37). While the quote includes a reference to divine punishment if David's descendants should fail to walk in God's ways (vv. 30–32), the emphasis is on God's total commitment to His promise.

"Nevertheless My
    lovingkindness I will not
    utterly take from him.
Nor allow My faithfulness to
    fail.
My covenant I will not break,
    nor alter the word that has
    gone out of my lips" (Ps. 89:33,
    34).

The third part of the psalm is a complaint (vv. 38–45). In spite of God's promises, "You have cast off and abhorred, You have been furious with Your anointed" (v. 38). The dire condition of the Southern Kingdom might possibly be taken as a repudiation by God not only of David's line, but of the Lord's own word!

In a final segment, the psalmist rejected this interpretation of events, and asked, "How long, LORD?" (vv. 46–52). Life is short, and Ethan longed to see God act before he died. The last verse in the psalm is an affirmation of faith. Whatever might happen, Ethan was determined to bless the Lord forever.

Qualities of God. The quality of God on which Ethan focused was His faithfulness. God will be true to His Word. Specifically, God will keep the covenant promises that He has made.

This conviction is easy to hold when everything is going well. But Ethan was living in a time of national decline, when it seemed that God had renounced His covenant (v. 39). Judah and its ruler were viewed with contempt, and the nation had known defeat and humiliation at the hand of its enemies. While Ethan knew that the covenant promise included a warning of judgment for disobedience, the present plight of Judah was so extreme that God's covenant commitment itself might be called into question.

Yet in quoting God's Word, Ethan reminded himself that God remains committed to His people. Deliverance is not a matter of "if" but "when." Ethan hoped he would live long enough to see God act.

Prayer's transforming power. Ethan introduced us to yet another resource which will enrich our prayer lives. He not only praised God for His faithfulness and power; he also quoted God's promises. This gave Ethan a basis for his appeal to God as well as a perspective on his situation. In spite of appearances, the nation's plight could not be viewed as abandonment of God's people.

Personal application. The use of Scripture in prayer has many benefits. It turns our thoughts to God. It provides a basis on which we can appeal to Him. God's promises encourage us and give us confidence. Perhaps most significant, God's Word gives us a perspective on our present situation which we often lack. However dark circumstances appear to be, God is faithful. We can claim and count on His promises, looking forward to that day when God will act.

PSALM 90
"Let Your work appear to Your servants."

Setting. This is the only prayer of Moses included in the Psalms (see the comment on the

title of Psalm 17, p. 59). In this psalm, Moses prayed for and as a member of God's covenant community. No specific historical context is indicated in the superscription.

Moses' emotions and needs. Moses compared the mortality of human beings with the eternity of God. At best, a person can expect seventy or eighty years of life, but to God a thousand years seem as fleeting as a single day. While Israel's sins have merited the troubles which God's people have known, Moses longed for God to have compassion, "that we may rejoice and be glad all our days!" (v. 14).

Qualities of God. Moses was overwhelmed by a sense of the eternity of God. The theme is set immediately in the psalm's opening verses:

> Before the mountains were
>   brought forth,
> Or ever You had formed the
>   earth and the world,
> Even from everlasting to
>   everlasting, You are God
>   (Ps. 90:2).

Compared to God, human beings are as finite as sleep or the grass that grows in the morning and withers in the evening (vv. 5, 6). The brevity of human life makes it even more tragic that "all our days have passed away in Your wrath" (v. 9).

Yet the Lord is a God of compassion (v. 13) and mercy (v. 14). So Moses appealed to God to let His (saving) "work appear to Your servants, and Your glory to their children" by establishing the work of their hands (vv. 16, 17).

Prayer's transforming power. The key verse in this psalm is "teach us to number our days, that we may gain a heart of wisdom" (v. 12). We human beings tend to measure all things by our own experience. We assume that our time is the most momentous in history; we approach life as though what we experience has ultimate meaning. Moses reminds us that God's plans and purposes are being worked

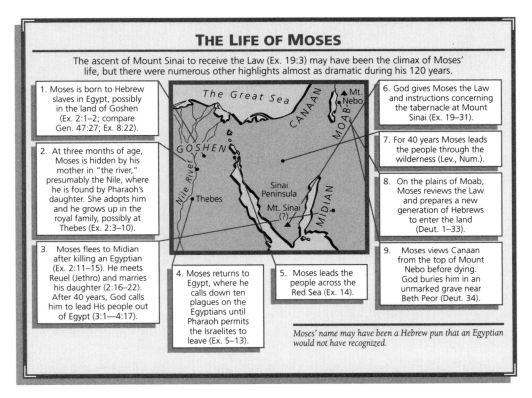

THE LIFE OF MOSES

The ascent of Mount Sinai to receive the Law (Ex. 19:3) may have been the climax of Moses' life, but there were numerous other highlights almost as dramatic during his 120 years.

1. Moses is born to Hebrew slaves in Egypt, possibly in the land of Goshen (Ex. 2:1–2; compare Gen. 47:27; Ex. 8:22).

2. At three months of age, Moses is hidden by his mother in "the river," presumably the Nile, where he is found by Pharaoh's daughter. She adopts him and he grows up in the royal family, possibly at Thebes (Ex. 2:3–10).

3. Moses flees to Midian after killing an Egyptian (Ex. 2:11–15). He meets Reuel (Jethro) and marries his daughter (2:16–22). After 40 years, God calls him to lead His people out of Egypt (3:1—4:17).

4. Moses returns to Egypt, where he calls down ten plagues on the Egyptians until Pharaoh permits the Israelites to leave (Ex. 5–13).

5. Moses leads the people across the Red Sea (Ex. 14).

6. God gives Moses the Law and instructions concerning the tabernacle at Mount Sinai (Ex. 19–31).

7. For 40 years Moses leads the people through the wilderness (Lev., Num.).

8. On the plains of Moab, Moses reviews the Law and prepares a new generation of Hebrews to enter the land (Deut. 1–33).

9. Moses views Canaan from the top of Mount Nebo before dying. God buries him in an unmarked grave near Beth Peor (Deut. 34).

Moses' name may have been a Hebrew pun that an Egyptian would not have recognized.

---

out across eons, not decades. We find the meaning of our lives not in accomplishing our purposes but in seeing God's work in history. We should look to God to establish what we do within the framework of His eternal plan.

Personal application. We can seek to discern our place in God's eternal purposes and pray with Moses,

> Let the beauty of the LORD
>   our God be upon us,
> And establish the work of our
>   hands for us;
> Yes, establish the work of our
>   hands (Ps. 90:17).

PSALM 94
"The LORD has been my defense."

Setting. No setting for this psalm is described.

The psalmist's emotions and needs. Verse 19 sums up the two contrary emotions which are

expressed in this psalm: "In the multitude of my anxieties within me, Your comforts delight my soul." Although the wicked seemed to dominate at the moment, the psalmist was confident that the Lord would "cut them off in their own wickedness" (vv. 22, 23).

Qualities of God. The psalmist honored God as Judge. Senseless people do not realize that the One who planted the ear hears them, or that the One who designed the eye must surely see them. But because God is who He is, the person whom the Lord instructs is blessed (v. 12), for God will cut off the evil in their own wickedness (v. 23).

Prayer's transforming power. The juxtaposition of "anxieties within" and "delight" in this psalm seems contradictory at first. But the psalmist blends these reactions by showing how our circumstances are responsible for our anxieties while our awareness of God's mercy delights our souls. Believers through the ages have discovered that the more threatening the circumstances, the greater the delight we take in the Lord and in our relationship with Him. Contemplation of God as the Judge who hears and sees all brings comfort and delight.

Personal application. When we bring our complaints and petitions to the Lord, we need to affirm God for who He is at the same time. The conviction that "the LORD will not cast off His people, nor will he forsake His inheritance" is the foundation of the confidence we have in bringing our prayers to Him.

PSALM 101
"I will behave wisely."

The setting. This psalm of David is recorded without mention of its historical setting.

David's emotions and needs. We think of prayer in familiar categories: Petition, intercession, complaint, praise, etc. This prayer of David adds another category to our list—commitment. David praised God for His mercy and justice. And David responded to the Lord by making commitments of his own. David will:

- "walk within my house with a perfect heart" (v. 2)
- "set nothing wicked before my eyes" (v. 3)
- "not know wickedness" (v. 4)
- "destroy whoever secretly slanders his neighbor" (v. 5)
- "not endure one who has "a haughty look and a proud heart" (v. 5)
- favor "the faithful of the land" (v. 6)
- "cut off evildoers from the city of the LORD" (v. 8).

Qualities of God. David had been blessed by the mercy and justice of God, so he praised Him. David realized that the best gift he could give the Lord in response to all His mercies was to imitate His moral qualities and commitments. In this very special prayer psalm, David promised to do just that.

Prayer's transforming power. David set goals for his life by pledging himself to live in ways that would please God. David was not perfect.

Like all of us, David fell short in many ways. But making such commitments to God and renewing them is a significant motivator to godly living.

Personal application. In view of God's mercy, we are privileged not only to sing His praises but also to pledge ourselves to honor Him by the way we live.

PSALM 102
"He shall regard the prayer of the destitute."

The setting. This is one of five psalms designated "a prayer" (see Psalm 17, p. 59). It is an appropriate model for any person who feels afflicted and overwhelmed and who "pours out his complaint before the LORD."

The psalmist's emotions and needs. The superscription describes the psalmist's state. He was afflicted and he felt overwhelmed. The depth of his despair is reflected in verses 4, 5:

> My heart is stricken and
>   withered like grass,
> So that I forget to eat my bread.
> Because of the sound of my
>   groaning,
> My bones cling to my skin.

Surrounded by enemies, apparently cast off by God, the psalmist's days were lived under a lengthening shadow (v. 11).

Qualities of God. The first eleven verses of this psalm express the psalmist's emotions and register his complaint. Then in verses 12–17, the psalmist shifted his focus to the Lord. In these verses, he considered the fact that God would endure forever. Surely in the future God would "arise and have mercy on Zion" (v. 13). The whole world would "fear the name of the LORD" (v. 15) when "He shall appear in His glory" (v. 16).

Prayer's transforming power. The psalmist's thoughts about God changed his attitude. God might not act in his lifetime. But God *will* act. This was so certain that the psalmist could

"My heart is stricken. . . . You have . . . cast me away."

write from the perspective of generations yet to come, as if describing what God *had* done rather than what He will do (vv. 18–22).

In a personal vein, the psalmist asked God not to shorten his own days (life). Yet whatever happened to him, God would endure, and "the children of Your servants will continue, and their descendants will be established before you" (v. 28).

Personal application. How often in our prayers do we thank God ahead of time for granting our requests? How often do we stand back from our own troubles, to look beyond ourselves and identify with God's eternal purposes? God will accomplish all that we ask and far more, but in His own time and way. As this psalm reminds us,

> Of old You laid the foundation
>   of the earth,
> And the heavens are the work
>   of Your hands.

They will perish, but You will
    endure;
Yes, they will all grow old like
    a garment,
Like a cloak you will change
    them,
And they will be changed (Ps.
    102:25, 26).

Yet God will endure, and His purposes will be accomplished. God's servants will continue, and their descendants will be established before Him (v. 28).

Whatever happens to us in this life, the future is ours. And our prayers *have been* answered!

PSALM 103
"Forget not all His benefits."

The setting. This is another of David's many general prayers recorded for us in the psalms.

David's emotions and needs. We can classify this psalm as pure praise. The formula, "Bless the LORD," as noted on pages 44–46, is an expression of gratitude, parallel in meaning to "praise the LORD."

In this psalm, David listed many reasons that he had to praise the Lord. In nearly every verse, David recounted another benefit which was his as one of God's children. We feel lifted up with David to praise our God as we read his inspired words.

Qualities of God. The psalm is launched with a list of benefits (vv. 2–6). Then David considered the benefits once again, this time in view of God's character. The root of our blessings is found in the nature of God: in His righteousness, mercy, forgiveness, compassion, faithfulness, and sovereign dominion over all.

Prayer's transforming power. How good it is to worship and praise God for who He is, without any consideration of our needs at the time. Simply talking to the Lord, expressing our thanks and wonder, pleases Him—it draws us closer to Him.

Evidence of God's power is seen throughout His world.

◆

Personal application. Praying this psalm each day for one month will work wonders for our appreciation of the Lord and awaken our awareness of His presence in our lives.

PSALM 104
"O LORD my God, You are very great."

The setting. No superscription is provided with this psalm.

The psalmist's emotions and needs. Like Psalm 103, this is a prayer of unmixed praise. But in this psalm, God is not praised for His benefits. Rather, the psalmist expressed his awe at nature's witness to God's mighty power and loving care. God is the world's designer as well as the One who sustains all living creatures.

Qualities of God. The creation witnesses to the wisdom and power of its maker, while God's provision for living creatures suggests compassion. In spite of sin's impact on the natural world, the eye of faith clearly sees nature's testimony to the glory of God.

Prayer's transforming power. Contemplation of nature leads to praise of God as Creator and sustainer. Believers who give themselves to praise will experience a lightened heart, as did the psalmist:

> I will sing to the LORD as long
>   as I live;
> I will sing praise to my God
>   while I have my being.
> May my meditation be sweet
>   to Him;
> I will be glad in the LORD (Ps.
>   104:33, 34).

Personal application. May our eyes be opened to the glory of God as it shines all around us. And may our hearts be lifted to Him in praise.

PSALM 108
"Through God we will do valiantly."

The setting. This poem of David was set to music as a song. No particular occasion for its writing is mentioned in the superscription.

David's emotions and needs. David's dominant emotion in this psalm is awe of our God, whose "mercy is great above the heavens" (v. 4). David alluded to Genesis 49 and paraphrased God's promises to His people in verses 7–9. While the help of man was useless, Israel's future triumph was sure, for "through God we will do valiantly, for it is He who shall tread down our enemies" (v. 13).

Qualities of God. David praised God as the deliverer of His beloved, counting on the Lord to bring about the promised triumph of Israel.

Prayer's transforming power. Although David referred to past defeats, he was confident that God would provide him with victories. David's confidence was well placed. During his 40-year reign, he saw all the surrounding nations defeated, and he extended the land controlled by Israel tenfold!

Personal application. God is committed to us as His people. How appropriate it would be for us to join David and "sing praises to You among the nations."

PSALM 123
"Have mercy on us, O LORD"

The setting. The superscription identifies this as a "Song of Ascents." Most believe the psalms with this designation (120—134) were processionals, sung by worshipers as they came to Jerusalem for national religious festivals.

The psalmist's emotions and needs. The psalm is a communal complaint, in which the worshipers appealed for mercy and expressed dependence on the Lord. The worshipers were disturbed by the scorn of those who viewed them with contempt.

Qualities of God. The phrase "You who dwell in [or 'are enthroned in'] the heavens" acknowledges God's kingship. He is able to have mercy if He chooses. He is able to come to the aid of His people.

Prayer's transforming power. This brief psalm is a simple statement of the Israelites' complaints. But it is also a call to trust a sovereign God. Its calming message for those under stress is simply that God is still in control.

Personal application. When the actions of others upset us, our first response should be to look to the Lord.

PSALM 131
"I have calmed and quieted my soul"

The setting. This is another of the processional hymns associated with the three festivals which brought the Israelites to Jerusalem to worship. The superscription tells us it was written by David.

David's emotions and needs. The psalm expresses a childlike confidence in God, won in spite of an inner struggle with pride and self-

will. David has learned to rely on God completely, as a weaned child (a three-year-old) relies on his or her parents.

Qualities of God. While the psalm focuses attention on that childlike faith in God which brings calmness to the soul, it implies the fatherhood of God. Jesus fully developed the implications of reliance on God as Father, as illustrated in Matthew 6:25–34 and Luke 11:9–13.

Prayer's transforming power. Prayers like this psalm are healthy reminders of our dependence on God and our need to rely completely on Him.

Personal application. True spirituality involves a humble submission to the will of our Father God.

PSALM 138
"I will praise You with my whole heart"

The setting. The superscription links this psalm to a collection of Davidic poems.

David's emotions and needs. David was overcome by wonder and gratitude. Although God was "on high," and greater than all the kings of the earth, His majesty was allied with grace. What was most special to David was the fact that God had shown grace to him, and was deeply involved in David's life. This personal experience of God's grace moved the psalmist to intense appreciation. He was aware that he must never lose his sense of wonder at the goodness of the Lord.

Qualities of God. Although the Lord is on high, "yet He regards the lowly" (v. 6). God's active involvement on behalf of human beings is clear evidence of His "lovingkindness" (v. 2)—the NKJV term used to translate a Hebrew word that is rendered in other contemporary English versions by "grace." Together with "mercy" (v. 8), lovingkindness sums up God's readiness to help human beings, not because of our merits, but because He is moved by compassion.

What moved David most deeply, however, was that he had experienced God's gracious involvement in his own life. He had personally experienced God's grace as the Lord had delivered him from his enemies, reviving and restoring him.

Prayer's transforming power. This praise prayer was a response stimulated by David's previous experience of God's transforming power. How appropriate it is to praise God when we have experienced His grace.

Personal application. We can know objectively that God is gracious and merciful. But how we are moved to praise Him when we experience His grace on a personal level.

PSALM 141
"Against the deeds of the wicked"

The setting. The superscription identifies this psalm as Davidic.

"Let my prayer be set before You as incense."

David's emotions and needs. David was especially sensitive to the influence of what we today call peer pressure. He looked to God to protect him from the temptation to speak as the wicked spoke and to act as they acted, buying into their values (vv. 3–4). Rather than the delicacies of the wicked, David preferred the rebukes of the righteous, knowing these are of greater value (v. 5). No matter how difficult the circumstances, David was ready to take a stand against the deeds of the wicked (vv. 5b–7).

David concluded by looking to the Lord, confident that God would act and vindicate his trust in Him (vv. 9–10).

Qualities of God. The psalm presupposes that God is aware of and involved in human affairs.

Prayer's transforming power. The first verses of this psalm capture David's desire to please God. He wanted his prayers to be as the incense used in worship—an odor pleasing to the Lord. Ultimately, it was this desire to please God that moved David to separate himself from the wicked and to choose friendship with those who were committed to God's ways. In this psalm, prayer flowed out of an experience of God's transforming power.

Personal application. Like this psalm, the book of Revelation portrays prayer as sweet-smelling incense offered to God (see Rev. 8:3, 4). How humbling to think of our prayers as an offering that is pleasing to the Lord!

PSALM 142
"No one cares for my soul"

The setting. This psalm is described as a contemplation of David and as a prayer (see Psalm 17, p. 59). The superscription tells us that it reflects David's thoughts and feelings "when he was in the cave."

The reference is to events described in 1 Samuel 22. David had fled from Saul and taken refuge in the cave of Adullam. Even David's parents and brothers were threatened and forced to take refuge in Moab. Although joined by "everyone who was discontented,"

David felt totally abandoned. These emotions of despair are reflected in this psalm.

David's emotions and needs. David's prayer expressed his feelings as he poured out his complaint before the Lord. Expressions such as "my spirit was overwhelmed within me" (v. 3), "no one cares for my soul" (v. 4), and "I am brought very low" (v. 6) reflect the deep depression which gripped David during this period of his life.

Qualities of God. David identified no particular quality of God on which he focused during this time. Yet David experienced God as his refuge. All else might be lost, but David still had God as "my portion in the land of the living" (v. 5).

Prayer's transforming power. David spoke of pouring out his complaint to God, and declaring "before Him my trouble" (v. 2). After making his final appeal to God, David seemed convinced that God had heard him and that He would do as he had asked. David's last words were, "for You shall deal bountifully with me."

Personal application. How good to be able to bring every complaint to God. But when we do, let's remember that the Lord still is our portion. And let's have confidence that He will yet "deal bountifully" with us.

PSALM 143
"Revive me, O LORD."

The setting. No historical context is identified for this psalm of David.

David's emotions and needs. David expressed the emotions of a victim of ruthless persecution. His life was threatened, and he found himself in a state of shock and distress. Yet there was a source for the stability that David so desperately needed, and David turned his thoughts to God's past saving acts.

> I remember the days of old;
> I meditate on all Your works;

A BELIEVERS' GUIDE TO PRIVATE PRAYER

The book of Psalms has served for centuries as a guide to personal and private prayer. Use the following chart to locate psalms which reflect your own personal experiences or emotions. Then turn to the psalm, and either pray along with the psalmist, or use the psalm as a model to write and utter your own prayer to the Lord.

Emotions or Situations	Psalms
Abandoned	142
Afflicted	102
Anger	7, 35, 83
Dedication, commitment	101
Depressed	123
Desolate	25
Distressed	25
Doubting	10
Envious	73
Fearful, anxious	3, 71, 83, 94
Frustrated	7
Grief, mourning	43
Guilt	38
Joy	28, 30
Persecuted	7
Praise	28, 30, 108
Sorrowing	13
Stressed	142
Thankfulness	16, 27, 138
Troubled by injustice	10
Uncertainty	3
Victimized by injustice	13, 143

> I muse on the work of Your
>   hands.
> I spread out my hands to You;
> My soul longs for You like a
>   thirsty land (Ps. 143:5, 6).

Qualities of God. David focused his thoughts on God as One who has performed miracles, or saving works, in history. For reassurance, David meditated on God as One who intervenes on behalf of His people.

Prayer's transforming power. The psalm is divided into two sections, verses 1–6 and verses 7–12. In the first part, David expressed his complaint and contemplated God's historic interventions on behalf of His covenant people. In the second half, David addressed specific requests to God. Reassured by the record of what God had done for His people David called on the Lord to act for him. Specifically, David cried out:

- "Answer me speedily, O LORD" (v. 7)
- "Cause me to hear Your lovingkindness in the morning" (v. 8)
- "Deliver me, O LORD, from my enemies" (v. 9)
- "Teach me to do Your will" (v. 10)
- "Revive me, O LORD, for Your name's sake" (v. 11.)
- In Your mercy cut off my enemies" (v. 12).

David no longer focused on what his enemies were doing, but rather looked to God expectantly. Prayer can help us look beyond today's troubles, filling us with hope. And hope, in Scripture, is the confident expectation that what we look to God for will surely be ours.

Personal application. Remembering what God has done, we have the confidence to make very specific requests in our prayers. And we have confidence that God will answer our prayers as well.

PSALM 144
"Blessed be the LORD my rock."

The setting. While the superscription identifies this as a royal psalm, no historical roots for its writing are described.

David's emotions and needs. The first eleven verses of this psalm celebrate God's power in contrast to human weakness. David cried out to God for help, confident that "the One who gives salvation to kings" would answer (v. 10).

The meaning of God's deliverance for future generations is described in verses 12–15. God would multiply His people, their flocks, and the produce of the land. "Happy," the psalmist says, "are the people who are in such a state; happy are the people whose God is the LORD" (v. 15).

Qualities of God. David used a number of images which portrayed God as source of strength and security (vv. 1, 2). He called on God to act as Savior and deliverer again, that David might praise Him with a new song (vv. 9, 10).

Prayer's transforming power. This psalm focuses on God's power to act in our world, and so to transform our situation. God's action in history will open up a blessed future for generations to come.

Personal application. How appropriate to conclude our exploration of personal prayer poems in the psalms with this reminder. Prayer does have great subjective value, as we turn our thoughts to God and find inner peace. But prayer has more than subjective value. God does answer prayer. And God acts in our lives, because we bring our requests to Him.

CHAPTER 6

"TO THE CHIEF MUSICIAN"

PUBLIC PRAYER IN THE PSALMS

Psalms 1—150

Much contemporary Christian music tends to focus on worship. And many of our favorite worship songs are drawn from the psalms. We may not even realize their origin. But on Sunday mornings in the church I attend, we're likely to sing,

> The LORD lives!
> Blessed be my Rock!
> And let the God of my salvation
>   be exalted.

I wonder how many in our congregation realize that when we sing these words, we're repeating thoughts some three thousand years old, recorded in Psalm 18:46.

THE USE OF PSALMS IN PUBLIC WORSHIP

In this chapter on public prayers in the psalms, we will look at those prayer psalms whose superscriptions indicate they became a part of Israel's worship liturgy. Many, like the prayer psalms examined in chapters 4 and 5, were written in the first person singular. While at times the singular may represent the whole nation, as in Exodus 15, many of these psalms were originally private prayers, adopted for use by the believing community.

Reuven Hammer noted that the psalms have played an important role in shaping Jewish worship. In Jesus' day, a different psalm was sung each day of the week in the temple. And psalms 113 through 118 were chanted during festivals. While today's synagogue liturgy incorporates many prayers written by rabbis, Hammer points out that without the Psalter, contemporary Jewish services would be far different.

As Hammer noted, it is particularly striking that psalms intended for public worship shaped the prayers of Old Testament personalities.

This is the case of Jonah's prayer (Jon. 2:3–10) and that ascribed to Hannah, the mother of Samuel (1 Sam. 2:1–10). This can mean either that individuals, even as early as the period of the judges, used psalms composed for use in worship in the Tabernacle when they came to pray, or that the later writers of these books put such psalms into the mouths of their speakers when relating earlier events (Reuven Hammer, *Entering Jewish Prayer,* 1994, p. 55).

In either case, it is clear that psalms used in public worship had an impact on individual believers' view of and relationship with the Lord. It is the same today, as the psalms we sing in worship touch our hearts, focusing our thoughts on the Lord.

How do we identify public prayer psalms? These psalms are addressed to the Lord, not to the reader. And prayer psalms are identified in the superscriptions as delivered to the chief musician or other worship leader. In discussing the public prayer psalms, we will use the same analytical structure to which we subjected the private prayer psalms. We will note:

- the setting of the psalm;
- the psalmist's emotions and needs;
- qualities of God emphasized in the psalm;
- prayer's transforming power as illustrated in the psalm; and
- personal application.

As we enter into these ancient prayers used in worship by the gathered people of God, may our own relationship with God be revitalized.

PUBLIC PRAYERS IN THE PSALMS

PSALM 5
"I will look up."

The setting. The superscription indicates that this psalm of David was delivered to the "chief musician." The heading "to the chief musician," or music director, suggests this psalm was used in public worship. The superscription also tells us it was to be set to flute music.

We do not know whether this liturgical use was intended when the psalm was written.

David's emotions and needs. Psalm 5 has been called by some a "psalm of innocence." David reflected the worshiper's complete trust in and reliance on the Lord. It was trust that moved David to look up to the Lord in the morning (vv. 1–3), and to rejoice in the confidence that God "will surround [those He loves] as with a shield" (v. 12).

While David mentioned the wicked in this psalm, he was not particularly troubled by them. He knew that God took no pleasure in their actions (vv. 4–6), and he called on God to "pronounce them guilty" (vv. 9–10). What was important to David was expressed in verse 7:

> But as for me, I will come into
> Your house in the multitude
> of Your mercy;
> In fear of You I will worship
> toward Your holy temple.

Qualities of God. David spoke to the Lord as "My King and my God," and made specific reference to His commitment to righteousness. Because God is the sovereign Ruler of His universe, David was confident that the Lord would "pronounce [the wicked] guilty" and "cast them out in the multitude of their transgressions."

Prayer's transforming power. The depiction of the psalmist as an innocent person highlights its value in worship. God *can* be trusted. And trust in God is not only appropriate; it has many wonderful benefits. God blesses the innocent, so as the psalm says,

> Let all those rejoice who put
> their trust in You;
> Let them ever shout for joy,
> because You defend them;
> Let those also who love Your
> name
> Be joyful in You (Ps. 5:11).

Personal application. The sophisticated may sneer at a childlike trust in God. But the believer who rests in God as totally trustworthy knows peace and joy.

PSALM 6
"O LORD, heal me."

The setting. This psalm was also sent to the music director for arrangement and use in public worship. The early church traditionally

Serious illness caused David to face his own mortality.

---❖---

sang this psalm and six others on Ash Wednesday (Pss. 32; 38; 51; 102; 130; 143).

David's emotions and needs. The psalmist was so seriously ill that death seemed imminent. He was physically weak (v. 2) and emotionally drained (v. 3). The phrase "all night I make my bed swim" is explained in part by reference to David's tears, but may suggest heavy sweating as well. Clearly sickness had forced David to face his mortality, and he cried out to God for mercy and healing.

The tone of the psalm changes dramatically at verse 8. David was made aware that "the LORD has heard my supplication" (v. 9). David either had recovered, or had been assured that he would recover. How disappointing for his enemies, who had hoped for his death (v. 10).

Qualities of God. David was suffering intensely, perhaps more anguished at the prospect of death than by the physical pains. In this state, he found it difficult to concen-

trate on any quality of his God. Yet David turned instinctively to the Lord for help. What does this tell us? Simply that David had confidence in God's ability to heal him. God had unlimited power and was able to intervene if He chose. David's appeal to God for mercy reminds us that David had a right to ask for healing. If God responded, it would be because He had mercy on [compassion for] His servant, not because He was obligated to do so (v. 2).

Prayer's transforming power. Why would this prayer psalm be included among those used in public worship? Perhaps one of its values was to remind God's people of their mortality. Contemplating the nearness of death may call forth appreciation for life.

There is also great value in the example David set in looking to the Lord for healing. Second Chronicles 16:12 tells us that in spite of a severe disease, Asa, one of Judah's kings, "did not seek the LORD, but the physicians" (2 Chron. 16:12). It was not wrong for Asa to seek medical treatment, but his failure to appeal to God demonstrated a lack of reliance on the Lord.

Personal application. In Exodus 15:26, God says of Himself, "I am the LORD who heals you." No wonder God's people still look to Him when sickness comes.

PSALM 9
"The LORD is known by the judgment He executes."

The setting. This praise prayer was also given to the music director for use in public worship. The superscription notes, "To *the tune* of Death of [to] the Son." This translation assumes that the five Hebrew letters form two words. If the five letters are taken as a single word, the superscription would indicate "by soprano voices." No specific historical setting is given for this psalm of David.

David's emotions and needs. Psalm 9 is a prayer of praise directed to the Lord in anticipation of God's judgment of His people's enemies. Verses 1 and 2 give us special insight into the nature of praise. Praise flowed from the glad heart of the worshiper, and it involved telling of God's marvelous works and singing praises to His name.

Qualities of God. David knew God through the marvelous works that God had done. God had "rebuked the nations" and "destroyed the wicked" (v. 5). He had not "forsaken those who seek You" (v. 10). Clearly God was on the throne, "judging in righteousness" (v. 4).

David announced that "the LORD is known by the judgment He executes" (v. 16). And God's past acts of judgment have also demonstrated mercy shown His own people. Based on God's historic revelation of Himself, David's heart was filled with confidence and praise. Surely,

> The LORD also will be a
> > refuge for the oppressed,
> A refuge in times of trouble.
> And those who know Your
> > name will put their trust in
> > You;
> For You, LORD, have not
> > forsaken those who seek
> > You (Ps. 9:9, 10).

Prayer's transforming power. David's heart was filled with joy as he meditated on God's historic revelations of Himself as mankind's Judge. Based on who God is, David was able to anticipate the failure of his enemies. While at the moment the needy were oppressed, David was filled with confidence as he looked to the future.

> The wicked shall be turned into
> > hell,
> And all the nations that
> > forget God.
> For the needy shall not always
> > be forgotten;
> The expectation of the poor
> > shall not perish forever
> > (Ps. 9:17, 18).

Personal application. The future is not determined by the present situation but by who God is and what He intends. When we praise God as history's sovereign Lord, our hearts will also be filled with praise.

PSALM 18
"My God, my strength"

The setting. The superscription of this psalm provides many interesting details. It was sent by David to the music director for use in public worship. This prayer of praise and thanksgiving was stimulated by a specific event: The death of Saul in battle. While David mourned the king who had been his enemy (see 2 Sam. 1:17–27), David also felt a sense of joy and release when Saul was killed. David's months and years of living as a fugitive in the wilderness were over, and he would soon be able to take his place as king of the Hebrew people. David was moved to affirm his love for the Lord, who had protected and delivered him.

David's emotions and needs. David's emotions of love and gratitude infused the first verses of this long prayer poem.

> I will love You, O LORD, my
> > strength.
> The LORD is my rock and my
> > fortress and my deliverer;
> My God, my strength, in
> > whom I will trust;
> My shield and the horn of my
> > salvation, my stronghold
> > (Ps. 18:1, 2).

As the psalm continued, David reviewed his relationship with the Lord. David "cried out to my God" and was answered (v. 6). Awed at God's answer to his prayer, David pictured the Lord in all His power stepping into the material universe to deal with David's enemies (vv. 7–19).

How could David explain the mercy extended to him by the Lord? David looked back over his relationship with Saul and was able to say that he "was blameless before Him" (v. 23). God, who is merciful to the merciful (v. 25), showed mercy to His servant David. Filled with joy at this evidence of God's favor, David exulted:

> For by You I can run against
>   a troop,
> By my God I can leap over a
>   a wall (Ps. 18:29).

Nothing seemed impossible to David, for it was God who had armed him with strength (v. 32).

While David believed that his own commitment to the Lord had made it possible for God to bless him, David realized that all credit for his accomplishments belonged to the Lord. After all, it was God who had given David "the shield of [my] salvation" (v. 35), and God who had "armed me with strength" (v. 39). Surely God was the One who "subdues the peoples under me" and "delivers me from my enemies" (vv. 47, 48).

> Therefore I will give thanks to
>   You, O LORD, among the
>   Gentiles,
> And sing praises to Your name (Ps.
>   18:49).

Qualities of God. David's praise was evoked not simply by the deliverance he had just experienced but most significantly by his vision of God. God meant everything to David. God was his salvation, his fortress, his deliverer. God answered David's prayers, put down David's enemies, and gave David strength. God provided the light David needed to see in the darkness and His trustworthy word to guide him. No wonder David burst out in praise,

> The LORD lives!
> Blessed be my Rock!
> Let the God of my salvation be
>   exalted (Ps. 18:46).

Prayer's transforming power. In Psalm 9, David praised God in anticipation of His intervention. In Psalm 18 God had acted, freeing David from the stress that King Saul had placed upon him. No wonder David's heart leaped within him, and he was filled with gratitude and joy.

Personal application. The length of David's praise prayer is impressive. It reminds us to spend as much time in thanksgiving and praise for answered prayer as we do in bringing our requests to the Lord.

PSALM 20
"Some trust in chariots."

The setting. The superscription indicates this unusual psalm was used in public worship. The content of the psalm suggests it was part of a prayer ceremony before Israel's kings went to war.

The psalmist's emotions and needs. The first verses utilize an oblique form of petition, made here by the people on behalf of their king before he set out to do battle (vv. 1–5). Verse 6 is a response, perhaps offered by a priest, announcing that God will answer from heaven with "saving strength." The congregation then responded to this announcement, expressing confidence in the Lord and calling on Him to save (vv. 7–9).

Qualities of God. God is pictured in this psalm as Savior and deliverer. While some people trust in chariots (military might), God's people rely on His aid when they must do battle.

Prayer's transforming power. There may be no more tense time for a people than when their nation goes to war. This public prayer focused the attention of Israel on the Lord, reminding them of the special relationship God had established not only with the Hebrew people but also with the Davidic line (see 2 Sam. 7). The prayer's structure was designed to turn the eyes of the people to the Lord, providing a vehicle through which they could affirm their trust in Him.

Personal application. Like other liturgical prayers, this prayer of David reminds us of the importance of affirming our confidence in the Lord together, as a people of God.

PSALM 22
"Why have You forsaken Me?"

The setting. Again, the superscription identifies this psalm as a lament to be used in public worship, apparently set to a familiar tune. While the feelings David expressed are his own, they also foreshadow the experience of Christ. In his commentary on Psalms 1–50, Peter C. Craigie (1983) observed,

It is clear from the recorded words of Jesus on the cross that He identified His own loneliness and suffering with that of the psalmist (Matt. 27:46; Mark 15:34). And it is clear that the evangelists interpreted the crucifixion in the light of the psalm, utilizing its words in their description of the scene (Matt. 27:39; Mark 15:29; cf. Luke 23:35; Ps. 22:8). Indeed, the psalm takes on the appearance of anticipatory prophecy; the high priests, scribes and elders employ the modes of words of the psalmist's enemies against Jesus (Ps. 22:19; cf. John 19:24; Matt. 27:35; Mark 15:24; Luke 23:34). It is not without reason that the psalm has been called the "Fifth Gospel" account of the crucifixion (p. 202).

David's emotions and needs. In the first 21 verses, David lamented his situation. He felt forsaken by all, including God (vv. 1–11). Surrounded by troubles, David felt feeble and helpless (vv. 12–18). In his extremity, David cried out to the Lord (vv. 19–21).

The second major section of the psalm shows a dramatic change in mood. David's prayers had been answered, and David promised to declare God's name to his brothers (vv. 22–26). Surely,

All the ends of the world
Shall remember and turn to the
    LORD,
And all the families of the
    nations
Shall worship before You (Ps. 22:27).

Qualities of God. In spite of his troubles, the psalmist honored God as holy, and as One who was to be trusted (vv. 3, 4). From his mother's womb, "You have been My God" (v. 10).

Prayer's transforming power. The last section of the psalm depicts the psalmist's prayers to God as answered. This was more than a change of attitude; it was a change of condition. As a result of God's answer to prayer "all the ends of the world shall remember and turn to the LORD" (v. 27), and "they will come and declare His righteousness to a people who will be born, that He has done this" (v. 31).

Personal application. From the perspective of the Cross and the Resurrection, nearly every verse of this great prayer psalm bursts with significance. While we can accept the fact that the psalm originally reflected David's emotions, we can hardly read it today without our thoughts being directed to the Savior. Surely the significance of this psalm, such a familiar part of first-century worship liturgy, must have been an especially powerful witness to Jesus in the days following His resurrection.

PSALM 31
"The LORD preserves the faithful"

The setting. Psalm 31 is another lengthy psalm forwarded to the chief musician for use in public worship.

David's emotions and needs. While the psalm includes a graphic lament over troubles and grief, overall the psalm serves as a testimony to God's faithfulness. David had trusted in God, and his trust had been well placed.

The first part of the psalm is carefully patterned, with the lament (vv. 9–13) enclosed by affirmations of trust (vv. 3–8, 14), and by opening and closing prayers (vv. 1–2, 15–18). A proclamation of God's great goodness (vv. 19–20) introduces the final section of the psalm—a joyful expression of thanksgiving and praise (vv. 21–24).

It is significant that Jesus on the Cross quoted Psalm 31:5, "Into Your hands I commit

"Into Your hands I commit My spirit."

My spirit" (see Luke 23:46). The deliverance from death which David celebrated foreshadowed the greater deliverance won for us by Christ, who guarantees our resurrection.

Qualities of God. David had a clear vision of the God whom he trusted. God was a righteous Savior (v. 1), a rock of refuge (vv. 2, 3). God was David's redeemer (v. 5) and David had complete confidence in His mercy (v. 7). God was Sovereign, in absolute control of David's times and able to deliver him (v. 15). How great God's goodness is toward those who trust Him (v. 19), for He preserves the faithful (v. 23).

Prayer's transforming power. This praise prayer of David is a testimony to the greatness and goodness of the Lord. Everything that David knew about God convinced him to trust the Lord, whatever his situation. Again and again David expressed his trust, and as he did so his heart was filled with confidence and joy.

Personal application. It is a good thing to thank God when He has answered our prayers. It is an even better thing to express our trust and thanksgiving before He answers.

Then we will be doubly blessed. We will be blessed immediately with peace and with joy later when our prayers have been answered.

PSALM 44
"Do not cast us off forever."

The setting. The sending of this psalm to the music director indicates this lament was part of Israel's worship liturgy. The content of the psalm and its distinctive structure indicate that it was used in worship following a significant military defeat.

The alternation of the first person singular and first person plural probably indicates the parts given to different speakers. If so, the prayer service would follow this pattern:

Liturgy of acknowledgment
- The people recited God's past acts (vv. 1–3).
- The king called on God (v. 4).
- The people expressed confidence in God (v. 5).
- The king declared his trust in God (v. 6).
- The people expressed their confidence (vv. 7, 8).

Lament
- The people grieved the recent defeat (vv. 9–14).
- The king confessed his shame at the defeat (v. 15, 16).
- The people proclaimed innocence (vv. 17–22).

Appeal

- People and king joined in appealing for God not to cast them off forever, but to help them soon (vv. 23–26).

The psalmist's emotions and needs. The military defeat described in verses 10–16 had shaken God's people as well as devastated the nation. Although the nation had been faithful to the Lord (vv. 20–22), their enemies had been victorious. The nation had a desperate need to reaffirm trust in God and to reconcile the defeat with the covenant-keeping character of the Lord.

Qualities of God. The nation knew God through His acts in history and acknowledged Him as king. While there was no answer to the question of why God permitted the present reverse, God's people still trusted Him and called on Him to act.

Prayer's transforming power. When we experience sudden reverses in national or personal life, we need some way to deal with them. This psalm provided a way for ancient Israel to deal with a military defeat. The people came together, reaffirmed their belief in God, dealt together with their failure to understand "why," and recommitted themselves to the Lord in prayer.

Personal application. In a sense, this psalm served the same purpose for Israel that a funeral serves for families. The people had experienced a great loss. It was important that they face the reality of the defeat, relate it to their beliefs, and reaffirm their faith in the Lord. Like our funerals—in which individuals face the reality of the death of loved ones and relate death to God—the religious service outlined in this psalm helped Israel deal with military defeat without a loss of faith.

How vital it is that we relate every major event of our lives—from birth to marriage to death—to our God. And that we share these major events with others in the community of faith.

PSALM 51
"Blot out my transgressions"

The setting. It is significant that this personal prayer of confession was handed over by David to the music director for use in public worship. The superscription makes the occasion of the prayer clear. David had sinned in committing adultery with Bathsheba, another man's wife (2 Sam. 11). He compounded his sin by arranging for the death of her husband Uriah in battle. David then married Bathsheba, who was already pregnant with his child.

David attempted to cover up his sin. Finally, David was confronted by Nathan the prophet, and at last he acknowledged his sin and guilt.

Psalm 51 is David's prayer of confession to God. Its inclusion in the Psalter served as public acknowledgment of a sin that—in the Jerusalem of David's day with only about 3,500 inhabitants—could hardly have been kept secret. David realized that public sin requires public as well as private confession. In turning this great prayer poem over to the chief musician, David provided one of the greatest model prayers to be found in the Old Testament.

(For comments on this psalm, its content and its significance to us today, see pp. 41 and 112, 113.)

PSALM 54
"Strangers have risen up against me."

The setting. This brief psalm of David was to be sung as part of Israel's worship liturgy. The superscription tells us that it was a contemplation on a specific event, "when the Ziphites said to Saul, 'Is David not hiding with us?'"

The event mentioned is described in 1 Samuel 23. David, pursued by Saul, hid in the wilderness of Ziph. The local citizens hurried to Saul to betray David's location, and they were sent back by Saul to spy out all of David's hiding places. This followed closely on David's discovery that the people of Keilah, who

David had saved from the Philistines, would also quickly hand him over to Saul. Truly these men of Judah, David's own tribe, were "strangers." David could not grasp what would motivate such a betrayal.

In this brief prayer psalm, David turned to God, aware that he could not trust human beings who failed to "set God before them."

David's emotions and needs. David had experienced betrayal, and he had realized he couldn't count on persons whom he might have had reason to trust. Strikingly, David didn't seem discouraged as he turned to the Lord.

Qualities of God. Unlike supposed friends who suddenly revealed themselves to be strangers, David was sure he could count on the Lord. God was David's helper, who had delivered him in the past. David was certain that God would "repay my enemies for their evil" (v. 5).

Prayer's transforming power. We are vulnerable to rejection and hurt when those whom we trust let us down. But in this instance, David set hurt and anger aside. He appealed to God, confident that the Lord was his helper (v. 4).

Personal application. It does hurt when our friends turn on us. A cruel or thoughtless remark can wound as easily as intentional betrayal. How greatly we need to follow David's example when others let us down, remembering that God is a helper who will always be by our side.

PSALM 55
"Violence and strife in the city."

The setting. Although this psalm portrays the lament of an individual, it was intended for use by the chief musician in public worship. Two things about this psalm are striking: It describes urban life in a wicked city, and the psalmist was shaken by the betrayal of one on whom he had counted as a friend.

David's emotions and needs. A number of phrases describe the intense emotions of the psalmist. He moaned as he appealed to God because of oppression by the wicked (vv. 2, 3). He wrote,

> My heart is severely pained
> within me,
> And the terrors of death have
> fallen upon me.
> Fearfulness and trembling
> have come upon me (Ps. 55:4, 5).

Life in the city is full of terrors because

> Destruction is in its midst;
> Oppression and deceit do not
> depart from its streets
> (Ps. 55:11).

What bothered the psalmist even more was his betrayal by a friend. He could have dealt with the hostility of an enemy, but the person who had harmed him was a close companion. "We took sweet counsel together," he said, "and walked to the house of God in the throng" (v. 14).

Crushed by his experience, the psalmist at first alternated between a desire to flee the city for the simpler life of the country (vv. 6, 7), and impassioned calls for God to judge.

> Let death seize them;
> Let them go down alive into
> hell,
> For wickedness is in their
> dwellings and among them
> (Ps. 55:15).

Qualities of God. While the psalm began with an appeal to God to hear his prayer, it was only in the last third of the psalm that David focused his thoughts on the Lord. When David thought on the Lord, he remembered that God, who had redeemed his soul, had heard his prayers and would save him (vv. 16–18). David also remembered that God as Judge was aware of the actions of the wicked and would "afflict them" (v. 19). God would judge "bloodthirsty and deceitful men," and David would "trust in you" (v. 23).

"Violence," "strife," "destruction," "oppression"—some aspects of the inner city.

David's contemplation of his troubles led him to a conclusion which he shared with his readers.

> Cast your burden on the LORD,
> And He shall sustain you,
> He shall never permit the
>   righteous to be moved
>   (Ps. 55:22).

Prayer's transforming power. This psalm, like others, invites us to share in a healing process. It takes us into the heart of a hurt and angry man, who wanted nothing so much as to get away from the situation that tormented him. We are gripped by the intensity of the psalmist's fears and his frustration. But then we see him call upon God.

As the psalmist focused his attention on the Lord, his fears were quieted and gradually replaced by a sense of peace. God would judge those who had troubled him. He cast his burden on the Lord, confident that God would sustain him and "never permit the righteous to be moved."

Personal application. The wicked city of this psalm is never identified, but its description reminds us of the dangers present in our own inner cities. We can identify with the loneliness and vulnerability of the person who lives among crowds of strangers. In the city it is so essential to have a close friend. But how much worse it is if such a friend should betray us.

Ultimately, God is the only source of peace for the city dweller. We must rely on God for our security and turn to Him to judge those who would prey on us. Our friends may abandon us. But God we can trust.

PSALM 56
"What can man do to me?"

The setting. The superscription describes the experience which led David to write this psalm, which was later delivered to the music director for use in public worship.

The psalm reflects David's feelings "when the Philistines captured him in Gath." The incident is related in 1 Samuel 21. David had just fled, alone, from Saul's capital. Stopping along the way to pick up a weapon, he had been given the sword once worn by Goliath. David then entered Philistine territory and slipped into the city of Gath. This was not a particularly wise choice. Goliath had come from Gath, and the giant's sword would have been immediately recognized! David was also recognized, and his presence was reported to the king of Gath.

Aware of the danger, David "changed his behavior before them" and pretended to be insane. Disgusted by David's behavior, the ruler of Gath rebuked his servants and dismissed David as a madman. Escaping Gath, David then returned to Israel, where he went into hiding.

David's emotions and needs. In Gath, David was in danger. There is no question that David was afraid (v. 3). Yet the psalm does not emphasize fear, but trust. Twice in its 13 verses, David commited himself to trust God, adding, "I will not fear. What can flesh do to me" (v. 4) and "I will not be afraid. What can man do to me?" (v. 11).

Of special note is David's saying, "Whenever I am afraid, I will trust in you" (v. 3). David had discovered what many Christians have yet to learn. Being afraid does not demonstrate a failure to trust God. Being afraid provides an *opportunity* for us to trust God. In his fear, David discovered that he truly did trust the Lord. And this was a wonderful discovery indeed.

Qualities of God. David twice mentioned God's Word in the immediate context of trust (vv. 3, 4, 10, 11). He was confident that when he cried out to the Lord, "then my enemies will turn back." David added, "This I know, because God is for me" (v. 9).

Prayer's transforming power. In looking to God with trust, David found an antidote to fear.

Personal application. It is important for us to realize, as David did, that fear or discouragement are not in themselves indications of lack of trust and spirituality. Like David, we need to see them as opportunities to trust God and so deepen our reliance on the Lord.

PSALM 57
"He shall send from heaven and save me."

The setting. This is another prayer of David which found its way into worship liturgy. In the superscription, "Do not destroy" probably indicates a popular tune to which the psalm was set. The meaning of "michtam" is uncertain, but it may mean "written for public use."

The superscription links this psalm to David's experience "when he fled from Saul into the cave." While some relate this to David's initial flight from Saul as recorded in 1 Samuel 21, it is better taken as a reference to events recorded in 1 Samuel 24. David and his men were hiding in a cave when Saul entered the cave to relieve himself. David's men urged him to strike Saul, but David refused to "stretch out my hand against" Saul, whom God had chosen as king. David also restrained his men, who wanted to kill Saul.

The content of the psalm fits this event well, as it reflects David's commitment to wait on God to remove Saul.

> I will cry out to God Most High,
> To God, who performs all
>   things for me.
> He reproaches the one who
>   would swallow me up
>   (Ps. 57:2, 3).

David's emotions and needs. Although Saul was intent on killing David, David refused to act against Saul. Perhaps surprisingly, the psalm is filled with expressions of confidence and joy. David had done what he knew was right. He had honored the Lord, and God had filled his heart with songs of praise.

Qualities of God. The name *God Most High* (v. 2) emphasizes God's sovereignty. By his restraint, David showed his trust in God as sovereign. The Lord had chosen Saul, and the Lord must be the One to depose him.

Personal application. This psalm reveals the transforming power of obedience. David was convinced that it would be wrong to strike

With God as his guardian—and a little help from his wife—David eluded Saul's soldiers.

Saul. He honored God by his restraint, and the Lord filled his heart with a sense of joy and praise. Prayer will often quiet our fears and bring peace. But if we would know joy in the Lord, we need to make life's hard choices and determine to please Him in all we do.

PSALM 59
"They lie in wait for my life."

The setting. This is another psalm drawn from David's personal experience, which came to be used in public worship. (See the setting of Psalm 57, p. 93).

The occasion the psalm recalls is when Saul sent men to watch David's house in order to kill him when he left. The story is told in 1 Samuel 19:11–17. Aware of the danger,

David's wife Michal helped David slip away through a window. Later, when Saul's men reported that David had not left the house, Saul told them to go in and bring David to him, so he could kill David himself. The delay helped David get far away from Saul's capital and make his escape.

David's emotions and needs. David appealed to God to defend him from those who "gather against me, not for my transgression nor for my sin" (v. 5).

David did not seem particularly terrified of his enemies, although they were "bloodthirsty men" (v. 2). He did call for God to act against them, but only so they may know "that God rules in Jacob to the ends of the earth" (v. 13).

Qualities of God. David affirmed God as ruler and "God of hosts" (armies, v. 5). In His unlimited power, God would defend David (vv. 1, 9, 16, 17) and bring down his enemies. Twice David addressed God as his strength (vv. 9, 17), and also referred to Him as "My God of mercy" (v. 17). In view of the power of the God who defended David, the psalm shows that David had little fear of his enemies.

Prayer's transforming power. David's knowledge of God and his confidence in God were expressed both in his petition, and in the conclusion he reached after considering God's character.

> But I will sing of Your power;
> Yes, I will sing aloud of Your
>   mercy in the morning;
> For You have been my defense
> And refuge in the day of my
>   trouble;
> To You, O my Strength, I will
>   sing praises;
> For God is my defense,
> My God of mercy (Ps. 59:16, 17).

PSALM 61
"He shall abide before God forever."

The setting. This psalm of David was set to music by the chief musician for use in worship.

David's emotions and needs. The psalm celebrates the king's relationship with the Lord. A strong note of praise echoes through the psalm, which is also marked by expressions of trust (v. 4) and commitment (vv. 5, 8).

This psalm appears to be an individual prayer, but it is likely that it was used in public worship as an affirmation of messianic hope. God had given His covenant promise to David, and He would surely exalt David's promised descendant to "abide before God forever."

Qualities of God. God had sheltered the psalmist and His people and made covenant

THEMES OF PUBLIC PRAYER PSALMS

Psalm	Theme
5	Trust
6	Healing
9	Praise
18	Thanksgiving
20	War
22	Suffering
44	Grief
51	Forgiveness
55	Stress
56	Fear
57	Obedience
59	Confidence
61	Hope
67	Confidence
69	Suffering
70	Dependence
80	Restoration
84	Joy
85	Blessing
140	Deliverance

commitments to them. The psalmist and those who used his words in worship responded with trust (v. 4) and praise (v. 8).

Prayer's transforming power. If the commentators are correct, this psalm was used as a reminder of God's promise to send His Messiah to Israel. What a blessing it must have been to the few Jews in the holy land to recall God's commitment as they called upon Him to prepare the mercy and truth for which they longed (v. 7).

Personal application. Remembering God's promises and affirming them together remains a source of hope and confidence among the Lord's people.

PSALM 67
"God shall bless us."

The setting. This brief, joyfilled psalm is designated both a psalm and a song, to be accompanied on stringed instruments. Usually the word "song" refers to a secular song. Joined, the two terms indicate a "song-type psalm."

The psalmist's emotions and needs. The psalm opens with a brief community prayer that God's way and salvation may be known on earth (vv. 1, 2). This is followed by a joyful call to praise, in which the community joins the psalmist in affirming, God shall bless us, And all the ends of the earth shall fear Him (Ps. 67:7).

Qualities of God. The psalmist saw God as merciful, and His mercy as the source of blessings. Confidence is also drawn from the fact that God will "judge the people righteously, and govern the nations on earth" (v. 4). Because God is committed to Israel as His people, His own character guarantees their blessing.

Prayer's transforming power. We can find as much joy in affirming what God will do as in naming the blessings He has already given us.

PSALM 69
"Reproach has broken my heart."

The setting. This lengthy psalm communicates the psalmist's lament and complaint in vivid metaphors. Drawn from the Davidic collection, it was delivered to the chief musician for use in public worship, "set to 'The Lilies.'" The word translated "lilies" is a musical notation, but its exact meaning is unknown.

David's emotions and needs. While David expressed his own emotions, this psalm has long been understood to have messianic overtones. The description of the enemies who plagued and taunted the devoted servant of God depicts Christ's opponents, as applied by the evangelists (see Matt. 23:28, 29; 27:34, 48; Mark 15:36; Luke 23:36; John 2:17; 15:25; 19:29, 30).

Several of the psalm's major sections emphasize the pain suffered by God's servant. The psalmist:

- Prays for deliverance from a   vv. 2–5 desperate situation.
- Protests his innocence and his   vv. 6–14b enemies' guilt.
- Urgently begs for God's saving   vv. 14c–18 intervention.

- Complains of the hatred of   vv. 19–22 the enemies who humiliate him.
- Asks God to punish the enemies vv. 23–26 in his anger.
- Utters a final complaint and   vv. 27–29 asks God to punish the enemies.
- Concludes with expressions   vv. 30–37 of praise and confidence in the Lord.

The anguish of the psalmist is reflected in such phrases as "I am weary with my crying" (v. 3), "my reproach, my shame, and my dishonor" (v. 19), and "reproach has broken my heart, and I am full of heaviness" (v. 20). A sense of urgency is expressed in this series of appeals:

- "Hear me" (v. 16).
- "Turn to me" (v. 16).
- "Do not hide Your face" (v. 17).
- "Hear me speedily" (v. 17).
- "Draw near to my soul" (v. 18).
- "Deliver me" (v. 18).

Qualities of God. The psalmist depicted himself as a servant of God. Even though he was surrounded by enemies, he was confident that God would intervene "in the acceptable time . . . in the multitude of Your mercies" (v. 13).

As God of Hosts, the Lord has sovereign power (v. 6a); as God of Israel, the Lord is a covenant-making and covenant-keeping God (v. 6b). The psalmist was well acquainted with God's lovingkindness ["grace"] (v. 16), and knew that God was fully aware both of his own innocence and of the wicked hearts of his oppressors (v. 19). As Savior, God would surely intervene, to deliver him and to punish his enemies (v. 29).

Prayer's transforming power. The first 29 verses of the psalm are overshadowed by the psalmist's anguish. But verses 30–36 conclude on a note of praise and thanksgiving. God who "hears the poor" (v. 33) will surely answer the psalmist's prayers. The final verses of the psalm convey utter confidence.

Let heaven and earth praise
     Him,

The seas and everything that
    moves in them.
For God will save Zion
And build the cities of Judah,
That they may dwell there and
    possess it.
Also, the descendants of His
    servants shall inherit it,
And those who love His name
    shall dwell in it (Ps. 69:34–36).

Personal application. Believers are encouraged to bring their burdens to the Lord and leave them there. When we know God as well as David did, we will also leave our sessions of prayer filled with joy and thanksgiving, certain that God will do what is best.

PSALM 70
"Make haste, O God."

The setting. This brief memorial psalm was sung as a reminder to worshipers of their dependence on the Lord. No historical setting is provided for this psalm of David.

David's emotions and needs. The psalm urges the Lord to hurry to the worshiper's aid. A sense of dependence is clearly expressed in the last verse:

But I am poor and needy;
Make haste to me, O God!
You are my help and my
    deliverer;
O LORD, do not delay (Ps. 70:5).

Qualities of God. The psalmist honored God as the One who is able to save by turning back His enemies.

Prayer's transforming power. Throughout this psalm, the psalmist kept his focus on God. Although enemies threatened, the psalmist did not doubt that God would help. His prayer was that God would act quickly.

Personal application. When we remember who God is, we are confident of His help. We will not wonder if God *will* act, but *when!*

PSALM 80
"Restore us, O God of Hosts."

The setting. This is another prayer psalm used in public worship. It was to be sung by the worshiping community to a familiar tune ("lilies"). The designation "a testimony" is taken to mean "covenant" or "a reminder." While no specific historical setting is indicated, it is clear from the content that this was a national lament—a prayer suited to a time of national disaster.

The psalmist's emotions and needs. God's people longed for protection and the restoration of security. The present situation was depicted in two different but equally powerful images. The first image is captured in verse 5:

You have fed them with the
    bread of tears,
And have given them tears to drink
    in great measure.

The second image is a familiar one, used most powerfully in Isaiah 7. Israel was a vine planted in the holy land. But now, God's people asked,

Why have You broken down
    her hedges,
So that all who pass by the way
    pluck her fruit?
The boar out of the woods
    uproots it,
And the wild beast of the field
    devours it (Ps. 80:12, 13).

Crushed and desperate, God's people begged the Lord to restore them (vv. 3, 7, 19).

It is notable that this lament does not include any confession of sins. Not every national or personal disaster should be viewed as God's punishment.

Qualities of God. The psalm assumes that the present disaster was possible because God had, for some reason, withdrawn His favor. In the mind of the psalmist, God was in sover-

If Israel is the vine, a wild boar represents big trouble.

pens. The conviction that God remains in control may make it hard to understand why He lets us suffer. Yet that conviction is a source of hope. We can appeal to God to restore and revive us, confident that He is fully able to answer our prayers.

Personal application. It is so easy to misunderstand the doctrine of divine sovereignty, assuming that God's control of all events turns human beings into puppets with no choice of their own. In fact, the doctrine of God's sovereignty is freeing. Because the Lord is in control of history and of the events of our lives, we are never the helpless victims of circumstance. All that happens to us is filtered through God's wise love. And we can always appeal to God in prayer that the good times be restored.

PSALM 84
"The LORD will give grace and glory."

The setting. The psalm is a work of the "sons of Korah," who, according to 2 Chronicles 20:19, were a guild of temple singers. This particular psalm expresses the joy of believers who have come together to worship the Lord.

The psalmist's emotions and needs. The psalm is filled with expressions of joy at the privilege of worshiping God.

Qualities of God. The psalmist took delight in God Himself. God is wonderful,

> For the LORD God is a sun and
>   shield;
> The LORD will give grace and
>   glory;
> No good thing will He withhold
> From those who walk
>   uprightly.
> O LORD of hosts,
> Blessed is the man who trusts
>   in You! (Ps. 84:11, 12).

eign control. Thus, He was the one who had fed God's people "the bread of tears" (v. 5). Israel may not be able to trace current events to specific national sins, but what they had experienced felt like the anger of God (v. 4).

But the God who had caused (or permitted) the national disaster was able to restore. "Cause Your face to shine" the people cried, "and we shall be saved!" (v. 3). This affirmation is repeated three times; here, and in verses 7 and 19.

How significant that what had happened to the nation had not shaken the people's faith in God's *ability* to act. If we suffer, it is not because God is unable to aid us. The psalmist's heartfelt appeals to the Lord also make it clear that disaster had not shaken the belief that God *will* act in the future to revive His people.

Prayer's transforming power. It is so easy to give in to doubt or depression. This prayer, crafted for a time of national disaster, reminds us that God is in charge, no matter what hap-

Prayer's transforming power. In this case, the worshipers' focus on God has transformed their prayer. Prayer is seen in its purest form—as joy-filled praise. The person whose

"As the deer pants for the water brooks, . . . my soul thirsts for God."

soul "longs, yes, even faints for the courts of the LORD" (v. 2) will find praise a door which opens into His presence.

Personal application. The psalms often express the believer's longing for God as well as the joy to be found in His presence. Here are two such expressions:

> One thing I have desired of the
>   LORD,
> That will I seek;
> That I may dwell in the house
>   of the LORD
> All the days of my life,
> To behold the beauty of the LORD,
> And to inquire in His temple
>   (Ps. 27:4).

> As the deer pants for the
>   water brooks,
> So pants my soul for You,
>   O God.

> My soul thirsts for God, for the
>   living God.
> When shall I come and appear
>   before God? (Ps. 42:1, 2).

When our hearts are moved to worship the Lord and we want to praise Him, we can use psalms such as this as our guide. Then we will be able to say with the saints of old, "A day in Your courts is better than a thousand" (v. 10).

PSALM 85
"The LORD will give what is good."

The setting. The "sons of Korah" were a guild of temple singers (see the setting of Psalm 84, above). This psalm was also part of the official worship repertoire of Israel.

The psalmist's emotions and needs. The psalm is a confident prayer for divine aid, expressed in verse 7:

> Show us Your mercy, LORD,
> And grant us Your salvation.

Unlike other psalms which emphasize the desperate situation in which God's people find themselves, this psalm focuses on past experiences of God's saving work and then looks ahead in confident expectation. The God who has "brought back the captivity of Jacob" and "forgiven the iniquity of Your people" (vv. 1, 2) surely "will speak peace to His people and to His saints" (v. 8).

Qualities of God. The psalmist pictured qualities of God as personal agents that would restore life to His people. Verses 10 and 11 contain this fascinating imagery. God's qualities are pictured as kings, meeting together and agreeing on a course of action. The ruling characteristics of the Lord so portrayed are mercy, truth, righteousness, and peace. And what course of action do these four determine to take? "The LORD will give what is good."

Prayer's transforming power. What great confidence we can have in God. We can remember His goodness to us in the past. But even more than that, we can focus on the kind of person He is. His qualities of mercy, truth, righteousness and peace assure us that the Lord surely will "give what is good."

Personal application. We need only spend more time looking to God than we do looking at our circumstances. When we do, we will pray—and live—with confidence.

PSALM 140
"Deliver me, O Lord."

The setting. The superscription tells us that this psalm of David was delivered to the chief musician, intended for use in public worship.

David's emotions and needs. This psalm fits the pattern of many prayers of complaint, also called laments. The psalmist was deeply disturbed by violent and evil men who persecuted him (vv. 1–3). He begged God to thwart the malicious plans of his enemies, and

> Let not a slanderer be
> established in the earth;
> Let evil hunt the violent man
> to overthrow him (Ps. 140:11).

Yet at heart of the psalm is an expression of David's confidence in the Lord. The key verses are 6 and 7:

> I said to the Lord: "You are my
> God;
> Hear the voice of my
> supplications, O Lord,

> O God the Lord, the strength
> of my salvation,
> You have covered my head in
> the day of battle.

The confidence that grows out of knowing that the Lord is our God is echoed in the last verses' of the psalm, as David declared, "I know that the Lord will maintain the cause of the afflicted" (v. 12).

Qualities of God. David found relief in knowing that the Lord was his God. While God was known for His justice and salvation, the thing that thrilled David the most was that he had a personal relationship with the Lord. "You are my God," David said—and knowing this was enough.

Prayer's transforming power. Prayer is an affirmation of relationship. We come to God with the assurance that He cares about us. While we may come to God's throne anxious and concerned, we leave with a peace that the final words of this psalm portray:

> I know that the Lord will
> maintain
> The cause of the afflicted,
> And justice for the poor.
> Surely the righteous shall give
> thanks to Your name;
> The upright shall dwell in Your
> presence.

Personal application. Anxiety is God's invitation to approach Him. Peace is our assurance that He has heard.

CHAPTER 7

MIGHTY IN PRAYER

LEARNING FROM ABRAHAM, MOSES, HANNAH, AND DAVID

Genesis; Exodus; 1 Samuel

P at was one of the elders in our church in Phoenix. He was an engineer at one of the local radio stations, skilled mechanically, but not otherwise gifted. Pat was one of those persons who couldn't quite find words to explain the biblical principles of church life we were committed to. I can't remember a single meeting of the elders in which Pat contributed a significant insight. But he could pray.

When Pat led our elder team in prayer, or led our congregation on Sunday mornings, we all sensed his unique contribution to our lives. Pat slipped easily into the presence of the Lord, and he brought us with him. Simply by praying, Pat enriched each of us and provided a model of meaningful prayer.

Not every Christian knows a Pat who can teach him or her to pray simply by praying. But all of us have, in the Scriptures, men and women of faith whose prayer lives can enrich us today. In this chapter, we will visit them and let them teach us to pray.

ABRAHAM, THE MAN OF FAITH

The first thing we want to notice about Abraham is that in his early life, he was a pagan. The Lord even reminded Israel that

Your fathers, including Terah, the father of Abraham and the father of Nahor, dwelt on the other side of the River in old times; and they served other gods. Then I took your father Abraham from the other side of the River, led him throughout all the land of Canaan, and multiplied his descendants (Josh. 24:2, 3).

Abraham had no one to show him how to pray. He had to take his own first stumbling steps in prayer with no one to guide him. It is striking that in nearly every case where Abraham's prayers are recorded, God rather than Abraham was the initiator.

FIRST CONTACT (GENESIS 12)

God first spoke to Abram when he lived in that land on "the other side of the river." There God gave Abram a series of stunning promises, telling him to go to a "land that I will show you" (v. 1). Abram followed God's instructions. When he finally reached Canaan, the Lord appeared to him again and promised, "To your descendants I will give this land" (v. 7). The next verse tells us that Abram built an altar there, and "called on the name of the LORD" (v. 8).

Jewish commentators have focused much attention on this phrase, rendered in the Tanakh (a contemporary Jewish translation), as "invoked the LORD by name." One theme the rabbis consistently emphasize is that in this act Abram "publicly proclaimed God's name." Abram may not have known the protocols of prayer, but God had spoken to Abram. From that moment, all of Abram's hope and worship was focused on the Lord.

REVEALING A TROUBLED HEART (GENESIS 15)

Abram maintained his commitment to God during the following years. When kings from the north took Abram's nephew Lot captive along with the population of several cities in the Jordan valley, Abram went to the rescue. Afterward when he was offered the recaptured wealth, Abram refused. Abram would depend on "the LORD, God Most High, the Possessor of heaven and earth" (Gen. 14:23). He would not let any person take credit for making Abram rich.

After this incident, God spoke to Abram again and announced "I am your shield, your exceeding great reward" (Gen. 15:1). No earthly wealth could compare to Abram's personal relationship with the Lord.

Abram's response to this affirmation by the Lord may seem surprising. He revealed his troubled heart. "LORD God, what will You give me, seeing I go childless, and the heir of my house is Eliezer of Damascus" (v. 2). Not a word of thanks. Just a cry. Surely Abram was a stranger to the protocols of prayer!

But Abram's outburst was understandable. God had promised that Abram's descendants would inherit Canaan. Yet Abram had no children. According to custom, his chief servant would inherit Abram's flocks and herds. The words of this first prayer of Abraham's expressed the concern that troubled his heart. What could any "reward" mean to Abram if he died childless?

In response, God again promised Abram descendants. "One who will come from your own body shall be your heir" (v. 4). God then brought Abram outside, pointed to the heavens, and told Abram to "count the stars if you are able to number them. So shall your de-

Can you count the stars? God promised Abram that many descendants.

scendants be" (15:5). In one of the truly pivotal verses in Scripture, the Bible declares, "And he believed in the LORD, and He accounted it to him for righteousness" (v. 7).

But this was not the end of the incident. The LORD told Abram, "I am the LORD, who brought you out of Ur of the Chaldeans, to give you this land to inherit it." God had always intended to give Canaan to Abram and his descendants. But Abram responded, "LORD God, how shall I know that I will inherit it?" (v. 8).

Since Scripture tells us that Abram believed, what was Abram asking? The rabbis suggest that Abram was asking *How will I inherit it? During which generation? How much of it will be mine?* Or perhaps more likely, *What objective evidence of Your grant will confirm my witness to Your promise?* As the story continues, we see that God did provide objective confirmation of His promise to Abram. Following established custom, God entered into the most binding of ancient covenants (contracts, legally binding oaths) with Abram (vv. 12–21). In making this covenant, God affirmed, "To your descendants I *have given* this land" (italics mine). God's word is so trustworthy that when He speaks of the future, that future is as sure as if the events had already come to pass!

But what do we learn of prayer from this experience of Abram's? Looking at the incident, we sense how deeply Abram was troubled about his childless state. He had come to Canaan at God's command. He had been promised the land would be his and his descendants' after him. But as the weeks and months and years passed, and no child was born, his yearning for a son grew until it dominated Abram's thoughts. And when God spoke to him again, even so great a promise as we have in verse 1 meant little. Abram expressed the concern that troubled him deeply.

God responded graciously by reaffirming His promise. And Abram did believe God. But there is room for doubt in the firmest faith. Abram trusted God, but he couldn't understand what God was doing or exactly how God intended to fulfill His promises. So in grace God underlined His promise with a legally binding oath, that Abram might be *certain.*

We can paraphrase this first of Abram's prayer conversations with God this way:

God: "Knowing Me is your great reward."
Abram: "Speaking of rewards, You promised that my descendants would inherit this land. But You've given me no child."
God: "I'll give you more descendants than you can count."
Abram: (Abram believed God.)
God: "I brought you out of Ur to give you this land to inherit."
Abram: "LORD, I believe You. But how will I *know?*"
God: (Instructed Abram to prepare for a legally binding, covenant-making ceremony).

If we understand such conversations with God as prayer, simply because they are conversations *with God,* we begin to sense something important. For Abram, prayer was uncharted territory. So Abram simply plunged in, sharing his deepest concern. He trusted God. He believed God. But he didn't understand what God was doing, and so he asked. And he was reassured.

EXPRESSING THE HEART'S DESIRE (GENESIS 17)

The next recorded prayer of Abram is found in Genesis 17. Years had passed since the incident recorded in Genesis 15. In the meantime, Abram had a son with Hagar, his wife's maid. That son, Ishmael, was 13 years old when God spoke to Abram and repeated the promises He had made earlier.

I will establish My covenant between Me and you and your descendants after you in their generations, for an everlasting covenant, to be God to you and your descendants after you. Also I give to you and your descendants after you the land in which you are a stranger, all the land of Canaan, as an everlasting possession; and I will be their God (Gen. 17:7, 8).

The Lord went on to tell Abram, now called Abraham, that he would have another son, this time by his wife Sarah, who was 89 years old. And Abraham blurted out his heart's desire: "Oh, that Ishmael might live before You!"

Abraham had invested so much love in Ishmael over the past 13 years. He had imagined Ishmael's future, picturing future generations who would know the blessing of God springing from this son. So the Lord's announcement shook Abraham. Why another son? Why not Ishmael? And so Abraham blurted out his request. "Lord, make it Ishmael!"

God's answer was, "No." He told Abraham "No, Sarah your wife shall bear you a son, and you shall call his name Isaac; I will establish My covenant with him (v. 19).

Abraham had spontaneously expressed his heart's desire. But in this case, his heart's desire was out of harmony with God's plan.

Later Abraham learned to love Isaac deeply (see Gen. 22:2). But at the moment, Abraham's heart must have broken as all his dreams for Ishmael were shattered.

Like Abraham, we always have the freedom to express our heart's desire to the Lord. But like Abraham, we must learn to accept God's "No" in the realization that the Lord has something better in store.

QUESTIONING GOD'S MORALITY (GENESIS 18)

God again visited Abraham, this time accompanied by two angels. The promised son would be born to Sarah within the year. When leaving, God took Abraham aside and told him of His intent to judge the cities of Sodom and Gomorrah.

The news greatly disturbed Abraham, and he posed this question:

Would You also destroy the righteous with the wicked? Suppose there were fifty righteous within the city; would You also destroy the place and not spare it for the fifty righteous that were in it? Far be it from You to do such a thing as this, to slay the righteous with the wicked, so that the righteous should be as the wicked; far be it from You! (Gen. 18:23–25).

The possibility that God might act in a way that violated Abraham's sense of right and wrong was deeply disturbing, and Abraham brought his concern to the Lord. Abraham's expression of concern evoked a promise: "If I find in Sodom fifty righteous within the city, then I will spare all the place for their sakes" (v. 26).

But Abraham, now uncertain of his speaking in such tones with the Lord, continued. "Indeed now, I who am but dust and ashes have taken it upon myself to speak to the LORD" (v. 27). Then he went on to ask God to reduce the necessary number of righteous to forty, then thirty, then twenty. Finally, concerned that he had gone too far, Abraham prayed "Let not the LORD be angry, and I will speak but once more: Suppose ten should be found there" (v. 32)?

The investigating angels who went to Sodom found only one righteous man there: Lot. God didn't spare the city. But God did make sure that Lot and his family were saved from the destruction. When raging fires destroyed Sodom and Gomorrah, only the wicked remained.

Abraham had no examples to follow; no guidelines to tell him what was acceptable in prayer. Did he dare express concern about the morality of God's intentions? Clearly Abraham himself had doubts that a mere human being should question God's judgments. But how much Abraham learned, and how much he teaches us. We live in a world marked by tragedy and loss. There are times when each of us wonders, How could God permit this calamity, that suffering? Abraham's prayer reminds us that God is not angered by our concern for others. But we learn far more.

Ultimately, Abraham was ready to accept the deaths of ten righteous people as the cost of punishing the wicked. *But God was not!* God would not let even the one innocent person in Sodom suffer with the wicked.

It's important for us to remember this incident when our sensibilities are offended and we find ourselves questioning the morality of God's acts. Events ultimately proved that God had a deeper concern for others than Abraham did. In spite of the questioning nature of Abraham's prayers, the Lord must have been pleased with His follower. Abraham's prayer showed that, like God, he really did care for people.

SUBMITTING IN SILENCE (GENESIS 22)

Before we reach Genesis 22, there are two other references to Abraham's prayers (Gen. 20:7, 17; 21:33). But the twenty-second chapter of Genesis contains the last incident in which we actually listen in on Abraham's conversations with God.

When this last conversation took place, Isaac was a youth (the rabbis claim Isaac was 37 years old). Once again, God spoke to Abraham first. Abraham replied, "Here I am." The

When Abraham and Isaac started out to make a sacrifice to God, Isaac did not know he was to be it.

❖

phrase is idiomatic, to be understood as an expression of readiness and submission. And God's next words surely tested Abraham's submission severely. God said "Take now your son, your only son Isaac, whom you love, and go to the land of Moriah, and offer him there as a burnt offering on one of the mountains of which I shall tell you" (22:2).

Stunned, Abraham had nothing to say. Yet his actions spoke for him. The text says, "So Abraham rose *early in the morning* and saddled his donkey . . . and went to the place of which God had told him" (v. 3, *italics mine*).

There are times when the only prayer we can offer is silence—when our readiness to obey expresses what is in our hearts in a way that words never could. But how can we come to the place where we are able to offer such a prayer? Only as Abraham did.

Abraham's years with God had developed in him an unshakable trust in the Lord. We see that trust expressed in verse 5. When Abraham and Isaac approached the mountain,

Abraham told the two servants who accompanied them, "Stay here . . . The lad and I will go yonder and worship, *and we will come back* to you" (italics mine). The writer of Hebrews explains this statement. Abraham remembered God's promise, " 'in Isaac your seed shall be called,' concluding that God was able to raise him up, even from the dead" (Heb. 11:18, 19). Abraham did not understand what God intended. But Abraham trusted God so much that he was sure God would find a way to save his son.

LESSONS FROM ABRAHAM'S PRAYER LIFE

God spoke to Abraham when he was still a pagan worshiping idols in Mesopotamia, and He launched him on a grand adventure. No road map existed to lead Abraham to Canaan; no guide existed that could teach Abraham how to relate to God. But one thing Abraham knew: The Lord was God; Abraham would invoke the Lord only.

When opportunities came to speak with the Lord, Abraham made the most of them. His recorded prayers are spontaneous and heartfelt. Abraham shared the concern that troubled his heart. He freely expressed his deepest desire in heartfelt petition. Abraham even questioned God about His morality. But ultimately he submitted in silence to God's command—not reluctantly but eagerly—intent on seeing how God would keep His promise to do him good. Through it all, God showed His patience with Abraham as well as His grace.

God is also patient with us. In grace, God listens as we share our troubled hearts, our deepest desires, the questions that disturb us, and the silences which mark our own obedience as expectant trust.

MOSES, FAITHFUL IN GOD'S HOUSE

It's not surprising that more narrative passages record the prayers of Moses than any other person in the Bible. After all, Moses is the dominant figure in four of the first five books of the Old Testament—about one-sixth of the entire Old Testament! His experiences with God and with Israel are recorded in significant detail, including accounts of a number of his conversations with God. As we look at these accounts, several aspects of Moses' prayer life seem especially significant.

MOSES REMAINED HUMBLE BEFORE GOD (EXODUS 3, 4)

Moses did not begin life as a humble man. He was raised in Egypt's royal family, trained in "all the wisdom of the Egyptians, and was mighty in words and deed" (Acts 7:22). He identified with the Hebrew people and saw himself as the hero who would deliver them from slavery one day. For the first forty years of his life, Moses was certainly not a man of humility.

One day he killed an Egyptian taskmaster who was mistreating a Hebrew slave, then hid the body. When Moses realized that others knew what he had done, he fled Egypt. For the next forty years, Moses lived as a fugitive, herding a few sheep in the Sinai wilderness. The harsh desert winds gradually eroded his pride as his dream of greatness evaporated in the hot sun. At age 80, Moses truly had become a humbled man.

Numbers 12:3 notes, "The man Moses was very humble, more than all men who were on the face of the earth." The adjective is derived from the Hebrew verb 'anah, which suggests a state of submission brought about by affliction and suffering. The proud young prince had been worn away, leaving an old man stripped of all pretensions as well as self-confidence—in short, leaving a man whom God could use.

But with Moses as with the rest of us, our greatest strength may also be our weakness. We see this in Moses' first encounter with God and in the extended dialogue which—because the conversation was *with God*—we may consider prayer (Ex. 3, 4). We know the story from Sunday school.

God spoke to Moses from within a burning bush, reviving Moses' dream. God announced that He had at last come down to deliver Israel, and said "Come now . . . and I will send you to Pharaoh that you may bring My people, the children of Israel, out of Egypt" (Ex. 3:10).

Just as Moses had dreamed!

But now the dream was dead, and Moses was humbled. The interaction that followed shows how humble Moses had become. Again and again, Moses objected, insisting that he was inadequate for the task. And again and again, God reminded Moses that He, the Lord, was adequate.

Moses	God
"Who am I, that I should go to Pharaoh?" (3:11).	"I will certainly be with you" (3:12).
"When I come to the children of Israel . . . what shall I say to them?" (3:13).	"Say to the children of Israel, 'I AM has sent me to you'" (3:14).
"But suppose they will not believe me?" (4:1).	[God gave to Moses miraculous signs.]
"LORD, I am not eloquent. . .but I am slow of speech" (4:10).	"I will be with your mouth and teach you what you shall say" (4:12).
"O my LORD, please send by the hand of whomever else You may send" (4:13).	[Angry (4:14)] God still gave Moses his brother Aaron to serve as spokesman, but insisted "I will be with your mouth . . . and I will teach you what you shall do" (v. 15).

Moses' humility protected him from the danger of self-reliance, keeping him dependent on the Lord. Yet the same humility made Moses reluctant to step out in faith. But by expressing his doubts and hesitations Moses gave the Lord the opportunity to encourage him. Finally, Moses bowed to God's will. In spite of his doubts about himself, he set out on the mission that would make him one of the most honored of history's saints.

How wonderfully prayer provides us with the opportunity to express our doubts about ourselves. And in the process, prayer reminds us that God's strength is made perfect in human weakness. We can carry humility too far. But without humility, our prayers may take the form of seeking to bend God to our will rather than expressing our willingness to do His.

MOSES REMAINED MINDFUL OF GOD'S SOVEREIGNTY (EXODUS 5:22; 6:12, 30; 14:14)

One of the most fascinating contrasts between Moses and the people he led out of slavery is seen in the reaction of both to reverses. When things seemed to go wrong, the Israelites grumbled and complained against Moses (see Ex. 15:24; 16:2; 17:2–4). Not so Moses! When Moses' efforts to free Israel were not met with immediate success, Moses went to God with his questions and complaints.

The first time Moses approached Pharaoh, it was with God's demand to let Israel go a little distance into the wilderness and worship Him. Pharaoh, contemptuous of this God of his slaves, responded by making their labor even more burdensome. And the Israelites blamed Moses (Ex. 5:21)! Moses then showed his respect for God and His sovereignty by asking, "LORD, why have You brought trouble on this people? Why is it You have sent me?" (Ex. 5:22).

Some may see this complaint as presumptuous. In fact, Moses' reaction showed his respect for the Lord. God could have done differently. Why then did God, who had stated His intent to free Israel, permit their situation to become worse? And why did God permit this reverse, which seemed to destroy Moses' credibility with his own people? Surely if the Israelites would not heed Moses, how could Moses expect Pharaoh to pay attention to him (Ex. 6:12, 30)?

God explained to Moses what was going on. Pharaoh's refusal to listen to Moses was part of His plan. God would use Pharaoh's resistance to His will to display His power over Egypt's deities and as an everlasting witness to God's commitment to His covenant people. The explanation helped Moses develop even

more trust in God and in His control of events.

Moses would soon have opportunities to exercise that trust. He spoke boldly to announce imminent plagues and to promise their removal. And when the Egyptians were trapped between the Red Sea and an Egyptian army, Moses reassured the people by telling them to "stand still and see the salvation of the LORD" even before God revealed His intention to divide the waters (Ex. 14:13–16).

Moses' prayer to the Lord reminds us that it is better to question God than to complain about our circumstances. In our thoughts and prayers, we need to remain mindful of God's sovereignty and look to Him in tragedy and triumph.

MOSES SHOWED CONCERN FOR GOD'S HONOR (EXODUS 32; NUMBERS 14)

Moses' years as the leader of Israel were filled with stress. More than once Israel pushed even the Lord to the brink. The first occasion was while Moses was on Mount Sinai receiving the Ten Commandments. At the foot of the mountain, Aaron succumbed to the urging of the people and fashioned a golden calf. The people worshiped it and sacrificed to it, saying, "This is your God, O Israel, that brought you out of the land of Egypt!" (Ex. 32:8).

God told Moses what was happening and offered to make a great nation out of Moses. But Moses pleaded with the Lord:

LORD, why does Your wrath burn hot against Your people whom You have brought out of the land of Egypt with great power and with a mighty hand? Why should the Egyptians speak, and say, 'He brought them out to harm them, to kill them in the mountains, and to consume them from the face of the earth'? Turn from Your fierce wrath, and relent from this harm to Your people.

Remember Abraham, Isaac and Israel, Your servants, to whom You swore by Your own self, and said to them, "I will multiply your descendants as the stars of heaven and all this land that I have spoken of I give to your descendants, and they shall inherit it forever" (Ex. 32:10–13).

Lest we think this prayer was made lightly, in Deuteronomy 9:25 Moses related: "I prostrated myself before the LORD; forty days and forty nights I kept prostrating myself, because the LORD had said He would destroy you." Moses *labored* in prayer, driven by a desire to see God honored.

Later, God commanded the Exodus generation to enter Canaan. Moses, Aaron, Joshua, and Caleb urged the people to trust God, but the Israelites rebelled again. Once again, God offered to make a great nation of Moses. And once again, Moses pleaded with God for Israel:

> Then the Egyptians will hear it, for by Your might You brought these people up from among them, and they will tell it to the inhabitants of this land. They have heard that You, LORD, are among these people; that You, LORD, are seen face to face and Your cloud stands above them, and You go before them in a pillar of cloud by day and in a pillar of fire by night.
>
> Now if you kill these people as one man, then the nations which have heard of Your fame will speak, saying, "Because the LORD was not able to bring this people to the land which He swore to give them, therefore He killed them in the wilderness."
>
> Pardon the iniquity of this people, I pray, according to the greatness of Your mercy, just as You

have forgiven this people from Egypt even until now (Num. 14:13–16, 19).

In each of these prayers, Moses showed concern for God's honor. He had a greater concern for the honor of God and for God's reputation than for any benefit that might accrue to him as the leader of the nation.

How powerful our prayers become when our heart's desire is to see God glorified!

MOSES WAS MOVED BY A DESIRE TO KNOW GOD BETTER (EXODUS 33)

This chapter of Exodus depicts a special relationship which Moses enjoyed with God. When Moses went to the tabernacle, all the people went to their tent doors to watch. When Moses entered, they could see the cloudy-fiery pillar that was the visible mark of God's presence descending and hovering at the door of the tabernacle. The text tells us, "So the LORD spoke to Moses face to face, as a man speaks to his friend" (Ex. 33:11).

Nahum M. Sarna's commentary on Exodus (1991) notes that "this figurative language is intended to convey the preeminence and uniqueness of Moses as a prophetic figure who experiences a special mode of revelation.

The experience is personal and direct, not mediated through visions or dreams, and the message is always plain and straightforward, free of cryptic utterances" (p. 212).

But in spite of his privileged relationship, Moses yearned to know God even better. And so Moses prayed, "Please, show me Your glory" (Ex. 33:18). What Moses yearned to see was not evidence of the presence of God, as in the pillar of cloud, but God Himself. Moses' request to see the glory of God was a plea to see God unshielded, fully revealed in His essential being.

This is a desire shared by Jewish and Christian mystics through the ages—a yearning to experience God in himself, unmediated by words or deeds. God's response to Moses was disappointing, for the Lord said, "You cannot see My face, for no man shall see Me, and live" (Ex. 33:21). In His essence, God is so awesome that mortal flesh would dissolve in His unshielded presence. But God did reveal more of Himself to Moses. Hiding Moses in a crevice in Sinai's rocky face, the Lord passed by, calling out His name, and announcing His character as merciful, gracious, long-suffering, abounding in goodness and truth.

Moses could not see God in His essential glory, but Moses knew God by name. He would continue to experience the mercy, grace, patience, and abounding goodness of God. And through these experiences, he would come to know the Lord better day by day.

The desire to know God better is one that we can also express in prayer. Even more, this desire *will move us to pray.* While we cannot see God in His essential being, we can grow to know Him better as we experience His mercy, grace, patience, and goodness in our lives.

LESSONS FROM MOSES' PRAYER LIFE

There are some important lessons to be drawn from Moses' prayer life. But these seem to be dominant themes in the walk with God that Moses enjoyed the last forty years of his life. Moses began that relationship humbly,

and he continued to be humble and submissive to God.

Moses remained mindful of God's sovereignty. In every situation, Moses brought his complaints and requests directly to He who could deal with them. Moses showed a deep concern for God's honor. His prayers were not selfish, but they reflected his desire to see God glorified and respected by all. And, through the years, Moses was moved by a desire to know God better. What a wonderful example for us to follow as we come to God in prayer.

HANNAH, THE BROKEN-HEARTED

How many mothers have followed the example of Hannah, dedicating a child to the Lord before he or she was born? Certainly Hannah set an example that many have followed. Yet becoming an example was not her motivation as she rocked to and fro, pouring out her heart before the tabernacle.

AN INTENSE PRAYER (1 SAMUEL 1:10–16)

Hannah was childless. Although she was loved by her husband, she was constantly humiliated by her husband's second wife, Peninnah, who had borne children. The Old Testament tells us that Hannah "was in bitterness of soul" as she prayed to the Lord and "wept in anguish" (1 Sam. 1:10). One need so dominated Hannah's thoughts that she was unable to appreciate the blessings which she had.

Hannah stayed crumpled on the ground for a long time, praying continually, her lips moving but the words flowing only from her heart. The high priest Eli, watching her, assumed that she was drunk and rebuked her. But Hannah's answer revealed the intensity of her desire.

No, my lord, I am a woman of sorrowful spirit. I have drunk neither wine nor intoxicating drink, but have poured out my soul before the LORD. . . . Out of the abundance of my complaint and grief I have spoken until now (1 Sam. 1:15, 16).

Reading the description and noting the words Hannah used to describe her emotions, we are impressed with the intensity with which Hannah prayed. This was no perfunctory prayer, in which a request was placed thoughtlessly before the Lord. This was a prayer filled with longing, anguish, and grief. This was a prayer in which Hannah poured out her heart and soul—her entire being—before the Lord.

AN UNSELFISH PRAYER (1 SAMUEL 1:11)

It may seem strange to view Hannah's prayer as unselfish. Women in most ancient Near Eastern cultures saw having children as their purpose in life. As girls grew into womanhood, they dreamed of marriage and a family. Hannah loved her husband, and the fact that she had been unable to give him a son was breaking her heart. The sneers of her rival, her husband's other wife, added to the burden and made her life almost unbearable.

Hannah's prayer, in which she begged God to give her a son and vowed to dedicate the son to God's service, has been misinterpreted as "bargaining with God." But Hannah begged God to "look upon the affliction of Your maidservant." This was clearly an appeal to God's mercy and His grace, not bargaining. Her vow to dedicate the son whom God would give to the Lord was an indication of her unselfishness. Hannah was desperate to have children. But she did not want a son to keep for herself. She wanted him as a gift to give to her husband, and ultimately as a gift for God.

This is the way it should be with us and our children. The common joke that features a parent taking pride in "my son, the lawyer" or "my daughter, the doctor," distorts the nature of parenthood. Children are loaned to us by the Lord. They are not given to us to enhance our reputation, but that we might nurture them for a time, until they become their own persons—and God's.

Hannah understood this, so her prayer was not selfish at all. She yearned for the opportunity to find fulfillment in the role assigned to women of her day, and for the chance to *give*—to her husband, to her son, and to God.

It is impossible for us to understand fully how deep Hannah's need was. But we misunderstand the nature of her prayer if we charge her with selfishness, or misunderstand her appeal for mercy as a form of bargaining with God.

A VOW FULFILLED (1 SAMUEL 1:17–28)

After Eli heard Hannah's explanation of her behavior, he pronounced a blessing on her. As high priest, Eli's blessing amounted to a promise that God would grant Hannah's prayer. This was how Hannah understood his words, so she "went her way and ate, and her face was no longer sad" (1 Sam. 1:18).

In God's time, a son was born to Hannah. She named him Samuel, which means "heard by God." When Samuel was weaned, probably at about three years of age, Hannah kept her vow. She brought her son to the tabernacle and delivered him to Eli.

For this child I prayed, and the LORD has granted me my petition which I asked of Him. Therefore I also have lent him to the LORD; as long as he lives he shall be lent to the LORD (1 Sam. 1:27, 28).

A PRAYER OF PURE PRAISE (1 SAMUEL 2:1–10)

Hannah's praise prayer is one of the most striking in the Bible. Note that it was not offered when Hannah's anguished appeal for a son was answered and Samuel was born. The words recorded here were spoken by Hannah after she dedicated Samuel to the Lord and left him at Shiloh with Eli and God's tabernacle!

Strikingly, Hannah's prayer is not an expression of thanks. Rather, Hannah's prayer is filled with expressions that revealed her joy in the Lord!

My heart rejoices in the LORD;
My horn is exalted in the
   LORD.
I smile at my enemies,

Hannah rejoiced in the birth of her son, Samuel, and later, when he was old enough, she brought him to live at the tabernacle with Eli.

Because I rejoice in Your
    salvation.
No one is holy like the LORD,
For there is none besides You,
Nor is there any rock like our
    God (1 Sam. 2:1, 2).

And the prayer continues, joyfully contemplating the wonder of who God is, honoring Him for His greatness, and expressing confidence in Him.

Hannah's prayer had been answered. But she discovered that the true source of her joy was not the gift from God, but the Giver Himself.

God was gracious to Hannah. The text tells us that God later gave Hannah three more sons and two daughters (1 Sam. 2:21). But this praise-filled prayer of Hannah tells us that Hannah had discovered the true source of the believer's joy. Joy is not found in the prayers God answers, no matter how deeply felt those prayers may be. Joy is not found in the gifts God gives, no matter how wonderful these gifts are. The true source of the believer's joy is the Giver.

LESSONS FROM HANNAH'S PRAYERS

Hannah is the Old Testament's best example of a person who was totally immersed in prayer. Every fiber of her being was focused on God as she poured out her pain and begged Him to act.

There may be a few times in our lives when we are moved to pray with Hannah's intensity. How good to know that in our times of greatest need, we can turn to God with our hearts and souls. Hannah's prayer life reminds us that even at such moments as these, our prayers can be unselfish.

Perhaps most significant of all, Hannah's prayers teach us that we will find our joy not in the requests that God grants, but in the Lord Himself.

DAVID, THE SINNING SAINT

We have already examined David's many psalms. Don't these provide enough insight into his prayer life? In reality they do: David poured so much of himself into his prayer poems that we can read his every emotion, his every thought. Yet we need to visit David's prayers recorded in the historical books if we are to learn a vital lesson from Israel's shepherd king.

The historical books record David's lengthy prose prayer of wonder at God's special covenant promise which guaranteed that the Christ would come from his line (2 Sam. 7, see p. 25). They also record a brief spontaneous prayer uttered by David as he fled from Absalom (2 Sam. 15:31).

Significantly, the historical books record nine times that David "inquired of the LORD." These repeated requests for guidance display David's constant reliance on God—one of the keys to his success as a leader as well as David's character.

Yet one of the most significant lessons on prayer is taught in relationship to an incident that showed David as a sinning saint.

DAVID'S SIN (2 SAMUEL 11)

The story of David's sin with Bathsheba is a familiar one. Some persist in casting David more as a victim than a sinner. Yet the biblical account makes it clear that David took the initiative and was fully responsible for what happened. Bathsheba was bathing at night in the courtyard of her own home when David, who had been unable to sleep, saw her from the roof of his palace. Lust took control of David. The text tells us that after inquiring about her, David "sent messengers, and took her" (2 Sam. 11:4). There was no way that Bathsheba—a woman alone, her husband away on the battlefield—could have resisted the will of the king.

After a night of passion, David sent her home. He apparently gave no more thought to her until she sent a message telling him that she was pregnant. David's first thought was to cover up his involvement. He sent to the battlefield for Bathsheba's husband, Uriah, assuming that he would spend the night with his wife and that the child could then be passed off as Uriah's. But Uriah was a dedicated officer, unwilling to accept any comforts denied his men at the front. He refused to go home!

So David, desperate to cover up his sin, sent a message to the commander of his forces. Uriah was to be placed in a vulnerable position where he would be killed by the enemy. David's orders were followed, and Uriah was killed.

Still intent on covering up his sin, David brought Bathsheba into his palace and married her, adding her to his harem. How relieved David must have been. He had sinned. But now no one would know! His reputation as a godly ruler was safe!

THE AGONY OF UNACKNOWLEDGED SIN

David's relief was short-lived. His frantic efforts to conceal his sin only *appeared* successful. No one mentioned what David had done. And David pretended nothing had changed as he went about his duties as ruler. But in fact, everything had changed. God

knew what David had done, and He was displeased. David knew what he had done, and Psalm 32 bears witness to the anguish caused by the guilt he had plotted to conceal (see Ps. 32:3, 4).

In all likelihood, everyone knew what David had done. In a city with a population estimated at only about 3,500 in David's day, it would have been hard to keep his actions a secret. Certainly those he had asked about the woman, and the messengers he had sent to bring her to him, knew what David had done. And no "secret" held by so many can be kept a secret long.

But still David pretended. God's hand was heavy on David's heart, but David would not acknowledge his sin.

Finally, God had to send the prophet Nathan to confront David. Only then did David face the reality of what he had done.

THE CONSEQUENCES OF DAVID'S SIN (PSALM 51)

Nathan's bold words to David must have been like a sword piercing his heart. David could not hide from or deny his guilt. Nor could David avoid the consequences that would flow from his sin as Nathan spelled them out.

Why have you despised the commandment of the LORD, to do evil in his sight? You have killed Uriah the Hittite with the sword; you have taken his wife to be your wife, and have killed him with the sword of the people of Ammon. Now therefore, the sword shall never depart from your house, because you have despised Me, and have taken the wife of Uriah the Hittite to be your wife (2 Sam. 12:9, 10).

Exposed, David pretended no longer. He admitted, "I have sinned against the LORD." Nathan announced that God had put away David's sin so that he would not die. But the effects of David's sin would ripple through his family from then on.

Later when David's son Amnon raped his half-sister Tamar, David—perhaps paralyzed by the knowledge of his own guilt—did nothing. When Amnon was assassinated by

Tamar's brother Absalom, David again failed to react. David's abdication of moral authority in his family led to Absalom's subsequent rebellion and the death of many in the civil war which followed. Even though David publicly confessed his sin and celebrated God's forgiveness in Psalm 51, David and his family suffered from his sin.

There was one other effect of David's sin, which led to a time of prayer from which we have much to learn. The text tells us that "the LORD struck the child that Uriah's wife bore to David, and it became ill" (2 Sam. 12:15). David immediately began to plead with the Lord for the life of the child. David's actions show the intensity of his prayer.

David "fasted and went in and lay all night on the ground." In spite of the pleas of David's friends and officials, David refused to touch food. Day after day, David pleaded with the Lord, until finally the child died.

David's officials were afraid to tell the king about the death. But David noticed their behavior, realized what had happened, and stopped praying. He bathed and changed his clothes, "went into the house of the LORD, and worshiped," and then went home and ate.

When his officials expressed surprise, David explained. "While the child was alive, I fasted and wept: for I said, 'Who can tell whether the LORD will be gracious to me, that the child may live?' But now he is dead; why should I fast? Can I bring him back again? I shall go to him, but he shall not return to me" (2 Sam. 12:21, 22).

David's experience teaches us several lessons about prayer.

First, we are to pray as long as there is hope. We never know ahead of time what God will do. No matter how hopeless a situation may appear, God can intervene. Perhaps God will answer our prayers.

Second, however, when events show that God has told us "No," we are to get on with our lives. Like David, we are to accept God's will, worship Him, and go back to the business of living. God's "No" is as much an answer to prayer as His "Yes."

For seven days and nights David begged the Lord to spare Bathsheba's son.

❖

There is a third lesson as well. Sin will have consequences that even the most earnest of prayers will not change. We live in a moral universe, subject to God's moral and ethical laws. God may forgive our sins. But the most earnest prayer cannot reverse the effect of sin on our personalities or those closest to us.

THE HEALING POWER OF CONFESSION (2 SAMUEL 12:24; PSALM 51:10–19)

Listening to Nathan's announcement of the consequences that would follow David's sin, we might get the wrong impression. What is the value of confessing sin if the prayer of confession does not cancel the consequences of our sins? David's experience and his prayer of confession help us sort out several issues.

Confession does heal. The words used in the Old and New Testaments to depict confession of sins mean "to acknowledge" sin. In Psalm 32:3, 4, David related, "when I kept silent, my bones grew old . . . my vitality was turned into

BIBLE BACKGROUND:

DID GOD PUNISH THE BABY FOR DAVID'S SIN?

Many have been troubled by the death of David's child by Bathsheba. Why would a good God punish an innocent baby for David's sin? This seems at first glance to be implied by 2 Samuel 12:14:

"Because by this deed you have given great occasion to the enemies of the LORD to blaspheme, the child also who is born to you shall surely die."

The passage continues, "And the LORD struck the child . . . and it became ill" (v. 15).

But it does not necessarily follow that the child was *punished* for David's sin. Indeed, it can be argued that the death of the child was an act of divine grace. Imagine what it would have been like if the child had survived. Every time David or Bathsheba saw him, they would have been reminded of their sin. The little boy would surely have felt the pain he caused his parents. He would have been the object of gossip in the court, and a victim of disguised ridicule. A barrier alienating the child from his parents would have existed, unseen but surely felt by all.

When the Bible says that God visits the iniquity of the fathers upon the children and the children's children to the third and fourth generation (Ex. 34:7), it is *not* suggesting that God *punishes* children for their fathers' sins. Rather, the point is that our sins so influence our attitudes and behavior that our sins have an impact on the experience of our children and even our great-grandchildren. We can perhaps imagine how terrible the impact of this sin of David might have been on his and Bathsheba's son. And imagining it, we can see God's grace in taking the child as an infant, in spite of David's fervent prayers.

the drought of summer." David stonewalled, unwilling to take responsibility for his fault. But then David went on,

I acknowledged my sin to You,
And my iniquity I have not
hidden.

I said, "I will confess my
transgressions to the LORD,"
And You forgave the iniquity of
my sin (Ps. 32:5).

The acknowledgment of sin to God opened the door to an experience of forgiveness. When we understand that one consequence of sin is alienation and the interruption of a believer's fellowship with the Lord, we realize how important confession of sin is. Confession brings forgiveness and the restoration of fellowship with God.

More healing available to us. Our relationship with God also governs our relationships with others. When we sin against another person, there is no prospect of healing without acknowledgment of our guilt. We cannot expect to avoid the interpersonal consequences of sin apart from a full confession of our wrongdoing.

In David's case, his confession to Nathan the prophet and in Psalm 51 made possible a healing of his relationship with Bathsheba. That relationship had been born in lust and violation. Yet we read in Scripture that the two had four other sons, and 1 Kings 1 shows that David and Bathsheba came to love each other deeply. In taking responsibility for what he had done and acknowledging his guilt publicly, David made it possible for Bathsheba to forgive as well.

We may not be able to avoid all the consequences of our sins, but confession can help heal relationships that have been broken by sin.

Other benefits of confession of sin. Reading through Psalm 51, we discover other benefits of confession. In getting right with God, David recovered his sense of joy (Ps. 51:8, 12). God cleansed his heart and again upheld him (Ps. 51:12). God also restored to David the privilege of ministry, that he might teach transgressors God's ways and that sinners might be converted to Him (Ps. 51:13).

Through this experience, David learned that what God desires in us is not so much our service as a broken and contrite heart. And the sacrifice that pleases God most is a righteous life. In spite of the fact that David's life and family would be forever marked by the consequences of his sin, David truly had been spiritually restored.

LESSONS FROM THE PRAYER LIFE OF DAVID

There are many lessons about prayer that we can learn from David's psalms. But perhaps the most significant lessons are learned through the great sin that marred David's walk with God and scarred his family. In the prayers David offered on that occasion, we are reminded that there are limits to what prayer can accomplish. While we are to pray until events reveal that God's answer is "No," when His answer comes we are to get on with our lives.

We also learn that the most fervent prayer cannot change the consequences that flow from our sins. Sins will have an impact on our personalities and on others who are close to us. Yet the prayer of confession has wondrous power to restore the vitality of our relationship with God. And, if we model our relationship with others on our relationship with God, acknowledging and taking responsibility for the sins which have injured others will open the door to restore interpersonal relationships as well.

These are some of the most important lessons we can learn in life.

MIGHTY IN PRAYER

LEARNING FROM ELIJAH, NEHEMIAH, DANIEL, AND JEREMIAH

1 Kings; Nehemiah; Daniel; Jeremiah

It was something my mother laughed about. When sitting in a car, I always cocked my head just a little to the left. What made it funny was that my dad, who had been injured in a fall, sat just that way when he drove our car. Sitting behind him in the back seat, I had picked up his mannerism without being aware of it.

We do learn from the company we keep. That's why it's important for us to keep company with Old Testament saints who had significant prayer lives. We can learn from them, even without being consciously aware of their influence. Of course, when we study their prayer lives intentionally, we may learn even more. Certainly the four persons we looked at in the last chapter, and the four we will visit now, have important lessons to teach.

ELIJAH, GOD'S WARRIOR PROPHET

Elijah wasn't the kind of warrior we usually picture, clad in armor and carrying a sword. Elijah looked like a very ordinary eighth-century B.C. Jewish man. His beard was long, his clothing typical. But throughout his life, Elijah was deeply involved in spiritual warfare.

Ahab, the ruler of the northern Hebrew kingdom, Israel, had married Jezebel, the daughter of the king of Sidon. Together they set out to replace worship of the Lord in Israel with worship of the pagan deity Baal. Ahab built a temple to Baal in his capital city, Samaria, and placed a wooden image there. As part of their campaign, the two also murdered all the prophets of the Lord they could find. They imported 850 prophets of Baal and his consort, Asherah, to "evangelize" Israel.

The aggressive persecution of believers instituted by the royal pair had an impact on the nation. Many followed the politically correct path by choosing to worship Baal. Others, who refused to turn their backs on the Lord, were forced to worship Him in secret. The great majority stood back, confused, uncertain about which deity was the true God.

The Lord sent Elijah the Tishbite to stand against this apostasy. As a first step, God told Elijah to find Ahab and to announce that the entire land was to be struck with a terrible drought that would last for years. Elijah was then told to go into hiding. As the land dried up, Ahab and Jezebel would become desperate to get their hands on Elijah.

The Old Testament records three special prayers of Elijah, God's "warrior prophet." One prayer reveals the prophet at war with tragedy, a second shows him at war with his nation's unbelief, and a third portrays him at war with his own depression.

At war with tragedy (1 Kings 17:8–24). For part of the three and one-half years that Israel had suffered from the drought, the prophet was hidden in the home of a widow in Zerephath. Ironically, Zerephath lay in Sidonian territory. Elijah hid in the homeland of the queen who was so intent on corrupting Israel's faith!

While Elijah was with the widow, her small supply of flour and olive oil was miraculously extended to feed the widow and her son as well as Elijah. But after some time, the son became seriously ill and died. Deeply moved by the widow's pain, Elijah carried the boy to his room and cried out to the Lord.

"O LORD my God, have You also brought tragedy on the widow with whom I lodge, by killing her son?" (1 Kings 17:20).

Elijah then stretched out on the child's body and cried out three times,

"O LORD, my God, I pray, let this child's soul come back to him" (1 Kings 17:21).

The Bible tells us that the Lord heard the voice of Elijah and that the soul of the child came back to him. The child revived, and Elijah brought him down from his room and presented him to his mother.

The story is a simple one, yet it reminds us of a great truth. In this world where tragic incidents occur daily, believers are called to spiritual warfare on behalf of the sufferers. Like Elijah, we are called to care for the hurting and, when possible, to alleviate their suffering. This is a challenge that calls for action—but action bathed in prayer. Ultimately, only the God who gives life to the dying can heal a broken heart. Our part is to be with others, to act for them and, like Elijah, to pray.

At war with the nation's unbelief (1 Kings 18). When about three and one-half years had passed, God sent Eljah to confront Ahab again. Elijah challenged Ahab to a test. The king was to bring his own 450 prophets of Baal and Jezebel's 400 prophets of Asherah to Mount Carmel. Elijah would meet them there. He would call on the Lord, and they could call on their god. The deity who answered the prayers of his servants would be acknowledged as the true God.

Surprisingly, Ahab accepted the challenge and sent for the 450 prophets of Baal. In this, Ahab showed himself a true believer. But Jezebel did not send her 400 prophets to the contest. By this action, she showed that she was using religion as a pretext to strengthen her own position. Although she was from Sidon, the source of the cult, she was not a true believer at all!

As word spread, a multitude of Israelites came to witness the contest. Two altars were prepared, and Elijah invited the prophets of Baal to call on their god first. The hours passed as the prophets cried out and cavorted—all to no avail. When noon came, Elijah began to mock them. Perhaps Baal was on a journey. Perhaps he was asleep, and if the prophets cried louder they could awaken him. As the sun drifted toward the western horizon, the desperate prophets of Baal cut themselves with knives. They believed that Baal delighted in the smell of fresh blood.

At last, Elijah declared it was his turn. He prepared his sacrifice and even soaked it in water. Then Elijah cried out to the Lord. His prayer was brief and simple:

"LORD God of Abraham, Isaac, and Israel, let it be known this day that You are God in Israel and I am Your servant, and that I have done all these things at Your word. Hear me, O LORD, hear me, that this people may know that You are the LORD God, and that You have turned their hearts back to You again" (1 Kings 18:36, 37).

Fire fell from heaven immediately, consuming not only the sacrifice but the water and even the stones of the altar.

The people who witnessed the contest were convinced. They shouted, "The LORD, He is God. The LORD, He is God" (1 Kings 18:39). And then, at Elijah's command, the people seized the prophets of Baal, and executed them.

Elijah's public prayer and God's answer turned the nation back to God. Then clouds formed on the horizon, and the rains fell on the parched land of Israel.

We also live in a day when competing beliefs and values are at war with God. Some

For three years there was no dew or rain in Israel; then Elijah prayed, and God sent a rainstorm.

❖

who seek to do away with biblical faith are, like Ahab, "true believers," honestly convinced that their way is best. Others, like Jezebel, manipulate the nation for their own benefit. Whatever such leaders' motives, our nation is today drifting away from its spiritual moorings.

How we need prayer warriors like Elijah—men and women of prayer who have faith enough to take a stand. Who have faith enough to contend with popular views and put truth to the test by expecting God to answer prayer and call our nation back to him.

At war with depression (*1 Kings 19*). Elijah had won the people back to God. But then Jezebel sent a messenger to the prophet: Before a day passed, she would see Elijah dead!

We can't explain Elijah's reaction. The warrior prophet ran for his life! Finally, completely exhausted, Elijah collapsed under a broom tree and prayed,

"It is enough! Now, LORD, take my life, for I am no better than my fathers" (1 Kings 19:4).

At the moment of his greatest public triumph, Elijah experienced depression and defeat.

There was no logic to Elijah's reaction. He had just experienced the awesome power of God. Yet he fell almost immediately into deep depression. How ashamed he was that he had fled in terror. Surely he was weak and useless, no better than his fathers. Gripped by despair, Elijah fled for another 40 days until he reached Mount Horeb (Sinai).

Still in the grip of depression, Elijah expressed his feelings to the Lord:

I have been very zealous for the LORD God of hosts; for the children of Israel have forsaken Your covenant, torn down Your altars, and killed Your prophets with the sword. I alone am left; and they seek to take my life (1 Kings 19:10).

Elijah's words are consistent with deep depression. Every perception was colored by the dark pit in which he felt himself. The victory on Carmel was forgotten. Black images of the unbelief against which he struggled dominated the prophet's thoughts. The situation seemed hopeless, and Elijah's emotions exaggerated his isolation so deeply that he felt alone and abandoned. "I alone am left, and they seek to take my life."

When depression tightens its grip, even the boldest spiritual warrior may find himself or herself sharing Elijah's emotions. Then even our prayers, like Elijah's, will reflect our sense of hopelessness.

But even when our prayers are lifeless and without hope, God responds to us. In Elijah's case, God helped his prophet find his way back by taking several specific steps:

When Elijah's depression led him to despair, and he ran from his ministry, God was not angry. Instead God actually *provided food to sustain* Elijah while he ran (1 Kings 19:6–9). Then God *spoke* to Elijah *in a "gentle whisper"* (9:12). God gave Elijah *a simple task* to do, and also *reassured Elijah* that there were others who were faithful to the Lord (19:15, 16, 18). Finally, God *gave Elijah a companion,* who would be with him and would one day take on his prophetic ministry (*The Believer's Guidebook*, 1983, p. 183).

When we must battle our own human weaknesses, we need not pretend to be strong. We can pour out our sense of helplessness before the Lord. And He will come to our aid.

Lessons from Elijah's prayer life. Elijah was called to be God's prayer warrior, fighting against the pain of human tragedy as well as hostile forces which dragged his nation toward unbelief. We learn from Elijah's prayers how to stand through the suffering, opposing the forces that threaten the foundations of a nation.

But Scripture also shows us the human face of Elijah, revealing his vulnerability to despair and hopelessness. We are reminded that God hears our prayers when we feel inadequate, and that in the Lord we have the promise of victory over ourselves.

NEHEMIAH, GOD'S LEADER

Nehemiah was a high official in the court of the emperor of Persia. But first of all, Nehemiah was a Jew who identified himself with God's people. When Nehemiah heard that the walls of Jerusalem had not been repaired, he was greatly distressed. In that age, only a walled city was viewed with respect. To Nehemiah, it seemed a scandal that Jerusalem, the site of God's rebuilt temple and the future capital of God's Messiah, should remain unwalled.

Nehemiah was moved by the distress of the little colony of Jews who had returned from Babylonian captivity some decades before. Obtaining a royal commission as governor of Judah, he set out to correct the situation. The book of Nehemiah, which tells the story of his governorship, is generally viewed as a source of insight into leadership. The book pictures Nehemiah the leader as a man of prayer—a person whose prayer life might serve as a model for spiritual leaders of any time.

Nehemiah identified with the people and with God (Nehemiah 1:4–11). The prayer recorded in the first chapter of Nehemiah shows first that Nehemiah identified with the needs of God's people. Nehemiah prayed "day and night, for the children of Israel your Servants" (v. 6).

But even as he was sympathetic with the needs of God's people, Nehemiah also identified with God. He confessed the sins that had led God to exile the Israelites from the promised land (vv. 7, 8), and reminded God of His promise to gather His people and bring them back to the place which He had chosen (v. 9).

This is the first qualification for spiritual leadership. The leader must represent the people before God, and he must represent God to the people. Caring deeply about people while caring just as deeply about God's purposes and His glory are essential qualities of spiritual leadership.

Nehemiah bathed his work in prayer. Nehemiah was a man of action as well as a visionary leader. He saw what needed to be done, and he set out to do it. As he took each step, Nehemiah prayed. He prayed when he asked the king of Persia for the governorship of Judea (Neh. 2:4). When Nehemiah arrived in Jerusalem, he surveyed the task and challenged the people to undertake it. When opposition developed as the walls were going up, Nehemiah prayed (4:4). When enemies threatened to attack, Nehemiah had half the workers continue the construction while the other half stood with weapons drawn, ready to fight. And Nehemiah prayed (4:9).

When the Jews' enemies threatened to report the Jews to the Persian rulers, Nehemiah prayed that God would strengthen his hands—and he kept on working (6:9). And when the work was completed and the people gathered to celebrate, Nehemiah led the people in praising God.

In all this, Nehemiah demonstrated a good leader's attention to detail, his ability to motivate, and his commitment to the task—along with a dependence on God expressed in his constant attention to prayer.

Nehemiah looked to God for his reward (Nehemiah 13). Chapter 13 of Nehemiah contains

Work on Jerusalem's wall continued after Nehemiah introduced a rotation plan for guarding against intruders.

a recurring phrase that has troubled some people. As Nehemiah reviewed what he had accomplished, he asked again and again, "Remember me, O my God, concerning this."

Remember me, O my God, concerning this, and do not wipe out my good deeds that I have done for the house of my God, and for its services! (13:14).

I commanded the Levites that they should cleanse themselves, and that they should go and guard the gates, to sanctify the Sabbath day. Remember me, O my God, concerning this also, and spare me according to the greatness of Your mercy! (13:22).

I cleansed them of everything pagan. I also assigned duties to the priests and the Levites, each to his service. . . . Remember me, O my God, for good! (13:30, 31).

In Hebrew idiom, "remember" means "to act in accord with." When the Bible says that God will "not remember your sins" (Isa. 43:25), it is not suggesting that God will literally forget what we have done. Instead, it is promising that God will not *treat us as our sins deserve*. So here Nehemiah's prayer that God would "remember" is a request that God would reward him in accordance with his good deeds.

Some have been critical of Nehemiah, seeing these prayers as selfish. Instead, we ought to appreciate the purity of Nehemiah's motives. Nehemiah did not seek a leadership role for any other reason than a desire to serve God and his people. Nehemiah, unlike many of us, wanted no reward that those whom he led could offer. He sought neither wealth nor praise from men. The only reward that Nehemiah cared about was God's "well done."

Lessons from Nehemiah's prayer life. Nehemiah was an effective leader. He was skilled in planning, motivating, organizing, delegating, and all the other functions of leadership. But the real secret of Nehemiah's effectiveness was not his skills but his prayers. In his prayers, he identified with the needs of the people whom he led as well as God's purposes. Nehemiah was a man of action, yet his prayers show that he relied on God. Finally, this effective leader showed that he served not for any reward that God's people could provide but for the approval of the God whom he worshiped and loved.

DANIEL, THE SECULAR SERVANT

Daniel is one of the most appealing characters in the entire Old Testament. As a teenager, Daniel was taken to Babylon with a group of Jewish captives. Here he was enrolled as a student in a school that King Nebuchadnezzar of Babylonia had created to train young men from across his empire to serve in government. Daniel's adventures, as recorded in the first six chapters of the book that carries his name, have fascinated generations of Sunday school students. Daniel's visions, contained in chapters 7–13 of the book, have been studied just as intently by students of prophecy.

Daniel completed his studies and served in significant posts in the bureaucracy of succeeding world empires. He lived, just as we do, as a believer in a secular society. During his life, Daniel remained faithful to God and at the same time faithful to the government duties he was assigned. He was indeed a secular saint. And throughout his life, prayer was important to him.

Prayer in a time of crisis (*Daniel 2*). Shortly after Daniel and three other young Jewish men completed their studies at the king's school, Nebuchadnezzar had a disturbing dream. But when he awoke, he was unable to remember it. So Nebuchadnezzar called for his wise men, demanding that they tell him the dream and its meaning. The request was unreasonable, but Nebuchadnezzar was in no mood to quibble. If his wise men couldn't tell him the dream, what good were they? Furious, the king ordered all men in the class of "Chaldeans" killed. And the executions began.

Daniel and his three Jewish companions were also considered "Chaldeans." When the captain of the king's guard found Daniel, Daniel went to Nebuchadnezzar and asked for time, "that he might tell the king the interpretation" (2:16). Daniel found his companions, explained the situation, and the four young men prayed together.

That night God revealed the dream and its meaning to Daniel. And so the time of urgent petition turned into a praise meeting, as Daniel blessed the God of heaven, saying:

Blessed be the name of God
forever and ever,

With God's help, Daniel interpreted the king's dream when no one else could.

For wisdom and might are His.
. . . .
I thank You and praise You,
O God of my fathers;
You have given me wisdom
    and might,
And have now made known to
    me what we asked of You,
For You have made known to
    us the king's demand (Dan.
    2:20, 23).

Daniel went to the king and, giving God the credit, revealed the dream and its meaning. The killing of Babylon's wise men stopped. Nebuchadnezzar, impressed with Daniel's God and with Daniel himself, promoted Daniel to chief administrator of the province of Babylon.

Daniel had faced a crisis because he lived in a secular world, and was part of that world. This was not a case in which Daniel and his friends were being persecuted because of their faith. The danger to them arose only because

Daniel's daily prayer time gave his enemies an opening to charge him with disloyalty to the king.

———————————❖———————————

they were members of a group whose identity was secular, not sacred. But in spite of the secular source of the danger, their only recourse was to prayer.

Recently a friend of ours was promoted and transferred to the headquarters of a company for which he worked. Two weeks later the company was sold to another company in the same business. The buyer intended to help pay for the acquisition by letting many employees of the old company go. Our friend is in danger of losing his job, not because he is a Christian, but because in the secular world he is a member of a group that has suddenly become expendable.

Like Daniel and our friend, each of us is vulnerable to forces in our society which are purely secular. Like Daniel and our friend, when such forces place us in danger, the only thing we might be able to do is to pray. But when we pray, it is wise to follow Daniel's example and to pray *with others*. There is strength in having prayer partners, who will join us in bringing our burdens to the Lord.

While the source of danger may lie in a secular realm over which we have no personal control, "wisdom and power" do belong to God. He is able to give us the wisdom and power we need to live successfully. As we do so, we bring honor and witness to him.

Prayer as a daily habit (*Daniel 6*). Much later, commitment to prayer got Daniel in trouble. In the Persian Empire which followed the Babylonian Empire, Daniel served on a team of three which supervised governors of 120 provinces, called satrapies. The incorruptible Daniel made it difficult for those under him to build personal fortunes, and they decided to get rid of him. But they could find nothing of which to accuse Daniel.

Finally, one of these officials suggested that Daniel's habit of daily prayer might be used against him. They manipulated the Persian ruler to issue a decree that for 30 days, no one could make any request of man or god other than the king. When the Persian ruler finally recognized the trap, it was too late. Daniel's subordinates had accused Daniel of the "crime." And because of a peculiarity of Persian law, a ruler's decree could not be set aside once it had been issued—not even by the ruler himself.

It had been Daniel's habit to pray three times daily. Daniel was not obvious in his prayers. He did not feel a need to flaunt his faith. So he would go home, open a window, and pray toward Jerusalem. But Daniel was not to be intimidated either. Even after the decree was made, Daniel opened his window just as he had always done and prayed to the Lord. And so Daniel's prayer was noticed by others, and he was accused.

We know the rest of the story. Daniel was thrown into a den of lions. Early the next morning the anxious Persian king hurried to the den to see if Daniel's God had saved him. He had. Daniel was lifted out of the lion's den unscathed. And then the men who had plotted against Daniel where thrown to the lions and killed.

What is so impressive about Daniel's prayer life is its consistency. He was dedicated to the discipline of prayer. He felt the need to approach God at least three times each day. Daniel was not ostentatious in his prayer life. He wasn't out to impress anyone. But neither was he ashamed of being a man dedicated to prayer. He refused to change the pattern he had established, whatever the cost.

Prayer as searching (Daniel 9). Daniel 9 reports an incident in "the first year of Darius the son of Ahasuerus, of the lineage of the Medes" (9:1). While reading Scripture, Daniel discovered in the book of Jeremiah that the Jews' captivity in Babylon would last seventy years. Daniel was excited. The seventy years were about up! What would God do now?

Daniel looked to God for an answer. In a powerful prayer recorded in Daniel 9, the prophet reviewed the history of Israel's relationship with God. Daniel praised God for His covenant keeping, confessed Israel's sin, and appealed to God's mercy and forgiveness. He acknowledged God's rightness in punishing His people, but added,

O Lord, according to all your righteousness, I pray, let Your anger and Your fury be turned away from Your city Jerusalem, Your holy mountain; because for our sins, and for the iniquities of our fathers, Jerusalem and Your people are a reproach to all those around us. Now therefore, our God, hear the prayer of Your servant, and his supplications, and for the Lord's sake cause Your face to shine on Your sanctuary, which is desolate (Dan. 9:16, 17).

Even though Daniel was involved each day in secular matters of national importance, he searched the Scriptures and prayed over the issues he found there. Secular concerns never replaced spiritual concerns as the center of Daniel's life. Through Bible study and prayer, Daniel kept his focus on God's larger plans.

The details of his daily life and work were kept in perspective by his concern to understand God's will, and to pray about those things that were important to the Lord.

Lessons from Daniel's prayer life. Most of us, like Daniel, also live secular lives. The troubles we face usually do not arise because we are

Christians, but because of some role we have in society. How important it is to pray with others about experiences that are shaped by purely secular forces. It is also essential, no matter how involved we are with making a living, that we discipline ourselves to set aside regular times for prayer. Maintaining a habit of prayer is vital if we are be God's people in the secular world.

It is also important that the agendas of our lives not be set by secular concerns, but by God's purposes. We need to be in the Scriptures, as Daniel was. As we discover concerns that are important to the Lord, we should make these a matter of prayer.

The lessons we learn from Daniel's prayer life can help us live balanced lives—lives in which God has the highest priority and first claim on our hearts.

JEREMIAH, THE WEEPING PROPHET

Jeremiah ministered in Judah during the last forty years of the southern Hebrew kingdom. His mission was to announce God's judgment on His people, urging submission to the Babylonians. Jeremiah faithfully carried out this commission despite the hostility of his countrymen. Ridiculed and persecuted, accused of being a traitor, Jeremiah was imprisoned and even threatened with death.

In the book that bears his name, we experience Jeremiah as a lonely and tragic figure. Denied by God the comforts of marriage and a family, and increasingly isolated from the crowds that filled the streets of Jerusalem, Jeremiah remained faithful to the Lord. He eventually saw all his predictions fulfilled. But the lonely prophet must have known little satisfaction in his vindication, for it came at a terrible cost.

The city where he had preached lay in ruins; the temple where he had worshiped was razed; and the bloated corpses of the people he had tried to save lay scattered on the ground. Most of those who survived were taken to Babylon as captives. The remnant that had remained disobeyed God's command

and fled to Egypt, only to disappear from the stage of history.

In public Jeremiah preserved a stern appearance, as he presented God's case against His people and portrayed the judgment that was sure to come. But in his heart, Jeremiah was a far different man. A number of cries to God express the torment that Jeremiah felt as he preached to his countrymen. Jeremiah's ministry took a terrible toll—a toll we can sense in the words which he poured out in private to the Lord. These words contain a number of lessons for us today.

God limited Jeremiah's prayer *(Jeremiah 7:16; 11:11, 14; 14:11)*. Jeremiah's preaching frequently expressed God's invitation to His sinning people to return to Him. Yet when the people of Judah denied God's case against them and ignored His indictment of their sins, Jeremiah was told not to pray for his listeners. This instruction was repeated several times.

"Therefore do not pray for this people, nor lift up a cry or prayer for them, nor make intercession to Me; for I will not hear you" (Jer. 7:16).

"Behold, I will surely bring calamity on them which they will not be able to escape; and though they cry out to Me, I will not listen to them. . . . So do not pray for this people, or lift up a cry or prayer for them; for I will not hear them in the time that they cry out to Me because of their trouble (Jer. 11:11, 14).

> Thus says the LORD to this people;
> "Thus they have loved to
>   wander;
> They have not restrained their
>   feet.
> Therefore the LORD does not
>   accept them;
> He will remember their
>   iniquity now,
> And punish their sins."

Then the LORD said to me, "Do not pray for this people, for their good" (Jer. 14:10, 11).

God's people had passed a point of no return. They refused to hear God's word, and instead placed their confidence in lies told by

"prophets" whom God had not sent. The problem was not that God would reject the repentant. The problem was that the people were so hardened that they would not repent. And so Jeremiah was warned not to pray for the good of his countrymen, so that God would not be forced to turn away from Jeremiah's prayers.

There is a hint of this same situation in the New Testament. First John 5 contains these verses:

If anyone sees his brother sinning a sin which does not lead to death, he will ask, and he will give him life for those who commit sin not leading to death. There is sin leading to death. I do not say that he should pray about that (1 John 5:16).

What do these verses mean? John makes it clear that he was writing about fellow-Christians, believers. It follows that "death" here is not spiritual, but biological. We have just such a situation described in 1 Corinthians 5. There a brother openly flaunted an illicit sexual relationship condemned even by pagans, and Paul called on the church to deliver him "to Satan for the destruction of the flesh, that his spirit may be saved in the day of the Lord Jesus" (1 Cor. 5:5).

In this case, however, the brother did repent, was forgiven, and was welcomed back into fellowship. Paul had been wrong in assuming that this brother had committed "a sin leading to death." Discipline by the church accomplished what even prayer was not expected to do!

The passage in 1 John and the case recorded in 1 Corinthians help us put God's command to Jeremiah in perspective. Jeremiah *wanted* to pray for the good of his people. God had to warn him three times not to do so, making it clear to Jeremiah that the people of Judah had passed the point of no return. While the New Testament tells us that there will be times when Christians give themselves so fully to sin that they forfeit our prayers, we must be careful not to stop praying for any person too quickly. We must be especially sensitive to the Holy Spirit and pray for others until God makes it as clear to us as He did to Jeremiah that we are to pray no longer.

Cries from Jeremiah's heart (Jeremiah 11; 12; 15; 17; 18; 20). Among the most striking features of the book of Jeremiah are a number of cries addressed to God, torn from Jeremiah's heart. As we trace them, we can sense how the pain Jeremiah experienced drove him to the Lord again and again. Later Jeremiah was given a secretary, Baruch, who recorded his messages. But for most of his ministry, the prophet was cut off from others by the nature of his mission. With only God to turn to, Jeremiah poured out his thoughts and feelings to the Lord.

Jeremiah and the men of Anathoth (Jer 11:18— 12:6). Anathoth was Jeremiah's home town. Jeremiah could hardly believe it when he learned that those he had known from childhood were plotting to kill him. This passage contains two parallel laments. Each contains the same elements.

Jeremiah cried out to God in anguish over the plot against him.

	1st cry	2nd cry
Invocation	11:18	12:1a
Complaint	11:19	12:1b, 2
Prayer	11:20	12:3, 4
God's response	11:21–23	12:5, 6

Jeremiah complained that although he was as innocent as a lamb, the men of his hometown plotted to destroy him (11:19). How unfair it was that these wicked men, who pretended to be religious, should prosper (12:1b, 2).

Jeremiah then prayed, begging God to act as the righteous Judge:

But O Lord of hosts,
You who judge righteously,
Testing the mind and the
heart,
Let me see Your vengeance
on them,
For to You I have revealed my
cause (Jer. 11:20).

God responded to Jeremiah's prayer, assuring His prophet that "I will bring catastro-

phe on the men of Anathoth, even the year of their punishment (11:23). Meanwhile, Jeremiah was to learn from this experience not to put any confidence in the people of his time.

For even your brothers, the
house of your father,
Even they have dealt
treacherously with you;
Yes, they have called a
multitude after you.
Do not believe them,
Even though they speak
smooth words to you
(Jer. 12:6).

Jeremiah had no one to trust but the Lord. In his loneliness, Jeremiah could only draw closer to God.

Jeremiah pleaded God's case (Jer. 15:10–21). In this passage, Jeremiah presented himself as a man of "strife" and "contention." The two terms are often used in legal contexts. Jeremiah had served as God's lawyer, presenting His indictment of the people of Judah. But at the same time, Jeremiah had a case to plead against God. For although God's word "was to me the joy and rejoicing of my heart," Jeremiah's call to proclaim it had isolated him from his people. Jeremiah has "sat alone because of Your hand" (15:16, 17).

God responded to Jeremiah's lament (15:10) by stating that the prophet's opponents would know a time of adversity (15:11–13), but that Jeremiah must suffer with them when the foreign enemy invaded (15:14). But Jeremiah complained again. In spite of his faithfulness to God, "You filled me with indignation" (Jer. 15:17). God was faithful to Jeremiah, but it didn't feel this way to the prophet.

"Why is my pain perpetual
And my wound incurable,
Which refuses to be healed?
Will you surely be to me
     like an unreliable stream,
As waters that fail?" (Jer. 15:18).

Again God responded. Jeremiah could not avoid the mission to which he had been called or the suffering this service involved. But even though His own people were at war with Jeremiah,

"They shall not prevail
     against you;
For I am with you to save you
And deliver you," says the LORD.
"I will deliver you from the hand
     of the wicked,
And I will redeem you from the
     grip of the terrible" (Jer. 15:20b,
     21).

There are times when we pray for relief and relief is not possible, because God has a mission for us that involves suffering. At such times, we can take heart from God's promises to be with Jeremiah, and in the end to deliver from the hand of the wicked.

Jeremiah, "they," and You (Jeremiah 17:14–18). In this complaint, Jeremiah contrasted his innocence with the guilt of "they" who say, "Where is the word of the LORD? Let it come now!" These sayings were ridicule. All of Jeremiah's passionate warnings of judgment to come and all his pleading of the Lord's case against the wicked in Judah had left the listeners untouched. Indeed, they mocked Jeremiah's words, and thus mocked God.

Jeremiah's plea has two elements. Jeremiah begged God, "Heal me, O LORD, and I shall be healed" (17:14). And Jeremiah begged, "Let them be ashamed who persecute me" (Jer. 17:17). The prophet thus urged God to vindicate His messenger by bringing on Judah the doom that Jeremiah had pronounced.

God responded to many of the confessional prayers of Jeremiah, making the biblical record read like a dialogue. But Jeremiah recorded no divine response to this plea. God remained silent. Jeremiah would have to wait for events to unfold to find out what God intended.

God may expect us to wait as Jeremiah did to find out how He will answer our prayers. But God's silence never means that He has not heard.

Jeremiah prayed against the people of Judah (Jeremiah 18:19–23). God had told Jeremiah not to pray *for* the people of Judah. Now events convinced Jeremiah that the people would never repent, and thus Jeremiah found himself praying for the divine judgment to appear.

Jeremiah 18:18 introduces the prayer. The people had consulted together on how to oppose Jeremiah. They knew they could not shut him up, for as the saying goes, "The law shall not perish from the priest, nor counsel from the wise, nor the word from the prophet." So the people of Judah determined (1) to attack him with words and (2) not [to] give heed to any of his words.

Jeremiah then turned to the Lord, and begged God to heed him. Jeremiah's intention had been to "speak good for them" (18:20). He desperately hoped that his warnings of judgment would bring repentance and save his people from a terrible fate. But rather than listen, his countrymen had "dug a pit for my life" (18:20).

Verse 21 depicts the turning point. "Therefore," Jeremiah said, in view of Judah's failure to respond, "deliver up their children to the famine, and pour out their blood." Jeremiah, convinced that judgment must come before any healing was possible, finally asked God to "deal thus with them, in the time of Your anger" (15:23).

There are few times in our lives when we will be led to pray *against* others. Our calling is to serve others for their good. But as Jeremiah discovered, there are some situations in which the only appropriate prayer is that God will judge.

Jeremiah's emotional roller coaster (Jeremiah 20:7–18). Prayer in Jeremiah 20 is introduced by a story. Pashur, a priest who was a high temple official, became angry at Jeremiah's prophecies of impending doom. He struck Jeremiah and put him in stocks, subjecting the prophet to public ridicule. Jeremiah then pronounced judgment on Pashur in God's name. Pashur would live to see his friends slaughtered, and Pashur himself would be carried into captivity in Babylon, where he would die and be buried.

The experience stirred up conflicting emotions in Jeremiah. These emotions are powerfully expressed in the rest of the chapter. While many commentators take Jeremiah 20:7–13 and Jeremiah 20:14–18 as separate prayers, it seems better to see the passage as a unit, revealing how vulnerable Jeremiah was to his own surging emotions. And through Jeremiah, we recognize how vulnerable we are as well.

Jeremiah's initial reaction was to reflect on his life. God, who was too strong for Jeremiah, called him to cry out against Judah's sin. But this only earned Jeremiah reproach and daily derision (Jer. 20:7, 8). Jeremiah had reacted by trying to keep silent and speaking no more in God's name. His enemies were de-

lighted and felt that they had won. But Jeremiah found he could not keep still: "I was weary of holding it back, and I could not" (20:9).

How wonderful it felt to speak out again. Jeremiah sensed the Lord with him "as a mighty, awesome One." He *knew* that his persecutors would not prevail! And so Jeremiah cried out

> O LORD of hosts,
> You who test the righteous,
> And see the mind and heart,
> Let me see Your vengeance on
>   them;
> For I have pleaded my cause
>   before You.
> Sing to the LORD! Praise the
>   LORD!
> For He has delivered the life
>   of the poor
> From the hand of evildoers (Jer.
>   20:12, 13).

But then Jeremiah was overcome by deep despair. He felt his life had been worse than meaningless, and he expressed his wish that he had never been born. In one of the most powerful cries of despair recorded in any literature, Jeremiah declared,

> Cursed be the day in which I
>   was born!
> Let the day not be blessed in
>   which my mother bore me!
> Let the man be cursed
> Who brought news to my
>   father, saying,
> "A male child has been born to
>   you!"
> Making him very glad (Jer. 20:14,
>   15).

Jeremiah went on to lament that he had not been aborted, and that the womb that gave him birth was not also his grave. Deeply depressed, Jeremiah said,

Why did I come forth from the
   womb to see labor and
   sorrow,
That my days should be
   consumed with shame? (Jer.
   20:18).

Like Jeremiah, we may also have mood swings
that take us from the heights to the depths,
and back again. We are sensitive to the circumstances of our lives, perhaps too much so.
Yet there is comfort in the fact that even while
our emotions are in constant flux, the Lord is
with us. God does eventually deliver the poor
from the hand of evildoers.

Jeremiah's gift of hope (Jeremiah 32:16–44). The
invaders were already in Judah and Jerusalem
was being besieged when God spoke to Jeremiah. A cousin would soon approach Jeremiah, who was in prison. This relative would
ask the prophet to buy a field in Anathoth, his
home town. Jeremiah was to buy the land,
seal the deed in an earthen jar, and then bury
the jar. Although Jeremiah couldn't understand why he should buy land that was already overrun by the Babylonians, Jeremiah
did as God commanded.

Later Jeremiah prayed. His prayer,
recorded in Jeremiah 32:16–25, acknowledged God's greatness and His lovingkindess
(32:16–22). Jeremiah also acknowledged the
fact that Judah's sins had "caused all this
calamity to come upon them" (32:23). But
then Jeremiah got to the issue that so puzzled
him.

Look, the siege mounds! They have come to the
city to take it, and the city has been given into the
hand of the Chaldeans who fight against it, because
of the sword and famine and pestilence. What You
have spoken has happened; there You see it! And
you have said to me, O LORD God, "Buy the field
for money, and take witnesses!"—yet the city has
been given into the hand of the Chaldeans (Jer.
32:24, 25).

Jeremiah simply could not make sense of what
God had told him to do.

But then God explained. Jerusalem would
be destroyed, her people would be deported,

Jeremiah's purchase of land in the midst of the
Babylonian invasion became a sign of hope for
Israel's future.

and the field that Jeremiah had purchased
would be overrun with weeds. But a day
would come when "I will bring them back to
this place, and I will cause them to dwell
safely. They shall be My people, and I will be
their God" (Jer. 32:37, 38).

Jeremiah's purchase of the field was symbolic. Just as surely as God had kept His
promise to devastate Judah and decimate her
people, God would bring a remnant back to
the land. In spite of Judah's unfaithfulness,
God would remain faithful to His covenant
promises and to the people whom He loved.

Jeremiah had not grasped the meaning of
the purchase, but he had obeyed God's command. Later, in answer to Jeremiah's prayer,
God explained. And Jeremiah was finally able
to look beyond the judgment that he had
preached to a time of hope.

It is important to note the role that prayer
played in this incident as well as the role it did
not play. Jeremiah heard God's command and

obeyed. Only after he had obeyed did Jeremiah ask God for understanding. We too must be careful to obey *before* we ask God "Why?" When God speaks, His people are to respond with obedience, not questions. But after we have done the will of God, then we are free to ask Him to explain the meaning of what we have been told to do.

Lessons from the prayer life of Jeremiah. So many prayers are woven into Jeremiah's book of prophecies. And we have so much to learn from them. One lesson, emphasized three times, is that there are certain situations in which we are *not* to pray for others. We need to look to God to sensitize us to such times, for they will be few.

Jeremiah learned an important lesson when the people of his home town plotted to kill him. While we can always trust God, we must not rely heavily on other human beings. What an important resource prayer is when we have been let down by others and feel isolated and alone.

Jeremiah also learned that sometimes suffering is a necessary consequence of serving God. We human beings will always be vulnerable to pain caused by others. While we can pray that God will vindicate us, prayer may not avail against the pain involved in sacrificial ministry.

Like Jeremiah, we may find ourselves at times on an emotional roller coaster, subject to wide mood swings. We should not be shaken if this happens to us or expect prayer to moderate every emotion.

Finally, we learn from Jeremiah that we are never to substitute prayer for obedience. The godly will hear God's word, obey it, and then seek understanding in prayer. We must never vary this sequence. We should put prayer for understanding ahead of obedience. When we keep prayer in its proper place, we will be blessed indeed.

❖

JESUS' FIRST PRINCIPLES OF PRAYER

MATTHEW

In 1994 Harper-Collins published the *Book of Prayers*. Billed as a treasury of prayers through the ages and compiled by Robert Van de Weyer, the book is a collection of recorded prayers. It includes prayers of obscure Christians of the early church as well as recognized saints like Francis of Assisi. Prayers of moderns, like Mother Teresa, are included, as are prayers of believers of other religions.

This collection was probably intended to provide inspiration for the spiritually minded, and perhaps to instruct by providing examples of "good" prayers. Yet it's strange that none of the prayers of Bible personalities are included. It's even more strange that no reference is made to a prayer taught or offered by Jesus. For if anyone is an authority on prayer, it is Christ. Jesus lived His human life immersed in prayer to the Father. Jesus often taught about prayer. And the recorded prayers of Jesus provide deep insight into the nature of prayer. Jesus even promised that prayer addressed to the Father in His name would surely be answered.

We have much to learn about prayer from the prayers recorded in the Old Testament. We may even learn by reading and meditating on the prayers of mature Christians. But if we truly want to understand prayer and to prac-

tice it effectively, we must learn from Jesus.

And so we come to an exciting section of this study of *Every Prayer and Petition in the Bible*. In this chapter and those which follow, we will learn the secrets of Christian prayer from the Master.

Five chapters are devoted to the study of Jesus on prayer. In this chapter, we look at Jesus' "first principles" of prayer. In chapter 10, we study Jesus' instructions about prayer. In chapter 11, we draw together Jesus' prayer promises. In chapter 12, we look at some strange incidents involving prayer from the ministry of Jesus. And in chapter 13, we study Jesus' own recorded prayers.

I'm sure there is some value in works like the *Book of Prayers*. But if we really want to learn to pray, we must look to Jesus.

JESUS' RIGHT TO TEACH ABOUT PRAYER

Many people have claimed the right to teach on prayer. What makes us rely more on Jesus' teaching on prayer than on any others?

Jesus received and answered prayer (Matthew 8, 9). If we were to read quickly through the synoptic Gospels, one thing that would impress us is the number of times that ordinary people came to Jesus to ask for something which only God could provide.

For example, consider Matthew 8–9, which summarizes Jesus' early itinerant ministry in Galilee. The first incident is found in Matthew 8:2.

And behold, a leper came and worshiped Him, saying, "Lord, if You are willing, You can make me clean" (Matt. 8:2).

Some might be inclined to argue that the leper used "Lord" in its ordinary sense as an expression of respect, like our "Sir." But no one would argue that anyone in his or her right mind would expect an ordinary person to cure leprosy. Yet this is exactly what the leper expected. He clearly confessed his belief that, if Jesus were willing, He could make a leper clean.

We see the same conviction expressed in several incidents that follow.

Now when Jesus had entered Capernaum, a centurion came to Him pleading with Him, saying, "Lord, my servant is lying at home paralyzed, dreadfully tormented" (Matt. 8:5, 6).

Then His disciples came to Him and awoke Him, saying, "Lord, save us! We are perishing!" (Matt. 8:25).

So the demons begged Him, saying, "If You cast us out, permit us to go away into the herd of swine" (Matt. 8:31).

And while he spoke these things to them, behold, a ruler came and worshiped him, saying, "My daughter has just died, but come and lay Your hand on her and she will live" (Matt. 9:18).

When Jesus departed from there, two blind men followed Him, crying out and saying, "Son of David, have mercy on us!" And when He had come into the house, the blind men came to Him. And Jesus said to them, "Do you believe that I am able to do this?" They said to Him, "Yes, Lord" (Matt. 9:27, 28).

As we read through the synoptic Gospels [Matthew, Mark, and Luke] we run across scene after scene just like these. A person with a great need—typically a physical problem that no doctor could resolve or a demon which no exorcist could expel—approached

A leper told Jesus, "Lord, if You are willing, You can make me clean."

Jesus. The person addressed Jesus as Lord, and asked Christ to do something for him or her that only God could do. And, frequently, the text tells us that the petitioner prostrated himself or herself before Jesus, thus "worshiping" Him.

Clearly those who came to Jesus did not view Him as an ordinary man. They may not have grasped His true identity—few did during the early days of Jesus' ministry—but it was abundantly clear that Jesus was special. There can be little doubt that at least some of those who appealed to Christ used the word *Lord* in a theological sense, acknowledging Him as God.

It is just as clear, as we see Jesus respond to such requests, that He actually performed miraculous healings. Jesus cleansed the leper, restored paralyzed limbs, gave sight to the blind, and even restored life to those who had died. Jesus did what only God can do.

The multiplied examples in the Gospels of just this kind of request, followed by

PRAYERS ADDRESSED
TO JESUS

RECORDED IN THE SYNOPTIC GOSPELS

Matt. 8:2	Mark 5:10	Luke 4:38
Matt. 8:6	Mark 5:18	Luke 5:8
Matt. 8:25	Mark 5:23	Luke 8:24
Matt. 8:31	Mark 6:56	Luke 8:31
Matt. 9:18	Mark 7:32	Luke 8:38
Matt. 9:27	Mark 8:22	Luke 8:41
Matt. 14:30	Mark 9:24	
Matt. 14:36	Mark 10:35f	
Matt. 15:25		
Matt. 17:15		
Matt. 20:21		
Matt. 20:30f		

demonstrations of supernatural power, are convincing. The people of Jesus' day actually *prayed to Jesus as if He were God*. And Jesus granted their requests, *because He was God*.

Surely we can find no one better able to mentor us in prayer than a person who both accepts and answers the prayers of human beings.

Jesus claimed to be God (*Matthew 16:13–17; John 5:1–23; 8:48–59*). One of the fictions promoted by modern critics of Christianity is that Jesus was an extraordinary man, but nothing more. Some go so far as to argue that Jesus never claimed to be anything more than a Jewish rabbi, consumed as other rabbis with a desire to interpret and teach God's Word.

While Jesus was special, this theory goes, His teachings should be considered alongside the teachings of other great religions leaders of the world.

In making this argument, the critics overlook or dismiss claims that Jesus made about Himself. Three Gospel passages illustrate these claims.

Matthew 16:13–17. Jesus had spent years in Galilee and Judea, teaching and performing miracles. One day He asked His disciples whom people said He was. The disciples circulated through the crowds that followed Jesus, listening. They returned to report that "some say John the Baptist, some Elijah, and others Jeremiah or one of the prophets" (Matt. 16:14). Clearly, the Jewish people had great respect for Jesus, ranking Him among the greatest of the Old Testament prophets. But then Jesus asked, "But who do *you* say that I am?" (Matt. 16:15, italics mine). Peter answered for the Twelve. "You are the Christ, the Son of the living God" (Matt. 16:16).

Peter was correct, and Christ commended him. "Blessed are you, Simon Bar-Jonah, for flesh and blood has not revealed this to you, but My father who is in heaven" (Matt. 16:17).

John 5:1–23. Jesus' enemies certainly understood what He claimed about Himself. After Christ healed a paralyzed man on the Sabbath, the religious leaders considered killing Him, for they classified His healing as "work" which was not to be performed on the holy day. But Jesus told them, "My Father has been working until now, and I have been working" (John 5:17). John tells us that "therefore the Jews [a term used in John to designate the religious leaders, not the whole people] sought all the more to kill Him, because He not only broke the Sabbath, but also said that God was His Father, making Himself equal with God" (John 5:19).

John 8:48–59. Perhaps the strongest claim Jesus made about Himself is recorded in John 8. Near the end of a lengthy dispute, Christ's enemies ridiculed Him for assuming He was "greater than our father Abraham" (John 8:53). Jesus claimed that Abraham had foreseen Christ's day, and was glad. Again relying on ridicule and sarcasm, the leaders said to Him, "You are not yet fifty years old, and have You seen Abraham?" (John 8:57).

Christ's answer stunned His hearers. He not only claimed to have existed before Abraham, but to be the "I AM" of the Old Testament (John 8:58; cf. Ex. 3:13, 14). The immediate response of the leaders was to pick up stones to throw at Him (John 8:59). The "stones" were paving stones, and the Jews intended to stone Him to death for blasphemy.

So the notion that Jesus never claimed to be anything more than a humble rabbi does not fit the biblical facts. Christ not only performed miracles of healing; He also presented Himself to the Jewish people as the Savior promised in the Old Testament—a Savior who was God Himself.

Jesus' resurrection demonstrated His deity

(*John 1; Romans 1:4*). The Gospel of John begins with a strong possible affirmation of the deity of Jesus Christ. John writes,

In the beginning was the Word, and the Word was with God, and the Word was God. He was in the beginning with God. All things were made through Him, and without Him nothing was made that was made. In Him was life, and the life was the light of men. . . . And the Word became flesh and dwelt among us, and we beheld His glory, the glory as of the only begotten of the Father, full of grace and truth" (John 1:1–4, 14).

The use of the term "word," or *logos,* is significant. It suggests that one person of the Trinity took the lead in revelation. Throughout history, this "Word" who was both with God, and at the same time was God, communicated with human beings.

We meet this person in the Old Testament in the guise of the Angel of the Lord. We hear His voice as Yahweh, the "I AM" of the older revelation. And finally in Jesus Christ, the Word took on human flesh. The Word—who is God the Creator, God the source of life,

God the revealer, God the Son, who existed from eternity alongside and equal with God the Father—became incarnate as the human being we know as Jesus of Nazareth.

This is a stunning claim. Yet it is in complete harmony with all that Jesus claimed for Himself. And it is in complete harmony with the final proof offered by God—a proof which forever seals as certain the identity of Jesus Christ.

We all know the story of Jesus. We know how He lived a perfect life here on earth. We know how He was rejected by His own people and turned over to the Roman governor for trial and execution. We know that although He was innocent, He was condemned to death, and that He died a death reserved for the worst of criminals—crucifixion. If the story ended here, we would be justified in mourning Jesus, even as we shook our heads over the unbelievable claims He made about Himself.

But the story does not end here. It has never ended! After three days in a borrowed tomb, Jesus rose from the dead! He was seen by many witnesses, believed in by disciples whose sorrow was turned to joy, and was received into heaven. Today, Jesus stands at the right hand of God the Father, the living head of the church here on earth.

It is the resurrection which puts Jesus in final perspective, for as Paul wrote in Romans, Jesus was "declared to be the Son of God with power according to the Spirit of holiness, by the resurrection from the dead" (Rom. 1:4).

The resurrection is proof that Jesus was who He claimed to be, and that, as God the Son, Jesus is our authority in all things.

And so we conclude that Jesus does have the right to instruct us on prayer. Jesus received and answered prayer during His life here on earth. Indeed, Jesus claimed to be God. And in the resurrection, we have proof that Jesus *is* God.

Who better to teach us about prayer than the one to whom we pray?—the one who even now answers the prayers we offer in His name.

An empty tomb testifies to the resurrection of Jesus, the Son of God.

JESUS' FIRST PRINCIPLES OF PRAYER

Every discipline has its "first principles." These are truths that are basic or foundational. In the case of prayer, we can distinguish Jesus' first principles by looking at His earliest teachings on prayer, recorded by Matthew in the Sermon on the Mount (Matt. 5—7), and in Luke in private instruction which Jesus gave to His disciples (Luke 12).

FIRST PRINCIPLES IN JESUS' SERMON ON THE MOUNT

Jesus' Sermon on the Mount is recorded in Matthew 5:1—7:29. It is so named because Matthew 5:1 tells us that Jesus "went up on a mountain" where He "taught them" (Matt. 5:1, 2). The conclusion of the sermon is clearly identified. The text tells us that Jesus "ended these sayings" (Matt. 7:28), and that He then came "down from the mountain" (Matt. 8:1).

It is important to note that in this sermon, Jesus spoke not only to the disciples but also to the "multitudes." At this time, great crowds gathered to see Jesus perform miracles and to hear His teaching. Jesus did not begin to speak until His disciples were gathered

around Him (Matt. 5:1). But His words were addressed to all, for "the people were astonished at his teaching" (Matt. 7:28).

What was the Sermon on the Mount about? Jesus told the crowds that He had come to "fulfill" the Law. In Jesus' time, it was the dream of every rabbi to fulfill the Law, for the phrase meant to explain the Law's true and full meaning. In His teaching, Jesus explained to the Jews what the Law given to Moses was all about!

Jesus had many important points to make in His sermon.

- Jesus pronounced blessings on those whose values were based on God's requirements rather than the practices of sinful human society (the Beatitudes; Matt. 5:3–16).

- Jesus explained that the righteousness required by the Law was far different from the righteousness of the scribes and Pharisees, who thought they had only to act correctly. Jesus gave a series of illustrations to show that God is concerned with our hearts, not just our actions. What human beings need is a changed heart, for only people like this can be like the heavenly Father (Matt. 5:17–47).

- Jesus contrasted the public piety of the Pharisees with the private, personal relationships which believers are to nurture with God (Matt. 6:1–18).
- Jesus called for a commitment to God that is rooted in total trust of the Lord as a Father who knows and will meet our needs (Matt. 6:1–34).
- Jesus described characteristics of the fruit that such a relationship with God will produce in those who hear and respond to His words (Matt. 7:1–27).

Jesus' first principles of prayer are developed in the section of the Sermon on the Mount that contrasts public and private piety (Matt. 6:1–18).

A first negative principle: What prayer is not *(Matthew 6:1–5).* Jesus began this section of His sermon by warning, "Take heed that you do not do your charitable deeds before men,

to be seen by them. Otherwise you have no reward from your Father in heaven" (Matt. 6:1). Jesus' opening statement was surprising. In Christ's time, it was generally believed that giving alms to the poor—doing charitable deeds—was especially pleasing to God.

One authority notes how important charity was and is in rabbinic thought.

> There is a notation in the Talmud about an argument—whether real or apocryphal is not known—between Rabbi Akiba and Turnus (Tineius) Rufus, the governor of Judea. The Roman asked Rabbi Akiba: "If, as you say, your god loves the poor, why then does he not support them?" A reasonable question, certainly! Rabbi Akiba replied that if God left the care of the poor to the benevolence of the Jews themselves it was purposely "so that we may be saved by its merits from the punishment of Genhinnom [Gehenna or Purgatory]" (Nathan Ausubel in *The Book of Jewish Knowledge*, 1964, p. 82).

In view of this, it is not surprising that in Jesus' day the general population thought the wealthy were doubly blessed. They were rich

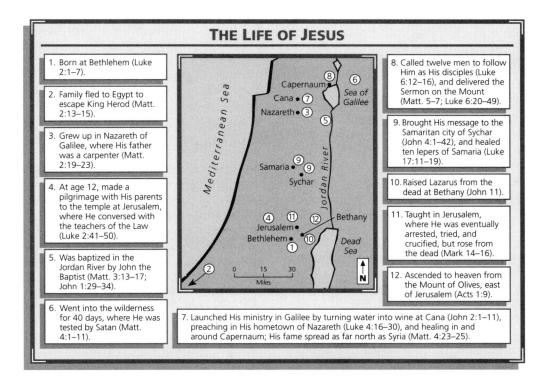

THE LIFE OF JESUS

1. Born at Bethlehem (Luke 2:1–7).

2. Family fled to Egypt to escape King Herod (Matt. 2:13–15).

3. Grew up in Nazareth of Galilee, where His father was a carpenter (Matt. 2:19–23).

4. At age 12, made a pilgrimage with His parents to the temple at Jerusalem, where He conversed with the teachers of the Law (Luke 2:41–50).

5. Was baptized in the Jordan River by John the Baptist (Matt. 3:13–17; John 1:29–34).

6. Went into the wilderness for 40 days, where He was tested by Satan (Matt. 4:1–11).

7. Launched His ministry in Galilee by turning water into wine at Cana (John 2:1–11), preaching in His hometown of Nazareth (Luke 4:16–30), and healing in and around Capernaum; His fame spread as far north as Syria (Matt. 4:23–25).

8. Called twelve men to follow Him as His disciples (Luke 6:12–16), and delivered the Sermon on the Mount (Matt. 5–7; Luke 6:20–49).

9. Brought His message to the Samaritan city of Sychar (John 4:1–42), and healed ten lepers of Samaria (Luke 17:11–19).

10. Raised Lazarus from the dead at Bethany (John 11).

11. Taught in Jerusalem, where He was eventually arrested, tried, and crucified, but rose from the dead (Mark 14–16).

12. Ascended to heaven from the Mount of Olives, east of Jerusalem (Acts 1:9).

and comfortable in this world. And they had the wealth needed to be generous to the poor. Thus, they were guaranteed salvation in the world to come.

Against this background, Jesus' words were surprising. Not do charitable deeds in public? Why, many of the wealthy even had servants announce their deeds of charity by blowing trumpets in the streets. The poor would flock to the sound, and the rich man who distributed the charity would gain a reputation for piety as well as gain merit with God. The idea that doing charitable deeds "to be seen by men" merited no reward from God was shocking.

Jesus intended to shock. His words about giving were intended to lay a foundation for what He was about to teach about relationship with God, and especially about prayer. So Jesus continued:

Therefore, when you do a charitable deed, do not sound a trumpet before you as the hypocrites do in the synagogues and in the streets, that they may have glory from men. Assuredly, I say to you, they have their reward. But when you do a charitable deed, do not let your left hand know what your right hand is doing, that your charitable deed may be in secret; and your Father who sees in secret will Himself reward you openly (Matt. 6:2–4).

The central point Christ made here is that relationship with God is a uniquely *personal* thing. It is a *one-on-one* relationship; it is an *"in secret"* relationship between the individual and God alone. Even the poor were not to know who their benefactor was. In this way, the purity of one's desire to please God alone might be maintained.

What the wealthy people of first-century Jerusalem were doing was denying the nature of personal relationship with God. They sought a public rather than a private relationship. Rather than seeking a one-on-one relationship, the wealthy sought a one-before-the-crowds relationship, with God a distant observer. The motivation for this kind of charity was not a desire to please God, but a hypocritical desire that others might consider them pious. Thus, the hypocrite had the reward he

valued—not the approval of God, but the esteem of others.

Jesus applied this illustration from charity to prayer. Just as hypocrites loved to do charitable deeds to be seen of men, so they loved to make public prayers (Matt. 6:5)—for the same reason and with the same outcome. They received the reward they valued—not God's answer to their prayers but the esteem of their fellows who considered them especially pious.

A first positive principle: What prayer is (Matthew 6:6). Jesus then presented what He considered a first principle of prayer.

But you, when you pray, go into your room, and when you have shut your door, pray to your Father who is in the secret place, and your Father who sees in secret will reward you openly.

This instruction summarizes what Jesus had been saying. Prayer is first of all an expression of a personal, private relationship with God as Father. It is a one-on-one relationship between a believer and God. Because it is essentially a one-on-one relationship, it is also an "in secret" relationship.

Prayer is a transaction that takes place between a person and God. As such, it is the business only of that individual and the Lord.

Jesus was not suggesting that it is wrong to pray with others. Prayer meetings have been a vital element of the church's relationship with the Savior from the beginning (cf. Acts 1:14; 2:42). What Jesus was saying is that we are to be careful to guard our hearts against mixed motives. We are to direct our prayers to God alone—for the purpose of communicating with Him rather than trying to influence how others might perceive us.

God who knows everything will honor those who seek Him in the secret recesses of their hearts. These are the people whom God will reward openly.

A second negative principle: No "vain repetitions" (Matthew 6:7, 8). While the "religious" people in Israel viewed public prayer as a means to a reputation for piety, pagan peoples thought of prayer as a way of persuading their gods to give them some material benefit. In *Backgrounds of Early Christianity* (1993), Everett Ferguson noted that Hellenistic prayers contained three parts: "invocation, praise, and petition. Sometimes a reminder of the piety of the worshiper preceded the requests. When the sacrifice or festival was ended, the god was asked to return his favors to those who honored him." Ferguson observes that "the attitude was that of self-interest. Only the prayers of philosophers were more disinterested" (p. 181).

Jesus characterized pagan prayers as "vain repetitions" when He said,

And when you pray, do not use vain repetitions as the heathen do. For they think that they will be heard for their many words. Therefore do not be like them. For your Father knows the things you have need of before you ask Him (Matt. 6:7, 8).

The Greek word translated "vain repetitions" is *battalogeo,* meaning "continuous babbling." While commentators normally connect this verb to the "many words" which Jesus suggested pagans address to their deities, neither repetition nor length of prayers is the real issue. Pagan prayers were mere babbling because they were addressed to lifeless idols.

The pagan assumption that by addressing many words to the gods, one could get what he or she wanted was an empty one indeed. Jesus told His listeners, "Do not be like them." Their assumptions about prayer were faulty.

The problem is that believers even today can buy into pagan assumptions about prayer. We may have faulty ideas about the God to whom we pray, assuming that our words draw His attention to needs of which He was unaware. In saying "your Father knows the things you have need of before you ask Him," Jesus introduced a contrasting set of assumptions that are basic to the prayer lives of true believers.

Again, what were the false assumptions underlying pagan prayer?

- The god or goddess was a stranger, invoked because of his or her supposed ability to help.
- Prayer involved asking this god or goddess for something wanted or needed.
- Prayer required alerting the deity to something he or she did not know about.
- The words of the prayer—its form, the gift presented to the deity—provided the basis on which the god's favor might be won.

A second positive principle: Prayer is addressed to God as Father (Matthew 6:8). In Matthew 6:8, Jesus introduced a stunning concept. The one-on-one relationship about which He had been speaking was the relationship of a child to his or her parent.

The significance of the fatherliness of God. A number of scholars have pointed out that God is spoken of as "Father" in the Old Testament. For instance, Malachi 2:10 reads, "Have we not all one Father? Has not one God created us?" But in this context, the term *Father* is equated with "Creator," and it conveys the idea of "source" or "originator."

Geza Vermes, a contemporary Jewish scholar, has gone to considerable lengths to show that Jesus should be understood as a rabbi operating within first-century Judaism, rather than as the Son of God. In his efforts to humanize Christ, Vermes has searched ancient literature and pointed out that ancient Judaism addressed God as "Father" before Jesus' day.

Most frequently in Jewish prayer, however, "Father" is used with other terms of respect, such as Ruler, Lord, and God. When Ben Sira, who wrote some 200 years before Christ, addressed God as "my Father" He explained, "for thou art the Hero of My salvation" (Ecclus. 51:10). He would not address God simply as Father without further explanation.

Prayer in the Jewish synagogue did at times appeal to God as "our Father." But again, God is "Father" in the sense of the covenant which made Israel His people. Commenting on the pre-Christian use of references to God as Father, one authority stated that the term

"lacks vitality because it does not express a radical appreciation of the fatherliness of God. It seems to be confined within the very different system of a legalism which contradicts fatherly freedom. What Israel possesses in this name looks ahead to a view which goes incomparably deeper, which transcends mere formality, which is no longer tied to the idea of merit, which no longer thinks in terms of the privilege of an elite or of respected teachers. The materials are there, but the spirit of true faith in the Father is still lacking" (*Theological Dictionary of the New Testament,* Vol. V, 1963, pp. 981–982).

It is just this—a "radical appreciation of the fatherliness of God"—which Jesus presents as a first principle of prayer.

The God to whom believers pray is not simply a Father, but is fatherly—one who "knows the things you have need of before you ask him" (Matt. 6:8). Those who appreciate this reality pray to God "in secret," assured that He knows our needs and heeds our prayers. We are heard, not because of our "many words," but because God has a fatherly concern for us.

How stunning this principle of prayer is. God knows and loves us! God has a fatherly concern for us. We relate to Him not simply as one of His creatures, or as one of His covenant people in good standing, but as *family!* And because we are family, our prayers need not follow the pagan pattern of request upon request. In our prayers, we are freed to speak to God as a child speaks to his or her loving father.

An illustration of the fatherliness of God (Matthew 7:7–11). A little later in his Sermon on the Mount, Jesus further developed the implications of the fatherliness of God.

Ask, and it will be given to you; seek, and you will find; knock, and it will be opened to you. For everyone who asks receives, and he who seeks finds, and to him who knocks it will be opened. Or what man is there among you who, if his son asks for bread, will he give him a stone? Or if he asks for a fish, will he give him a serpent? If you then, being evil, know how to give good gifts to your children, how much more will your Father who is in heaven give good things to those who ask Him! (Matt. 7:7–11).

Jesus builds on the first principle of God's fatherliness in teaching about prayer. We are

Knocking is the first step toward an opened door.

heard, and God responds to us when we ask, seek, and knock—not because of our much speaking. Not because of the form of our words. Not because we have done favors for God. Not because we *deserve* what we request. We are heard and God responds to us because—like a human father—God is committed to give "good things" when His children ask him.

The third positive principle: Here is how to pray *(Matthew 6:9–13).* As Jesus continued His Sermon on the Mount, He gave His listeners a Model Prayer, which we generally call the Lord's Prayer. It answers an important question. If God is our Father who has a fatherly concern for us, how are we His children to nurture our "in secret" one-on-one relationship with Him?

It is important to note two things before we explore this familiar prayer. First, Jesus did not say, "This is *what* you should pray," but to pray "in this manner" (Matt. 6:9). The Lord's

Prayer is a pattern for prayer, not a liturgical prayer. It establishes a pattern we are to follow in praying; it does not provide the words we are to recite in private or in church.

Second, Jesus' instructions in verses 5–8 emphasize "you," in contrast to the rest of humankind. Jesus' instructions on prayer are for His followers alone, as distinct from pagans as well as unbelieving Israel. The Lord's Prayer is to serve as a model for His followers.

How did Jesus teach us to pray? Matthew's version of the Lord's Prayer says,

> Our Father in heaven,
> > Hallowed be Your name.
> Your kingdom come,
> > Your will be done
> > On earth as it is in heaven.
> Give us this day our daily
> > bread,
> And forgive us our debts,
> > As we forgive our debtors.
> And do not lead us into
> > temptation,
> > But deliver us from the evil
> > one,
> > For Yours is the kingdom and
> > the power and the glory
> > forever. Amen
> (Matt. 6:9–14).

General observations on the Lord's Prayer. Jesus' Model Prayer is divided into two parts. The first part, and the believer's first priority, deals with God's glory. In prayer, we are first of all to focus on hallowing God's name, extending God's kingdom, and doing God's will. The second part of the prayer concerns our needs. Luther saw three petitions here, while Calvin and those in the Reformed tradition divide verse 13 and count four. But what is significant is to note the major divisions of the Model Prayer. Our prayers are to enhance God's glory, expressing our dependence on Him for all our needs.

Our Father in heaven (Matthew 6:9). These opening words remind us of the kind of God to whom we pray and of our relationship with

Him. God is the Father of Jesus' followers in the most intimate sense (see the significance of the fatherliness of God, page 138).

The words *in heaven* remind us that the one with whom we have a personal family relationship is actually God the Creator and sovereign ruler of the universe.

These initial words are not intended merely as a form of address. They are a reminder of the awesome privilege we have in Christ of addressing the Creator Himself as Father. Relationally, God is "Father" only of those who have trusted Christ, although in the sense of "source" He is the "Father" of all.

Hallowed be Your name" (Matthew 6:9). God's "name" captures to some extent who He actually is. To say "hallowed be Your name" is not a request that God become holy, but rather that He may be respected and treated as holy. When we come to God in prayer, we are to do so in an appropriate frame of mind. We are to come with awareness of and respect for who He is.

While God is our Father, we are never to forget that He is God.

Your kingdom come (Matthew 6:10). In biblical times, a "kingdom" was not viewed primarily as a geographical area. Rather, a kingdom existed where persons were subject to the rule of a king. It was the relationship between a ruler and his subjects that constituted a kingdom.

The Old Testament prophets looked forward to the eschatological kingdom of God's Messiah, through which God's rule would be extended over the entire earth. All humankind at last would become subject to Messiah's rule. While Jerusalem was to be the capital of the Messiah, and Israel the world's premier nation, the essence of the eschatological kingdom would be Messiah's worldwide rule.

But in Jesus, the Messiah has now appeared! True, not all humanity is subject to Him yet. *But He does rule now in the hearts and lives of those who acknowledge Him as King.* So the prayer "your kingdom come" looks ahead as well as to the present. Until Christ returns to rule over all, we are to pray that God's rule will be extended here and now, as more and more persons through faith subject themselves to God's Son.

Your will be done on earth as it is in heaven (Matthew 6:10). The word translated "will" in this passage is *thelema.* It expresses not what God *wants* but what He has *willed* or determined. This includes both God's revelation of what is right and His purposes for human beings.

When we pray "your will be done," we identify ourselves with God's will and commit ourselves to do it. Thus, to pray "your will be done" is both a personal commitment to moral obedience and a commitment to participate in the fulfillment of God's purposes here on earth.

But the verse adds, "On earth as it is in heaven." How is God's will done "in heaven"? Today only earth is in rebellion against God. In heaven, God's will is done fully, joyfully, and spontaneously. In heaven, there is no hesitation in doing God's will. In heaven, there are no competing wills. How wonderful to desire only what God wants and what He knows is best.

Give us this day our daily bread (Matthew 6:11). In biblical times, the term *bread* included all foods. In this context, "bread" stands for everything a person needs to sustain life.

While the prayer asks God to "give" our daily bread, this does not relieve us of our responsibility to work for what we receive. God supplied manna to the Exodus generation on a daily basis, but each person was required to gather what God had placed on the ground.

The phrase "daily bread" not only looked back to the Exodus generation, but also reflected a reality of first-century life. Workers were paid on a daily basis, and wages were just enough to sustain a family. The family of a person who became sick and could not work for a few days was in desperate straits. The prayer Jesus taught reminds us that we are to depend on God constantly, always looking to Him for what we need. All good things, including our ability to work, come from the Lord.

There is another thought here as well. We are to count on God to supply our *needs*—not our *greeds.* We are to be satisfied with what God provides rather than yearn for what He has not chosen to give.

And forgive our debts, as we forgive our debtors (Matthew 6:12). The word translated "debts" (*opheilema*) is rare in biblical Greek, occurring only two times in the New Testament (here and in Romans 4:4, where it means "obligation"). This word is also found four times in the Septuagint. In Aramaic, the language in which Jesus taught, the word means "sin" or "transgression." Given this and Luke 11:4 ("forgive us our sins"), we can be confident Jesus was referring to forgiveness of sins.

Some people have assumed from this passage that Jesus was teaching that we must earn God's forgiveness by being forgiving. Instead, as the Greek scholar C. F. D. Moule pointed out, Jesus is referring to an attitude which makes forgiveness possible. When we sense the enormity of the sins for which God has forgiven us, we find it possible to forgive the far lesser sins which others have committed against us.

We human beings tend to exaggerate the sins of others and to minimize our own. Christ encourages us to look to God for forgiveness, being so sensitive to our failings that the grace He extends to us will overflow to others.

"And do not lead us into temptation, but deliver us from the evil one" (Matthew 6:13a). In ordinary Greek as it was spoken in the first century, *peirasmos,* rendered "temptation" in this passage, meant "testing." New Testament usage frequently focuses attention on a specific kind of testing, such as temptation or enticement to sin. The book of James tells us that while we may respond to situations as if they were enticements to sin, the problem does not lie in the circumstances but in our sinful nature. God, James says, "cannot be tempted by evil, nor does He himself tempt anyone" (James 1:13).

Yet we know from Scripture that believers are called to face tests of many kinds and that we are to meet them with joy (1 Cor. 10:13; James 1:2). It would seem strange to pray that God will not do what He cannot do (entice us to sin), and equally strange to pray that God will not do what Scripture says He has chosen to do (test us)!

One suggested solution lies in understanding the verb *into* to reflect the fact that Jesus taught in Hebrew or Aramaic. Hebrew verbs, unlike the Greek, can distinguish between being led "to" testing and being led "into" testing. In this language, being led "into" testing would imply *succumbing to* the temptation. Jesus may have been teaching us to pray that we be spared from failing the test rather than spared the test of temptation itself. In this case, to "deliver us from" would mean "preserve us in" the difficult situation.

A second suggested solution views the verb as causative and sees the first phrase closely linked with the second. In this case, we are to pray that we will not be led into temptations to sin which the devil has organized! While God cannot tempt anyone by appealing to the sin nature, Satan certainly can! And in this case, "deliver us from" would be understood as "spare us the experience."

A third possibility is that the prayer simply encourages us to maintain a humble attitude. God is not asking us to seek martyrdom or to prove our faith by rushing headlong to test it. As Paul suggested in 1 Timothy 2:2, the church is to pray for those in authority, "that we may lead a quiet and peaceable life in all godliness and reverence." There is challenge enough in leading ordinary lives and glorifying God by godly living.

For Yours is the kingdom and the power and the glory forever. Amen (Matthew 6:13b). The prayer ends with a doxology which most feel was not included in the original text.

Jesus' first principles of prayer as seen in the Sermon on the Mount. We can summarize the "first principles" of prayer as Jesus taught them in the Sermon on the Mount.

1. True prayer is an expression of a person's personal relationship with God.
2. True prayer involves reliance on the fatherliness of God.
3. True prayer involves an expression by those who know God through Jesus of . . .
   (a) respect for God as holy;
   (b) submission to God's sovereign right to rule;
   (c) commitment to moral obedience and to fulfilling God's purposes;
   (d) daily dependence on God;
   (e) determination to live as a forgiven and forgiving person; and
   (f) reliance on God for strength to meet successfully any testing which He devises.

FIRST PRINCIPLES IN JESUS' TEACHING OF HIS DISCIPLES

A prayer much like the Lord's Prayer as recorded in Matthew 6 is found in Luke 11. Some scholars assume that either Matthew's or Luke's version is the original, and that the other is a variation. Others believe both were derived from a prayer recorded in some lost documentary source.

The truth is probably far simpler. Jesus traveled throughout Palestine and taught for about three years. He must have taught on prayer many times, just as He told His stories and parables over and over again. The two "versions" of the Lord's Prayer that we have in Matthew and Luke are both accurate reports of what Jesus said about prayer at different times and in different places.

Even a superficial reading of the two accounts makes this clear. The teaching on prayer in Matthew 6 is imbedded in the Sermon on the Mount. The teaching on prayer in Luke 11 took place when Jesus' disciples, impressed by Christ's own commitment to prayer, asked Him to teach *them* to pray (Luke 11:1). In the Sermon on the Mount, Jesus returned to the theme of prayer only briefly (Matt. 7:7–11). In Luke 11, Jesus continued on the theme after providing His disciples with a model showing them how to pray.

While the NKJV version of Luke's prayer does include words and phrases that were taken from Matthew, the best Greek manuscripts report a simpler, more direct version of what Jesus taught. Luke's original version is "streamlined." However, there is no *essential* difference in these two records of Jesus' teaching.

What did Jesus say to the disciples, as recorded in the best Greek manuscripts?

> Father,
> Hallowed be Your name.
> Your kingdom come.
> Give us day by day our daily
>   bread,
> And forgive us our sins,
>   for we also forgive everyone
>   who is indebted to us.
> And do not lead us into temptation
>   (Luke 11:2–4).

First principles of prayer in Luke's version. Most comments on the Matthew 6 version of Jesus' instructions on how to pray fit here as well (see pages 134–141).

"Father" (Luke 11:2). In both prayers, God is "Father," and Jesus' radical vision of the father-liness of God is affirmed. Luke's version is especially striking. While the believer approaches God with respect, he or she also approaches confidently, secure in the knowledge that he or she is now God's child.

God's fatherliness is emphasized in Luke 11:9–13, as in Matthew 7:7–11, by reference to the fact that even sinful human beings give good gifts to their children. How, then, could anyone imagine that God would not give good gifts to His children when they ask, seek, and knock?

"Hallowed be Your name" (Luke 11:2). The words are the same as in Matthew. Yet their juxtaposition next to "Father" may convey a note of worship rather than petition.

"Your kingdom come" (Luke 11:2). Here the second petition directed to God's glory serves the same function as the second and third in Matthew. To express a desire for God's kingdom rule implies submission to His will, which is stated explicitly in Matthew 6.

"Give us day by day our daily bread" (Luke 11:3). Luke's version of the Model Prayer emphasizes the need for constant dependence on the

Jesus' disciples were the first to receive His principles of prayer.

Lord. This need is clearly stated in Matthew. It is more strongly underlined here.

"And forgive us our sins, for we also forgive everyone who is indebted to us" (Luke 11:4). The same thought in Matthew is expressed here. The forgiveness we extend to others is not the basis on which we ask God for forgiveness, but it is an outcome of the forgiveness we have already received. We rely on God for a forgiveness that enables us to walk in fellowship with Him day by day. Our forgiveness of others is an appropriate expression of the fellowship we enjoy with the Lord.

"And do not lead us into temptation" (Luke 11:4). Here too the word used is *peirasmos,* and it means testing rather than enticement to sin. Again, the desire expressed is most likely for strength to avoid failing the trials that come.

Each version of the Lord's Prayer thus (1) emphasizes the fatherliness of God, (2) instructs us when we pray to put God's issues first, and (3) calls on us when we pray to express our dependence on the Lord in all things.

Another illustration *(Luke 11:5–8).* Luke 11 introduces a new simile. Jesus invited His disciples to consider what would happen if a visitor arrived late at night, and the host happened to be low on bread. In biblical times, hospitality demanded that food be found for the visitor.

So the disciples were to picture themselves going to a friend for the bread they needed, and asking for three loaves.

True, it was late. The friend was in bed, and he grumbled "don't bother me" when he first heard the knock. Most English versions assume that the word *anaideia* should be translated "persistence," and that Jesus was picturing a person who kept on knocking until the neighbor provided the bread just to get rid of him!

But there is another meaning of *anaideia,* which better fits both first-century customs and God's character. In the first century, visitors were considered the responsibility of the whole community, not just of the family they stayed with. And *anaideia* can mean "avoidance of shame." If this is the meaning here, Jesus was pointing out that the neighbor would surely get up and lend the bread *because he was obligated to do so, as it was the right thing for a neighbor to do.*

What Jesus taught was that God will surely respond to our prayers, simply because God will always do what is appropriate and consistent with His character. We can expect our heavenly Father to be fatherly and to supply our needs!

And so in both versions of the Lord's Prayer and in their contexts, the same "first principles of prayer" are emphasized.

1. True prayer *is* an expression of a human being's personal relationship with God.
2. True prayer involves reliance on the fatherliness of God.
3. True prayer involves an expression by those who know God through Jesus of:
    (a) respect for God as holy;
    (b) submission to God's sovereign right to rule;
    (c) commitment to moral obedience and to fulfilling God's purposes;
    (d) daily dependence on God;
    (e) determination to live as a forgiven and forgiving person; and
    (f) reliance on God for strength to meet successfully any testing which He devises.

God is our Father and always does what is right. We can count on Him to give what is good in response to our requests as His children.

JESUS' LIFE-CHANGING TEACHINGS ON PRAYER

MATTHEW—JOHN

Our daughter Sarah has just started college. One of her teachers has impressed my wife. His syllabus is so well organized. It explains just what he intends to teach, and when. It clearly states what each student's responsibilities will be, and how work will be graded. When this teacher gives an assignment, step-by-step instructions are written out and distributed. There's no mistaking what he expects.

Sarah has been fortunate to get a really good classroom teacher her first semester in college. But there is a better way to teach when the goal is to change lives.

That better way is the way Jesus taught. He didn't invite His disciples into a classroom. He didn't hand out assignments, or require papers. Jesus didn't even organize His teaching into a course. Instead, Jesus wove His teaching into the experiences He shared with His disciples and others. He let life itself organize the curriculum. And when a teachable moment came, Jesus showed His disciples how to respond in a way that changed their lives as well as the lives of others.

In this chapter we look at a number of these teachable moments and how Jesus used them to teach His followers—and us—about prayer.

PRAYER AND THE REAL MEANING OF GOD'S LAW

But I say to you, love your enemies, bless those who curse you, do good to those who hate you, and pray for those who spitefully use you and persecute you (Matt. 5:44; cf. Luke 6:28).

The teachable moment (Matthew 5:1–42). There were times when Jesus created His own teachable moment. One of the clearest examples of this is found here.

Jesus had just shocked the crowds that had gathered to hear Him teach. He began by calling "blessed" the people whom most thought of as deprived. Warning His listeners not to misunderstand what He was about to say, Jesus promised He would "fulfill" Moses' Law. His promise, misunderstood by moderns, was clear to first-century Jews, whose rabbis were intent on the same mission. To "fulfill" the Law meant to reveal its true, deepest meaning.

But then Jesus stunned His listeners again, this time by stating that to catch a glimpse of God's kingdom, a person's righteousness must exceed that of the scribes and Pharisees. This amazed His listeners, for the scribes were experts in Old Testament Law. And the Pharisees were highly respected for their commitment to keeping even its most minute commandment as interpreted by the rabbis.

What was Jesus talking about? A righteousness that exceeded that of men who were totally committed to doing the Law?

Jesus explained by providing a series of examples. Each example is introduced with the phrase, "You have heard that it was said," and then a statement of the Law *as understood by the rabbis.* Jesus then announced, "But I say to you," providing His own authoritative interpretation of the original law's intent. In each case, Christ shifted the focus from *behavior* to *intent.* He emphasized what a person *does* rather than what a person is like *inside.*

The law said, "Do not murder." Jesus pointed out that the anger and hostility which lead to murder are also sin (Matt. 5:21, 22). The law said, "Do not commit adultery." Jesus taught that this commandment was really addressed to the lust that moved a man to treat a woman as an object (Matt. 5:27, 28). In each of Jesus' illustrations, He showed that God's Law, while it defines wrong behavior, is actually addressed to the inward sin which corrupts and leads to the act.

The scribes might define right action, and the Pharisees might determine to act as the scribes prescribed. But God required a transformed and purified heart.

Only later, as the true meaning of Christ's mission to earth was revealed, did the implications of this early teaching of our Lord become clear. Christ would eventually die to pay for our sins and to win God's forgiveness for humankind. Then He would rise from the dead, offering to all who believe in Him the gift of a righteous standing with God and a transformed heart.

The teaching (*Matthew 5:44, 45*). Christ's words about prayer are contained in one of the illustrations Jesus used to make His point about the real meaning of law. He began with the usual formula, "You have heard that it was said," and continued, " '*You shall love your neighbor* and hate your enemy.' " The italicized part of the saying is in the Old Testament (Lev. 19:18). The second part—and hate your enemy—is *not* found in the Old Testament. This was an addition the rabbis thought of as implied.

Jesus went on. "But I say to you, love your enemies." The "neighbor" of the Old Testament is not to be understood as a "friend," but as anyone with whom we come in contact. Even enemies are neighbors. So God's intent in Leviticus 19:18 was that His people should love everyone, even enemies. Love for enemies calls us to return blessings for curses, good for hatred, and prayer for persecution!

Christ went on to explain further what God expects of His followers. He pointed out that our Father in heaven is good to those who hate Him. He sheds the warmth of His sun on the evil as well as the good. He waters the fields of the unjust with rain even as He waters the fields of the just. Our calling is to be like our Father in heaven. Believers are to bear a resemblance to our Father and to express it by praying for those who "spitefully use you and persecute you."

The life-changing impact. When I moved to Phoenix, we contracted with a landscaper to develop a desert backyard. He took several advance payments but failed to do the work. I discovered that he had lied about how these funds were used. I was angry and upset, and I felt "spitefully used."

But then God brought this passage of Scripture to mind. I shared with the family what the landscaper had done, and we prayed for this man who had showed himself to be an enemy. A few days later I confronted our landscaper with what I had learned, but I told him we would still work with him.

It turned out that this man had just been through a series of amazing experiences. His partner had stolen the company funds, his wife had thrown him out of the house, he had been fired from his other jobs, his truck had broken down, and he had broken an ankle trying to push it off the road. One day he turned the radio dial past a Christian station, heard a hymn from his childhood, and tried to sing along. No sound came from his mouth, and he decided God had given up on him.

That was about the time I confronted him, but I promised to work with him in spite of what he had done. He left the house thinking, "Maybe God hasn't given up on me after all." A few days later in a little church down the road, he accepted Christ as his Savior.

Jesus' teaching had led me to pray for an enemy, and God had used that prayer and a simple demonstration of love to bring our landscaper to repentance and faith. Jesus' teaching on love and prayer for enemies had softened my heart and opened another's heart to the gospel. Christ's teachings are life-shaping indeed!

PRAYER AND EVANGELISM

The harvest truly is plentiful, but the laborers are few. Therefore pray the Lord of the harvest to send out laborers into His harvest (Matt. 9:37, 38; cf. Luke 10:2).

The teachable moment (Matthew 9:31–36). Matthew 9 records a number of healings that Jesus performed for people who came to ask from Him what only God could do. It's not surprising to read that when those who were healed departed, "they spread the news about Him in all that country" (Matt. 9:31).

Jesus then threw Himself into His ministry. He "went about all the cities and villages" teaching, preaching, and healing (Matt. 9:35). Everywhere He went, great crowds gathered. As Christ and His disciples watched the multitudes milling about—so many wearied, so many uncertain in spite of the hope Jesus raised in their hearts—Christ was "moved with compassion" (Matt. 9:36). His disciples, standing beside Him, felt something of the emotion that moved Him, and they must have been moved themselves. It was another teachable moment.

The teaching (Matthew 9:37, 38). Looking around, Jesus saw needy people. He urged His

"Pray the Lord of the harvest to send out laborers."

disciples to pray that God would "send out laborers into His harvest." It is important to note several things in this passage.

First, compassion for the lost, "weary and scattered, like sheep having no shepherd," motivated this prayer.

Second, this was a prayer for harvesters. The image is familiar. Harvesters go into the fields to gather the ripe grain. In similar fashion, God's harvesters go to those whom the Holy Spirit has prepared with the gospel. God uses the gospel and the concern of believers to bring other persons to Himself.

Third, the very persons whom Jesus told to pray for harvesters—his disciples—*became the harvesters!* Those who are so moved by their compassion for people that they pray for them are likely to reach out to the objects of their prayers.

The life-changing impact. The fact that the disciples whom Jesus instructed to pray for harvesters became harvesters is significant. When we pray for others, God will often use us to reach them.

This principle provided the foundation for a unique prayer ministry that was begun in India. Indian Christians designate their homes as "neighborhood houses of prayer." They visit their neighbors, asking permission to pray for them and soliciting their prayer requests. During follow-up visits, they learn of answers to prayer and gather more prayer requests. As God answers Christians' prayers, the hearts of their neighbors are opened and the gospel is shared.

This prayer ministry has led to the conversion of more than one million people in India, and it has recently been launched in the United States (Neighborhood Houses of Prayer, P.O. Box 141312, Grand Rapids, MI 49514).

As Christians are moved by compassion to pray for the needs of their neighbors, we can expect hearts to be opened. We can also expect believers who have prayed for harvesters to become God's answer to their own prayers.

PRAYER AND FAITH

Then the disciples came to Jesus privately and said, "Why could we not cast it [a demon] out?" So Jesus said to them, "Because of your unbelief; for assuredly, I say to you, if you have faith as a mustard seed, you will say to this mountain, "Move from here to there" and it will move; and nothing will be impossible for you. However, this kind does not go out except by prayer and fasting (Matt. 17:19–21; cf. Mark 9:14–21; Luke 9:37–43).

The teachable moment (Matthew 17:14–21). Each of the three Gospel accounts places this incident immediately following Jesus' transfiguration. Christ had been accompanied to the top of a mountain by His disciples Peter, James, and John. When they arrived, Jesus was transfigured. Matthew tells us: "His face shone like the sun, and His clothes became as white as the light" (Matt. 17:2). On the mountain Jesus was joined by Moses and Elijah. As the awed disciples looked on, a voice from heaven announced, "This is My beloved Son" (Matt. 17:5).

Meanwhile, a different drama was being played out in the valley below. The other nine

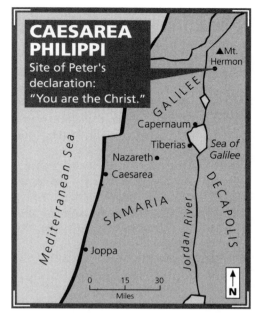

Many scholars believe that the Transfiguration occurred on Mount Hermon, the highest point near Caesarea Philippi.

disciples were approached by a distraught father, whose son was demon-possessed. The symptoms of his demonization were like those of epilepsy (Matt. 17:15), but the father had no doubts about the real cause. Mark 9 describes the real cause as a spirit, recording the father's report that "often he [the demon] has thrown him [the son] into the fire and into the water to destroy him" (Mark 9:22). The desperate father, hearing of Christ's powers, had come to Jesus for help. But since Jesus was not there, he turned to the disciples for help.

When Christ came down from the mountain, crowds gathered around the man and his son and Jesus' other nine disciples. The nine had tried to cast out the demon, but they had failed. And everyone had seen their failure.

The father reported the failure to Jesus, who told the father, "Bring him here to Me." Matthew reports that "Jesus rebuked the demon, and it came out of him; and the child was cured from that very hour" (Matt. 17:18).

As soon as the disciples had the chance, they asked Jesus privately, "Why could we not cast it out?"

To understand their question, we need to remember that Jesus had given His disciples "power over unclean spirits, to cast them out, and to heal all kinds of sickness and all kinds of disease" (Matt. 10:1). When the father brought his son to the disciples, each of them had successfully represented Jesus when sent out to preach, heal the sick, and cast out demons. So Jesus' disciples *expected* to cast out the demon easily. Yet they failed! No wonder they asked Jesus, "Why could we not cast it out?"

The teachable moment in this situation was created by the disciples' failure to accomplish something they fully expected they could do!

The teaching (Matthew 17:20, 21). Jesus' answer, and His teaching on prayer, has three parts.

"Because of your unbelief" (Matthew 17:20a). Earlier Jesus had observed the crowds that watched eagerly to see what would happen. He had expressed His disappointment in the people for being a "faithless and perverse generation." The word translated "faithless" is *apistos,* meaning "without faith." It is modified by *diestrammene,* "perverse." Jesus was disappointed in the failure of that generation to trust Him, in spite of the evidence of His miracles and His teachings.

It is important to note that a very different word is used in Matthew 17:20, where Christ told His disciples that they had no power over the demon because of unbelief. The Greek word translated "unbelief" is *oligopistia.* While the prefix *oligo* usually means "little," *oligopistia* is better rendered "flawed faith." There was a flaw in the disciples' faith which made them ineffective in exercising the authority Jesus had given them.

"If you have faith as a mustard seed" (Matthew 17:20). Jesus then went on to point out that the "quantity" of one's faith is not the issue. The mustard seed was the smallest of the seeds used in Jewish herb gardens. Using the familiar image of moving mountains—a common first-century simile for a difficult task—Jesus stated that nothing is impossible to a person who has the tiniest amount of unflawed faith.

It is important to note that *as yet* Jesus had said nothing about prayer. Jesus Himself had not prayed that the demon would leave; He had commanded the demon to go and it had obeyed. The disciples had not prayed that the demon would be cast out. They had acted on the assumption that because Jesus had given them power over evil spirits, they could just command the demon to leave—and he would! But when they had tried to cast it out, the demon hadn't moved!

When they asked why they had failed, Jesus explained that their faith was flawed. He did not say just how their faith was flawed, but they had apparently begun to believe they could cast out demons because of their past successes. They needed to come back to the truth that they should count on God to act through them.

"However, this kind does not go out except by prayer and fasting" (Matthew 17:21). Only now did Jesus mention prayer. Dealing with "this kind" of demon—one as powerful as the demon that possessed the child—requires prayer and fasting. The prayer and fasting were required not to cast out the demon, but to repair the disciples' flawed faith! Then they would be able to exercise the authority Jesus had given them!

(For an in-depth discussion of demon possession and this passage, see another book in this series, *Every Good and Evil Angel in the Bible,* Nelson, 1998).

With their faith restored by renewed concentration on God and by a deepened trust in Him, the disciples would again be able to cast out even the most powerful demons!

The life-changing impact. As we trace the experience of the apostles on into the book of Acts, we see an exciting transformation. The miracle-working powers of healing and exorcism that

PRAYER AND FASTING

"Fasting" was going without food as a spiritual discipline. Most fasts in biblical times lasted from sunrise to sunset. In Jesus' day, many Pharisees showed their religious zeal by fasting each Monday and Thursday (cf. Luke 18:12). Four typical reasons for fasting are suggested in the Old Testament.

(1) Fasts were undertaken to express the depths of a person's grief or mourning (1 Sam. 31:13). (2) Fasts were undertaken as part of the nation's or an individual's most urgent prayers to the Lord (2 Chron. 20:1–29; 2 Sam. 12:16–22). (3) Fasts were undertaken to show the sincerity of a person's repentance (1 Kings 21:27). (4) The only fast commanded in Scripture was for the Day of Atonement, and it was intended to underline the solemnity of the day (Lev. 16:29, 31).

The New Testament records Jesus' own 40-day fast in the wilderness just before being tempted by Satan (Matt. 4:1, 2; Luke 4:1–3).

When we take this evidence together, we see a common thread. A person who undertook a fast set aside the time to focus entirely on the Lord. While no command to fast appears in the epistles, fasts are mentioned as adjuncts to prayer or worship not only here (in Matt. 17:21; Mark 9:29) but also in Luke 2:37, Acts 13:2, and Acts 14:23.

Jesus gave to the Twelve began to function again! The disciples healed (Acts 3:6–9) and cast out demons as well (Acts 5:13–16).

This passage and what Jesus was teaching about prayer have frequently been misunderstood. Christ was not saying that demons are cast out by prayer or that mountains can be moved by a person who prays with enough faith. Just as Jesus cast out demons because of His authority over them, so exorcisms are performed in the power and authority of Jesus.

The role of prayer and fasting is to restore a flawed faith by concentrating on the Lord, so that we will be able to exercise the authority he has granted to us. Prayer and fasting as a means of purifying faith can make any Christian more effective in carrying out ministries for which he or she is gifted. The closer we are to the Lord, the more we rely on Him and the more effective any service we offer Him will be.

PRAYER AND WORSHIP

Then He taught, saying to them, "Is it not written, 'My house shall be called a house of prayer for all nations?' But you have made it a 'den of thieves'" (Mark 11:17; cf. Matt. 21:13; Luke 19:46; John 2:13–16).

The teachable moment. Jesus and His disciples had come to Jerusalem. One of their first priorities was a visit to the magnificent temple that dominated the city. From ancient times, the temple had been the focal point of Jewish worship. People from all over the world assembled each year for Judaism's three great religious festivals.

When Christ entered the temple grounds, He saw a familiar scene. Under the governance of the family of the high priest, crowds milled around the court of the Gentiles where business was conducted. Animals and doves certified "without blemish" were sold to worshipers for sacrifice. Shops owned by the high priest's family lined the aqueduct and intruded into the temple area. Money changers had set up tables where they exchanged foreign coins for Tyran drachmas, the only coins which the priests decreed acceptable for payment of the temple tax imposed on all male Jews. Exorbitant prices charged for this exchange were scandalous, amounting to exploitation of the poor.

The scene offended Jesus. The text tells us that He "began to drive out" the merchants and "overturned the tables of the money changers and the seats of those who sold doves" (Mark 11:15). They scattered before Christ's fury as the people looked on in amazement. Jesus' actions was a direct challenge to the high priest and the temple hierarchy which supervised the traders and shared the profits. Their reaction shows how furious

Jesus quoted Isaiah: "My house shall be called a house of prayer."

they were: When they heard what Jesus had done, they "sought how they might destroy him" (Mark 11:18).

When the merchants had been driven out of the temple courts, Jesus turned to His disciples and the amazed onlookers. Everyone waited eagerly to hear Jesus explain what He had done.

The teaching. Jesus' teaching consisted of quotes from two Old Testament prophets. Quoting from Isaiah 56, Jesus reminded His hearers that God had said, "My house shall be called a house of prayer for all nations." The Isaiah passage is messianic, providing a vision of God's purposes for humanity. Not only would the Jews who had been scattered throughout the nations be restored to the land; God would also bring "others besides" who would love and worship Him.

Isaiah's vision of the future is contrasted by Jesus with a description in Jeremiah 7 of a different situation. God's people "oppress the stranger, the fatherless, and the widow" (Jer. 7:6) and walk after other gods, and then dare to come to God's temple! What Israel had done was to turn the temple into a "den of thieves,"—a hiding place where robbers gathered to count their loot.

In blending these quotes, Jesus made a vital point. In Old Testament faith, the temple was the place where Israel approached God. But the attitude with which a person approached the temple was critical. What God intended to be a house of prayer for all could actually be turned into a den of thieves! Those who came to the temple expecting to find God's blessing might instead experience His judgment!

The life-changing impact. It is striking that the New Testament records two cleansings of the temple. John reports a cleansing that took place one Passover at the beginning of Jesus' public ministry (John 2:13–16). The other three Gospels report the second cleansing, which took place another Passover season, about three years later. Between these two incidents, Jesus had preached, taught, and performed His miracles. Yet nothing Jesus had done had changed the hearts of the religious leaders—still intent on worldly gain, still eager to make a profit from the poor who came to Jerusalem to worship the Lord.

Within a week of the second cleansing of the temple, Jesus was taken by those whose corrupt motives He exposed, and He was crucified. When He rose again, it was with the promise of inner cleansing for all who trusted Him as Savior.

The greed—the lack of concern for others that characterized the merchants in the temple courts—left no place for worship. Neither should these have any place in our lives. Jesus died that our hearts might become a temple— a house of prayer—dedicated to Him.

PRAYER AND THE PRETENSE

Woe to you, scribes and Pharisees, hypocrites! For you devour widows' houses, and for a pretense make long prayers. Therefore you will receive greater condemnation (Matt. 23:14; cf. Mark 12:40).

The teachable moment. In Matthew 23 Jesus spoke directly to the scribes and Pharisees. In Mark 12 He spoke about them to onlookers. In each Gospel the same sequence of events led up to the denunciation.

It was near the end of Christ's ministry, and the religious leaders were attempting to discredit Jesus. One group tried to trap Jesus with a question about taxes. If He told the people to pay taxes to the hated Romans, He would lose popular support. If He told the people not to pay taxes, they could report His sedition to the Roman governor.

Jesus avoided this trap (Matt. 22:15–22), but He was then asked a trick question by the Sadducees. The question was a challenge to Jesus as a master of God's law. But Christ answered in a way that showed His opponents did not understand either the Scriptures or the power of God (Matt. 22: 23–33).

Then the Pharisees took their turn. One of their experts in Scripture [a "lawyer"] asked Jesus to identify the "great commandment in the law." As a challenge, the question was weak, for the rabbis of Jesus' day had often discussed ways to summarize or prioritize Old Testament laws.

Christ's answer—that the command to love God was greatest and to love one's neighbor was the second greatest—was not a surprise (Matt. 22:34–40). Luke, in reporting a similar incident, portrays Jesus turning the same question back on a challenger, who gave the same answer that Jesus did in this passage (Luke 10:25–28).

In conjunction, the two passages show that the religious leaders, like Jesus, were aware of the importance of loving God! This awareness was at the base of the charges that Jesus was about to lodge against the leaders who sought to show Him up before the people.

But first Jesus challenged His challengers. The rabbis claimed that they alone "sat in Moses seat" as authoritative interpreters of God's Word. So Jesus posed a question concerning the Messiah. The only possible answer to this question was that this descendant of David must be divine (Matt. 22:41–45). Not one of Jesus' opponents would even attempt to answer. Christ had passed every test the religious leaders had applied, while they had failed His.

Then Jesus condemned the people whom all respected as spiritual leaders. In a series of devastating charges, Jesus stripped away the layers of pretense, revealing how far short of loving God and neighbors these men came.

Their motivation was not to please God, but "all their works they do to be seen by men" (Matt. 23:5). What they really loved was "the best places at feasts, the best seats in the synagogues, greetings in the marketplaces, and to be called by men, 'Rabbi, Rabbi' " (Matt. 23:6, 7).

Some Pharisees were sincere, and a number were later converted and became members of the early church. But the movement itself was flawed because of its emphasis on works as a means of pleasing God.

The teaching *(Matthew 23:14)*. This pronouncement of woe ["doom"] on the scribes is one in a series of condemnations of their hypocrisy. While in private the Pharisees were busy devouring [foreclosing on] widows' houses, they at the same time stood on street corners "and for a pretense make long prayers."

"For a pretense." The public prayers of the Pharisees were not offered to God but were directed toward influencing public opinion. The Pharisees were not focused on praising God or even on seeking His blessing. Instead, they were intent on building their reputation for piety.

The Pharisees succeeded in reaching this goal. The first-century historian Josephus described the Pharisees as "extremely influential among the townsfolk; and all prayers and sacred rites of divine worship are performed according to their exposition. This is the great tribute that the inhabitants of the cities, by practicing the highest ideals both in their way of living and in their discourses, have paid to the excellence of the Pharisees" (*Antiquities,* 18:15).

Private morality and prayer. But Jesus' criticism of the Pharisees went still deeper. Their motives were wrong. But even worse, in private they foreclosed on "widow's houses." Rather than showing compassion for the needy, many of the Pharisees exploited and profited from them. Centuries before, God through the prophet Micah had cried,

Rather than demonstrating true religious leadership, some Pharisees might be seen foreclosing on the house of a poor widow.

He has shown you, O man,
    what is good;
And what does the LORD
    require of you
But to do justly,
To love mercy,
And to walk humbly with your
    God? (Mic. 6:8).

The Pharisees of Jesus' time were intent on walking proudly among their fellow Jews, while loving money, not mercy.

The life-changing impact. Nothing Christ said or did changed the opinions of the religious leaders who opposed Him. They would not submit to the Son of God. But for those of us who do love and honor Jesus, what Christ said to the Pharisees has life-changing import. What Jesus said on that occasion reminds us that our first priority is to love God and our second priority is to love others. If we love God, our prayers will be shaped by our desire to praise and please Him. Our greatest desire will be to have God think well of us, not to have others consider us pious.

If we love others, we will neither exploit nor oppress them. Our private morality will be shaped by a love of mercy, not money. We will have no need for pretense, for our love for God will overflow in love for others.

This is what happened in the early church. When love for God and for others shaped its fellowship, God's people were powerful in prayer (see Acts 4:31; 4:32–35).

PRAYER AND HISTORY'S END

And pray that your flight may not be in winter or on the Sabbath (Matt. 24:20; cf. Mark 13:18).

Take heed, watch and pray; for you do not know when the time is (Mark 13:33; cf. Luke 21:36; Matt. 24:36–44).

The teachable moment. Each of the three synoptic Gospels contains an account of Jesus' teaching about the future. Each locates Christ's discourse on history's end in the last week of His life on earth. Matthew gives the most complete account.

Jesus was leaving the temple with His disciples after a devastating attack on the religious leaders (see Matt. 23). He had ended that attack with a warning. Punishment due past generations who had rejected and killed God's messengers was about to strike Jerusalem. The disciples had apparently been unmoved by Jesus' accusations. As they left, the disciples, like tourists, pointed out the wonders of the temple complex. Jesus brought them up short, telling them plainly that soon "not one stone shall be left here upon another, that shall not be thrown down" (Matt. 24:2).

This prediction shook the disciples, and they began to question Jesus. When would the temple be razed? What sign would mark Jesus' coming (to rule)? And, when would the world end? Jesus did not answer their first question. Within four decades, all would know the answer to that, for in A.D. 70 the Romans under Titus burned Jerusalem and tore the temple buildings down.

But Jesus did speak of history's end and events leading up to it. In this context, Jesus made His first remark about prayer. When those living saw the signs that marked the end, they were to flee Jerusalem. And they were to pray that conditions would be right for the speediest of departures!

While students of prophecy debate the meaning of Jesus' vision of history's end, they do not debate Christ's warning to believers looking ahead to that grand event. While God's plan for bringing history to an end has been made, we do not know *when* the end will come. "Therefore," Jesus concluded, "Watch . . . you do not know what hour your Lord is coming" (Matt. 24:42). Other Gospel writers add "and pray" to Christ's instructions.

The teaching (Mark 13:33). What Jesus said was, "Take heed, watch and pray; for you do not know when the time is." Each phrase is significant.

"Take heed." The phrase means "be on guard!" It is easy while waiting for Jesus to return to let our attention drift and to focus on the cares of this world.

"Watch." The second exhortation echoes the first. We are to "be vigilant." This call to remain alert is reflected throughout the passage, reflecting the fact that no one knows

- that day or hour (v. 32),
- the critical moment (v. 33), or
- when the lord of the household comes (v. 35).

This is not a call for vigilance at the time Christ returns, but for vigilance during the years and decades of waiting.

"And pray." Some manuscripts lack the phrase "and pray," which is found in Mark. But there is no doubt that prayer is included in Luke's account of this teaching. Certainly prayers are essential for those who await Christ's return.

In Matthew's longer version, Jesus' teaching on history's end is followed by an even more lengthy series of stories and warnings, each of which repeats the theme of actively looking for the Savior's return.

The story of the servant left in charge of an absent ruler's household emphasizes the importance of carrying out his duties toward his fellow servants rather than exploiting them. The story of ten virgins waiting for a bridegroom to arrive emphasizes the need to make sure each always has a full supply of oil for the lamps. The story of the talents emphasizes the fact that those left in charge of the master's resources are to use them for his benefit during the interim.

Why then do Mark and Luke, when relating Christ's urging that we "watch," include prayer?

The answer is that we are to guard against being distracted from our service to God by the things of this world. We must keep our focus on God and His kingdom. And it is prayer, daily communion with the Lord, which will keep our attention focused on Him.

The life-changing impact. Human beings are not particularly good at waiting. Especially today, when TV dramas imply that every conflict can be resolved and every goal reached in thirty minutes or an hour, waiting is hard for us. The longer gratification is delayed, the more likely we are to turn away and fix our hopes on something we can have now. And there are so many worldly things that are attractive to us.

We need to keep our focus on God and the hope of what Christ brings to us at His return. And the best way to keep our focus on God is to pray.

PRAYER AND WEAKNESS

Watch and pray, lest you enter into temptation. The spirit indeed is willing, but the flesh is weak (Matt. 26:41; cf. Mark 14:32–42; Luke 22:40, 46).

The teachable moment (Matthew 26:1–46). It was the last night before the Crucifixion. Jesus had shared an emotional Passover meal with His disciples, and it was filled with teaching.

Afterward they left Jerusalem. They wound their way down into the valley that separated Jerusalem from a familiar hillside where there was an olive grove—Gethsemane. Jesus told His disciples to sit down and wait while He went on a little way to pray.

Peter, James, and John walked on a little further with Him. They could see that Jesus was upset and distressed. Jesus shared with these dear friends how sorrowful He felt, and He asked them to wait and hold vigil with Him. Luke notes that even before Christ went on alone, He urged His disciples to "pray that you will not fall into temptation." (Luke 22:40). Then Christ went on a little further while the three waited. They had sensed Jesus' pain, and they really were concerned. But they were tired. Rather than pray, they sat down to wait. And all three dozed off.

After praying for a time, Jesus returned and found the three sleeping. His disappointment is reflected in His words: "What? Could you not watch with Me one hour?"

Jesus again encouraged them in the words of our key verse: "Watch and pray, lest you enter into temptation. The spirit indeed is willing, but the flesh is weak." Yet when Jesus left them to pray again, the three sat down and promptly fell asleep.

The teaching (Matthew 26:41). Jesus' exhortation to watch and pray was accompanied by a warning that has implications beyond the immediate situation. As we examine the passage, we note several important things.

The disciples were insensitive to a critical moment. Everything that happened that night should have alerted the disciples that a critical moment had arrived. They had sensed Jesus' own intensity and, as they drew near Gethesemane, they saw that He was disturbed and sorrowful. Yet somehow they did not respond to Christ's emotions; they failed to obey His instruction to watch and pray.

The disciples failed to follow Jesus' instructions. In biblical times, the normal position for prayer was standing. In times of extreme urgency, a

Peter, James, and John were with Jesus in Gethsemane, but during their Lord's time of crisis they fell asleep.

person might fall on his face to pray before the Lord, but normally one stood (Luke 18:11–13), often with raised hands (1 Tim. 2:8). If the disciples had obeyed Christ's instructions to pray, they would have remained standing rather than sitting on the ground.

The disciples did care about Jesus and His needs. In stating that "the spirit is willing," Jesus reminds us not to condemn the disciples' motives. It would be easy to judge the three as insensitive, uncaring persons.

We might wonder, "How could they possibly sleep while Jesus experienced the anguish He felt that night?" And we might conclude, "These men just didn't *care.*"

But Christ's words, "The spirit is willing," protects the three from this charge. The disciples did care about Jesus. They didn't fail Jesus that night because they didn't care.

The disciples were subject to natural human weaknesses. In the New Testament epistles, the phrase "the flesh" is often used in a theological sense to identify humankind's sin nature. But Jesus used the phrase here in a very different sense. By "the flesh," Jesus underscored the truth that people are "human." We are limited,

imperfect, and weak. There is so much we want to be and do but often we are thwarted by our own inadequacies.

The disciples wanted to be supportive of Jesus. But they were tired. Instead of being there for Jesus in His most painful hour—instead of remaining standing to pray—they sat down. And they fell asleep. Their motives were good, but their flesh was weak.

Tests vs. temptations. Jesus urged His disciples to watch and pray "lest you enter into temptation." Again the word translated "temptation" may also be rendered "test." Here, however, we sense that what was intended as a test became a temptation because "the flesh is weak." Jesus had shared His emotions and touched the disciples' hearts. Jesus had also instructed the three to "watch and pray." Even though the disciples cared about Jesus, they had disregarded His instructions, had sat on the ground, and had fallen asleep. The test had become a temptation and the disciples had succumbed.

The disciples' prayer mission. It is fascinating that Jesus did not ask the three to pray for Him. They were to pray for *themselves,* "that you do not enter into temptation." What was at issue was their own weakness and their need for God's help.

The life-changing impact of Jesus' teaching. This experience was immediately followed by another which illustrates the terrible reality underlying Jesus' instructions to the disciples. As the disciples left the upper room, Peter had vowed undying loyalty to Jesus. Yet as Jesus had told Peter he would, before that night was over, Peter had denied Jesus three times. Truly our human nature is weak. Only when we accept our weakness and rely on the Lord completely can we expect triumph in testing and victory over temptation.

Jesus' command to watch and pray reminds us first of all that obedience is vital if we are to overcome our human weaknesses. If the three disciples had obeyed Jesus and remained standing, they would not have fallen asleep. If they had prayed as Jesus told them, they might have responded differently to the events that followed. We must also obey Jesus if we are not to fall victim to our own weaknesses. We too must "pray, lest you enter into temptation."

These words express a truth that applies to all believers. In prayer we turn our eyes away from ourselves and our situation to focus our attention on the Lord. We acknowl-

edge our dependence and call on Him for strength. Through prayer we not only strengthen our willing spirits; we also open our lives to the Holy Spirit of power.

A familiar Old Testament passage contains a promise that combines awareness of the weakness of the flesh and states the promise implied in the words "watch and pray."

> He gives power to the weak,
> And to those who have no
>   might He increases strength.
> Even the youths shall faint and
>   be weary,
> And the young men shall
>   utterly fall,
> But those who wait on the
>   LORD
> Shall renew their strength;
> They shall mount up with
>   wings like eagles,
> They shall run and not be
>   weary,
> They shall walk and not faint (Isa.
>   40:29–31).

Today we need to watch and pray lest we enter into temptation. As we rely on the Lord, He will provide the strength we need to run and not be weary, to walk and not faint.

JESUS' PRAYER PROMISES

MATTHEW—JOHN

I've been fascinated by books that give all sorts of reasons why God will *not* answer prayer. Lists of obstacles to answered prayer are drawn from Old and New Testaments, and the writers explain what we must do for God to be able to hear us.

For instance, "If I regard iniquity in my heart, the LORD will not hear" (Ps. 66:18). This verse is usually interpreted in the obstacle books to mean, "If you have *any sin* in your life, forget it. God won't hear *you!*"

Another favored verse is, "Whatever things you ask when you pray, believe that you receive them, and you will have them" (Mark 11:24). Most "obstacles" books turn this promise into a threat. "You better believe—*really* believe—when you pray, or God won't give you *anything*."

These books tend to turn praying into a sort of "spiritual obstacle course." They convey the impression that God is sitting back with a checklist. If you don't get over every hurdle, He has a great excuse for not hearing you. You can almost hear the heavenly calculator clicking.

"OK, no iniquity in the heart."
Check. "Hmmm. Believing. No, she's not believing hard enough. That's only five out of seven. Guess I can't answer that prayer."

What bothers me is that the "obstacles to answered prayer" books make it seem that everything depends on us. If we do all the right things, God simply has to do what we ask. Under this philosophy, prayer is not an outgrowth of the relationship of a child to his or her heavenly Father.

Prayer as an obstacle course drains prayer of its essence, demeans God's love and grace, and makes answers to prayer dependent on our performance. In prayer as an obstacle course, there's no room for a loving Father's response to a child who appeals to Him.

Now, it is true that there are things that interrupt our fellowship with the Lord and are inconsistent with prayer. And we need to be aware of them. But we are not to see them as conditions which, if met, guarantee that God will answer prayer in just the way we expect or desire.

HINDRANCES TO ANSWERED PRAYER

Old Testament passages do indicate that God may refuse to hear prayer. If we skim the Old Testament, we find a number of verses that convey a similar message.

You will cry out in that day because of your king whom you have chosen for yourselves, and the LORD will not hear you in that day (1 Sam. 8:18).

The eyes of the LORD are on the righteous, and His ears are open to their cry. The face of the LORD is against those who do evil (Ps. 34:15, 16).

If I regard iniquity in my heart, the LORD will not hear (Ps. 66:18).

> Then they will call on me,
>   but I will not answer;
> They will seek me diligently,
>   but they will not find me.
> Because they hated knowledge
> And did not choose the fear
>   of the LORD.
> They would have none of my
>   counsel
> And despised my every rebuke.
> Therefore they shall eat the
>   fruit of their own way,
> And be filled to the full with
>   their own fancies
>   (Prov. 1:28–31).

> When you spread out your hands,
>   I will hide My eyes from you;
> Even though you make many
>   prayers,
>   I will not hear.
> Your hands are full of blood
>   (Isa. 1:15).

> But your iniquities have
>   separated you from your God;
> And your sins have hidden His
>   face from you,
> So that He will not hear (Isa. 59:2).

"They have turned back to the iniquities of their forefathers who refused to hear My words, and they have gone after other gods to serve them; the house of Israel and the house of Judah have broken My covenant which I made with their fathers." Therefore thus says the LORD: "Behold, I will surely bring calamity on them which they will not be able to escape; and though they cry out to Me, I will not listen to them" (Jer. 11:10, 11).

"When they fast, I will not hear their cry; and when they offer burnt offering and grain offering, I will not accept them. But I will consume them by the sword, by the famine, and by the pestilence" (Jer. 14:12).

Then they will cry to the LORD, but He will not hear them; He will even hide His face from them at that time, because they have been evil in their deeds (Mic. 3:4).

These Old Testament passages refer to the rebellious and wicked. Glancing back over these verses and examining the context of each, it's clear that each describes God's response to what is essentially the same behavior. A generation of God's covenant people had persisted in rebelling against Him.

The people of Samuel's time insisted on a human king and rejected the direct rule of God. God gave them a king, but warned them that when they complained about their king, He would not listen.

Psalm 34 promises that God will hear the cry [prayer] of "the righteous." That phrase is equivalent in this psalm to "the believer," while "those who do evil" are those who refuse to submit to God. Similarly, the person who "regards iniquity" is not one who sins in spite of his commitment to the Lord, but a person who *chooses* iniquity as a way of life.

This is especially clear in Proverbs 1:28–31. The wisdom writer was describing a person who had refused to respect God and who had shown it by "having none of" God's word. God would not intervene to protect such persons from the consequences of their choices.

Isaiah was very clear in warning the people of his day. God would not listen because "your hands are full of blood" (Isa. 1:15) and as a result "your iniquities have separated you from your God" (Isa. 59:2). A people committed to sinful ways have no claim on God's attention. Micah, a contemporary of Isaiah, echoed the great prophet's point. A people who have been "evil in their deeds" have no right to expect God to hear them.

All the prophets' warnings failed to move God's people. Despite infrequent revivals in Judah, that nation's people again and again turned their back on the Lord. They worshiped pagan deities and violated God's laws concerning personal and social morality. As Babylonian forces assembled to crush Judah, Jeremiah made it clear that they could expect no help from God. Judgment was unavoidable.

Identifying the rebellious and wicked whom God will not hear. It's important to understand such passages in the context of the Old Testament. That context is defined by covenants that God made first with Abraham, and then extended to Israel.

God made a number of promises to Abraham which are recorded in Genesis 12:1–3 and Genesis 7. These are restated in Genesis 15 and 17. These promises were eschatological in nature. They looked forward to history's end, when everything God told Abraham He would do would be fulfilled in every detail.

Centuries later God provided clear instructions to Israel in the Mosaic covenant, also called the Law covenant. The spiritual heart of the Law is complete love and loyalty to the Lord, while the moral heart of the Law is the practice of love and loyalty to one's neighbor (see Lev. 19:3–4, 18).

In calling Israel to a holy lifestyle, the Law covenant featured two sets of promises. God promised that if a given generation of Israelites would honor His commandments, thus showing love and loyalty to Him and to each other, that generation would experience many of the blessings intended for history's end!

But God also promised that if a generation of Israelites refused to honor His commandments, thus rebelling against God's call to love and loyalty, God would discipline that generation. Rather than enjoying promised blessings, these rebellious generations would experience famine and poverty and their land would be overrun by foreign enemies.

These promises of blessings for obedience and punishment for disobedience were made to the whole people. They were *national* promises. And the Old Testament passages quoted above are also national. When God's people rebelled against Him and refused to follow His guidelines, judgment could not be avoided. These were times when prayer would not be heard.

As we trace the history of Judah's existence as a nation, we do read of infrequent revivals. Even after turning to pagan gods and violating God's laws, when a godly king like Hezekiah or Josiah led a religious revival, God would respond to His people's prayers. God continually showed Himself to be gracious. But finally in both the Northern Kingdom and the Southern Kingdom, judgment could not be avoided. The people *refused* to respond to the prophets whom God sent to call them back to Him.

In the context of Old Testament history, the rebellious and the wicked whose prayers God would not hear were unrepentant generations of Israelites. And God's refusal to hear prayer was national rather than personal.

Personal implications of God's refusal to hear His people's prayers. We must interpret the passages quoted above as pronouncements against the nation. At the same time, we must admit individual and personal application. God is under no obligation to hear the prayers of any person who rejects Him or who refuses to follow His will.

Iniquities will still separate individuals from God. The person who neither trusts God nor intends to obey Him has no standing with God. Only repentance and a saving faith in Christ can bring such a person into a personal relationship with the Lord. This gives that person the standing with God that guarantees his or her prayers will be heard and answered.

While God in grace may answer the prayers of unbelievers at times, there is no guarantee that He will hear the prayers of the unsaved. The Old Testament passages quoted above suggest that God *will not* respond to the prayers of a person who is intentionally hostile to Him or who rebels against the gospel.

We can say with confidence that Jesus' prayer promises were given to believers only. And we should take to heart the truth that the habitual practice of sin leads to God's judgment—not answers to prayer.

JESUS' PROMISES TO BELIEVERS IN FELLOWSHIP WITH HIM

The Old Testament's stern announcements that God would no longer hear His people's prayers was based on His own rejection by a generation of His covenant people. When sin separated Israel and God, the privilege of access to God was revoked. Understanding this context is vital if we are to assess obstacles to answered prayer correctly.

We also need to understand the context of New Testament prayer promises. These promises are made to people who have a personal relationship with God, and who live in fellowship with Christ.

THE NEW TESTAMENT CONTEXT OF PRAYER PROMISES

Both the Old Testament and the New Testament portray human beings as sinners alienated from God. Both testaments describe God as taking the initiative to rescue members of our fallen race. The New Testament is the story of Jesus who, although God the Son, became a human being to die for our sins and provide forgiveness to all believers.

While the Old Testament focuses on the relationship of the nation to God, the New Testament emphasizes the relationship of individuals to the Lord. Old Testament verses that describe withholding answers to prayer are national in character, and New Testament verses dealing with prayer tend to be individual. The individual who trusts Christ as Savior has a personal relationship with God as Father. Prayer promises are generally made not to the church as a whole, but to individual believers.

As we examine Jesus' prayer promises, it is important to keep this distinction in mind.

Continuous connection—like a branch to a vine—is the key to spiritual growth and blessing.

We need to remember that prayer promises are made *to people who have a personal relationship with God through Christ, and who remain in fellowship with the Lord.*

Nowhere is this principle stated more clearly than in John 15, where Jesus likened His relationship with believers to that of a vine with its branches. As Christ developed this analogy, He emphasized the need for the branches to "abide in" the vine. The Greek verb for "abide," *meno,* means to remain in—to maintain an intimate connection with—the vine. Jesus made it clear that only a believer who lives an obedient life has the intimate connection with Him that makes fruitfulness possible—and that guarantees answers to prayer. Note how these themes are developed.

Abide in Me, and I in you. As the branch cannot bear fruit of itself, unless it abides in the vine, neither can you, unless you abide in Me. I am the vine, you are the branches. He who abides in Me, and I in him, bears much fruit, for without Me you can do nothing.

If you abide in Me, and My words abide in you, you will ask what you desire, and it shall be done for you.

As the Father loved Me, I also have loved you; abide in My love. If you keep My commandments, you will abide in My love, just as I have kept My Father's commandments and abide in His love (John 15:4–5, 7, 9–10).

When we read any prayer promise made by Jesus, we want to keep in mind that Christ Himself defined a specific relational context here in John 15. Jesus' prayer promises assume that the person or persons who are given the promise have a personal relationship with God through faith in Him. And these prayer promises can be claimed only by those who are living in a responsive, obedient relationship with Jesus Christ.

Only when we define as Jesus did the relational context of New Testament prayer promises can we understand what Jesus is saying to us today.

EVERYONE WHO ASKS, SEEKS, AND KNOCKS—RECEIVES

Ask, and it will be given to you; seek, and you will find; knock, and it will be opened to you. For everyone who asks receives, and he who seeks finds, and to him who knocks it will be opened.

Or what man is there among you who, if his son asks for bread, will give him a stone? Or if he asks for a fish, will he give him a serpent?

If you then, being evil, know how to give good gifts to your children, how much more will your Father who is in heaven give good things to those who ask Him! (Matt. 7:7–11; cf. Luke 11:9–13).

These verses are found in Christ's Sermon on the Mount. There are a number of implications that may be drawn from the location of this promise within the Sermon on the Mount.

The sermon is a description of God's kingdom (Matthew 5—7). In the Sermon on the Mount, Jesus emphasized the kingdom and glory of God. Christ explored the attitudes to be adopted by those who live as citizens of His kingdom (Matt. 5:3–12), the righteousness that characterizes these citizens (Matt. 5:13–48), and the personal "in-secret" relationship with God which they maintain (Matt. 6:1–34). The citizens Jesus describes are persons who "seek first the kingdom of God and His righteousness" (Matt. 6:33).

Clearly, the prayers of such persons will not be selfish, but they will be directed toward God's purpose. It is not at all unlikely that the "good gifts" which kingdom citizens ask for, seek, and knock to obtain are the very qualities that a relationship with Jesus makes possible for them.

Note that a variation of this illustration, given at a different time and place, confirms this interpretation. At another time, Jesus concluded His teaching with these words: "How much more will your heavenly Father give the Holy Spirit to those who ask Him" (Luke 11:13). How does this ending confirm our interpretation? The Holy Spirit is One whom Christ has given to us. His mission is to produce in us the attitudes, righteousness, and love for God and others which Jesus spoke about!

Thus, the context of the promise (the Sermon on the Mount) does limit and define the promise. And the context protects us from the unwarranted assumption that God guarantees an answer to every one of our prayers, whether selfish or unselfish.

The gifts offered are for "everyone" who asks, seeks, and knocks (Matthew 7:8). The context also defines the "everyone" to whom the promise is addressed. This is not a promise given to those who reject Christ's lordship, or who set their hearts on "all these things the Gentiles seek" (Matt. 6:32). The "everyone" Jesus has in mind is everyone who asks for, seeks, and knocks to obtain the precious gifts which kingdom citizenship offers to Jesus' followers.

This is a truly precious promise. A person may be persistent in his attempts to gain worldly wealth, but continue to live in poverty. But any person who persistently begs God for the kind of gifts He offers to kingdom citizens will surely receive!

The promise is guaranteed by God's fatherly love *(Matthew 7:9–11)*. In His earlier teaching on prayer in Matthew 6, Jesus made a point of telling His listeners to address God as "Father." Thus, the context presupposes a personal relationship between the person praying and God as Father—a personal relationship which can be established only through faith in Christ.

It would be wrong to assume that a believer's prayers are answered simply because of his persistence. Jesus' illustration of a human father who gives good rather than harmful gifts to his children reminds us that our prayers are answered because God has a fatherly concern for our well-being.

Jesus' illustration develops two points. First, parents do love their children and respond to their requests. As God is our Father, we can count on Him to respond when we ask, seek, and knock.

But second, Jesus portrays human beings as "evil." This word not only implies that human parents are sinful and may even abuse their children, but also that human parents are limited. Earthly parents may give gifts which are not in a child's best interest. In contrast, God—who is pure goodness—will give only good gifts to believers.

The illustration and the truths it rests upon reinforce our conviction that context imposes limitations on this promise. God answers the prayers of kingdom citizens—His children—when we ask for kingdom qualities. God is not in the business of answering selfish prayers. God realizes that we might be harmed if we were given our selfish desires.

God is too much a Father—and much too good—to provide anything that would harm us, no matter how urgently we might ask, seek, and knock.

THE PROMISE TO TWO OR THREE GATHERED IN JESUS' NAME

Again I say to you that if two of you agree on earth concerning anything that they ask, it will be done for them by My Father in heaven. For where two or

"If you then, being evil, know how to give good gifts to your children, how much more will your Father who is in heaven give good things to those who ask Him!"

three are gathered together in My name, I am there in the midst of them (Matt. 18:19, 20).

These verses are commonly taken as a promise that when a few Christians "agree" on any request, God commits Himself to answer their prayer. The problem is that this understanding of these verses is incorrect.

Again, context helps us define what Jesus is teaching. And a study of these verses in context leads us to a very different interpretation.

The judicial setting of the promise *(Matthew 18:15–20)*. The verses in question follow Jesus' explanation of a process that believers are to follow to settle interpersonal disputes. What should we do if a brother sins against us? We are to go to Him alone (Matt. 18:15). If he refuses to hear us, we are to take others and go back to him again and try to be reconciled (Matt. 18:16). If he still refuses to listen, we are to bring the matter to the church (Matt. 18:17). But what if such a person still refuses to work toward a resolution? Jesus taught that he is to be treated "like a heathen and a tax collector" (cut off from fellowship in the believing community).

Immediately after Jesus outlined this judicial process, He said, "Assuredly, I say to you, whatever you bind on earth will be bound in heaven, and whatever you loose on earth will be loosed in heaven" (Matt. 18:18).

This puzzling statement is best understood when we note that *"you* bind" and *"you* loose" are plural. It is community action that "binds" or "looses" the believer being disciplined. When the process is followed as Jesus taught, the joint action of the church will be confirmed in heaven. In following this judicial process for resolving conflicts in the church, believers will be doing heaven's will, and the outcome of following the process will be guided and confirmed by God Himself.

In essence, then, the promise in verse 18 is a commitment by God that He will be personally involved as we seek to resolve conflicts Jesus' way! The goal of church discipline is never punishment but the restoration of the sinning believer to fellowship with God and the local community (see 2 Cor. 2:5–8; 1 Cor. 5:1–5).

The link between Matthew 18:15–18 and 18:19–20. There are two reasons why Matthew 18:19–20 has been taken as a prayer promise. The first reason is that interpreters have assumed that there is no link between these verses and Jesus' outlining of the judicial process in verses 15–18. The second reason is that the Greek verb *aiteisthai* can mean "asking in prayer." Fixing on this frequent meaning of *aiteisthai*, commentators have assumed that Jesus introduced another subject in verses 19–20. But there are several reasons not to jump to this conclusion.

"Again I say to you" (v. 19). This phrase clearly indicates that a connection *does* exist between verses 15–18 and 19–20. Not only does the phrase make an immediate connection; it even helps to define that connection. Christ promised in verse 18 that God would be involved in the judicial process intended to bring reconciliation. The "again" points up the fact that Jesus is *further explaining* the promise He had just made!

The judicial meaning of aiteisthai *(Matthew 18:19).* While *aiteisthai* can mean "asking in prayer," this word is also used in judicial settings. In a legal judicial setting, the term has the sense of "pursuing a claim." In Matthew 18, Jesus urged individuals to seek resolution of conflicts, first individually, and as a last resort bringing the church into the process. Verse 18 describes what happens if one person in the dispute will not agree to work toward resolution. Matthew 18:19–20 describes what will happen if both parties to the dispute decide to pursue their claim before the church.

The promise of Christ's active participation in the judicial process (Matthew 18:19, 20). Our conviction that Matthew 18:19–20 is not a prayer promise at all is confirmed by its perfect "fit" with the conflict-resolution theme of the preceding verses.

Verses 19 and 20 promise God's involvement in the process if the two should agree to submit to a resolution of the conflict to be worked out by the church! As background, we look again to 1 Corinthians and Paul's demand that when one believer has a matter against another, they are to submit the dispute to Christians rather than go before secular law courts (1 Cor. 6:1–6). Jesus promised that when disputants (the "two of you") "agree on earth" to submit their case to a church court, God will see to it that the problem *will be* resolved. "It will be done for them by My Father in heaven" (Matt. 18:19).

Jesus then explained in Matthew 18:20 *why* the situation will be resolved. Whenever two or three (asked by the church to serve as judges to suggest a solution) gather in Christ's name, Jesus is with the judges. He will provide the wisdom needed to reach an appropriate solution!

The promise in Matthew 18:19–20 is a precious promise indeed. But it is *not* a promise guaranteeing an answer to group prayer.

THE EFFICACY OF BELIEVING PRAYER

"Assuredly, I say to you, if you have faith and do not doubt, you will not only do what was done to the fig tree, but also if you say to this mountain, 'Be removed and be cast into the sea,' it will be done. And whatever things you ask in prayer, believing, you will receive" (Matt. 21:21–22; cf. Mark 11:24).

Jesus' promise that "whatever things you ask in prayer, believing," is often transformed into an obstacle. But it is actually an encouragement. At first glance, the obstacle view seems reasonable. After all, in speaking of the withered fig tree, Jesus did say, "If you have faith and do not doubt." Doubt, then, must be an obstacle that hinders answers to our prayers. Or did Jesus really mean to make us wonder if we have enough faith to have our prayers answered?

To understand the passage, we must again look at the context in which Jesus spoke.

The significance of the withered fig tree *(Matthew 21:18–22).* This event happened during the last days of Jesus' life on earth. He and His disciples came to Jerusalem to celebrate the Passover. Christ drove money changers and merchants from the temple (Matt. 21:12–13). Jesus was confronted by the religious leaders of His people (Matt. 21:23–45). Just before His arrest and trial, Christ condemned the leaders who plotted to have Him killed because of their hypocrisy (Matt. 23).

During the Passover celebration, the population of Jerusalem doubled or tripled, as people from all over the Mediterranean world flocked to the temple. It was Jesus' practice during the three annual religious festivals at which all Jews were to appear to stay with friends at Bethany, two miles east of Jerusalem. Matthew describes what happened on one particular morning as Jesus and His disciples walked from Bethany to Jerusalem.

He was hungry. And seeing a fig tree by the road, He came to it and found nothing on it but leaves, and said to it, "Let no fruit grow on you ever again." (Matt. 21:18, 19a).

The text says that "immediately the fig tree withered away" (21:19b). Mark's account differs slightly. Jesus cursed the fig tree one morning, and by the next morning it had withered away. The two accounts are not necessarily in conflict. The Greek word *parachrama,* "immediately," may also be translated "soon" or "presently." While Mark separates the cursing and withering by a day, Matthew may well have chosen to combine curse and fulfillment in order to keep the link between them absolutely clear. In no other detail do the descriptions vary.

But what was the significance of this miracle? Interpreters agree that the event was symbolic. A fig tree in full leaf would normally carry ripe figs. In a sense, the tree was a hypocrite, pretending to offer sustenance, but in fact barren and empty. In a similar way, the scribes, chief priests, and Pharisees promised a way to God, but in fact their approach to religion left people disappointed and empty. Jesus condemned them as hypocrites, or pretenders (see Matt. 23).

However, the significance of the withered fig tree is not the central issue here. What is central is the relationship of Christ's response to the amazement of the disciples, and the response to Christ's prayer promise.

Christ's response to the awe of the disciples *(Matthew 21:21).* Christ had cursed the fig tree and it "immediately" withered away. The disciples were awed. "How did the fig tree wither away so quickly?" (Matt. 21:20).

Everyone knew that a tree might wither through blight or a lack of water. But the sudden wilting of a healthy tree was unnatural. By every normal measure, what happened to the tree was impossible. No wonder the disciples marveled.

Jesus, however, was not surprised. He had expected—He had known—that the fig tree would immediately die. So Jesus told His disciples, "If you have faith and do not doubt, you will not only do what was done to the fig tree, but also if you say to this mountain, 'Be removed and be cast into the sea,' it will be done" (Matt. 21:21).

A withered fig tree opened a discussion of faith and prayer to the God of the "impossible."

❖

"If you say to this mountain." Many commentators have pointed out that in the first century "moving mountains" was a common expression. It simply meant "doing the impossible." The definite article "this" suggests that Jesus may have pointed to the Mount of Olives across the valley or ahead to Mount Moriah where the temple stood. His disciples would have understood His imagery. Jesus was telling them that doing the impossible was not impossible. For Jesus, doing the impossible was not unusual at all.

"If you say." It is important to note that Jesus did not say, "If you *pray* that this mountain will be removed." Rather, Jesus spoke of commanding the mountain.

In modern thought, the material universe is real and the spiritual universe is unreal. To us, the material universe is fixed, and it can only be manipulated by material means. If a modern person wants to move a mountain, he thinks about renting a bulldozer.

The Bible has a totally different perspective. In Scripture, the material universe is a *derivative of* the spiritual. God spoke, and what "is" sprang into existence. The writer of Hebrews put it beautifully. "By faith we understand that the worlds were framed by the word of God, so that the things which are seen were not made of things which are visible" (Heb. 11:3).

But there is more. In Scripture, we see that the material universe is *subject to* the spiritual. The miracles of the Bible demonstrate God's ability to shape the normal processes of cause and effect in such a way that the material universe serves His ends.

Given this perspective, the withering of the fig tree is not amazing at all. It is simply another demonstration of an ultimate truth: The spiritual takes priority over the material.

"If you say." It was not surprising that the fig tree withered at Jesus' command. What is surprising are the words, "If *you* say." We human beings are subject to the laws that govern the material universe. Certainly, Jesus can simply speak and the material universe will yield to His command. But how can *we* exercise spiritual control over the material universe?

It is fascinating to remember that these disciples *already had* exercised just this kind of control. Matthew 10:1 indicates that Jesus gave His twelve disciples "power . . . to heal all kinds of sickness and all kinds of disease."

Sent out two by two by the Lord, they had not only seen but performed healing miracles. Natural processes in the physical universe had already yielded at their command. The disciples had done the impossible already!

"If you have faith." Faith is the source of spiritual power. But what validates faith is its object. Pagans may have faith in a charm or an idol, but that faith is worthless. For faith to have validity, its object must be the Lord as He has revealed Himself.

In the New Testament's use of words in the "faith" (*pistis*) word group, only 12 verses have God as the object of faith (see John 12:44; 14:1; Acts 16:34; Rom. 4:3, 5, 17, 24; Gal. 3:6; 1 Thess. 1:8; Titus 3:8; Heb. 6:1; 1 Peter 1:21). Usually the object of faith is Jesus, who is the One through whom we have access to the Father (John 14:6). What the New Testament teaches is that trust in God as He is known through Jesus gives us access to the spiritual realm and its powers.

"And do not doubt." While faith's validity is established by its object, the exercise of faith has a subjective dimension. Jesus made this point by adding, "And do not doubt." The word translated "doubt" here is *diakrithe,* a compound constructed from the preposition *dia* and *krino,* a word which has to do with evaluation and judgment. The *Theological Dictionary of the New Testament* (1965) notes that this doubt is

a specifically religious phenomenon. In Mk. 11:23; Mat. 21:21 man has the promise of God and he clings to it when he speaks the word of faith to God, or to the mountain. But he still thinks it is impossible, or at least not certain, that what he says should be done. He is at odds with himself. He believes, and yet he does not believe. . . . Jm. 1:6 gives a vivid description of the man of prayer who is a *diakrinomenos.* He does not stand firm on the promise of God but moves restlessly like a wave of the sea. He is double-minded and inconstant in all his conduct. (Vol. III, p. 947).

What Jesus is explaining, then, is that one's faith in God makes the impossible possible, because ultimately the spiritual realm controls the material. This is why a person with faith in God can do the impossible. But because of doubt, doing the impossible is not an everyday occurrence. Doubt—not as intellectual questioning but as confusion—robs us of the power we have been given. We who live in the physical world are accustomed to thinking of nature as *limiting*—so much so that even when we are absolutely convinced *theoretically* when we seek to put our faith into practice, we are often at odds with ourselves. We tell mountains to move while believing—yet not believing—that they will. And so the mountains remain where they are.

Jesus never experienced this kind of inner conflict. He lived His human life in intimate fellowship with the Father, doing always those things that pleased Him. When Jesus spoke, it was with an unalloyed faith—and so the fig tree withered away.

Jesus' explanation applied to prayer (*Matthew 21:22*). After Jesus had stated the principles found in Matthew 21:20, He applied them to prayer. "And whatever things you ask in prayer, believing, you will receive."

"Ask in prayer." We immediately see a difference between this promise and the words recorded in verse 20. There Jesus spoke of *commanding* mountains to move. Here He is talking about prayer.

"Ask in prayer, believing." The difference between commanding mountains and appealing to God in prayer is vast. It is one thing to believe without doubting that *we* can move mountains. It is another thing entirely to believe without doubting that *God* can move mountains! In this sense, believing prayer is an easier approach to accomplishing the impossible—not a harder one. Surely we can be utterly confident that God can do anything He chooses!

"Whatever you ask . . . you will receive." Few Christians have difficulty believing that God is able to do what we ask. The problem is having confidence that *what we ask* will be done! This has led many people to transform something

that is a wonderful encouragement to prayer into an obstacle we are supposed to overcome.

It may help if we will ask these questions: When Jesus said, "Whatever things you ask," did Christ mean "each and every thing you ask for" you will receive? Or did Christ mean, "Whatever kind of thing you ask for?" While the Greek grammar is not definitive, the words *panta osa* ("all whatever") are general rather than specific. What Jesus promises us is access to the One whom we *know* can do the impossible, whatever the "impossible" may be!

The overall context of prayer teachings. Earlier in this chapter, we looked at John 15 and saw that prayer is a privilege of those who know Christ. We also saw that abiding in Christ is vital for those who would pray. This is not a "condition" we must meet to be heard. Even this is a promise, for it reflects the fact that when we are living in fellowship with Christ, our prayers will be shaped by desires that grow out of our relationship with Him (pp. 160–161).

We noted the same thing in looking at the kingdom context of Christ's teaching on prayer found in the Sermon on the Mount. The citizen of the kingdom can be sure of receiving—when he or she asks, seeks, and knocks *for those good gifts which God makes available to those in whose hearts Jesus rules* (pp. 161–163). As we look at further teachings on the impact on prayer of abiding in His words and of praying in Jesus' name, we will find out even more about the prayer privileges God gives to us. And we will realize nothing Jesus taught raises obstacles for us to overcome— only promises to claim!

The *Expository Dictionary of Bible Words* (1985) reminds us of this in an observation on Matthew 21 and Mark 11:

In the Gospels, one vital fact is made clear in Jesus' words about faith: a lack of trust in the God in whom we have faith closes off life's possibilities. When we fail to believe, we do not experience the full range of God's activity (Mt 21:22). But when we trust, we open up our future to a full experience of God's power in and through us (Mt 17:20; 21:21;

Lk 7:9–10). All things are possible to the one who believes (p. 117).

PRAYING IN JESUS' NAME

And whatever you ask in My name, that I will do, that the Father may be glorified in the Son. If you ask anything in My name, I will do it (John 14:13, 14).

During His last supper with the disciples the night before the Crucifixion, Jesus gave them several prayer promises. This is the first.

The context of the promise (*John 14—16*). John was the only Gospel writer who recorded this private teaching that Jesus gave His disciples at their last supper. It has been called the "seedbed of the New Testament." So many of the truths Christ spoke of that night are developed further in the epistles of the New Testament.

For our study, it is critical to remember that Jesus was speaking to disciples who believed in and were committed to Him. Before Jesus began this discourse, Judas had left to fulfill his betrayal of Jesus. The words Christ spoke afterward were for His followers only. And they remain words addressed only to His own.

The content of the promise (*John 14:13, 14*). Several features of the promise Jesus made to His disciples must be considered.

"Whatever you ask." As noted above, the "you" to whom Jesus is speaking were disciples then and now. The "whatever" at first appears to make this a blanket promise to believers. "Whatever" has no limits! Yet "whatever" is more closely defined in the words which follow.

"Ask in My name." This is the first phrase that helps us define the "whatever."

In the biblical world, a "name" was more than a label or identifier. A name was intended to capture the essence of the thing named and to some extent express its character. The *Expository Dictionary of Bible Words* (1985, p. 454) notes that to pray in Jesus' name "means (1) to identify the content and

On their last evening together before the Crucifixion, Jesus shared several insights with His disciples.

the motivations of prayers with all that Jesus is and (2) to pray with full confidence in him as he has revealed himself." The "whatever" in this promise emerges as whatever is in harmony with Jesus' character and purposes.

"That the Father may be glorified in the Son." God is glorified by the fact that Jesus answers prayer. But more significantly, the prayers that Jesus answers, as all His activities, will reflect glory to God.

This is why "anything" *must* be defined in terms of Jesus' values and purposes. Nothing which reflects poorly on God or which fails to enhance His glory is a fit subject for a Christian's prayers. However, when we do truly pray in Jesus name—for anything which is in harmony with Him and which glorifies God—we can pray with confidence. God will not only hear such a prayer; Jesus will do what we ask.

PRAYING FOR WHAT WE DESIRE

"If you abide in Me, and My words abide in you, you will ask what you desire, and it shall be done for you" (John 15:7).

We have already commented on the significance of this verse when looking at the im-

pact of John 15 on understanding the context in which Jesus spoke about prayer (pp. 160–161). The phrase "ask what you desire," however, is critical to understanding this particular promise.

We think of a desire as something we want. But our desires change. As children, what we wanted most may have been a new sled or bicycle. As teens, our desire may have been focused on a date with that special guy or girl. Later, our desires may have been for a college education, a good job, marriage, and family. Desires change as we grow older, and our desires are shaped by our values as well as our character.

When Jesus said, "You will ask what you desire, and it will be done for you" He was not promising us bicycles or dates, or even good jobs or parties. Jesus said, "*If you abide in Me, and My words abide in you,* you will ask what you desire." That is, the promise is conditional. What Jesus promises is that He will do what we ask *when our desires are shaped by abiding in Him and His words.*

This is a truly wonderful part of this promise. It reminds us that when we abide in Christ, our relationship with Him will shape our desires! What Christ promises is that as we are transformed by our relationship with Him and His words, our desires will be different. We will grow to desire what He desires and to want what He wants. When we express these desires in prayer, "it shall be done for you."

This same thought is beautifully expressed in Psalm 37:4.

> Delight yourself also in the
> LORD,
> And He shall give you the
> desires of your heart.

God never promises to provide everything the human heart desires. But He does promise us the desires themselves. When we want what God wants, God will give us what we ask.

CHOSEN TO BEAR FRUIT

"You did not choose Me, but I chose you and appointed you that you should go and bear fruit, and that your fruit should remain, that whatever you ask the Father in My name He may give you" (John 15:16).

The immediate context of the promise *(John 15:16a).* Christ's first words in this passage state that He Himself had chosen and commissioned His disciples. The same is true of us (Eph. 1:1–11). And Christ sends those whom He has chosen on a mission—a mission to bear lasting fruit.

In the New Testament, "fruit" has a dual meaning. The primary focus is on the Christian character which the Holy Spirit produces in believers as He transforms us to reflect Jesus Christ (Gal. 5:22, 23; 2 Cor. 3:18). In Mark 4:20, converts are spoken of as fruit. Since in this passage the disciples were to "go and bear fruit" it seems most likely the mission Jesus had in mind was evangelism.

The promise itself *(John 15:16b).* The phrase "that whatever you ask" in this passage is specifically linked to fruit-bearing. The word translated "that" (*hina*) defines the following as either a result or purpose clause. Jesus has

chosen and ordained His followers to win others, and *in order that they might accomplish this purpose* God will give them whatever they ask in Jesus' name. What Jesus is saying is that prayer is a critical resource in winning others to Christ.

The expanded context. The immediate context of the promise helps us define the "whatever" Christ had in mind. Here the "whatever" prayers are prayers related to evangelism. These are prayers which we can offer confidently "in Christ's name" for He Himself came to seek and to save those who are lost.

We also need to remember the larger context of this promise. In John 15, effective prayer requires abiding in Christ, which calls for being obedient to Jesus' words (vv. 10, 14). As we live close to Jesus and His desires become ours, we will care and pray for the lost around us. And Christ will answer when we pray for them.

JESUS' PRAYER PROMISES: SUMMARY

Some Christians as well as non-Christians have a "magical" view of prayer. Many have taken Jesus' many prayer promises in a magical way. If we follow the formula—believing, not doubting, using Jesus' name—God must do anything we ask. After all, didn't Jesus *say* "whatsover"?

Even those who write of obstacles to answered prayer operate on the same basic assumption. To perform the magic, we have to follow the instructions exactly! If we do follow the directions, then we just ask for something, anything, and—poof—it appears!

But prayer is not magic. And Jesus' prayer promises must be understood on His terms. When we understand what Jesus taught about prayer, we discover that His words are promises indeed.

Prayer gives us access to powers beyond the imagining of those who see the physical universe as the ultimate reality. Prayer gives us access to God and the spiritual realm, to which the material creation is subject.

How do we gain this access? We begin by placing our trust in Jesus. He alone is the way, the truth, and the life. As Jesus said, "No one comes to the Father except through Me" (John 14:6).

Having begun, we find there are other keys to prayer's spiritual adventure. We are called to abide in Christ by living close to Him and responding to His word of guidance. We are called to identify with His purposes, to share His goals, and to let those goals shape our own desires. As we grow to value what Jesus values and to want what He wants, we will pray in His name. And our prayers *will* be answered.

As our relationship with Jesus deepens, we will lose the doubts that plague us. We will understand through personal experience that the spiritual realm is more authentic than the material world in which we live. With our focus on Christ and His power, we will ask— believing. And we will find that our prayers— prayers which glorify God and which are tuned to His purposes—are answered indeed.

JESUS' PRAYER PUZZLES

MATTHEW—JOHN

The hallway outside our 17-year-old's room is piled high. Clothes, CD's, posters, and all sorts of things add to the clutter. She is supposedly "cleaning" her room. But the overflow has rested in the hall lo these many days. And I'm not exactly pleased about it.

It's not that I'm compulsive. Unlike some people, I don't get upset if the cans in the cupboard aren't organized by soups, vegetables, and fruits. And I don't even line up the shirts in my closet so the collars all hang the same way. But seeing things just heaped up? Things that don't fit together at all? No, I don't like that.

Sometimes we run across stories or teachings in the Bible that seem out of place, too. They don't fit into any of the categories we've developed in thinking about a subject. And because they don't seem to fit, they make us uncomfortable.

For instance, take the teaching that prayer is for believers only. This is a belief that receives clear support from Scripture. Jesus' prayer promises, explored in chapter 11, were made to those who trust Him as Savior and who abide in Him as well. So when we read in Luke 8 and Mark 9 about a *demon* who prayed

to Jesus—and had his prayer answered—well, that just doesn't seem to fit what we think we know about prayer.

In this chapter, we will look at a number of prayers and comments about prayer that at first glance don't seem to fit with our ideas about prayer. And perhaps we will discover that in most cases the puzzling isn't so puzzling after all.

I. PUZZLING PRIORITIES IN PRAYER

LEAVE YOUR GIFT ON THE ALTAR

Therefore if you bring your gift to the altar, and there remember that your brother has something against you, leave your gift there before the altar, and go your way. First be reconciled to your brother, and then come and offer your gift (Matt. 5:23, 24).

Bringing a gift to the temple altar was a special form of Old Testament prayer: thanksgiving. The worshiper who wanted to express his or her thanks could bring an animal sacrifice. Even the poor could express thanks to God by bringing two doves, which cost only a penny. But in Matthew 5, Jesus tells His listeners that, if a person who comes to thank God is aware that a brother "has something against you," something more important than prayer has priority!

The context of the puzzling command (*Matthew 5:17–48*). This statement of Jesus is found in a part of the Sermon on the Mount where Jesus was explaining the true meaning of the Law. The righteousness God required far exceeded the righteousness of the scribes and Pharisees because God looked at the heart. Their emphasis was on behavior (see p. 134).

Jesus then provided a series of illustrations, first stating what the Law (as interpreted by the rabbis) said, and then showing what God was *really* concerned with. Yes, the Law defined right and wrong behavior. But behavior reflects what is in our hearts, and God examines the heart. The Law says, "Do not murder," but the roots of murder are anger, hostility, and enmity toward others (see Matt. 5:22). What the Law really teaches is that we are to love—not hate—one another. Living in harmony with one another is an expression of the love to which law points us all.

The content of the puzzling command (*Matthew 5:22, 23*). Jesus introduced His command to leave the gift on the altar with the word "therefore." Hostility, like the sin of murder, corrupts and endangers us. So, even if we are not hostile ourselves, but remember that someone has something against us, we are to take steps to be reconciled. And this takes priority over prayer!

The reason becomes clear when we look at another, puzzling teaching of Jesus about prayer.

FORGIVE TO BE FORGIVEN?

Mark 11 contains a teaching that is echoed in other passages as well. Jesus said,

And whenever you stand praying, if you have anything against anyone, forgive him, that your Father in heaven may also forgive you your trespasses. But if you do not forgive, neither will your Father in heaven forgive your trespasses (Mark 11:25, 26; cf. Matt. 6:12, 14–15, 18:35; Luke 6:37; 11:4).

The problem of conditional forgiveness. These passages are troubling to believers who

realize that God forgives all who trust Jesus as Savior unconditionally. Christ died on Calvary to pay for our sins. Our forgiveness depends on His merits, not ours. In Him, Colossians 1:14 says flatly, "We have redemption through His blood, the forgiveness of sins."

What then could Jesus have meant in making our forgiveness conditional on forgiving others? There are three possible answers.

Solution 1: Jesus meant experiencing forgiveness. Forgiveness has judicial and experiential dimensions. God pronounces people who have sinned "not guilty" on the basis of Christ's sacrifice. The charges are dismissed, because the penalty has been paid by another. This is judicial forgiveness.

But forgiveness has an experiential dimension, which is reflected in feelings of guilt and shame. The first possibility is that Jesus was not speaking of judicial but of experiential forgiveness. God may withhold from us the experience of feeling forgiven, while at the same time forgiving us judicially. If this is what He meant, there is no conflict of these sayings of Jesus with the gospel message.

Solution 2: Jesus spoke descriptively. This solution is much like the first, in that both look at forgiveness from a human point of view.

Christ's words make perfect sense if Jesus was speaking descriptively. They remind us that forgiveness is like a coin with two sides. "Heads" is forgiving others; "tails" is accepting forgiveness. Because both sides depend on a deep understanding of grace, only those people who are forgiving will know the release that an experience of forgiveness provides.

If this view is correct, here is how His remarks should be interpreted: When Jesus said that if we do not forgive, God will not forgive us, He was describing how we perceive our experience rather than attributing an unforgiving attitude to God.

Solution 3: Jesus' remarks are limited by the context of prayer. It is striking that most verses that link being forgiven with forgiving are found in passages where the subject is prayer.

We are even taught to pray, "Forgive us our debts, as we forgive our debtors" (Matt. 6:12; cf. Luke 11:4). And in Matthew's account, immediately after teaching this prayer, Jesus emphasized the significance of forgiving others (Matt. 6:14–15). It is possible that the context of prayer both defines and limits this teaching of our Lord.

If this is the case, the forgiveness we are denied is not the judicial forgiveness of all sins on the basis of Christ's death, but forgiveness of the specific sin of being unforgiving. This is a sin which has interrupted our fellowship with the Lord.

Old Testament echoes, New Testament emphasis *(Leviticus 6:1–5; John 15:12).* Note Jesus' words about leaving one's gift on the altar to go be reconciled to a brother and His teaching on forgiveness. Both of these emphases echo Old Testament principles. God's people were to live in harmony with one another. Any act against a brother that disrupted that harmony was a sin. While the person who sinned was to bring a sin offering to God, he was also to make restitution to his brother. In fact, as Leviticus 6 illustrates, it was only after restitution had been made and harmony restored that the person who sinned could approach God for His forgiveness.

When Jesus taught His disciples about the importance of abiding in Him (John 15, pp. 160–161), He promised that "if you abide in Me, and My words abide in you, you will ask what you desire, and it shall be done for you" (John 15:7). Abiding in Christ is at the heart of Christian prayer. But what is abiding in Christ? Jesus explained that "if you keep my commandments, you will abide in My love" (John 15:10). And Jesus went on to say, "This is My commandment, that you love one another as I have loved you" (John 15:12).

It is here that we understand the priority of reconciliation over thanksgiving and the need for those who seek God's forgiveness to forgive others. To abide in Christ means to love others. And loving others calls for us to maintain harmony with them, whether by

seeking reconciliation with those who have something against us or by extending forgiveness to those who have harmed us. To abide in Christ, we must be a forgiving as well as a forgiven people. Then our own prayers for forgiveness will be answered—and we will find peace.

JESUS' PUZZLING RESPONSES TO PRAYER

A DEMON'S PRAYER IS ANSWERED

When he [a demon-possessed man] saw Jesus, he cried out, fell down before Him, and with a loud voice said, "What have I to do with You, Jesus, Son of the Most High God? I beg You, do not torment Me!"

For he had commanded the unclean spirit to come out of the man. For it had often seized him, and he was kept under guard, bound with chains and shackles; and he broke the bonds and was driven by the demon into the wilderness.

Jesus asked him, saying, "What is your name?"

And he said, "Legion," because many demons had entered him. And they begged him that he would not command them to go out into the abyss.

Now a herd of many swine was feeding there on the mountain. So they begged Him that He would permit them to enter them. And He permitted them (Luke 8:28–32; cf. Mark 5:1–13).

The basis of prayer *(Matthew 6).* When Jesus taught His disciples to pray, He told them to address God as "Father." While God is the creator of all and thus the "father" of all in terms of our common origin, Jesus' use of "Father" implies family relationship (see chapter 9, pp. 135–138). As the New Testament puts it, we are all sons of God through faith in Christ Jesus (Gal. 3:26). It is this family relationship that gives us the standing with God which enables us to come to Him freely, relying on His fatherliness to move Him to meet our needs.

While our relationship with God in Christ provides the basis on which we can freely approach Him as our Father, this is not true of the lost. Their prayers are, in Jesus' words, "vain repetitions" (Matt. 6:7). Proverbs 15:8 puts it this way: "The sacrifice of the

Jesus' initial dealings with the man of Gedara were really with the demons who controlled him.

wicked is an abomination to the Lord, but the prayer of the upright is His delight."

What about demons, then? They are Satan's followers, hostile toward God, and committed in their opposition to God's children. Surely if God does not heed the prayers of the wicked, He would reject the prayers of demons. Yet Jesus *did not only heed but answered* the prayer of Legion!

God retains freedom to act as He chooses. It is true that God has promised to hear the prayers of His children. His fatherly love moves Him to listen to our prayers and to respond to them as He deems best.

But the fact that God is committed to hear His children's prayers does not mean He cannot respond to the prayers of others.

When the people of Nineveh repented at the warning of Noah, God withheld judgment on the capital of Assyria, Israel's bitter enemy. God had no covenant relationship with Assyria, and no obligation to heed their prayers. And yet He did. God simply chose to be gracious to these pagan people.

Naaman the leper came to Israel seeking healing and appealing to God's prophet. Naaman had no standing with God from which to plead for healing. But God did heed the prayer of this Syrian general, and Naaman was healed. God chose to be gracious.

And when the demon Legion appealed to Jesus, begging not to be sent to the abyss—a place where fallen angels awaiting judgment were bound—Jesus permitted them to go into a herd of pigs. The demons surely had no basis on which to appeal to Christ. Yet in grace, Jesus permitted the demons to go into the pigs. Jesus chose to be gracious.

All answers to prayer are gracious. The fact that God might choose to answer the prayers of pagans or even demons should not surprise us. God is free to be gracious to whomever He wishes. And we must remember that our own privileged access to God in Christ is rooted in His grace, not in our merits.

God *will* answer our prayers.

And God *may,* if He chooses, answer the prayers of others. He is free to do whatever seems good to Him.

A PRAYER OF THE
ONCE-DEMONIZED MAN
IS NOT ANSWERED

Now the man from whom the demons had departed begged Him that he might be with Him. But Jesus sent him away, saying, "Return to your own house, and tell what great things God has done for you." And he went his way and proclaimed throughout the whole city what great things Jesus had done for him (Luke 8:38–39; cf. Mark 5:18–19).

The mystery of unanswered prayer. Someone has noted that all our prayers are answered. It's just that sometimes the answer is "no" or "not now." Even so, it is striking to see Jesus permitting demons to do what they asked, and not allowing the man who was freed of the demons to do as he asked. We sometimes wonder why some prayers are answered while others are not—and why the requests of one person are granted but not the requests of another.

It's helpful in such cases to apply several tests: appropriateness, the asker's intent, and God's purpose.

Applying the tests to the demons and the man freed from them. When we test the two requests, we see the following.

THE PROBLEM OF
UNANSWERED PRAYER

In *Your Word Is Fire* (1977), a study of the views of Hassidic masters on contemplative prayer, Arthur Green and Barry W. Holtz give one answer to the problem of unanswered prayer suggested by the rabbis.

Why do the prayers of the righteous at times seem to go unanswered?

> There is a king who has two sons.
> Each of them comes to receive his gift
>   from the royal table.
> The first son appears at his father's door-
>   way, and as soon as he is seen, his
>   request is granted.
> The father holds this son in low esteem,
>   and is annoyed by his presence.
> The king orders that the gifts be handed
>   to his son at the door so that he will
>   not approach the table.
>
> Then the king's beloved son appears.
> The father takes great pleasure in this
>   son's arrival and does not want him
>   to leave too quickly.
> For this reason the king delays granting
>   his request, hoping that the son will
>   then draw near to him.
> The son comes closer, he feels the father's
>   love so deeply that he does not hesi-
>   tate to stretch forth his own hand to
>   the royal table (p. 24).

According to this story, the son whose prayer is not answered is privileged and most loved. Because he is not given what he asks, he comes closer and closer until he can sense the father's love.

The test of appropriateness. The demons, who were unclean spirits, begged Jesus to let them enter pigs. According to the Old Testament, swine were unclean animals. Their request was appropriate. If the demons had asked permission to enter another person, Jesus would never have permitted it. Since their request was appropriate, Jesus did permit them to do as they asked.

The man freed of these demons begged Jesus "that he might be with Him." This was also an appropriate request. The demonized man had been cleansed by Jesus, and he longed to be with his Deliverer. But even though the request was appropriate, Jesus said "no."

It is important that what we request in prayer be appropriate to the truth that we are to pray in Jesus' name. But appropriateness alone is not sufficient to guarantee a positive response.

The test of the asker's intent. The demons asked permission to enter the pigs for two reasons. First, there was something attractive to them about inhabiting a living being's body. There is no case in Scripture where a demon who had once invaded a person voluntarily left. Second, the demons were afraid that Jesus would assign them to the abyss. The abyss in Scripture and in first-century thought was a prison where spirits were kept while awaiting judgment. The demons had strong and selfish reasons for wanting to enter the pigs.

The man from whom the demons were exorcised sought to be with Jesus. He wanted not only to know more about the man who had delivered him from the grip of evil spirits but also to serve Him. He was thankful and eager to commit himself to Jesus. In addition, Jesus symbolized security and safety. If he were with Jesus, no demon would ever dominate him again. The man freed from the dominion of demons had very strong reasons for wanting to be with Jesus.

While Jesus permitted the demons to enter the pigs, he did not permit the man he had cured to travel with Him. Our reasons for making a request are not the primary criteria God uses in deciding whether to give us what we ask.

The test of God's purpose. The demons did enter the pigs. But the animals, sensing the inva-

sion of the evil spirits, ran headlong into the water and drowned. This incident, in spite of the healing of the demonized man, frightened the people of the district. The result was that they begged Jesus to leave!

In contrast, the demonized man was told by Jesus to go home and tell what God had done for him. As he traveled, he "proclaimed throughout the whole city what great things Jesus had done for him" (Luke 8:39). His desire to serve the Lord was honored, but not in the way he asked. Christ's "no" to the man's request was a different but better way of saying "yes!"

While we can apply these tests to any prayer, only the third is definitive. Is our request appropriate? We may or may not receive what we ask. Is our intent in asking to glorify God? If it is, God will honor our request. But still we may or may not receive what we ask. Is our request in harmony with God's purpose? *Ah, this is the key!* The answer we receive to our prayers will be in full harmony with the purposes of God. The answers that fit God's purpose will glorify God; they will be best for us as well.

When our requests seem to go unanswered, what a comfort to remember that God's intent is to do us good in ways that will glorify Him. This gives meaning and understanding to the answers that we receive.

PETER PRAYS: JESUS SAYS "NO"

When He had stopped speaking, he said to Simon, "Launch out into the deep and let down your nets for a catch."

But Simon answered and said to Him, "Master, we have toiled all night and caught nothing; nevertheless, at Your word I will let down the net." And when they had done this, they caught a great number of fish, and their net was breaking. So they signaled to their partners in the other boat to come and help them. And they came and filled both the boats, so that they began to sink.

When Simon Peter saw it, he fell down at Jesus' knees, saying, "Depart from me, for I am a sinful man, O Lord!" . . . And Jesus said to Simon, "Do not be afraid. From now on you will catch men" (Luke 5:4–8, 10).

When this incident happened, Peter and his fellow fishermen had spent much time with Jesus, whom they had met when they went to hear John the Baptist preach. Jesus had come back to Capernaum with them and spent time with Peter, James, John, Philip, and Nathaniel. So the fishermen knew Jesus well when he borrowed one of Peter's boats to teach crowds along the shore.

The test of appropriateness. Peter's prayer is, "Depart from me, for I am a sinful man" (Luke 5:8). Peter's association with Jesus led Peter to examine his own heart. In the miracle of the great catch of fish, Peter realized who Jesus was. Peter's prayer was appropriate. Any person who recognizes his own sinfulness and at the same time senses the holiness of God is bound to feel fear. Like Adam, his first reaction is to put distance between himself and the Lord.

Yet in another sense, Peter's prayer was not appropriate. Jesus had not come to condemn but to save. Our sense of sin should drive us to Jesus, not away from Him.

The test of intent. Peter's prayer represents a flawed solution to a sense of guilt. Peter's intent was to reduce his fear and deal with his guilt. But his fear drove him to deal with his guilt by putting distance between himself and the Lord.

The test of God's purpose. When we apply the test of God's purpose, we understand Jesus' response to Peter's prayer. Jesus had not come to condemn but to save. The person who realizes he or she is guilty before God does not need to avoid Jesus but to come to Him. When such a person comes to Christ, Jesus not only forgives but transforms. Jesus' words to Peter, "From now on you will catch men," beautifully expressed Jesus' purpose for Peter—and for us as well.

After the miraculous catch of fish, Simon Peter knelt before Jesus.

A DISTRAUGHT MOTHER'S REQUEST IS REFUSED

And behold, a woman of Canaan came from that region and cried out to Him, saying, "Have mercy on me, O Lord, Son of David! My daughter is severely demon-possessed!" But He answered her not a word. And His disciples came and urged Him, saying, "Send her away, for she cries out after us." But he answered and said, "I was not sent except to the lost sheep of the house of Israel."

Then she came and worshiped Him, saying, "Lord, help me!" But He answered and said, "It is not good to take the children's bread and throw it to the little dogs." And she said, "Yes, Lord, yet even the little dogs eat the crumbs which fall from their master's table."

Then Jesus answered and said to her, "O woman, great is your faith! Let it be to you as you desire." And her daughter was healed from that very hour (Matt. 15:22–28; cf. Mark 7:24–28).

This passage has disturbed readers. Why was Jesus so harsh with this woman who appealed to Him for her daughter? And what's all this about "little dogs"? Finally, what do we learn if we apply the three tests outlined above?

The test of appropriateness. The text tells us the woman approached Jesus twice. The first time she called out to Him, she addressed Jesus as "Son of David" (Matt. 15: 22). This was a messianic title, which acknowledged Christ as the promised King of the Jews.

Jesus failed to respond to her the first time because the woman, a Canaanite, had no claim to the rights and privileges of God's covenant people. We see this reflected in Christ's earlier commissioning of His disciples to go out and minister in His name and power. Jesus told the Twelve, "Do not go into the way of the Gentiles, and do not enter a city of the Samaritans. But go rather to the lost sheep of the house of Israel" (Matt. 10:5–6).

Jesus' message of hope and deliverance had to be presented to Israel first, that the Jews might have the opportunity to welcome or reject their Messiah. Thus, the woman's first appeal to Jesus was not appropriate, and Christ said nothing to her. She was a Gentile, and Israel's claim on the promised Messiah had to be addressed first.

Later the woman "came and worshiped Him, saying 'Lord, help me!'" (Matt. 15:25). This time her appeal had a different basis. She addressed Jesus simply as "Lord" and appealed for mercy.

Jesus' response to this appeal was intended to clarify the issue. His reference to children and "little dogs" (house pets in contrast to the wild scavengers that prowled the streets of first-century Palestinian cities) was not intended to insult. Jesus simply pointed out that children in a household had a right to expect food placed on the table. House pets did not. God's covenant people had a right to expect healing miracles from their Messiah (see Isa. 35:5–6). Pagans did not.

The woman's answer showed that she fully understood what Jesus was saying. She claimed no right to have her request answered. She simply pointed out that in Christ, God had provided more than enough for Is-

rael. As Lord, Jesus related to all people, not just to Israel. The woman's appeal for mercy showed that she believed—not that she had a right to request His aid.

Christ accepted her argument; now her prayer was appropriate. His gift of mercy was a response to her faith in Him, foreshadowing the gospel message that God would welcome into His family *whoever* believes in His Son.

The test of intent. The woman came to Jesus in her need, appealing for 'mercy for her daughter. It is never wrong to appeal to God when in desperate circumstances.

The test of God's purpose. We can see the outworking of God's purpose on several levels.

Christ presented Himself to Israel as the Jewish Messiah. In His early ministry He carefully maintained this role. While He did heal a Roman centurion's servant, that healing took place in Jewish territory with Jewish leaders interceding for the pious Roman (Matt. 8:5–13). In the Canaanite woman, we find Jesus' only healing of a Gentile outside of Jewish territory (see Matt. 15:21) during the time that Christ presented Himself to the Jews as their Messiah.

Christ's initial response to the woman was in harmony with God's purpose. And Jesus' response to the woman's second appeal was also in harmony with God's purpose. It was in harmony with His purpose of showing love and mercy to human beings whatever their relationship with Him. And it was in harmony with His intent to save those who responded to His promise with faith.

Jesus' "yes" to the woman's prayer glorified God as a God of love and mercy, demonstrating the truth that whoever comes to the Lord with faith in Him will be rewarded.

DISCIPLES' REQUESTS ARE REFUSED

Then the mother of Zebedee's sons came to Him with her sons, kneeling down and asking something from Him. And He said to her, "What do you wish?" She said to Him, "Grant that these two sons of mine may sit, one on Your right hand and the other on the left, in Your kingdom."

But Jesus answered and said, "You do not know what you ask. Are you able to drink the cup that I am about to drink, and be baptized with the baptism that I am baptized with?" They said to Him, "We are able."

So He said to them, "You will indeed drink My cup, and be baptized with the baptism that I am baptized with; but to sit on My right hand and on My left is not Mine to give, but it is for those for whom it is prepared by My Father" (Matt. 20:20–23).

This action of James and John aroused the anger of the other ten disciples, leading to Jesus' teaching that greatness in His kingdom is a matter of servanthood, not power.

The test of appropriateness. Self-promotion may be appropriate in the world. But it is not appropriate in our relationship with God or with other Christians. As Jesus went on to teach the Twelve, He pointed to Himself as an example of servanthood (Matt. 20:25–28). Christian leaders are to follow Jesus' example rather than seek power or position for themselves.

The test of intent. James and John, who enlisted their mother to plead with Jesus for them, expected Jesus to establish an earthly kingdom and to rule it as the Messiah. The two disciples looked ahead, seeking prominent places for themselves. To be at the right or left hand of an ancient ruler meant having access to Him. In earthly kingdoms, this guaranteed wealth and power.

Jesus' question about their ability to share His cup and baptism refer to participation in Christ's mission and His suffering. The disciples declared they were willing to pay the price they thought would bring them power.

The intent behind the request of these two disciples was seriously flawed.

The test of God's purpose. Christ's immediate purpose was not to establish the messianic kingdom but to call Jew and Gentile alike to God. Christ would first establish a spiritual kingdom, without geographical boundaries.

Faith alone would gain citizenship in Christ's spiritual kingdom. This kingdom would be marked by communities of love scattered across an unbelieving and hostile world. In Christ's spiritual kingdom, the great would serve rather than rule, comfort rather than command, and love others rather than love personal gain.

James and John would find their desires and motives turned upside down as they followed Jesus down a path marked by suffering and self-giving. And they would follow. But they would follow because they loved Him, not for any reward.

What place do these two disciples have in the eternal kingdom of our Lord? Only God knows. And with the dawning of the gospel age, James and John no longer cared.

JESUS IGNORES THE PRAYER OF PERSONS WHOM HE LOVED

Now a certain man was sick, Lazarus of Bethany, the town of Mary and her sister Martha. It was that Mary who anointed the Lord with fragrant oil and wiped His feet with her hair, whose brother Lazarus was sick. Therefore the sisters sent to Him, saying, "Lord, behold, he whom You love is sick."

When Jesus heard that, He said, "This sickness is not unto death, but for the glory of God, that the Son of God may be glorified through it." Now Jesus loved Martha and her sister and Lazarus. So, when He heard that he was sick, He stayed two more days in the place where He was (John 11:1–6).

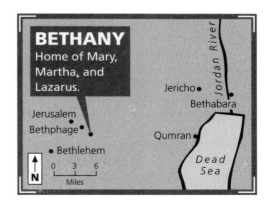

BETHANY
Home of Mary, Martha, and Lazarus.

Jordan River

Jericho •
Bethabara

Jerusalem •
Bethphage •

Qumran •

• Bethlehem

Dead Sea

0   3   6
Miles
N

The test of appropriateness. Mary and Martha were well aware of Jesus' power over sickness. For about three years, He had performed His healing miracles. They were also confident that they and their brother held a special place in Jesus' heart. So when Lazarus fell mortally ill, the first thing they thought of was to send word to Jesus. They were sure that if Jesus knew that Lazarus was near death, He would come and heal their brother.

The prayer was appropriate. But when Jesus received their message, He busied Himself for two days with other matters.

The test of intent. The sister's message was a cry for help. It was also an expression of complete faith in Jesus. There was no flaw in the intent of the sisters.

The test of God's purpose. During the days of waiting for Jesus to arrive, the sisters must have experienced growing anxiety. Why hadn't Jesus come? Why hadn't He responded to their desperate appeal? Then their brother died. And the two sisters *knew* that if Jesus had been there, Lazarus would not have died.

The pain of their loss must have been great because they knew if Jesus had intervened, Lazarus would have lived. And they must have wondered why. Why hadn't He responded to their desperate appeal? Today we understand why. As Jesus told His disciples, the sickness and death of Lazarus was intended to bring glory to God and to Jesus.

These stories in the Gospels about Jesus' puzzling answers to prayers of petition remind us of important truths.

- God is merciful and gracious even to those who have no standing with Him. As Jesus said, God "makes His sun rise on the evil and on the good, and sends rain on the just and the unjust" (Matt. 5:45). At times He even answers their prayers.
- Those who have a personal relationship with God through Jesus have standing with Him and a special privilege in prayer. We know that He hears our petitions and responds with fatherly love.

- Sometimes our petitions are appropriate, and sometimes they are inappropriate. While it is always appropriate to appeal to God for mercy, we need to test our prayers for harmony with God's known will.
- We also need to test the intent that lies behind our petitions. Why do we want what we are asking for? Motive is important to God and it should be to us.
- Finally, we need to understand that God answers our prayers of petition in ways that fit His purposes. As story after story illustrates, God's purposes never conflict with what is our own highest good.

PUZZLING PRAYER ILLUSTRATIONS

Jesus' teaching on prayer was sometimes direct and clear, as when he taught His disciples the Lord's prayer. At other times, Jesus used stories and illustrations that seem puzzling.

THE ILLUSTRATION OF THE PERSISTENT NEIGHBOR

"Which of you shall have a friend, and go to him at midnight and say to him, 'Friend, lend me three loaves; for a friend of mine has come to me on his journey, and I have nothing to set before him;' and he will answer from within and say, 'Do not trouble me; the door is now shut, and my children are with me in bed; I cannot rise and give to you.'

"I say to you, though he will not rise and give to him because he is his friend, yet because of his persistence he will rise and give him as many as he needs" (Luke 11:5–8).

The puzzle here is created by a mistranslation, which makes it appear that Jesus suggests we must be persistent in prayer, and that God will answer us because we continue to "bother" Him. In fact, the word *anaideia,* translated "persistence," also has the meaning of "avoidance of shame." And that meaning fits the culture in which Jesus lived.

In the Near East and in Jewish thought, hospitality was very important. A visitor was considered the responsibility of the family with which he stayed as well as the entire community. What Jesus was pointing out in this illustration was that the neighbor would get up and lend the bread because it was *the right thing for a neighbor to do*. It would shame him and the community not to provide for the needs of a visitor.

What was Jesus' point? If a neighbor would provide for a stranger because it was considered the right thing to do, how much more can we count on God to provide for His own children? We can surely expect our heavenly Father to act in a fatherly way. We can count on Him to answer our prayers!

THE ILLUSTRATION OF THE UNJUST JUDGE

"There was in a certain city a judge who did not fear God nor regard man. Now there was a widow in that city; and she came to him, saying 'Get justice for me from my adversary.' And he would not for a while; but afterward he said within himself, 'Though I do not fear God nor regard man, yet because this widow troubles me I will avenge her, lest by her continual coming she weary me.' "

Then the Lord said, "Hear what the unjust judge said. And shall God not avenge His own elect who cry out day and night to Him, though He bears long with them?" (Luke 18:2–7).

Luke introduces this parable by describing Jesus' intent. He wanted to teach "that men always ought to pray and not lose heart." But why use the illustration of an unjust judge?

In biblical times, rabbis served as judges who arbitrated disputes as well as interpreted biblical law. This judge was notable because of his character: He neither feared God nor respected men. These were the two primary motives for dispensing justice in first-century Judaism.

A pious judge feared God. Out of respect for God's commands to be impartial to poor and wealthy alike, he would do what was right. Even a judge who was not pious was sensitive to public opinion. The word translated "respect" is *entrepo,* which means to "be ashamed." In the passive form here, it means

to be sensitive to shame. Jesus was saying that the judge in His story was shameless, caring nothing for the opinion of man or God.

So when the widow appealed to this judge for justice, he ignored her. He didn't care what God thought. He didn't care what others thought. And he certainly didn't care about the widow.

But the widow in Jesus' story was persistent. She turned up everywhere the unjust judge went, shouting out her demand for justice. Finally, the judge acted, "lest by her continual coming she weary me." The word translated "weary" or "wear me out" is *hupopiaze*. It is taken from the sport of boxing, and it means literally "to give someone a black eye." As slang, it meant to blacken a person's face— to shame him or her in public.

So even the shameless judge who was proud of his insensitivity to public opinion became concerned for his reputation. Only then did he give the widow the justice she demanded.

In applying the parable, Jesus contrasted God with the unjust judge. The judge didn't care for anyone or anything. But God deeply loves "His own elect who cry out day and night." If an unjust judge can be forced to do justice by the persistent plea of a widow, how much more can we count on a just and merciful God to act on the plea of a person who presents a right cause to Him?

The wait may seem long to those who pray for justice and God may seem silent and far away, but He hears every prayer. And God will "avenge them speedily" (Luke 18:8), although what seems quick to God may seem long to us.

Understanding God's commitment to justice and to us, we are to continue to pray, confident that God *will* act.

THE ILLUSTRATION OF THE PHARISEE AND THE TAX COLLECTOR

"Two men went up to the temple to pray, one a Pharisee and the other a tax collector. The Pharisee stood and prayed thus with himself, 'God, I thank

The widow persistently begged the judge for justice.

You that I am not like other men—extortioners, unjust, adulterers, or even as this tax collector. I fast twice a week; I give tithes of all that I possess.' And the tax collector, standing afar off, would not so much as raise his eyes to heaven, but beat his breast, saying, 'God, be merciful to me a sinner!' I tell you, this man went down to his house justified rather than the other, for everyone who exalts himself will be humbled, and he who humbles himself will be exalted" (Luke 18:10–14).

Luke again explains the point of the illustration. He tells us that Jesus spoke this parable "to some who trusted in themselves that they were righteous, and despised others."

The parable was shocking to those who first heard Jesus tell it. The Pharisees were highly respected for their dedication to keeping every detail of the Law as it was interpreted by the sages. Both the ordinary people and the Pharisees themselves were sure that their prayers must be welcome in heaven. The popular conviction was expressed by a blind man whom Jesus healed, although in a different context: "We know that God does not hear sinners; but if anyone is a worshiper of God and does His will, He hears him" (John 9:31).

The Pharisee surely saw himself as one who worshiped God and did His will, and so he prayed proudly and with confidence.

The tax collector in first-century Judea was as thoroughly despised as the Pharisee was admired. Tax collectors collaborated with the Romans. Most made their money by extorting more than was due from their countrymen.

The actions of the tax collector showed intense inner anguish. Striking the breast is a traditional Middle Eastern gesture of women. A man would do so only when in the grip of intense emotion. Deeply aware of his sin and need, the publican would not even look up toward heaven, and his prayer was an appeal for mercy taken from Psalm 51:1.

The contrast between the two men is striking. One thought he was righteous; the other knew he was a sinner. One condemned his fellow men; the other condemned only himself. One stood proudly before God; the other stood humbly. One relied on his own works; the other relied only on God's mercy. And wonder of wonders, it was the sinner who left the temple justified [declared innocent] by God!

What a reminder for us! When we approach God in prayer, we come relying on Him alone rather than on anything we have done. It was Jesus who won access for us by His blood. Through faith in Him, we were born into God's family and we know Him as Father. His fatherly love and grace give us confidence that God will answer our prayers.

JESUS' OWN PRAYERS

MATTHEW; JOHN

It's strange that many people feel little need to pray. It is especially strange in view of the fact that Jesus Himself prayed often. If the Son of God felt a need to maintain a close relationship with the Father, how much more do we need to stay close to Him?

One of the significant questions we can ask, of course, is, "What did Jesus pray?" Did He just enjoy spending time with the Father? Or did Jesus, in His incarnation, depend on the Father as we are to depend on Him? These are questions we can answer, in part at least, by looking at the prayers of Jesus recorded in the Gospels.

JESUS' PRACTICE OF PRAYER

Each of the synoptic Gospels makes mention of Jesus slipping away from His disciples to pray. Luke, intent on portraying Jesus as the ideal human being, speaks most often of Christ's habit of prayer.

When all the people were baptized, it came to pass that Jesus also was baptized; and while He prayed, the heaven was opened. And the Holy Spirit descended in bodily form like a dove upon Him, and a voice came from heaven which said, "You are My beloved Son; in You I am well pleased" (Luke 3:21–22).

However, the report went around concerning Him all the more; and great multitudes came together to hear, and to be healed by Him of their infirmities. So He Himself often withdrew into the wilderness and prayed (Luke 5:15–16).

Now it came to pass in those days that He went out to the mountain to pray, and continued all night in prayer to God. And when it was day, He called His disciples to Himself; and from them He chose twelve whom He also named apostles (Luke 6:12–13).

And it happened, as He was alone praying, that His disciples joined Him, and He asked them, saying, "Who do the crowds say that I am?" (Luke 9:18).

Now it came to pass, about eight days after these sayings, that He took Peter, John, and James and went up on the mountain to pray. As He prayed, the appearance of His face was altered, and His robe became white and glistening (Luke 9:28, 29).

Now it came to pass, as He was praying in a certain place, when He ceased, that one of His disciples said to Him, "Lord, teach us to pray, as John also taught his disciples" (Luke 11:1).

It is clear from Luke's numerous references that prayer had a significant place in Jesus' life. But Luke's reports of occasions when Jesus withdrew to pray tell us even more.

Christ went to the Father, often praying all night, when He was about to take significant steps or when He faced critical decisions!

According to Luke, Christ prayed at the time of His baptism by John. Immediately following this, John identified Jesus to his own disciples as the Son of God (cf. John 1:29–34).

According to Luke, Jesus often withdrew to pray privately when crowds gathered to witness and experience His healing miracles. The strain of His ministry was too great to be conducted without the restorative power of prayer.

According to Luke, Jesus prayed the entire night before selecting the disciples who would later become the apostles who launched the Christian church. This choice was too critical to be made without hours of prayer.

According to Luke, Jesus prayed before asking His disciples to report what the crowds were saying about Him. This was a turning point in Christ's ministry. The crowd honored Him as a great prophet, but not as the promised Messiah and Son of God. From this point on, the focus of Jesus' teaching shifted from a presentation of the kingdom to Israel to conversations with His disciples about the Cross and personal discipleship.

According to Luke, Jesus was praying on a mountain when the Transfiguration took place. The three disciples with Him on this occasion were given a glimpse of His glory.

And according to Luke, it was Jesus' own dedication to prayer that moved His disciples to ask Him to teach them to pray. As He taught them, He introduced us to the Lord's Prayer.

While the other Gospel writers speak less often of Jesus' practice of private prayer, each mentions it at least once.

And when He had sent the multitudes away, He went up on the mountain by Himself to pray. Now when evening came, He was alone there (Matt. 14:23).

Now in the morning, having risen a long while before daylight, He went out and departed to a solitary place, and there He prayed (Mark 1:35).

For His times of personal prayer, Jesus usually sought out a secluded location, away from the crowds.

And when He had sent them away, He departed to the mountain to pray (Mark 6:46).

Even without knowing the specific content of Christ's prayers, the Gospels make it clear that prayer was vital to Him. For Jesus, prayer was more than fellowship with the Father. Prayer expressed His dependence on the Father as well as a deep awareness of His need for the Father's guidance and support.

THE RECORDED PRAYERS OF JESUS

Several of Jesus' own prayers have been recorded for us by the Gospel writers. We can learn much from each of them.

JESUS' PRAYER WHEN REJECTED

At that time Jesus answered and said, "I thank You, Father, Lord of heaven and earth, that You have hidden these things from the wise and prudent and have revealed them to babes. Even so, Father, for so it seemed good in Your sight. All things have been delivered to Me by My Father, and no one knows the Son except the Father. Nor does anyone know the Father except the Son, and the one to whom the Son wills to reveal Him (Matt. 11:25–27).

The context of the prayer *(Matthew 11:16–30).* Jesus had been teaching and healing in Galilee for over a year. While the crowds flocked to listen to His teaching and to witness His miracles, He had not been welcomed as the promised Messiah. Instead, the same people who found fault with John for being too stern and distant found fault with Jesus for being accessible to sinners (Matt. 11:16–19)!

Jesus rebuked the cities where His miracles were performed (Matthew 11:20–24). Jesus pronounced woe (judgment) on the cities, for if the pagan cities of Tyre and Sidon, or even Sodom, had witnessed the miracles that were performed in Galilean centers like Chorazin, Bethsaida, and Capernaum, they would have "repented long ago." The failure of the nation to acknowledge Jesus as Messiah had doomed its cities and towns.

Jesus thanked God for the role His rejection played in God's plan (Matthew 11:25–27). Jesus' prayer lauded God for the good which would come from the painful rejection He had experienced.

Jesus invited individuals to come to Him for rest (Matthew 11:28–30). The nation would not respond to Jesus as the Messiah, but He made it clear that individuals who came to Him heavy laden would find rest. While the door of opportunity was swinging shut for the nation, it was opening wide for any person who sensed his or her need and came to Jesus for rest.

Understanding this context helps us see the significance of Jesus' prayer of thanks.

The content of the prayer *(Matthew 11:25–27).* The wording of this prayer is more significant than might appear at first glance.

"I thank You, Father, Lord of heaven and earth" (Matthew 11:25a). The word translated "thank" here and "praise" in other English translations is *exomologoumai.* In Matthew 3:6, it is rendered as "confess" or "acknowledge." Used in reference to God, as here, it is best understood

"Come to Me, all you who labor and are heavy laden, and I will give you rest."

as acknowledging who God is—Jesus' Father and Lord of heaven and earth.

Christ thus began His prayer by acknowledging the sovereignty of God the Father. The rejection of His own people hurt Jesus deeply, but Christ affirmed that His rejection was in accord with the purposes of God. Thus, it merited praise rather than recrimination.

What an attitude for us to adopt when we are disappointed by circumstances or by others about whom we care!

"You have hidden these things from the wise and prudent and have revealed them to babes" (Matthew 11:25b). The phrase "wise and prudent" is irony. The generation that rejected Jesus considered itself wise and understanding; yet these people did not recognize the significance of the miracles that Jesus performed. The general "wise and prudent" populace is contrasted with "babes," literally "little children." While the "mature" group relied on its

own understanding, the "babes" were willing to learn from Jesus.

But Jesus seemed to ascribe these reactions to God's activity of concealing and revealing. Can the general population be blamed for failing to recognize Jesus as the Christ if this was concealed from them? To answer this challenge, we must place this statement in the context of the ministry of John the Baptist. John had called this same generation to repentance because of the imminent appearance of the Messiah.

John warned that unless there was repentance, there would be judgment. While some accepted His message and were baptized as a sign of repentance, most people did not. God's activity in concealing "these things" from the wise and understanding was an act of divine judgment on those who had *already rejected* God's word as expressed by John. God's activity in revealing "these things" to babies was a gracious response to those whose hearts were open to Him.

God may still conceal and reveal, but not to show favoritism. God has done what is right and what "seemed good in Your sight" (Matt. 11:26).

"No one knows the Son except the Father. Nor does anyone know the Father except the Son" (Matthew 11:27a). This claim of exclusive knowledge between the Father and the Son is significant. It reflects a phenomenon expressed in Deuteronomy 34:10, which said of Moses, "Since then there has not arisen in Israel a prophet like Moses, whom the LORD knew face to face." This was also a claim of exclusive reciprocal knowledge: Moses was known by God, and God revealed Himself to Moses in a "face-to-face" relationship.

The Jewish people honored Moses as the prophet *par excellence,* for the knowledge he had of God became knowledge for others as it was recorded in the Torah (the Law, the Scriptures). Now in Jesus' prayer, He claimed an even greater knowledge of the Father than Moses was given. By implication, Jesus was One through whom an even more perfect

knowledge of God would be revealed to humankind.

"Nor does anyone know the Father except the Son, and the one to whom the Son wills to reveal Him" (Matthew 11:27b). The exclusive knowledge of the Father claimed by Jesus is truly unique. Moses had reciprocal knowledge of God because that knowledge was revealed to Him by God. The knowledge of the Father that Jesus possessed was known directly, intimately, and forever, for Christ alone shared deity with the Father and the Holy Spirit.

There is even more. Jesus was revealing not just knowledge about the Father, but the Father Himself. The revelation that came through Moses was factual. The revelation that Jesus alone mediates is *personal.* And, as the revealer of the Father, Jesus is authorized to reveal the Father to whomever He wills.

These words of Jesus demanded that His hearers acknowledge not only Jesus' authority but His Person as well. He was the Messiah looked forward to by the Jews, but before they could grasp this reality, they had to acknowledge Him as the Son of God. Jesus is our Savior, but before we can grasp this reality, we too must acknowledge Him as the Son of God. It is only because Jesus is the Son of God that He is able to save. It is only because Jesus is the Son of God that He will return to rule in the future.

The open invitation: "Come to Me" (Matthew 11:28). In Jesus' prayer, He acknowledged the Father as sovereign and affirmed God's judgment on sinners as well as His grace. By virtue of His exclusive reciprocal knowledge of the Father gained as the Son of God, Jesus presented Himself in His prayer as the only One who can provide human beings with access to the Father. Jesus followed this prayer with an open invitation for people to come to Him and find rest in Him.

This invitation to the weary and burdened is open to us today. Whoever chooses to come to Jesus will find that he has also been chosen by Christ.

JESUS' PRAYER AT LAZARUS'S TOMB

Then they took away the stone from the place where the dead man was lying. And Jesus lifted up His eyes and said, "Father, I thank You that You have heard Me. And I know that You always hear Me, but because of the people who are standing by I said this, that they may believe that You sent Me." Now when He had said these things, He cried with a loud voice, "Lazarus, come forth!" (John 11:41–43).

This prayer of Jesus is unusual, not necessarily for its content but because it was uttered for the benefit of onlookers. At the same time, the content of the prayer underlined the reality of Jesus' constant communion with the Father.

The context of the prayer *(John 11)*. When Jesus was informed of Lazarus's sickness, He purposely waited for His friend's death before going to Bethany. There the two sisters, Mary and Martha, expressed their trust in Jesus. If Christ had been present, they declared, their brother would not have died.

Jesus challenged their faith by promising that their brother would rise again. Martha misunderstood, and she expressed her faith that Lazarus "will rise again in the resurrection at the last day" (John 11:24). In response, Jesus stated, "I am the resurrection and the life" (John 11:25). Christ did not seek theological correctness, but a total commitment to Him. Mary, her faith rising to the challenge, said, "Yes, Lord, I believe that You are the Christ, the Son of God" (John 11:27).

Jesus then led the family and the mourners to Lazarus's grave. After uttering the prayer recorded in 11:41, 42, He called Lazarus back to life.

This stunning miracle caused many people to believe in Jesus. But it also deepened the hostility of the leaders who feared and opposed Him. Their response to Christ's miraculous signs was not belief, but a determination to kill Jesus (John 11:48–50).

The content of the prayer *(John 11:41, 42)*. The prayer that Jesus spoke publicly, just like

the miracle, was intended to reveal Christ's uniqueness and to call those who witnessed this event to faith in Him.

"I thank You that You have heard Me" *(John 11:41b)*. Jesus had already communed with the Father concerning Lazarus, and His prayer for the raising of Lazarus had already been answered. Looking back at John 11:4, we see that Jesus was fully aware of the coming death of His friend. Jesus also knew that through this death and the events that would follow, both the Father and the Son would be glorified.

"I know that You always hear Me" *(John 11:42a)*. One interpreter had the following comments about this passage:

Jesus lives in constant prayer and communication with His Father. When He engages in vocal prayer, He is not entering, as we do, from a state of nonpraying into prayer. He is only giving overt expression to what is the ground and base of His life all along. He emerges from non-vocal to vocal prayer here in order to show that the power He needs for His ministry—and here specifically for the raising of Lazarus—depends on the gift of God. It is through prayer and communion and constant obedience to His Father's will that He is the channel of the Father's saving action. That is why the prayer is thanksgiving rather than petition. . . . Here we have the most profound aspect of John's treatment of the miracles. It places Jesus poles apart from the mere wonder-workers, and seeks to penetrate into the mystery of how he, though to all outward appearance an ordinary (or perhaps extraordinary) human being, is the One in whom is disclosed God's presence and His very self in saving action (R. H. Fuller, *Interpreting the Miracles*, 1957, pp. 107–108).

God always hears Jesus, and this demonstrates His union with God the Father and Their shared identity as God.

"Because of the people who are standing by I said this" *(John 11:42a)*. Jesus did not need to put His union with the Father to the test. His words were not verbalized because He needed confirmation of this relationship. He said them so the people standing by would grasp the significance of the miracle they were about to witness. If they understood its significance, they might, like Mary and Martha, "believe that You sent Me" (John 11:42b).

Jesus shared Mary and Martha's pain in the death of their brother, but He had good news for them!

The prayer verbalized a relationship that was about to be confirmed by indisputable proof.

The significance of Jesus' prayer. While the content of the prayer explains the reason why Jesus verbalized it, one of Christ's sentences expresses a basic truth about His prayer life. For Jesus, prayer was not infrequent and sporadic. Christ lived His entire life in the presence of God the Father, fully aware of the Father every moment. While Jesus withdrew on occasion for concentrated times of prayer, there was no moment when Christ functioned without a profound awareness of the Father and His will.

Any person who lives constantly in God's presence will naturally be immersed in prayer.

JESUS' PRAYERS FOR HIS DISCIPLES

We are given three insights into Jesus' prayers for His followers in the New Testament. Luke tells us that at the Last Supper when Christ predicted Peter's betrayal, He said,

Simon, Simon! Indeed, Satan has asked for you, that he may sift you as wheat. But I have prayed for you, that your faith should not fail; and when you have returned to Me, strengthen your brethren (Luke 22:31, 32).

It was Jesus' intercession for Peter—so weak in spite of his confidence in his own strength—that protected Peter from Satan and from himself. The incident reminds us of the wonderful truth expressed in 1 John 2:1, that "if anyone sins, we have an Advocate with the

Father, Jesus Christ the righteous." We may be disloyal to Christ, but He remains loyal to us—just as He was to Peter.

A second insight in the content of Jesus' prayers for His followers is found in John 14:16. Again, the occasion was the Last Supper that Jesus shared with His disciples just before the Crucifixion. Urging the disciples to show their love by keeping Jesus' commandments, He looked ahead to His resurrection and said,

And I will pray the Father and He will give you another Helper, that He may abide with you forever—the Spirit of truth, whom the world cannot receive (John 14:16, 17).

Jesus' prayer has been answered, and the Holy Spirit has been given as our Helper. And He stays with us, to aid us as we seek to keep Christ's commands.

The third prayer of Jesus for His followers is found in John 17. Here we have the prayer itself. This lengthy prayer is often called Jesus' "high priestly prayer." John tells us that this was the prayer Jesus offered at the close of His Last Supper teaching. It was a prayer not only for the disciples but for believers of every age.

Because of its length, we will examine it section by section.

Prayer for the glorification of the Son that He might be the source of eternal life *(John 17:1–5)*. The words *glory* and *glorify* appear frequently in this first section of Jesus' prayer. The biblical meaning of these terms is drawn from the Old Testament, and this meaning infuses the New Testament. The primary Hebrew word translated "glory" is *kabod,* which means "heavy" or "weighty." Used figuratively, as it most often is in the Old Testament, it indicates the impressive, powerful, and splendid.

While God is by nature glorious, we sense His glory only in His self-revelation. The mighty acts by which God won freedom from Egyptian slavery for Israel (Num. 14:22), the cloud which often accompanied His appearances (Ex. 40:34–35), the Creation itself (Ps. 19:1)—all of these reveal God's glory. Now, in

His high priestly prayer, Jesus asked God to reveal further His own splendor—not only in the Cross but also in the eternal life that Jesus was about to win for humankind.

Father, the hour has come. Glorify Your Son, that Your Son also may glorify You, as you have given Him authority over all flesh, that He should give eternal life to as many as You have given Him. And this is eternal life, that they may know You, the only true God, and Jesus Christ whom You have sent. I have glorified You on the earth. I have finished the work which You have given Me to do. And now, O Father, glorify Me together with Yourself, with the glory which I had with You before the world was (John 17:1–5).

"The hour has come" (17:1). The moment toward which Christ's whole mission on earth had been focused was at hand. The ultimate revelation of the deep love and justice of God was about to take place on a hill where criminals experienced a shameful death.

"That He should give eternal life" (17:2). God is glorified by the provision of eternal life and the transformation of sinful humankind which this gift implies. Only God could find a solution to the problem that human sinfulness created for One who was both completely loving and totally just.

"I have glorified You on the earth" (17:4). Living now in history's critical hour, Jesus looked back at His incarnation and said, "I have glorified You on the earth." Every word and deed of Jesus had revealed more of the Father. Soon in His sacrifice of Himself on the cross, the ultimate revelation would take place.

"With the glory which I had with You before the world was" (17:5). The incarnation called for Christ to "empty himself" (Phil. 2:7)—to set aside the splendor of His deity to live as an ordinary human being. On Christ's return to heaven, the full manifestation of the glory that was His from eternity was restored.

Prayer for the disciples *(John 17:6–19)*. The central section of Jesus' prayer was for the disciples. In this section, three themes are developed: (1) Jesus' reasons for praying for them, verses 6–11a; (2) prayer that they might be kept, verses 11b–16; and (3) prayer that they might be sanctified with Jesus, verses 17–19. While this section of the prayer was specifically for those who shared the Last Supper with Jesus, the prayer has application to us as well.

Jesus' reasons for praying for the disciples *(John 17:6–11a)*. Jesus was about to leave the disciples to face the challenges of ministry without His physical presence. How appropriate that Christ should pray for these special followers whom the Father had given Him.

Throughout this section of His prayer, Jesus referred to the "world." The particular word Jesus uses, *kosmos,* has a distinctive theological cast. When this word occurs in the New Testament, its usual reference is not to the earth or to mankind in general, but to human society as shaped by mankind's sinful nature. The "world" is that system of beliefs and values which grows out of and is driven by sin. In saving the disciples as well as us, Jesus transfers us from the world to His own kingdom, where we are to be driven by desires which grow out of our relationship with the Lord (Col. 1:13).

I have manifested Your name to the men whom You have given Me out of the world. They were Yours, You gave them to Me, and they have kept Your word. Now they have known that all things which You have given Me are from You. For I have given to them the words which You have given Me; and they have received them, and have known surely that I came forth from You; and they have believed that You sent Me. I pray for them. I do not pray for the world but for those whom you have given Me, for they are yours. And all Mine are Yours, and Yours are Mine, and I am glorified in them. Now I am no longer in the world, but these are in the world, and I come to You (John 17:6–11).

"The men whom You have given Me out of the world" (17:6). Several things in this prayer clarify what makes the disciples—and all believers—so special.

- They are God's gifts to Jesus (17:6).
- Jesus has revealed to them God's "name," i.e., His nature and character (17:6).

- They have welcomed and responded to the word Christ brought them (17:8).
- They have acknowledged that Jesus was sent by God (17:8).

"I do not pray for the world" (17:9). Jesus prayed here only "for those whom You have given Me," not for the world. Yet as Jesus' prayers for the disciples were answered, their ministry had a significant impact on the world. Through the disciples, thousands of people came to know Christ, the church was expanded, and the words that Christ spoke to them have been recorded for us.

"But these are in the world" (17:11). Jesus was on His way to the Father. It would be up to the disciples to carry on Christ's mission by sharing the gospel of salvation with all people.

Jesus' prayer that the disciples might be kept *(17:11b–16)*. The translation of the disciples from the world to Jesus' kingdom had made them vulnerable. The world that was hostile to Jesus would now be hostile to the disciples. So Jesus prayed that the Father would keep the disciples from the evil one when Jesus ascended to heaven.

Holy Father, keep through Your name those whom You have given Me, that they may be one as We are. While I was with them in the world, I kept them in Your name. Those whom You gave Me I have kept; and none of them is lost except the son of perdition, that the Scripture might be fulfilled. But now I come to You, and these things I speak in the world, that they may have My joy fulfilled in themselves. I have given them Your word; and the world has hated them because they are not of the world, just as I am not of the world. I do not pray that You should take them out of the world, but that You should keep them from the evil one. They are not of the world, just as I am not of the world (John 17:11–14).

"Holy Father" (17:11b). This is the only place in the Scriptures where Jesus addressed God as "holy Father." The biblical concept of the holiness of God involves more than moral perfection. "Holy" conveys a sense of the otherness—the awesomeness—of God as distinct

from and greater than His creation. In the Old Testament, a place, person, or object that was "holy" had been set apart for God's special use.

While Jesus' prayer blended transcendence and intimacy, the use of "holy" is particularly appropriate for this section of Christ's prayer. The disciples too were holy; they had been set apart from the world and dedicated to God's service. They were both instruments of God in the world and objects of His love separated from the world. It was imperative that Jesus' disciples be kept safe.

"That they may be one as We are" (17:11). The unity which Jesus spoke of here is a unity of thought and purpose. Jesus lived on earth in sensitivity to the Father's will, and totally committed to doing it. It is in this sense that believers may be one, not with each other, but one with God as Christ Himself was.

The oneness of which Jesus spoke here is frequently described in other sayings which John ascribes to Jesus.

Most assuredly, I say to you, the Son can do nothing of Himself, but what He sees the Father do; for whatever He does, the Son also does in like manner. For the Father loves the Son, and shows Him all things that He Himself does (John 5:19–20).

For I have come down from heaven, not to do My own will, but the will of Him who sent Me (John 6:38).

I do nothing of Myself, but as My Father taught Me, I speak these things. And He who sent Me is with Me. The Father has not left Me alone, for I always do those things that please Him (John 8:28, 29).

The words that I speak to you I do not speak on My own authority; but the Father who dwells in Me does the works. Believe Me that I am in the Father and the Father in Me (John 14:10, 11).

In none of these expressions was Jesus speaking of the unity that exists within the Trinity. Rather, He was describing an experiential oneness that depended on living His life in submission to God's will. It was this experience of oneness with God which Christ prayed His disciples would know.

"While I was with them . . ., I kept them" (17:12). When Jesus was physically present with the

Twelve, He was able to guard them. Christ was now about to leave, so He committed their care to the Father.

"None of them is lost except the son of perdition" (17:12). The only disciple who had not been faithful to Jesus was Judas. The phrase "son of perdition" may have several meanings. The same phrase is found in the Septuagint's rendering of Psalm 57:4, where it is used of unrighteous or wicked persons. It is also applied to the antichrist in 2 Thessalonians 2:3, where it probably describes his evil nature, although it may imply his certain destruction.

Judas was doomed not because of any failure of Christ but because he followed his own warped and twisted nature. He took sides with Satan against the Lord.

"That they may have My joy fulfilled in themselves" (17:13). In spite of the conflict and sufferings that mar every human life, there is joy for the person who lives close to the Lord. This was a joy which Jesus knew and which He requested for His own.

"The world has hated them" (17:14). Sinful human society, "the world," mirrors the passions and warped values of Satan. Even more, Scripture calls Satan the "ruler of this world" (John 12:31) and says that the whole world (*kosmos*) "lies under the sway of the wicked one" (1 John 5:19). Satan's hostility toward God is mirrored in the reaction of the world to believers.

Jesus specified two reasons for the world's hatred. (1) Jesus gave them God's word, and (2) their identity is now rooted in heaven, even as Christ's is. The word that the believer receives exposes the world's corruption; the new life given by Christ makes the believer stand out as one who is different, no longer "of the world." The hatred for the world is instinctive, the natural animosity of the sinful toward the holy, of lost humanity toward God (cf. Rom. 5:10).

No wonder Jesus said, "They are not of the world, just as I am not of the world."

Jesus' prayer that the disciples may be consecrated as He is (17:17–19). The key word in this section of Jesus' prayer is "sanctify." The Greek word used here is *hagiazon,* from the root *hagiazo,* "to make holy." In the Old Testament, the holy was separated from ordinary use so it might be dedicated to God. In the New Testament, God transformed the ordinary that it might be usable by Him. Thus, Jesus' prayer was one of consecration, asking God the Father to transform and use His disciples to His glory.

Sanctify them by Your truth. Your word is truth. As You sent me into the world, I also have sent them into the world. And for their sakes I sanctify Myself, that they also may be sanctified by the truth (John 17:17–19).

"Sanctify them by Your truth" (17:17). We might better catch the intent of these words if we translated them, "Consecrate them in Your truth." Jesus' disciples were no longer to live in the world, ruled by its passions. Instead, they were to live in the realm of God's truth, ruled by the governing principles unveiled in God's Word. Living in God's truth, the disciples would be fully equipped for their mission to the world.

"As You sent Me into the world, I also have sent them into the world" (17:18). The disciples were the fruit of Jesus' mission to the world. Now Jesus was sending them into the world to gather more fruit for Him.

"For their sakes I sanctify Myself, that they also may be sanctified by the truth" (17:19). In the Old Testament, the language of sanctification or consecration is intimately linked with sacrifice. In this passage, Jesus spoke of the sacrifice He was about to become, that through His death on their behalf His disciples might be consecrated to their mission.

Jesus prayed that all believers might be one (17:20–23). Of all the statements in Jesus' prayer, this is perhaps the most misunderstood. Many people have viewed it as a call to organizational unity. Many sermons have been preached and many well-intentioned movements have been launched on the interpretation of this statement.

However, Christ specifically asked that the disciples might be one "as You, Father, are in Me, and I in You" (17:21). The unity of which Jesus spoke is organic. His focus was on the unity which believers can have with the Lord—not with one other.

I do not pray for these alone, but also for those who will believe in Me through their word; that they all may be one, as You, Father, are in Me, and I in You; that they also may be one in Us, that the world may believe that You sent Me. And the glory which You gave Me I have given them, that they may be one just as We are one; I in them, and You in Me; that they may be made perfect in one, and that the world may know that You have sent Me, and have loved them as You have loved Me (John 17:20–23).

"I . . . pray . . . for those who will believe in Me through their word" (John 17:20). The focus of Christ's prayer shifted here from the disciples to future generations of believers. This section of Jesus' prayer relates to members of the church of all the ages.

"That they all may be one" (17:21). It is significant that this section contains a single request, which is stated again and again. Repetition alerts us to the significance of "being one." More to the point, within the verses the oneness prayed for is carefully defined:

- "as You, Father, are in Me, and I in You" (17:21);
- "that they also may be one in Us" (17:21); and
- "I in them, and You in Me" (17:23).

What Christ described here is a mutual indwelling, patterned on the relationship with God which Jesus experienced during His life on earth. This is the same request made in John 17:11 for the disciples, and it is to be understood in the same way. All the verses quoted with the comment on 17:11 above (p. 192) help us define the practical implications of mutual indwelling for believers, even as they define the practical implications of mutual indwelling in the case of the Father and the Son.

Again, Jesus was not asking the Father that the visible church on earth might experience organizational unity. His prayer was that all believers of all times would experience the same kind of organic unity with God which made it possible for Jesus to minister as He did.

"That the world may believe that You sent Me" (John 17:21). One outcome of organic unity with Christ is that Jesus will be seen in us. The most fundamental witness to the person of Jesus Christ is the transformed lives of believers.

"The glory which You gave Me I have given them" (John 17:22). As Jesus in His incarnation revealed the glory of God, so God now expresses Himself through the believer who lives out his or her union with Jesus.

"That they may be made perfect in one" (John 17:23). In Scripture, to be "made perfect" generally means to become mature or to be fully equipped for a particular service. Our oneness with Jesus equips us to continue Jesus' mission to the world and to communicate God's amazing love.

It is not enough that the people of the world hear about God. They need to *see the gospel enfleshed.* Because Jesus remained in union with God, His glory could be seen in Christ. As we live in union with our Lord, God's glory will be displayed in us as well.

Jesus prayed that believers might be with Him (17:24–26). The conclusion of Jesus' prayer echoes its beginning.

Father, I desire that they also whom You gave Me may be with Me where I am, that they may behold My glory which You have given Me; for You loved Me before the foundation of the world. O righteous Father! The world has not known You, but I have known You; and these have known that You sent Me. And I have declared to them Your name, and will declare it, that the love with which You loved Me may be in them, and I in them (John 17:24–26).

The wonder of our Lord's high priestly prayer is that it *has* been answered. The Holy Spirit unites us to Jesus Christ, for "by one Spirit we were all baptized into one body" (1 Cor. 12:13)—the body of Christ. No less than 87 times in 86 different verses, the New Testament speaks of believers as being "in Christ." And through this mystical relationship that we have with Jesus, we are kept, empowered, and enabled for life to the fullest in this world.

JESUS' PRAYER IN GETHSEMANE

Perhaps the second most familiar prayer of Jesus was offered shortly after He and His disciples left the room where they had shared the Last Supper and walked to the Garden of Gethsemane. Each of the synoptic Gospels gives us a report of what happened there.

Then Jesus came with them to a place called Gethsemane, and said to the disciples, "Sit here while I go and pray over there." And He took with him Peter and the two sons of Zebedee, and He began to be sorrowful and deeply distressed.

Then He said to them, "My soul is exceedingly sorrowful, even to death. Stay here and watch with Me." He went a little farther and fell on His face, and prayed, saying, "O My Father, if it is possible, let this cup pass from Me; nevertheless, not as I will, but as You will."

Then He came to the disciples and found them asleep, and said to Peter, "What? Could you not watch with Me one hour? Watch and pray, lest you enter into temptation. The spirit indeed is willing, but the flesh is weak."

Again, a second time, He went away and prayed, saying, "O My Father, if this cup cannot pass away from Me unless I drink it, Your will be done." And He came and found them asleep again, for their eyes were heavy. So He left them, went away again, and prayed the third time, saying the same words.

Then He came to His disciples and said to them, "Are you still sleeping and resting? Behold, the hour is at hand, and the Son of Man is being betrayed into the hands of sinners. Rise, let us be going. See, My betrayer is at hand" (Matt. 26:36–46; cf. Mark 14:32–42; Luke 22:39–46).

Earlier we looked at Gethsemane and explored Jesus' words to His drowsy disciples (see pp. 154–156). Here we want to focus on Christ's actual prayer in this experience.

Jesus' anguish (*Matthew 26:37–38*). One of the most significant questions we can ask is why

Jesus showed such emotion as He faced death. The stories of Jewish and Christian martyrs tell us how many faced terrible deaths with courage and even joy. Yet Jesus was gripped with such sorrow that He almost died, (26:38). Luke tells us that as Jesus prayed, "His sweat became like great drops of blood falling to the ground" (Luke 22:44). The depth of His anguish so affected His body that it was almost a killing sorrow!

It is important to remember that Jesus' death was unique. Christ knew that He would soon face a moment when He would be entirely alone. Jesus was to be the sacrificial lamb. In that moment when He bore in His own body the sins of the world, Jesus would be forsaken even by the Father (Matt. 27:46). The essential unity of the Godhead would be ripped apart, and this would be an event so unique that we cannot imagine its impact on the Father and the Son.

What we do know is that this moment paid the price required by all the sins of the human race—from Adam's fall to mankind's last surge of rebellion at history's end. Physical death held no terrors for Jesus. But what was about to take place on the cross caused Him an anguish we cannot begin to understand.

"Let this cup pass from Me" (*Matthew 26:39*). Only a superficial reading of the Bible would lead a person to suggest that the "cup" Jesus longed to avoid was physical death. "This cup" might serve as an image of any painful experience. But the imagery is frequently used in the Old Testament not merely of suffering and death (see Ps. 11:6; Jer. 25:15–16) but as a symbol of God's wrath. What Jesus begged for was an alternative—any alternative—to this means of carrying out His mission of redemption.

"Nevertheless, not as I will, but as You will" (*Matthew 26:39*). Throughout His time on earth, Jesus had gladly done the Father's will. Now Jesus faced the ultimate temptation. The almost unbearable pressure He felt is reflected in the anguish which He displayed.

In Gethsemane, we see the reversal of Eden. There Adam said, in effect, "Not Your will but mine," and so sin entered our race. Now Jesus said, "Not my will but yours." In the ultimate act of submission, He purged our sin, providing all who believe with eternal salvation.

"And prayed the third time, saying the same words" (*Matthew 26:44*). While the Gospels report slight variations in the wording of the three prayers, Matthew reminds us that each time Jesus said essentially the same thing. But why three prayers?

Submission to God's will is something we need to renew moment by moment. In Gethsemane, Jesus provided an example for moment-by-moment obedience, and He provided a reminder that our commitment to the Lord must be constantly renewed. Like Jesus, we need to reaffirm in every prayer, "Nevertheless, not my will, but Yours."

JESUS' UNPRAYED PRAYER

Scripture provides the content of one prayer that Jesus never uttered. It is a prayer that would have been answered, as all Christ's prayers were answered. But He chose not to pray this prayer.

Just after the prayers of submission offered at Gethsemane, Judas led a band into the garden to arrest Jesus. Peter's first reaction was to fight (cf. John 18:10). He pulled a sword, or knife (the same Greek word is used for both) and struck out at an official who represented the Jewish high priest. Jesus told Peter,

Put your sword in its place, for all who take the sword will perish by the sword. Or do you think that I cannot now pray to My Father, and he will provide Me with more than twelve legions of angels? (Matt. 26:52–53).

Instant relief to Jesus in this situation was available. Yet He never spoke the words which would have spared Him death on the cross.

Jesus' unspoken prayer reminds us that Christ was not a martyr, butchered at the instigation of evil men who thwarted His best attempts to unveil a God of grace and love. In

Jesus stopped Peter as he struck out at those who had come to arrest the Lord.

fact, Jesus chose the cross, and it was only in the cross that the fullest meaning of God's love and grace are seen.

THE PRAYERS FROM THE CROSS

If we chart the prayers recorded in the Gospels, we find a fascinating pattern. Luke records the prayer of a godly man named Simeon who recognized the baby Jesus as the promised Savior. Simeon praised God for letting his aged eyes see the Lord's salvation (Luke 2:34). Each of the synoptic Gospels records the Lord's Prayer, which Jesus taught His disciples. But there are few recorded prayers of Jesus Himself. And of those which are recorded, most were prayed during Christ's final days on earth.

Forgiveness for the guilty *(Luke 23:34).* "Father, forgive them, for they know not what they do."

The scene on Calvary has often been represented in Christian art. Luke's description is brief, but specific. When they had come to Calvary, "There they crucified him." These few words are suggestive. The military detail came to crucifixion hill. They had been there before,

often. They knew the drill. Without any hesitation they went about the familiar but tragic process. They drove nails into the hands of the condemned, nailing them to the crossbars the prisoners had been forced to carry. Two or three soldiers lifted them up, attached the crossbars to the poles already standing on the execution ground, and drove nails through the heels of the prisoners, fixing them as firmly to the pole. Then they sat down to wait.

Luke pictures them then, squatting around the cross to gamble for the prisoners' clothing, which the soldiers would later sell to supplement their wages, all indifferent to the suffering men over their heads.

But Jesus was sensitive to them despite their callousness. While they ignored Him and the two men crucified with Him, Jesus prayed for them. "Father, forgive them. They do not know what they do."

They did not know He was the Savior.

They did not realize that every human life was precious in God's sight.

They were not even aware that they themselves, despite their indifference to human suffering, were objects of God's love. But they were. And even as the Savior died, He

THE LOCATION AND LENGTH OF JESUS' PRAYERS

Baptism & early, mid-ministry	After 2–2 1/2 years of ministry	The last few days on earth
None	At rejection: Matt. 11 (3 verses)	High priestly: John 17 (26 verses)
		In Gethsemane Matt. 26 (3 verses)
		On the cross Matt. 27 (1 verse)

prayed for all who like them are unaware of man's true identity as creations of a God whose love for them knows no bounds at all.

The final recorded prayer of Jesus was His cry from the cross.

And about the ninth hour Jesus cried out with a loud voice, "E'li, E'li, lama sabachthani?" that is, "My God, My God, why have You forsaken Me?" (Matt. 27:46).

These words, which Matthew first set down in Aramaic and then translated into Greek, were uttered in the moment that Jesus feared most (see Gethsemane, above, pp. 194–195). At that moment He took upon Himself the sins of the world, and God the Father turned away from the Son, who was made sin for us.

How beautifully Elizabeth Barrett Browning's words sum up the meaning of this awful moment for us.

> Yea, once Immanuel's orphaned cry
>   his universe has shaken.
> It went up single, echoless, "My God,
>   I am forsaken!"
> It went up from the Holy's lips amid
>   his lost creation,
> That, of the lost, no son should use
>   those words of desolation.

Through Jesus the forsaken we have been forever reunited with God.

THE EARLY CHURCH AT PRAYER

ACTS

Our congregation has a prayer chain. When a special need arises, one phone call will quickly set the people in our congregation to praying, day or night. The first phone call goes to Trajan or to Gus and Dottie, who then alert the first person on each of our eight prayer teams.

My wife and I are on Team 2. So Trajan calls Tom or Jean Sbani, who passes the request to Vern and Marge Mitton, who call Margie Bowman, who calls Evelyn Kurvink, who calls our house, and we pass the request on to Jim or Marge Irvine, and so on.

Prayer chains are easy to organize, and they are an effective way to focus a congregation's prayers on needs as soon as they emerge.

It seems unlikely that the first-century church organized this kind of prayer chain. But even a quick look through the book of Acts makes it clear that prayer was an essential link in the early church. There are 21 references to prayer in the book of Acts, and the content of three prayers is recorded in this book for our enrichment.

EVERY REFERENCE TO PRAYER IN ACTS

ACTS 1:14:
Continual United Prayer

After Jesus returned to heaven, a little band of believers gathered in Jerusalem to wait for the promised coming of the Holy Spirit. Acts 1:15 tells us that about 120 believers, including the eleven remaining disciples, met together in an upper room. The company also included Mary the mother of Jesus and His brothers. Acts 1:14 states that "these all continued with one accord in prayer and supplication."

In a sense, this verse sets the tone for the prayer life of the early church. All were involved in prayer. And prayer was an essential, continuing element in first-century church life.

The believers "all continued" (v. 14). Prayer was not simply a personal exercise. Prayer was an important matter for the assembled community.

The believers were of "one accord" (v. 14). All agreed that prayer had priority in the life of the church. The relationship with God that had been won for believers by Christ was nurtured and affirmed in a shared commitment of prayer.

The believers were engaged in "prayer and supplication" (v. 14). While "prayer" is a general term that includes all conversation with God, "supplication" emphasizes requests and implies dependence on the Lord. While some early manuscripts omit "and supplication," references to prayer in Acts make it clear that members of the early church were deeply sensitive to their dependence on the Lord and were also confident of His powerful, living presence.

ACTS 1:24, 25:
Prayer Concerning Judas's Successor

See the discussion of this prayer on page 210.

ACTS 2:42:
Prayer's Central Role in Church Life

The coming of the Holy Spirit on the first believers, as recorded in Acts 2, drew a multitude to the scene (cf. Acts 2:6). Peter took the opportunity to preach history's first evangelistic sermon, and some three thousand persons responded to the gospel invitation. These believers bonded to form a fellowship marked by specific commitments. Acts 2:42 says that those converted that day "continued steadfastly in the apostles' doctrine and fellowship, in the breaking of bread, and in prayer."

The apostles' doctrine. The Greek word translated "doctrine" means "teaching." The apostles spoke authoritatively, and their teaching as recorded in the New Testament remains the standard of Christian belief and practice.

Fellowship. The Greek word is *koinonia*. It speaks of the common bond that unites a group as well as expressions of that common bond. What Christians have in common is a personal relationship with God through Jesus. This common bond is expressed in the love and care which believers have for one another. It is significant that in the New Testament the

word most commonly used to describe Christian giving is *koinonia*.

The breaking of bread. This reference may be to the practice of meeting frequently and the sharing of meals by first-century Christians. Many take this as a reference to celebration of the Lord's Supper, the Eucharist or Communion. It seems best, however, to understand this phrase as a reference to the intimacy that developed between members of the Christian community. It was expressed in their delight to be with each other.

"And in prayers." The fourth characteristic of the first-century church was its continuing commitment to prayer. The believers submitted to the authoritative teaching of the apostles, they were united in their commitment to each other, they met together daily, and they prayed when they met.

A vital Christian church of today will be characterized by these same commitments.

ACTS 3:1:
Personal Prayer Practiced

For some time the Christian community was viewed by Jew and Christian alike as a sect within Judaism. During this period, Christians were also practicing Jews. They kept the dietary and other lifestyle laws found in the Old Testament, and they worshiped as other Jews did at the Jerusalem temple.

Acts 3:1 depicts Peter and John going up to the temple to pray at one of the traditional hours of prayer. This was probably a time when a sacrifice was offered and people gathered for worship. On this occasion, Peter healed a lame man. When a crowd gathered, he preached a notable evangelistic sermon.

It would be wrong, however, to assume that the two disciples were going to the temple to preach. In fact, they were going to the temple as individuals, to worship God and to pray as part of their personal devotions.

While praying with other believers is vital to healthy church life, it is just as vital that believers have personal prayer lives as well.

ACTS 4:23–31:
Prayer for Boldness

See the discussion of this prayer on page 210.

ACTS 6:4:
Prayer Lives of Leaders

As the church grew, it became necessary for the apostles to delegate responsibilities. The first case of delegation is described in Acts 6.

One of the ways in which the first-century church showed love and concern for its members was to distribute food to widows and orphans and others who were unable to work to meet their own basic needs. Such a system of organized charity already existed in Jerusalem, and it was funded by gifts given to the temple. As long as Christians were considered good Jews by the authorities, needy believers shared in the existing "social security" program. But as the Christian community grew, the Jewish religious leaders ostracized believers. The church responded by setting up its own system for helping needy believers.

Acts 6 tells of a dispute that broke out in the church when some believers felt their widows and orphans were not receiving their fair share in the daily distribution. The solution was obvious. Someone would have to accept responsibility to oversee the distribution and make sure it was fair.

The real issue was: Was this a task for the apostles? Their answer was, "No." The reason is given in Acts 3:4: "We will give ourselves continually to prayer and to the ministry of the word."

The priorities set by the apostles are important for all in full-time ministry. Spiritual leadership requires an emphasis on prayer and ministry of the Word. It is fascinating to note that the apostles mentioned prayer first!

ACTS 6:6:
Prayer on Ordaining Workers

Read first the discussion of Acts 6:4, above.

The apostles' solution was to establish stringent qualifications for persons who would

The apostles commissioned certain believers to perform particular tasks—such as feeding the poor—for the church.

be put in charge of supervising the distribution to the needy. The congregation was then instructed to select persons who met these qualifications. Seven men were selected and brought to the apostles. The apostles prayed, confirmed the congregation's choices, and laid hands on the seven to ordain them for their ministry.

It is uncertain from the text if the apostles prayed for wisdom in order to confirm the congregation's choices, or if they prayed for the seven at a confirmation ceremony. It is clear, however, that prayer played an important part in this entire process. Surely anyone who is set apart for any ministry in the church deserves our prayers. And just as surely, prayer should play a significant role in their selection.

ACTS 7:59–60:
Stephen's Dying Prayer

See the discussion of this prayer on page 212–213.

ACTS 8:15:
A Unique Prayer for Converted Samaritans

In time, opposition to the Christian movement grew, and ordinary believers were forced to flee Jerusalem and Judea. As the believers scattered, they shared their faith and more people were converted. This included a number of Samaritans, descendants of pagans who had been resettled in Israelite territory by the Assyrians hundreds of years before. The Samaritans' claim to worship Israel's God was decisively rejected by the Jews. In the first century, a deep and mutual hostility existed between Jews and Samaritans.

Luke tells us that "when the apostles who were at Jerusalem heard that Samaria had received the word of God, they sent Peter and John to them" (Acts 8:14). The two actually formed an investigative committee, sent to find out what had really happened. Peter and John were quickly convinced that the Samaritans who professed faith in Jesus were actually converted. The next verses, Acts 8:15–16, state that the apostles then "prayed for them that they might receive the Holy Spirit, for as yet He had fallen upon none of them."

Prayer to receive the Holy Spirit? This verse has served as a proof text for those who believe in a "second work of grace." This teaching holds that a person must believe in Jesus to be saved. But salvation is only a first work of grace. The second work of grace is held to be the coming upon the believer of the Holy Spirit. Those who hold this view also typically claim that the coming of the Spirit will be demonstrated by speaking in tongues.

The authority of the epistles. The book of Acts is a report of what happened in the first-century church, and the Epistles are the New Testament's repository of doctrine. The distinction is important. Acts reports events. The Epistles contain authoritative teaching. We are to build our doctrine on the clear teaching of the Epistles. We should not try to construct doctrine from the reports of first-century experiences.

This principle is important because the New Testament epistles clearly teach that every believer is given the Holy Spirit on conversion. For instance, Romans 8:9 specifically states that "if anyone does not have the Spirit of Christ, he is not His."

Why didn't the Samaritans receive the Holy Spirit upon conversion? If we accept the teaching of the epistles as normative, we have to conclude that the experience of the Samaritans was an exception to Scripture's rule. And we need to ask, Why would God make an exception here?

There is a simple answer to this question. The Jews and Samaritans were hostile to each other. And religious differences provided the basis of the hostility! The Jews insisted that God was to be worshiped at the temple mount. The Samaritans claimed that God was to be worshiped on Mount Gerizim. In fact, the Samaritans had constructed a temple on Mount Gerizim. The Jews said that their version of the books of Moses was authoritative. The Samaritans had their own version of the Pentateuch. And the Samaritans claimed that their version was authoritative!

This hostility was so deeply rooted that there was no way Samaritans would submit to the religious authority of Jews. But the apostles were Jews! They were also Jesus' chosen leaders of His church, and their teaching was authoritative. What could move Samaritans to submit to the authority of Jewish apostles and maintain the unity of the Christian church?

Acts 8 gives us the answer. God, this one time, withheld the giving of the Holy Spirit until the apostles Peter and John came down from Jerusalem. The apostles accepted the Samaritans as true believers, and the Samaritans were given an unmistakable sign that the apostles' authority came from God. The Holy Spirit was given when the apostles prayed—and not before!

Is it valid to build a doctrine such as the second work of grace on the report in Acts of what happened in Samaria? Not at all. The epistles establish a very different doctrine. What Acts records is the experience of the first-century church, which in this case involved exceptions required by some unique and never-to-be-repeated historical situation. Acts is simply not to be used as a source from which to draw Christian doctrine.

ACTS 8:22:
Prayer for Forgiveness

Read first the article on Acts 8:15, above.

The coming of the gospel message to Samaria was supported by notable miracles performed by Philip the evangelist (Acts 8:6, 7). One of those shocked by Philip's miracles was a man named Simon, who had presented himself as a sorcerer, impressing many people in Samaria. Apparently, Simon was an illusionist—a "magician." When Simon saw Philip's real miracles, he was astounded, and he turned to Christ.

But when the apostles from Jerusalem prayed and believers received the Holy Spirit, Simon saw an opportunity for a financial killing! If Simon had this kind of power, he could make millions! So Simon, saved but spiritually immature, approached the apostles. He offered them money if they would give him the power to lay hands on people and pray and have them receive the Holy Spirit.

Peter rebuked Simon, warning him that his heart was not right with God. Inwardly Simon remained "poisoned by bitterness and bound by iniquity" (Acts 8:23). Peter warned Simon to repent and pray for forgiveness!

ACTS 8:24:
Intercessory Prayer Requested

Read first the articles on Acts 8:15 and 8:22, above.

Peter's stern rebuke frightened Simon. He then asked the apostle to "pray to the Lord for me, that none of the things which you have spoken may come upon me." Some argue that Simon was not truly converted, pointing (1) to his offer to buy supernatural powers, (2) to the content of Peter's rebuke, and (3) to Simon's appeal that Peter pray he would not suffer the consequences of which he had been warned. But the text tells us that Simon had

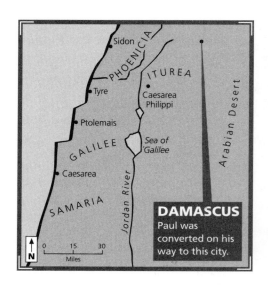

believed and had been baptized (8:13). We shouldn't expect a new believer to act like a mature Christian. It's better to take Simon's urgent request for prayer as a sign that he truly did believe and that he repented of his foolish request.

ACTS 9:11:
The Prayer of Redirected Faith

Acts 9 records the conversion of Saul of Tarsus, better known as Paul the apostle. A committed Pharisee, Saul felt an intense hostility toward first-century Christians. Convinced that they had rejected the Law of Moses and Judaism, Saul set out on a holy crusade to stamp out the "heresy." His persecution of the early Christians was rooted in zeal for God, as Saul understood God and His will.

Acts contains three accounts of Saul's sudden conversion while traveling on the road to Damascus with a commission from the Sanhedrin to capture Christians and bring them to Jerusalem for judgment. Stunned and blinded by a great light, Paul heard the voice of Jesus. He realized his zeal had actually led him to fight against God. Instructed to go to Damascus and wait to be told what he must do, Saul was led there, still blind, by his companions.

For three days, Saul fasted and prayed. We can only imagine his thoughts during those hours. What we can be sure of is that Saul's prayers were now redirected. Rather than praying the traditional prayers offered by the Pharisees, Saul's prayers were now as intensely personal as any of the Old Testament psalms. They were now offered in Jesus' name.

Paul's redirected and deeply personal prayers were heard. God spoke to a believer named Ananias and sent him to Saul of Tarsus, "for behold, he is praying."

God still answers heartfelt prayers offered in Jesus' name by believers.

ACTS 9:40:
Prayer for a Miracle

The book of Acts tells us that the flurry of miracles that marked Jesus' ministry continued in the first years of the Christian era. Authenticating miracles were performed by the apostles as well as by believers like Philip, who introduced the gospel into new lands (cf. Acts 8).

❖

The converted but still blind Saul was visited by Ananias.

Verses 36–43 of Acts 9 tell of a visit Peter made to Christians who lived along the coast of the Mediterranean Sea. While Peter was in the area, a beloved Christian woman died in the port city of Joppa. When Peter was told of the woman's many acts of mercy, he sent everyone from the room where the body lay and prayed. He then spoke and told the woman to arise . . . and she was restored to life.

Even this private miracle performed within the Christian community had an evangelistic impact. Many in Joppa heard what had happened, and they believed.

The apostles had dedicated themselves to "prayer and to the ministry of the word" (Acts 6:4). Here we see some of the results of their setting of that priority. They bathed all their activities in prayer, and they lived close to the Savior and were responsive to the Holy Spirit's guidance. The apostles not only laid the foundations of the Christian church but they were also infused with unmatched spiritual power.

ACTS 10:2, 4:
The Acceptable Prayers of a Roman Soldier

God's Old Testament people enjoyed a covenant relationship with the Lord that guaranteed access to Him in prayer by all believers. Until Jesus died and rose again, this special relationship with God was not available to non-Jews, all of whom were known as Gentiles.

Writing in Romans, the apostle Paul summed up the spiritual advantages enjoyed by Israel. Of Israelites alone it could be said, "To whom pertain the adoption, the glory, the covenants, the giving of the law, the service of God, and the promises" (Rom. 9:4).

But just as these privileges were no guarantee of salvation, so being a Gentile did not prevent a person from believing in the God of Israel and establishing a personal relationship with Him. Acts 10 introduces one such Gentile, a centurion in the Roman army who is described as "a devout man and one who feared God with all his household, who gave alms generously to the people, and prayed to God always" (Acts 10:2).

The technical term in first-century Judaism for such a Gentile was "God-fearer." Such persons did not undergo full conversion to Judaism, but they displayed a true faith in God by a life lived in harmony with God's moral law, by concern for the poor, and by "prayer to God always."

This military officer, named Cornelius, was to become the first Gentile Christian. Acts tells us that one day about the ninth hour (3:00 p.m.), an angel appeared to Cornelius. The hour is significant, for this was a time set apart in Judaism as a time for prayer (cf. Acts 3:1). The implication is that Cornelius was praying when the angel appeared "in a vision." But we have additional evidence. Later when Peter came to see Cornelius, the officer reported that "at the ninth hour I prayed in my house" (Acts 10:30–31). Cornelius *was* praying when the angel visited him.

The angel told Cornelius that his prayers and alms "have come up for a memorial before God." He instructed Cornelius to send for Peter, who would "tell you what you must do" (Acts 10:6).

Prayer was vital in preparing the heart of this Gentile, who believed in God and welcomed the gospel. God is not obligated to hear the prayers of pagans. But those who show spiritual sensitivity by praying may be preparing their hearts to welcome the gospel.

ACTS 10:9:
Prayer Preparation for a Change of Heart

Read first the article on Acts 10:2, 4, above.

Devout first-century Jews isolated themselves from Gentiles lest they become ritually unclean. A Jew in this condition could not participate in public worship until a day had passed and he or she had undergone ritual purification. Since uncleanness was transmitted by coming into contact with any unclean object or person, no devout Jew would visit the home of a Gentile. The risk of ritual contamination was too great.

Peter, who had lived all his life as a devout Jew, would not welcome an invitation to visit the home of Cornelius who, however godly, was still a Gentile.

Acts 10:9 tells us that the day after the angel spoke with Cornelius, Peter "went up on the housetop to pray, about the sixth hour" (noon). There Peter was given repeated visions in which God commanded Peter to kill and eat animals that the Old Testament classified as unclean. Each time Peter refused to eat, but he was told, "What God has cleansed you must not call common."

Even as Peter puzzled over the meaning of the vision, the messengers sent by Cornelius arrived. And Peter realized that God had been teaching him to set aside his prejudices and to go with these visitors.

It is significant that this vision came while Peter was praying. Prayer focuses our hearts and minds on the Lord, clearing a channel through which God can speak to our hearts. Even as prayer had prepared Cornelius for the angel's visit, so prayer prepared Peter to aban-

CAESAREA
Where Peter met Cornelius the centurion, and Gentiles believed.

Sidon

Tyre

Caesarea Philippi

Ptolemais   Capernaum

GALILEE
Tiberias   Sea of Galilee
Nazareth

SAMARIA

Samaria

Mediterranean Sea

Jordan River

DECAPOLIS

Joppa
Lydda   PEREA

0   15   30
Miles

N

don his deeply rooted prejudices and to accept Gentiles as full partners in the Christian community.

How vital prayer is as a way of opening our hearts to God's Spirit, that He might transform and teach us as well.

ACTS 11:5:
Peter's Report of His Experience

First read the articles on Acts 10:2, 4 and Acts 10:9, above.

A sense of their special identity as God's chosen people had shaped Jewish attitudes for centuries. The first-century Christians, who were also Jews, had been jolted by the conversion of Samaritans and their earlier integration into the church (see Acts 8). But no one had imagined that Gentiles might also be saved. The gospel, like the law, was assumed to be for Jews or near-Jews only.

As Peter visited the house of Cornelius, he was shocked when these Gentiles experienced conversion and spoke in tongues, signifying the Holy Spirit's presence in their lives. The same thing had happened to the disciples on the day of Pentecost! (Acts 2). Peter understood the significance both of his vision and of what he had witnessed. Later, when he was asked to explain his actions to the Jerusalem church, Peter told them the whole story. He told of the vision that came while he was praying, of Cornelius's angel encounter, and of the visible evidence of the Spirit's coming upon these Gentile believers. Peter concluded, "If therefore God gave them the same gift as He gave us when we believed on the Lord Jesus Christ, who was I that I could withstand God?" (Acts 11:17).

Peter's report convinced the church, and the early Christian community "glorified God, saying, 'Then God has also granted to the Gentiles repentance to life'" (Acts 11:18). This response was made by a praying church—a church which experienced daily fellowship with the Lord and so remained responsive and teachable (see the article on Acts 2:42, page 199).

ACTS 12:5, 12:
An Unexpected Answer to Prayer

One of the most fascinating prayer experiences reported in Acts is related to Peter's imprisonment.

Herod Antipas, Roman ruler over Palestine, had curried favor with his Jewish subjects by executing the apostle James. The response of the Jewish authorities was so favorable that Herod had Peter arrested, intending to execute him after the religious holidays. Peter was locked away and placed under heavy guard during the holiday season.

The Christians responded by appealing to God. Acts 12:5 tells us that "constant prayer was offered to God for him by the church." Every hour day and night Christians slipped into and out of this continuing prayer meeting.

God answered the church's prayer by sending an angel, who released Peter from his chains, led him outside the prison, and left him on the familiar streets of Jerusalem. When Peter realized he was truly free and had not been dreaming, he hurried to the home of Mary, the mother of John Mark, where the prayer meeting was being held (Acts 12:12).

When Peter knocked on the door, his voice was recognized by Rhoda, a young servant. She was so excited that she burst into the prayer meeting and shouted out the good news, leaving Peter at the door!

What is so fascinating is that the people who were praying did not believe Rhoda! When she insisted it was Peter's own voice, they still didn't believe. Their response reflected the common first-century view that a person's guardian angel resembled the person he guarded, and they insisted that "it is his angel" (Acts 12:15). These Christians couldn't believe that God had answered their prayers and had brought about Peter's release!

This incident is helpful in two ways. First, it suggests an answer to those who insist that to have any prayer answered a person must "believe." In this case, God answered the prayer of believers who prayed without the

The servant who answered Peter's knock was so excited about his release from prison that she forgot to let him in!

❖

"necessary" confidence that the Lord would do as they asked! Second, the incident reminds us that God does answer prayer. There are no limits on what God is able to do. When faced with the impossible, our only course is to bring the need to God's attention and ask Him to act.

ACTS 13:2, 3:
Prayer in Calling and Commissioning Missionaries

The first predominantly Gentile church emerged in Antioch. It was guided by a leadership team of prophets and teachers that included Saul of Tarsus, Barnabas, and three others. Like the apostles, this local leadership team gave priority to prayer and the ministry of the word of God (see article on Acts 6:4, page 200).

Acts tells us that "as they ministered to the Lord and fasted, the Holy Spirit said, 'Now

separate to Me Barnabas and Saul for the work to which I have called them'" (Acts 13:2). These two men would be the first missionaries to be sent specifically to Gentiles. They would spearhead that great first-century missionary movement which planted the Christian church throughout the Roman Empire.

It is important to note that the Holy Spirit spoke to the leaders "as they ministered to the Lord [prayed, worshiped] and fasted." Concentration on the Lord opened the hearts of these men to the Holy Spirit and made them sensitive to His leading. Such times of concentrated prayer are important if we are to develop sensitivity to the leading of the Holy Spirit. For more on the role of fasting, see the Bible Background feature on page 149.

Acts 13:3 continues the account. "Then, having fasted and prayed, and laid hands on them [Barnabas and Saul], they [the other members of the leadership team, probably with the participation of the whole Antioch congregation] sent them away." A time of concentrated prayer marked the commissioning as well as the call of Barnabas and Saul to their special ministry.

While we are not to take incidents in the book of Acts as normative for the church today, we may certainly learn from them. The example set by these early Christian leaders suggests that church leaders today should take time for concentrated prayer to develop sensitivity to the Spirit's leading—especially when commissioning believers for special ministries.

ACTS 14:23:
Prayer and the Appointing of Church Leaders

The missionary ministry of Barnabas and Saul, known in the rest of Acts as Paul, met with striking success. The two men visited a number of major population centers on their first missionary journey. In spite of difficulties, they established churches in each of these centers. Later Paul and Barnabas revisited the churches they had established and "appointed elders in every church, and prayed with fasting" (Acts 14:23).

The linkage of fasting with prayer again suggests that a period of concentrated prayer was associated with the commissioning of elders.

"Elders in every church." Both Acts and the epistles indicate that spiritual oversight of local churches was provided by a team of elders. It is important to understand the function of this team in the light of first-century conditions.

The "church in Ephesus" was not a congregation that met Sundays for worship in a special building. The "church in Ephesus" was made up of all believers in that major population center. These believers met in small groups in private homes on Sundays. While many believers might come together on special occasions for larger worship services, the small "house churches" served as the basic structure of the Christian movement for the first two and one-half centuries of the Christian era.

There were no "churches" as we know them today, with pastors and buildings and their own elders, deacons, or board members. In the first century, the elders oversaw the spiritual health and provided guidance for all the Christians in the larger community. When the apostles ordained elders for Ephesus or other cities, the men commissioned had a significant and full-time leadership ministry!

"Appointed elders in every church." The manner in which elders were appointed has been much debated. Even with the insight provided by Paul's later letters to Timothy and Titus concerning qualifications for spiritual leadership, Christians differ on the method of appointment.

Denominations in the Episcopal tradition assume that Paul and Barnabas chose and commissioned the elders, transmitting authority to them by the laying on of hands. This is the view held by Catholic and Anglican churches.

Most Protestant denominations assume that Paul and Barnabas simply confirmed as leaders those persons whom the Christians in a community had already elected. Selection by some kind of electoral process is typical in Calvinistic, Methodist, and Baptist traditions.

It is likely that neither approach accurately mirrors what happened in the first century. The New Testament makes it clear that spiritual leadership rests on character qualifications. That is, spiritual leaders are to be selected based on evidence of spiritual maturity, as well as ability to understand and teach revealed truth (cf. 1 Tim. 3:1–13). It was not possible for the missionaries to appoint leaders on their first missionary journey, simply because those who would mature quickly in the faith needed time to do so. By the time Paul and Barnabas revisited the churches, those with leadership qualities had begun to emerge and they were recognized by the other believers.

It is most likely that on revisiting a church, Paul and Barnabas sought the counsel of the Christian community to identify emerging leaders. It is *unlikely* that the Christians simply "voted" on their leaders.

The reference to "praying with fasting" once again alerts us to the fact that a period of concentrated prayer preceded the appointment of leaders. As noted in the discussion of Acts 13:2, 3 (p. 206), such times of prayer are associated with the Holy Spirit's guidance and with the calling and commissioning of persons to ministry. The two missionaries probably consulted with the Christian community, prayed for guidance, and then "appointed" leaders from a congregation's nominees.

The word *appointed* in this passage is *epitithimi*, which is often translated "ordain." The basic meaning, however, is "to give official recognition to." By laying hands on those selected to provide spiritual leadership, Paul and Barnabas gave them official standing as *the* leaders of the Christian community. And concentrated prayer was a vital element in confirming first-century church leaders.

ACTS 16:13:
Prayer Identifies a Potential Convert

The basic strategy that Paul and Barnabas used in spreading the faith was to visit area synagogues and to base their presentation of Jesus on the Scriptures. Two groups of people were contacted in this way—the Jews, from whom Christ came, and God-fearing Gentiles, who had been attracted to Judaism's vision of a single, all-powerful Creator who called human beings to a moral lifestyle. Typically, the Gentile population proved more open to the gospel than the Jewish people, but the earliest members of most first-century churches were drawn from these two groups.

When Paul and Barnabas came to Philippi—which had been settled by discharged Roman soldiers—they found no Jewish synagogue. The two missionaries found out "where prayer was customarily made" and simply talked with people who came there—in this case, women. People who pray, who have a spiritual sensitivity, may be more open to the gospel than materialists whose concern is for the things of this world.

The first convert in Philippi was Lydia, a woman with a Greek name, who "worshiped God." The Lord opened her heart, and she opened her home to the missionaries as a base of operations in her city.

ACTS 16:16:
Prayer Creates a Recognizable Aura

One of the most interesting references to prayer in Acts is found in this verse. Luke notes that "it happened, as we went to prayer, that a certain slave girl possessed with a spirit of divination met us."

The girl followed the missionaries for days, crying out that "these men are the servants of the Most High God, who proclaim to us the way of salvation" (Acts 16:17). Finally Paul, "greatly annoyed," cast the spirit out of her, an act which aroused the anger of the slave girl's owners and led to the missionaries' imprisonment.

But what is so fascinating is Luke's comment that the slave girl met and recognized them as the missionaries "went to prayer." Why did Luke link this spirit's recognition of the missionaries with prayer? Is it possible that when Christians pray, an aura visible to spirit beings forms around them? We cannot know for sure, but even as the flow of electricity disturbs the atmosphere, the flow of spiritual power may create a glow around us.

ACTS 16:25:
Prayer and Praise in Prison

Read first the discussion of Acts 16:16, above.

Paul's exorcism of the spirit that possessed the slave girl angered her owners. They had made a good living offering her services as a fortuneteller. With the spirit exorcised, the girl no longer had supernatural powers. The disturbance they caused led to a judicial beating of Paul and Silas, who were then thrown in prison. There, in the utter darkness of the innermost cell, through the pain caused by their restraints, the two missionaries were "praying and singing hymns to God."

As they prayed, an earthquake shook the prison and threw open its doors, initiating a sequence of events which led to the conversion of the Philippian jailer and the establishment of a Christian community in Philippi.

It is unlikely that Paul and Silas were praying for an earthquake. But they were praying. And God sometimes responds to our prayers in unexpected but wonderful ways.

ACTS 21:5:
A Prayerful Farewell

Paul undertook a number of missionary journeys to different parts of the Roman world. But after this third journey, he felt led by the Spirit to return to Jerusalem. He and others sensed that something out of the ordinary awaited him there. In Acts 21 we follow Paul on the way to Jerusalem, stopping briefly in cities where he had established churches, saying farewell to believers whom he loved. Perhaps these believers realized they would never see Paul again in this life.

In the depths of the Philippian jail, Paul and Silas prayed and sang hymns.

———————— ❖ ————————

Verse 5 of Acts 21 describes a poignant scene, as the Christians in Tyre followed Paul with their children, finally kneeling with him on the shore to pray before the apostle and his companions boarded ship and sailed away.

How wonderful it is that we can be linked by prayer to loved ones far away.

ACTS 22:17:
Prayer and Guidance

Read first the discussion of Acts 21:5, above.

In Jerusalem a riot started when Paul was falsely accused of bringing Gentiles into the temple. He was rescued by Roman soldiers. Later, on his request, he was allowed to speak to the crowds that had assaulted him. Paul related the story of his conversion and also told of an experience he had been through on his return to Jerusalem as a Christian. He told them of praying and falling into a trance. The Lord told Paul to leave Jerusalem, indicating

that he was destined to bring the gospel to the Gentiles.

This is another of several references in Acts which link prayer and divine guidance. In prayer, we open our hearts to the Lord and are more receptive to messages the Holy Spirit wants to impress on our hearts.

ACTS 27:29:
A Prayer that Was Not a Prayer

Accused falsely by the Jews, Paul exercised his right as a Roman citizen to be judged in the capital city of Rome. On the way to Rome, the ship was caught in a violent storm for two weeks. At last the sailors sensed the ship was being driven toward land. But it was midnight. Fearing they would be driven aground, the sailors dropped four anchors and waited. The text says they also "prayed for day to come." A note in the margin of the NKJV text suggests an alternative reading, which is to be preferred. They "*wished* for day to come."

Why is the alternative reading preferred? Jewish sages identified situations in which prayer was not warranted. For instance, if a man approached his hometown and saw smoke arising from a burning home, he was not to pray "Please, God, let it not be my home." Why? The sages pointed out that such a prayer is meaningless *because the event has already taken place.* The traveler's prayer would not change the past. If his house is on fire, prayer won't transfer the fire to someone else's home. It is too late for prayer.

The sailors were not asking God to shorten the night. If they were praying, it was a prayer that they would live to see the dawn. If the word translated "prayed" should be taken here as "wished," we have the same meaning. They hoped desperately that they would survive to see the dawn.

ACTS 28:8:
Prayer and Healing

Before reading, see the comment on Acts 27:29 above.

The dawn did come, and the ship was maneuvered safely through the coastal reefs. While the ship broke up in the stormy seas, everyone on board lived.

The crew and passengers found themselves on Malta, a small island in the Adriatic Sea. Luke tells us that the father of Malta's chief leader was seriously ill. Paul went in to him and prayed, and he laid his hands on him and healed him (Acts 28:8). This event led to many other healings. In response, the islanders provided whatever the ship's crew and passengers needed during their stay.

RECORDED PRAYERS IN ACTS

Along with the many references to prayer in Acts, Luke records the specific content of three petitions.

ACTS 1:24, 25:
The Apostles' Prayer for Guidance

When Jesus returned to heaven after the Resurrection, the disciples were instructed to wait in Jerusalem. Basing their action on Psalm 69:25 and Psalm 109:8, they set out to choose a replacement for Judas. Two men met the criteria established—that the replacement leader should have accompanied the disciples from John's baptism to the end and that he should be an eyewitness to Christ's resurrection. How would they be able to choose between the two candidates?

The disciples chose a method used infrequently in Old Testament times. It was based on a conviction reflected in Proverbs 16:33: "The lot is cast into the lap, but its every decision is from the Lord." That is, God exercised control over what human beings call "chance." So the disciples asked God to reveal His choice of one of the two when they cast lots! Their prayer is recorded in Acts 1:24, 25:

You, O Lord, who know the hearts of all, show which of these two You have chosen to take part in this ministry and apostleship from which Judas by transgression fell, that he might go to his own place.

After making this request of God, the apostles cast lots. A man named Matthias was chosen to serve as one of the twelve apostles.

Earlier in this chapter, we noted that we are not to derive doctrine from Acts, or to assume that the practices it reports are normative for all Christians. It is important *not to assume* that Christians today are to determine God's will by casting lots or throwing dice. When the apostles cast lots to select Matthias, the Holy Spirit had not yet come. In every case after the Spirit had been given, the apostles and others sought guidance from the Holy Spirit. Never again in Scripture was God asked to reveal His will through chance or any other visible sign.

ACTS 4:24–31:
A Petition for Boldness

In the days following the coming of the Spirit, the apostles gave enthusiastic witness to Christ's resurrection. Acts 4 tells of one incident triggered by Peter's healing of a man who had been lame from birth. Peter preached Christ to the crowd that gathered, and the number of believers grew to include about five thousand men, plus women and children. The number was impressive in a city whose population at the time probably numbered less than forty thousand.

The leaders who had plotted Jesus' death were alarmed. They called Peter and John before them and "severely threatened" them, insisting that they not "speak at all or teach in the name of Jesus" (Acts 4:17). The two apostles announced boldly that they would keep on preaching Jesus as God had commanded. Only the enthusiasm of the crowds that were praising God over the healing of the lame man kept the leaders from acting against Peter and John. Instead, the leaders threatened them again and reluctantly let the two go.

Peter and John reported what had happened to the other disciples ("their own companions," v. 23). The apostles went to prayer. Their prayer is recorded for us by Luke.

Lord, You are God, who made heaven and earth and the sea, and all that is in them, who by the mouth of Your servant David have said:

"Why did the nations rage,
  And the people plot vain
    things?
The kings of the earth took
    their stand;
And the rulers were gathered
    together
against the LORD and against
    His Christ."

For truly against Your holy Servant Jesus, whom You anointed, both Herod and Pontius Pilate, with the Gentiles and the people of Israel, were gathered together to do whatever Your hand and Your purpose determined before to be done.

Now, Lord, look on their threats, and grant to Your servants that with all boldness they may speak Your word, by stretching out Your hand to heal, and that signs and wonders may be done through Your holy Servant Jesus.

"Lord, You are God" (*v. 24*). The bulk of this prayer is not petition but a grand affirmation of God's greatness. This was most appropriate for the situation. The disciples were threatened by officials of great authority who had been able to bring about the execution of Jesus Himself. In contrast, the disciples had no worldly authority. They were vulnerable not only to the Jewish leaders but to governors posted by the world's most powerful empire, Rome.

This was certainly a fitting time for them to recall who God is and to affirm His power by acknowledging Him as Creator of all.

"Who by the mouth of . . . David have said" (*v. 25*). After affirming God as Creator, the apostles went on to affirm God as sovereign. The kings of this earth might array themselves against God and His Christ, but their opposition would prove futile. Even though Herod, Pontius Pilate, and even the people of Israel had turned against Jesus, they were able to do only "whatever Your hand and Your purpose determined before to be done" (*v. 28*). The apostles prayed with confidence because they realized that God was in charge of every event

that touched them, their lives, or their ministries.

These two great affirmations of God as the Creator who controls history provided the foundation for three specific requests.

"Look on their threats" (*v. 29*). The disciples asked God to be aware of the danger they faced from the Jewish officials. The phrase is tantamount to asking God to intervene and thwart any plans the leaders might make against them.

"Grant to Your servants that with all boldness they may speak Your word" (*v. 29*). The second specific request was for boldness. The apostles relied on God to give them a spirit of boldness, that they might speak God's word freely. Certainly the apostles' conviction that God is sovereign was essential to the boldness they realized they must maintain to carry out their mission.

"By stretching out Your hand to heal, and that signs and wonders may be done through the name of Your holy Servant Jesus" (*v. 30*). While Christ was present on earth, He performed miracles which authenticated His claims of authority. The very nature of the miracles Jesus performed also identified Him as the promised Messiah. Miracles by earlier prophets fell short of those the Old Testament foretold would be done by the coming Savior King (see Isa. 35:4, 5).

Previous outbreaks of authenticating miracles, such as those performed by Moses and by Elijah, were followed by supportive miracles which gave added proof that the truths they introduced truly were divine revelation. Now the apostles asked God to perform such supportive miracles through them, that their listeners might have additional evidence that the truths revealed by Jesus were from God.

For an extended study of the nature and role of miracles in Scripture, see the companion volume in this series, *Every Miracle and Wonder of the Bible.*

The apostles' prayer is answered (*Acts 4:31*). Luke reports that "when they had prayed, the place where they were assembled together was shaken; and they were all filled with the Holy Spirit, and they spoke the word of God with boldness." God gave them freely of His Spirit, the source of the boldness we all crave. And as the book of Acts continues, we see that God also answered their prayer that healings and miracles might be done through Jesus' name.

ACTS 7:59–60:
Stephen's Dying Prayer

The boldness for which the apostles had prayed was sorely needed. As the church grew, so did the opposition. A flurry of persecution was stimulated by the boldness of Stephen, who challenged opponents to debate and proved from the Old Testament Scriptures that Jesus truly is the Christ. Falsely accused of blasphemy, Stephen was called before the Sanhedrin, the Jewish governing counsel. His defense, recorded in Acts 7, took the form of a powerful argument based on Israel's historic refusal to respond to God. He condemned the hardness of heart displayed by the court before which he stood. Refusing to acknowledge Jesus, they arrested him on false charges and had him executed by the Roman authorities.

The accusation so infuriated the court that its members mobbed Stephen, dragged him outside the city, and stoned him to death. Thus, Stephen became the first Christian martyr. The prayer he offered as he died reflected that spirit of martyrs through the ages:

And they stoned Stephen as he was calling on God and saying, "Lord Jesus, receive my spirit." Then he knelt down and cried out with a loud voice, "Lord, do not charge them with this sin." And when he had said this, he fell asleep.

"Lord Jesus, receive my spirit" (v. 59). For the Christian, death is not the end. It is not saying "goodbye," but "hello." When a Christian dies, he or she is welcomed into glory, as his or her "spirit" (personality) joins Jesus and those believers who have gone on before.

"Lord, do not charge them with this sin" (v. 69). To the end Stephen maintained the spirit of forgiveness that moved Christ to offer up His life for our sake.

But could Stephen's prayer be answered? We have evidence in Acts 8 that it was. As Stephen's life was crushed from his body, a young Pharisee stood guard over the clothing of some of Stephen's executioners, showing

When angry Jews took up stones to attack him, Stephen prayed for them.

his approval of Stephen's murder. That young Pharisee was named Saul, and he was from the city of Tarsus. Later this young Pharisee would experience the forgiveness won for him by Jesus. He would go on to become the apostle Paul, Christianity's greatest missionary-theologian.

Stephen's dying prayer was answered indeed.

God does answer prayer. This truth is demonstrated again and again in the book of Acts. The apostles and others in the first-century church looked to prayer to deepen their relationship with God, to open their hearts to God's Spirit, and to seek God's help in time of need. We are also called to give ourselves to prayer as an expression of our trust in the Lord.

CHAPTER 15

PRAYER ACCORDING
TO THE APOSTLES

PRAYER TEACHINGS IN THE EPISTLES
Romans—Jude

Prayer is a thing of mystery. And most of us aren't comfortable with mystery. We tend to prefer clear, simple answers. It's not surprising that the Jewish sages, who dedicated their lives to understanding the mysteries of God, looked for omens to tell them whether their prayers would be answered.

Examples drawn from rabbinic writings illustrate this fact. One sage announced, "He who sneezes during prayer should regard it as a bad omen" (*Ber.24b*). The same document which recorded this belief reported that when Rabbi Channina ben Dusa was praying "on behalf of the sick, he would say, 'This one will live, that one will die.' They asked him, 'How do you know?' He replied, 'If my prayer is fluent in my mouth, I know that he is accepted; but if not, I know that he is rejected'" (ibid, v. 5).

The New Testament epistles suggest no such omens by which we might know whether prayers will be answered as asked. But the Epistles do contain much teaching on prayer.

GENERAL REFERENCES TO PRAYER IN THE EPISTLES

Prayer played a significant role in the lives of first-century Christians. We can sense something of the importance of prayer by the fact that references to prayer are found in nearly every New Testament letter.

The apostle Paul typically assured his readers early in his letters that he was praying for them (Rom. 1:8, 9; Eph. 1:16; Phil. 1:4; Col. 1:3; 1 Thess. 1:12; 2 Thess. 1:11; 2 Tim. 1:3; Philem. 4). Paul also typically requests his readers to pray for him (Rom. 15:30; 2 Cor. 1:11; 9:14; Eph. 6:19; Phil. 1:19; 1 Thess. 5:25). In the same vein, the writer of Hebrews wrote, "pray for us" (Heb. 13:18).

There are other general references to prayer that cannot be classified either as teaching on prayer or as prayers themselves. Paul mentioned his own persistent prayers for the salvation of Israel (Rom. 10:1) and encouraged his readers to be steadfast in prayer (Rom. 12:12). He expressed appreciation for those who had been helping him by praying (2 Cor. 1:11) and noted that one positive benefit of giving is that those who receive aid will be moved to pray for their benefactors (2 Cor. 9:14).

Paul also encouraged persistent prayer for all the saints as an essential element of spiritual warfare (Eph. 6:18). He listed faithfulness in prayer as a primary qualification for membership in the early church's ministry to widows (1 Tim. 5:5).

Such general references to prayer remind us of its importance. But the two great contributions of the Epistles to helping us understand the mystery of prayer are their explicit teachings on prayer and the recorded prayers of the apostle Paul.

TEACHING ON PRAYER IN THE EPISTLES

When we read the New Testament epistles, we find no hint of the "omens" approach to prayer that characterized some rabbinic writings. What we do find is teaching that helps us develop confidence that God does hear and answer our prayers. In the remainder of this chapter, we will examine specific teachings in the Epistles. In the next chapter, we will look at specific prayers recorded in the Epistles.

ROMANS 8:26, 27:
The Spirit Prays with Us

Prayer is a mystery to us. But not to God.

Likewise the Spirit also helps in our weakness. For we do not know what we should pray for as we ought, but the Spirit Himself makes intercession for us with groanings which cannot be uttered. Now He who searches our hearts knows what the mind of the Spirit is, because He makes intercession for the saints according to the will of God (Rom. 8:26, 27).

Romans 8 describes several ministries of the Holy Spirit. These two verses describe the Spirit's unique prayer ministry.

"Our weaknesses" (v. 26). Human beings are limited. We do not understand our own needs or the deep needs of others. Because of this, we do "not know what we should pray for." Our prayers are inadequate expressions of our true needs.

"The Spirit also helps" (v. 26). The word translated "helps" is found only one other place in the New Testament. It is a compound word that means literally to "take hold of one's end of a task." We are to pray. But as we pray, the Holy Spirit takes up His end of the task and prays along with us.

"With groanings which cannot be uttered" (v. 26). The prayers of the Spirit would sound to us like wordless groans. While we would sense their intensity and urgency, we would not grasp the content of the Spirit's prayers for us. But God, "who searches the hearts knows what the mind of the Spirit is." The prayers of the Holy Spirit are no mystery to God.

"Because He makes intercession . . . according to the will of God" (v. 27). In His prayers, the Holy Spirit not only takes into account all of our needs, but He also takes into account God's will. Carl Barth wrote that God "makes himself our advocate with himself" (*A Shorter Commentary on Romans,* p. 102).

Implications for our prayer lives. The fact that the Holy Spirit "helps us" suggests that the Spirit prays with and for us *when we pray.* What a blessing to picture the Holy Spirit praying with us each time we pause to pray. As inadequate as our prayers are and as uncertain as we may be about what we should pray for, the Holy Spirit takes up the burden of intercession with us. The Spirit knows our deepest needs—needs we could never express or even formulate. As the Spirit interprets our needs to God the Father, He makes appropriate requests that are in complete harmony with the Father's will.

How eagerly we should pray daily, for each time we pray the Holy Spirit prays for us.

1 CORINTHIANS 7:5:
Prayer and Married Love

In 1 Corinthians 7, the apostle Paul responded to some believers in Corinth who thought that "spiritual" Christians would refrain from sex in marriage. Paul corrected those who had this notion and commanded married persons not to "deprive one another" sexually. Paul did describe one exception to the rule of sexual availability. He wrote,

Do not deprive one another except with consent for a time, that you may give yourselves to fasting and prayer; and come together again so that Satan does not tempt you because of your lack of self-control (1 Cor 7:5).

"Fasting and prayer." As we noted earlier, when a New Testament writer links fasting with prayer, he has in mind a time of concentrated focus on the Lord. This is the implication in this passage. Only a mutual agreement to focus our thoughts and prayers on God can set aside the marital obligation husbands and wives have to each other.

"With consent for a time." Two conditions are placed on this exception. The husband and wife are to agree to give themselves to a special time of prayer. And they are to set a time limit. The length of the period is to be strictly limited. After the time has passed, the couple is to resume sexual intercourse.

"So that Satan does not tempt you." The rationale Paul gave is very practical. One reason God ordained marriage was to provide a context in which the sexual needs of human beings could be met (1 Cor. 7:2). To "deprive one another" too long might make some vulnerable to Satan's temptations.

Implications for our prayer lives. Paul's words of warning remind us that the "spiritual life" is not divorced from day-to-day living. We may need to set aside times for focused concentration on the Lord. But prayer will generally be woven into the fabric of our lives, with time given to our work, marriage, families, church, even recreation.

1 CORINTHIANS 11:4, 5, 13:
Women at Prayer in Church

The role of women in church ministries generates a lot of discussion today. And 1 Corinthians 11 is one of the passages frequently debated. Two things are clear from even a superficial reading of this passage: (1) God does make a distinction between men and women. (2) Women did pray and prophesy in the first-century church.

Every man praying or prophesying, having his head covered, dishonors his head. But every woman who prays or prophesies with her head uncovered dishonors her head, for that is one and the same as if her head were shaved (1 Cor. 11:4, 5).

Judge among yourselves. Is it proper for a woman to pray to God with her head uncovered? (1 Cor. 11:13).

The historical context. In the Jewish synagogue, men and women were strictly separated. Only men could constitute a quorum of worshipers. Men alone participated in the synagogue service; women kept silent. What was exciting for women in the newly formed Christian church was that like men, women were equipped with spiritual gifts. Just like men, they participated actively during church meetings.

The women in Corinth found this so exhilarating that they abandoned the tradition of covering their heads when gathering for worship. They shared privileges that once belonged only to men; they would advertise their new rights by uncovering their heads just as men did!

Paul rejected this symbolic act, arguing that God created human beings male and female and that the distinction is not to be blurred. Strikingly, he then says that "for this reason the woman ought to have a symbol of authority on her head, because of the angels" (1 Cor. 11:10). Paul's point is not that women are to cover their heads as a symbol of men's authority over them, as some have wrongly taken this phrase. Paul's point is that women are to cover their heads as a symbol of *the authority they now have* to pray and prophesy in the gathered church! What the angels need to see is women praying and prophesying *as women,* that all creation might witness the wonder of what God has done in the church in making all humanity one. Whether Jew or Greek, slave or free, male or female, each believer shares fully in Christ and each is gifted to minister to others in His name.

By failing to cover their heads, the women of Corinth had denied rather than affirmed their equality with men in the body of Christ!

"Every woman who prays or prophesies" (v. 5). While there are strong reasons to hold that the elder role in the church is reserved for

men, this and other passages make it clear that men and women alike share the privilege of leading groups of believers in prayer. And, if "prophesy" is to be understood here as presenting God's word rather than predicting the future, women also shared what God was teaching them in gatherings of the first-century church.

Implications for our prayer lives. Prayer is the privilege of every believer in Jesus Christ. And prayer is a gift that we are to share with one another as we meet together as the living body of Christ. Men, women, children—all have access to God in prayer. Anyone who can pray can lead others in public assemblies to the throne of grace.

1 CORINTHIANS 14:
Praying in Tongues

In 1 Corinthians 12–14, the apostle Paul corrected misunderstandings that developed in the Corinthian church concerning spirituality. That congregation had assumed that the ecstatic gift of speaking in an unknown spiritual language ("tongues") marked the possessor as more "spiritual" than other Christians. In 1 Corinthians 12, Paul pointed out that every spiritual gift is a manifestation of the Holy Spirit in the life of a believer and that all believers have at least one spiritual gift.

In 1 Corinthians 13, Paul pointed to love as the real measure of spirituality. The Christian who lives in close relationship with Jesus will be filled with Christ's love and will express that love in his or her relationships with others.

In 1 Corinthians 14, Paul looked at "practical" ways to evaluate the significance of spiritual gifts. Earlier he had noted that the Spirit's gifts were given "for the profit of all" (1 Cor. 12:7). The problem with "tongues" is that unless someone with the gift of interpretation is in the congregation, no one will know what is being said. The result is that the church does not gain anything from the experience. "Unless you utter by the tongue words easy to understand, how will it be known what is spo-

ken?" (1 Cor. 14:9). Judged this way, those spiritual gifts which are "for the edification of the church" are far more significant (1 Cor. 14:12) than other more spectacular gifts.

Paul then stated his conclusions in 1 Corinthians 14:13–19:

Therefore let him who speaks in a tongue pray that he may interpret. For if I pray in a tongue, my spirit prays, but my understanding is unfruitful. What is the conclusion then? I will pray with the spirit, and I will also pray with the understanding. I will sing with the spirit, and I will also sing with the understanding. Otherwise, if you bless with the spirit, how will he who occupies the place of the uninformed say "Amen" at your giving of thanks, since he does not understand what you say? For you indeed give thanks well, but the other is not edified. I thank my God that I speak with tongues more than you all; yet in the church I would rather speak five words with my understanding, that I may teach others also, than ten thousand words with a tongue (1 Cor 14:13–19).

Praying in tongues in private devotions. The passage above neither encourages nor discourages praying in tongues in private. The apostle Paul certainly prayed in tongues in his own devotions. He also prayed with his "understanding." Many people who have prayed in tongues testify that they felt closer to Jesus through the experience. There is no basis for challenging this testimony.

At the same time, Paul does make a distinction between praying with one's understanding and praying in tongues with one's spirit. "Spirit" as used here is not the Holy Spirit but the human spirit. Prayer with the spirit, even singing with the spirit (1 Cor. 14:15), are authentic expressions of relationship with God. Not only are these experiences authentic; they are also expressions of true worship.

But there is a critical difference. Praying in tongues in one's own spirit makes no contribution to our understanding. In Paul's words, such experiences may be wonderful, but "my understanding is unfruitful" (1 Cor. 14:14).

Realizing this, Paul stated, "I will pray with the spirit, and I will also pray with the understanding" (1 Cor. 14:15). *Paul did not intend to abandon praying in tongues,* and he did not suggest that any other believer abandon the exercise of this spiritual gift. What Paul intended was to continue to pray in tongues—and to pray in words with understanding as well.

Praying in tongues in the church. While Paul did not forbid prayer in tongues in the church, he did discourage it. When God's people gather, the goal is edification. Even if a person prays well in tongues, "the other [person] is not edified" (1 Cor. 14:17).

The result is that Paul did not pray in tongues in the church, but reserved this practice for his private devotions. As to the relative value of prayer in tongues and plain speech in the gathered congregation, Paul said, "I would rather speak five words with my understanding . . . than ten thousand words in a tongue" (1 Cor. 14:19).

While there is more in this chapter about the exercise of the gift of tongues, these verses sum up what the apostle taught about prayer in tongues.

Implications for our prayer lives. Private prayer is an expression of our personal relationship with God. We come to Him as His dependent children, confident that He is eager to hear not only our praise but also our requests. As they pray, some Christians experience a warming of heart and spirit and find themselves speaking to God in words they simply don't understand. This passage in Paul's letter to the Corinthians helps us understand such experiences as praying "with the spirit," and frees us to reach out to God with our spirit, without fear of what we are experiencing. Such prayer experiences need not come to every believer. But if they should come to us, we may welcome them, remembering that they are not to replace other forms of prayer.

But the Scriptures are clear that praying with the spirit, in tongues, is not to be encouraged in gatherings of the church. There we pray with the understanding, that all present

might be led by our words into the presence of God, and that all might join their hearts and minds in praise and worship of our Lord.

EPHESIANS 6:18:
Praying Always

The debate over this verse is whether it begins a new line of thought or whether it is linked to Paul's discussion of the spiritual armor with which God has equipped Christians. It is probably best to link Paul's exhortation to pray with the armor passage. After listing what God has provided, Paul urges us to be

praying always with all prayer and supplication in the Spirit, being watchful to this end with all perseverance and supplication for all the saints (Eph. 6:18).

"Praying always." The Greek indicates praying "on all occasions." Whatever the situation, and no matter what piece of God's armor the situation calls for, prayer is essential for any spiritual victory. We are to rely on God at all times.

"Prayer and supplication in the Spirit." The phrase "in the Spirit" means praying under the Holy Spirit's influence and with His aid. Romans 8:26–27 reminds us that the Holy Spirit takes up His end of the process when we pray, interpreting our deepest needs to God and making requests in harmony with the Father's will. When we pray, we are to reach out consciously and seek the Spirit's guidance and support.

"Being watchful to this end." While other verses urge us to be aware of things in our environment about which to pray, Paul urges us in this passage to develop an inner awareness of the Holy Spirit. He will prompt us to pray. He will also guide our prayers and take us into God's presence before the throne of grace.

Implications for our prayer lives. We need to learn to develop a prayerful attitude. What is a prayerful attitude? It is awareness of our dependence on God and of His presence with us. This awareness of His presence is expressed in bringing each emerging need to His attention, and in responding as the Spirit's inner voice calls us to share with Him. Praying "on every occasion" will be true of us only as we develop prayerful attitudes.

PHILIPPIANS 4:6, 7:
Prayer, Anxiety, and the Promise of Peace

When Paul wrote this letter, he was in prison and the Philippians were experiencing persecution. There were very real reasons for Christians to be anxious in the first century, even as there are troubles in our time that cause us to be anxious. Against this background, the apostle wrote,

Be anxious for nothing, but in everything by prayer and supplication, with thanksgiving, let your requests be made known to God; and the peace of God, which surpasses all understanding, will guard your hearts and minds through Christ Jesus (Phil. 4:6, 7).

"Be anxious for nothing" (v. 6). The Greek phrase means "stop worrying." The added "for nothing" leaves us with no exceptions. We prayed in my Sunday school class for a single mother of six, who will undergo surgery for ovarian cancer. Paul's instruction to her, and to others like her whose problems are real and potentially devastating, is to "stop worrying."

"Prayer, supplication, and requests" (v. 6). Paul used three different Greek words to teach us that the way to be anxious about nothing is to pray about everything. These words— *proseuche, deesis,* and *aitemata*—are synonyms, yet they express the personal nature of prayer as conversation with God, as pleas directed to God, and as requests made to Him. We are to inform the Lord of our situation, confident that He as the ruler of the universe is able to meet our every need.

"With thanksgiving" (v. 6). The surprising emphasis in the Greek construction is on thanksgiving. We are not only to pray to God but to praise Him. When we pray with thanksgiving, we honor God by expressing our trust in His loving care. As we give thanks

"Be anxious for nothing, but . . . let your requests be made known to God."

to God, we rest ourselves and our needs in Him.

"The peace of God" (v. 7). This phrase is found only here in the New Testament. Distinct from peace *with* God, the peace *of* God is an inner peace which God alone can give. And this peace is found within the very circumstances that cause others to be anxious.

"Which surpasses all understanding" (v. 7). This phrase can be taken in either of two ways. It may mean that God's peace is so overwhelming than no one can grasp its significance. Or, it could mean that God produces a peace that is far more wonderful than any human plan we might construct to solve our problems. The next phrase helps us see why this second meaning is more likely. God's peace guards our "hearts and minds." Not only our thoughts but our emotions are protected from the assaults of worry by the peace which God gives.

Implications for our prayer lives. Paul's command and His promise of peace are for us today as much as they were for first-century Christians. Prayer with thanksgiving affirms the lordship of Christ in our lives. We will find peace in Christ Jesus alone.

COLOSSIANS 4:2:
Continual, Vigilant Prayer

This exhortation is found in a series of brief statements in the last chapter of Colossians.

Continue earnestly in prayer, being vigilant in it with thanksgiving (Col. 4:2).

Three elements of this brief exhortation seem especially significant.

"Continue earnestly in prayer." The Greek verb in this context means "to adhere to" or "to persist in." It suggests a determination not to give up on prayer as the way to respond to every challenge in life. Our first reaction in any situation should be to turn to the Lord in prayer.

"Being vigilant." The Greek participle means "being watchful." It stands in contrast to being careless or mechanical about prayer. Christians are to remain alert, constantly aware of the spiritual warfare in which we as Jesus' people are engaged.

"With thanksgiving." Specific reference to thanksgiving suggests that the kind of "prayer" Paul had in mind was petition (compare Phil. 4:6, 7). We are to be alert to situations that call for prayer and to be committed to praying about them. And we are to pray with thanksgiving, confident that God hears and will respond.

Implications for our prayer lives. There is nothing wrong with setting aside regular times for daily prayer. This is one of the best ways to nurture our relationship with the Lord. But this verse reminds us to pray about each need as it arises—and to be alert to emerging needs.

1 THESSALONIANS 5:17:
Unceasing Prayer

This brief, three-word verse simply says, "pray without ceasing." The phrase reinforces Paul's exhortations in Ephesians 6:18 (page 218) and Colossians 4:2 (above).

1 TIMOTHY 2:1, 2, 8:
Prayer for Rulers

In his first letter to Timothy, the apostle Paul gave this second-generation Christian leader instructions on how Timothy was to guide the churches he oversaw. Special instructions on prayer were included in Paul's brief letter.

Therefore I exhort first of all that supplications, prayers, intercessions, and giving of thanks be made for all men, for kings and all who are in authority, that we may lead a quiet and peaceable life in all godliness and reverence.

. . .

I desire therefore that the men pray everywhere, lifting up holy hands, without wrath and doubting (1 Tim 2:1, 2, 8).

To understand the rationale for this call to prayer, we need to note that the subject of 1 Timothy 2 is not prayer but the universality of the gospel. This is made clear in verses 3–7 of this chapter, which emphasize God's desire for "all men to be saved and to come to the knowledge of the truth" (1 Tim. 2:4). The church is to pray for all people and especially for rulers, on whom the freedom of Christians to live quiet and godly lives depends. Paul's point was that in quiet times, when no persecution is directed against the church to inflame the populace against Christians, unsaved men and women will be more open to the gospel.

It is in this context, then, that Paul encouraged and directed the prayers of the church.

"First of all" (v. 1). This phrase indicates that what Paul urged was of great importance to God and the church. Prayer, and in particular *this prayer,* was to be given priority by the first-century church.

"Supplications, prayers, intercessions, and giving of thanks" (v. 1). Paul used three synonyms for petitionary prayer. Rather than look for shades of difference in the meaning of these three (*deesis, proseuchai, enteuxeis*), we should assume that Paul's intent was to emphasize the importance of prayer for leaders. As in Philippians 4:6, 7, Paul reminds us that we are to pray with thanksgiving, thus affirming our confidence in God's love and His power.

"Made for all men" (v. 1). Although Paul goes on in verse 2 to mention "kings and all who are in authority," this was truly prayer for "all men" (v. 1). Paul urged prayer for rulers because they control the political and social climate in which the gospel is presented. Paul was not concerned with politics. What Paul cared about is that "all men" ("all persons") have the best possible chance to hear and respond to the gospel.

"That we may lead a quiet and peaceable life in all godliness" (v. 2). While this prayer concerned rulers and those in authority, it was directed toward maintaining conditions which will enable Christians to live quiet and peaceable lives. Persecution was a real and present danger to Christians in the first century. Persecution of Christians was not empire-wide, nor was it ordered by early emperors. Instead, persecution developed locally. Whether Christians could lead peaceful lives depended on the attitude of local and provincial Roman governors. Where peaceful conditions were maintained and the Christians were not persecuted, the first-century church tended to grow rapidly.

"That the men pray everywhere" (v. 8). The use of the definite article with "men" as well as the phrase "also the women" in verse 9 indicates that Paul was writing here of men in distinction to women. It is probably correct to assume that Paul expected that men would take the lead in public worship.

"Lifting up holy hands" (v. 8). Jews and pagans as well as Christians frequently raised their arms when praying. The emphasis here, however, is on the adjective *holy*. The word

Paul urged prayer for "kings and all who are in authority."

here is *hosios* rather than the more common *hagios,* and it means "pleasing to God." The way in which we please God is defined in the next phrase.

"Without wrath and doubting" (v. 8). The word translated "doubting" is more likely "disputing." This verse picks up the theme of prayer from verse 2. We should probably understand it to encourage positive prayer for rulers rather than a prayer that expresses anger or concerns disputes Christians have with governing authorities. Our prayers for peaceable and quiet lives must come from thankful and confident hearts, purged of anger and hostility.

Implications for our prayer lives. Because God is concerned for us, we can trust our needs to Him, and we can concern ourselves with His purposes in our world. Rather than fearing or being angry with unjust governments, we are to pray for those governments to the end that Christians might be free to share the gospel with all people.

BIBLE BACKGROUND:

CHRISTIAN PERSECUTION

In A.D. 112, a Roman governor named Pliny wrote a letter about Christians, asking the Emperor Trajan for advice on how to deal with them. We have the correspondence between the two, parts of which are quoted below. The letters illustrate the political and social climate of the first century, showing why Paul considered prayer concerning rulers of such significance.

PLINY TO TRAJAN: AN INITIAL INQUIRY

I have never been present at an examination of Christians. Consequently, I do not know the nature or the extent of the punishments usually meted out to them, nor the grounds for starting an investigation and how far it should be pressed. Nor am I at all sure whether any distinction should be made between them on the grounds of age, or if young people and adults should be treated alike; whether a pardon ought to be granted to anyone retracting his beliefs, or if he has once professed Christianity, he shall gain nothing by renouncing it; and whether it is the mere name of Christian which is punishable, even if innocent of crime, or rather the crimes associated with the name.

PLINY REPORTING ON HIS INVESTIGATION

After investigation, Pliny concluded that Christians were members of a foreign cult but that they were not guilty of any specific crimes. He reported the results of his investigation to the emperor and asked for further instructions.

They declared that the sum total of their guilt or error amounted to no more than this; they had met regularly before dawn on a fixed day to chant verses alternately among themselves in honor of Christ as if to a god, and also to bind themselves by oath, not for any criminal purpose, but to abstain from theft, robbery, and adultery, to commit no breach of trust and not to deny a deposit when called upon to restore it. After this ceremony it had been their custom to disperse and reassemble later to take food of an ordinary harmless sort.

TRAJAN'S INSTRUCTIONS TO PLINY

Pliny had taken the relatively mild approach of giving Christians the opportunity to recant and worship the Roman emperor, after which they were freed without penalty. Those who would not recant were executed. Trajan affirmed what Pliny had done, adding the following guidelines.

You have followed the right course of procedure, my dear Pliny, in your examination of the cases of persons charged with being Christians, for it is impossible to lay down a general rule to a fixed formula. These people must not be hunted out; if they are brought before you and the charge against them is proved, they must be punished, but in the case of anyone who denies that he is a Christian, and makes it clear that he is not by offering prayers to our gods, he is to be pardoned as a result of his repentance however suspect his past conduct may be. But the pamphlets circulated anonymously must play no part in any accusation. They create the worst sort of precedent and are quite out of keeping with the spirit of our age (*Epistles of Pliny*, 96 through 10:97).

In an age when a person could be punished just for being a Christian, we can understand the urgency of Paul's instructions to pray for rulers!

---

1 TIMOTHY 4:4, 5:
Prayer's Sanctifying Effect

In chapter 4 of 1 Timothy, Paul warned against an asceticism that has its roots in the demonic rather than the Spirit. Speaking specifically about refraining from marriage and from eating certain foods, Paul wrote,

For every creature of God is good, and nothing is to be refused if it is received with thanksgiving; for it is sanctified by the word of God and prayer (1 Tim. 4:4, 5).

The word translated "refused" means to be thrown away or discarded. Paul is not teaching that such things are *made good* by prayer, for God created them good (cf. Gen. 1:10, 12, 18, 21, 25). The point is that it is as we acknowledge God's word and thank God for His provision that this provision becomes holy (sanctified) for us, thus freeing our conscience so we can partake of His bounty.

HEBREWS 7:25:
Christ's Intercession for Us

The purpose of the writer of the book of Hebrews was to show the new covenant instituted by Jesus was superior to the revelation which God gave through Moses. In chapter 7, he showed the superiority of Jesus, our High Priest, to the Old Testament's high priests. The critical point the writer made is that because Jesus "continues forever" He has an unchangeable priesthood. The conclusion?

Therefore He is also able to save to the uttermost those who come to God through Him, since He always lives to make intercession for them (Heb. 7:25).

This same truth is emphasized in 1 John 2:1, and it is associated with God's promise of forgiveness and cleansing when Christians confess (acknowledge) their sins. There John writes,

My little children, these things I write to you, so that you may not sin. And if anyone sins, we have an Advocate with the Father, Jesus Christ the righteous.

As our Advocate, Christ intercedes for us, pleading His shed blood before the Father's throne.

While Romans 8 indicates that the Holy Spirit intercedes for us as we pray, Hebrews 7:25 and 1 John 2:1 assure us that Christ Himself intercedes for us *when we are most in need of prayer,* whether we are praying or not.

JAMES 1:5–7:
Prayer for Wisdom

In Scripture, "wisdom" is the ability to apply spiritual truths to real life situations, so that we are able to determine and to choose God's will. Wisdom is needed for practical righteousness in daily life. James encouraged Christians to ask God when they lack wisdom. But he added an important warning.

If any of you lacks wisdom, let him ask of God, who gives to all liberally and without reproach, and it will be given to him. But let him ask in faith, with no doubting, for he who doubts is like a wave of the sea driven and tossed by the wind. For let not that man suppose that he will receive anything from the Lord; he is a double-minded man, unstable in all his ways (James 1:5–7).

These verses emphasize two aspects of the prayer for wisdom. On God's side, there is an immediate gracious response and He gives the gift of guidance that the believer needs. On our side, there must be a commitment to do God's will as He reveals it.

"If any of you lacks wisdom" (v. 5). The conditional clause, beginning with *ei de* makes it clear that James believed his readers *did* "lack wisdom." They lived in an increasingly hostile society, and they were forced to make many difficult moral choices. It was beyond them to know what they should do in every situation.

The lack of such wisdom is characteristic of us as well, as we struggle to apply our faith in daily life.

"Let him ask of God" (v. 5). James urged his readers to ask God for guidance. He will show us the right thing to do. Two special qualities of God encourage us to ask frequently: (1) God "gives to all liberally." By nature God is generous, and He will gladly and spontaneously provide the wisdom we need. (2) God gives "without reproach." Rather than being upset with us for our lack of wisdom, God is gracious and glad to help. Nothing in God's character or attitude keeps us from receiving the wisdom we need to make right choices.

"It will be given to him" (v. 5). This construction is often called "the divine passive." That is, the passive voice is often used to describe the hidden action of God. The phrase "it [wisdom] will be given" means, "God will give it to him."

"He who doubts is like a wave of the sea driven and tossed by the wind."

"But let him ask in faith, with no doubting" (v. 6). The only thing that can keep us from righteous living is a flaw in our own faith.

It is important to understand that the flaw is not that we lack faith when we *ask* God for wisdom. The flaw in our faith appears when we fail to apply the wisdom God provides. Most commentators argue that *diakrinesthai* found here in apposition to *pistis,* "faith," implies "doubting." But the basic meaning of the word is to separate, distinguish, decide, or judge. It seems better to understand James in this sense: He is contrasting our acceptance without question of the wisdom which God provides [e.g., faith] with our taking it upon ourselves to stand in judgment on God's guidance. When God gives us wisdom and shows us what to do, we are to commit ourselves to obey. We are not to stand in judgment on His guidance and decide whether we will obey.

"He who doubts is like a wave of the sea" (v. 6). Jewish literature often portrayed the wicked or hypocritical at the mercy of the ocean. Thus, Isaiah 57:20, 21 declared, "the wicked are like the troubled sea, when it can-

not rest, whose waters cast up mire and dirt. 'There is no peace,' says my God, 'for the wicked.' "

By using this allusion, James portrayed this failure of faith as extremely serious. It is, in fact, so serious that James went on to say, "Let not that man suppose that he will receive anything from the Lord."

"He is a double-minded man, unstable in all his ways" (v. 8). The word translated "double-minded" is *dipsuchos,* from *di,* "double," and *psuchos,* soul. While this word is used only here in the New Testament, it is modeled on similar terms used frequently in Greek literature: double-tongued, double-faced, double-hearted. The specific sense that James had in mind must be determined from context. Those who take *diakrinesthai* as "doubt" see the double-minded person as wavering, uncertain, between two opinions, uncertain of what to do. However, if we take *diakrinesthai* in its ordinary sense of judging or distinguishing, the double-minded person wants divine guidance, but at the same time he reserves for himself the right to decide whether to do what God reveals.

If we take this second view, we might paraphrase James's teaching in this way.

If any of you lack wisdom, ask God. God is generous and gracious, and will show you the right thing to do. But when you ask, make up your mind that you will follow God's guidance. The person who takes it on himself to decide whether to obey God is like a wave tossed back and forth by the sea. Don't ever imagine that God will reveal His will to you if you insist on the right to decide whether you will obey Him!

Implications for our prayer lives. When it comes to asking God to show us the right thing to do, we have a promise and a warning. The promise is that God *will* guide us. The warning is, Don't ask God for wisdom unless you are committed to doing His will. It is an insult to the Lord for a human being to claim the right to decide whether to obey Him.

A person who prays for guidance, while reserving the right to take or not take the path that God reveals, cannot expect to discern God's will. But if we commit ourselves to obey Him, God will give us the wisdom we need to make right choices in our daily lives.

JAMES 4:2, 3:
Why God Says "No"

There are many reasons why God may answer our prayers with a "No" or perhaps a "Not yet." James, however, dealt with one reason why God, who gives His children only good gifts (James 1:17), is sure to say "No."

You lust and do not have. You murder and covet and cannot obtain. You fight and war. Yet you do not have because you do not ask. You ask and do not receive, because you ask amiss, that you may spend it on your pleasures (James 4:2, 3).

"You lust" (v. 2). The Greek word lacks sexual connotation. It refers to any longing or intense desire. The *Theological Dictionary of the New Testament* describes this desire as "anxious self-seeking" (Vol. 3, p.171).

James saw such anxious self-seeking as the source of wars and fighting, and he linked it to the sins of coveting and murder.

"Yet you do not have because you do not ask" (v. 2). The most intense efforts to satisfy selfish desires are futile. The way for us to obtain what we truly desire is not to fight but to pray!

"You ask and do not receive" (v. 3). But often we pray for things that we do not receive. We want to be loved by that special person who doesn't know we're alive. We want to succeed. We want to prosper. Many Christians have prayed for just such things and have not received them. Why? If the way to get what we want is to pray rather than struggle for them, how does James explain frequent failures of prayer to produce what we want?

"You ask amiss" (v. 3). To ask "amiss" is to ask in the wrong spirit, with the wrong motives. Specifically, the motive in asking is to *get something* that we believe will bring pleasure. Strikingly, the same word translated "lusts" in verse two is translated "pleasures" in verse three. Such prayers are driven by selfish desires. This is why they are not answered by God.

Implications for our prayer lives. In an earlier chapter, we saw that God promises to answer prayers offered "in Jesus name." When we come to God through Jesus and ask in harmony with His character and will, God will grant our requests. When we ask for things in hopes of satisfying our own selfish desires, such prayers are *not* offered in Jesus' name.

The notion that *things* can ever satisfy the deepest needs of the human heart is wrong. God has created us for Himself, and He has re-created us in Christ that we might reflect the image of His Son. Our identity and our destiny are linked with God and not with anything that can be found in this world. When we realize this, our thoughts and desires are directed away from things—toward loving God and loving others. God will not give us things we ask for in hopes that our desires will be satisfied. He knows that things cannot satisfy the believer.

Only when we turn our prayers away from "anxious self-seeking" will the things we pray for satisfy our hearts.

JAMES 5:3–8:
The Prayers of the Oppressed

James has little sympathy for the rich. This is because in his society the rich obtained their wealth at the expense of the poor. God had given each Jewish family its own plot of land, which was to remain in the family forever. The great landowners of James's time had built their estates by forcing families off their land or by foreclosing on loans and making their fellow Jews virtual serfs or slaves. Old Testament law required that laborers be paid daily, so they could buy their daily food and provide for their families. But many held back the wages of laborers. As the gap between rich and poor in first-century Palestine widened, the rich became more and more oppressive.

In chapter 5, James warned the rich of judgment to come, and he encouraged the poor. Their prayers have been heard, but they are to be patient until the Lord returns to set things right.

JAMES 5:13–18:
Prayer for the Sick

This extended passage on prayer has been the source of much debate and misunderstanding.

Is anyone among you suffering? Let him pray. Is anyone cheerful? Let him sing psalms. Is anyone among you sick? Let him call for the elders of the church, and let them pray over him, anointing him with oil in the name of the Lord. And the prayer of faith will save the sick, and the Lord will raise him up. And if he has committed sins, he will be forgiven. Confess your trespasses to one another, and pray for one another, that you may be healed. The effective, fervent prayer of a righteous man avails much. Elijah was a man with a nature like ours, and he prayed earnestly that it would not rain; and it did not rain for three years and six months. And he prayed again, and the heaven gave rain, and the earth produced its fruit (James 5:13–18).

The passage describes circumstances that call for prayer, providing an example of the power of prayer. Prayer is called for (1) if anyone is suffering, (2) if anyone is cheerful, and (3) if anyone is sick.

JUDGMENT ON THE RICH?

Joachim Jeremias, in *Jerusalem in the Time of Jesus* (1969), relates the following about the rich widow of one high priest.

The aristocratic ladies of Jerusalem had a reputation for being very pampered. Martha, the widow of the high priest R. Joshua, is said to have been assured by the scribes of a daily allowance of two measures of wine, while the daughter-in-law of Naqdimon b. Borion was given two *se'ah*, or more than twenty-six litres, of wine per week (Lam.R. 1.50 on 1.16, Son. 1.47, 128; b. Ket. 65a). The daughter of Naqdimon is reported to have cursed the scribes because under the agreement for her widow's maintenance they allowed her only 400 gold denarii a day for luxuries (b. Ket. 66b' Lam.R. 1.51 on 1:16, Son. 1.48, 129, says 500 denarii). No wonder that the same Martha could not withstand the misery of the siege of Jerusalem in A.D. 70, and when at her last hour she threw all her gold and silver in the street, she learnt too late the worthlessness of money (b. Gitt. 36a).

Sometimes judgment does not await the return of Christ.

"Is anyone among you suffering?" (v. 13). The word *kakopatheias* might better be translated as "in trouble" or "facing adversity." Whatever misfortune or difficulty we face, our first response should be to pray about it.

"Is anyone cheerful? Let him sing psalms" (v. 13). Singing psalms to God is as much a way of communicating with him as making petitions. Just as troubles are to direct our hearts to the Lord, so are blessings.

"Is anyone among you sick?" (v. 14). In the event of trouble, James expected individuals to pray for themselves. If sickness should happen, James told his readers to "call for the elders of the church."

There are a number of teachings on prayer and sickness that this unusual prescription helps us to evaluate.

- *Healing is provided when we believe in Christ.* This view holds that healing is guaranteed to believers in the atonement. The idea is based on a phrase in Isaiah 53:5, "By His stripes we are healed." However, (1) Isaiah frequently uses sickness as a metaphor for sin, and healing as a metaphor for salvation (cf. Isa. 1:4–6). (2) While all human ills will be done away with in the resurrection, physical health is not guaranteed to believers before that time.
- *Healing is ours if claimed by faith.* This view is closely linked with the notion that Christ's death won healing as well as salvation for Christians. The fact that Christians become ill is explained as a lack of faith. This view has burdened many faithful believers with a sense of guilt as they blame their illness on their lack of faith.
- *God provides healing miraculously, through "faith-healers."* The idea that God heals miraculously through faith healers is rooted in a reference to healing as a spiritual gift in 1 Corinthians 12. It is true that the New Testament records healing miracles and that a gift of healing is mentioned in the New Testament. It is not necessary, however, to assume that God heals only through gifted individuals, or that the gift of healing calls for the working of miracles. That gift may well be found in medical professionals, who are trained in the science of healing.

How does James 5:14 help us evaluate these ideas? James did not tell the sick person to claim healing, to exercise faith, or to seek out a faith healer. Instead, James told the sick to "call for the elders of the church, and let them pray over him, anointing him with oil in the name of the Lord." Surely his prescription would be different if any of the three teachings outlined above accurately portrayed what the Bible teaches about human illness.

James urged sick believers to call for the ministry of the elders, including both prayer and anointing.

"Let them pray over him" *(v. 14)*. The phrase "pray over" may suggest a laying on of hands by the elders. It is certain, however, that prayer for the sick is a ministry conducted not by individual elders but by the elders as a group.

"Anointing him with oil in the name of the Lord" *(v. 14)*. The purpose of the use of oil has been much debated. We do know that in the New Testament era, medicines were commonly administered by mixing them with olive oil. We even have examples of this, as when the good Samaritan poured oil on the wounds of the injured man whom he stopped to help (Luke 10:34). In addition, there are two words in Greek which mean "anoint." The one which refers to anointing for symbolic or religious purposes is *not* used in this passage.

Finally, the phrase "in the name of the Lord" seems fitting if James's intent was to portray the use of medicine but at the same time to make it clear that the healing was due to God's action—not the medicine alone.

What we conclude is that James called for the use of whatever medicines were available, but he reminded us to credit God with the healing.

"And if he has committed sins, he will be forgiven" (v. 15). James recognized the possibility—though certainly not the certainty—that the sickness was a consequence of sin. If this is the case, spiritual as well as physical restoration are available to the sick person.

"Confess your trespasses to one another, and pray for one another, that you may be healed" (v. 16). James seems to suggest that keeping a clear conscience by confessing when we sin against another person is related to health and well being. Unconfessed sin may cause illness and hinder healing.

Many people in James's day saw sickness as punishment for sin. They assumed that a person who became ill was a secret sinner. James acknowledged that there *may be* a connection between illness and sin. But neither James nor the elders were to make this assumption. The implication is that should the sick person be aware of sin in his or her life, it should be confessed when the elders prayed and anointed with oil. And if he or she did, the sin would be forgiven and a hindrance to healing would be removed.

"The effective, fervent prayer of a righteous man avails much" (v. 16). What James said is that the prayer of a righteous man is "very powerful in its working." If Elijah's prayer could close and then open the heavens, the prayers of the elders of the church could heal the sick.

Implications for our prayer lives. This passage reminds us that we can come boldly to present our prayers before God's throne (cf. Heb. 4:16). But we need the prayers of our brothers and sisters in the church. Even as we intercede with God for others, so we should encourage others to pray for us. And when we fall ill, we need to ask the elders of the church specifically to pray for us.

1 PETER 3:7:
A Husband's Prayers

In chapter three of his first epistle, Peter wrote about how wives and husbands are to relate to each other. The first six verses are directed to women. Verse seven is directed to husbands.

Husbands, likewise, dwell with them in understanding; giving honor to the wife, as to the weaker vessel, and as being heirs together of the grace of life, that your prayers may not be hindered (1 Pet. 3:7).

Peter affirmed that if we fail to treat each other in the family as co-heirs, our prayers will be hindered. The only other mention in this letter of *proseuche,* "prayers," is in 4:7. The context (4:8–11) also emphasizes the importance of mutual love and ministry. When approaching God in prayer, it is important that we be in harmony with God's family here on earth (see the discussion of Matt. 5:23, 34 on page 161).

The "hindrance" to prayers is not spelled out. This may mean that without proper devotion to each other, we may not know how to pray. Or the hindrance may be linked to the fact that while "His ears are open to" the prayers of the righteous, "the face of the Lord is against those who do evil" (1 Pet. 3:12).

1 JOHN 3:22:
Prayer and Obedience

There is an intimate relationship between John's letters and his Gospel. The same themes recur again and again in both. John often quotes or paraphrases familiar words spoken by our Lord. This verse is one of those which clearly echoes truths taught by Jesus.

And whatever we ask we receive from Him, because we keep His commandments, and do those things that are pleasing in His sight (1 John 3:22).

For a discussion of this theme, see the discussion of Jesus' teachings on prayer in John 15, pages 160–161.

1 JOHN 5:14, 15:
Confidence Our Prayers Will Be Answered

First read the discussion of 1 John 3:22, above.

Here again, we have a theme that has been developed in John's Gospel which is reemphasized here. The principle John restates is initially stated in John 14:13, 14; 15:7, 16; and 16:23–24, 26. For a discussion of this principle, see pages 167–170.

JUDE 20, 21:
Prayer and Commitment

The brief book of Jude was written to urge believers to contend for the faith against the corrupting influences of false teachers who had infiltrated the church. After characterizing the false teachers and their teaching, Jude had this word of exhortation:

But you, beloved, building yourselves up on your most holy faith, praying in the Holy Spirit, keep yourselves in the love of God, looking for the mercy of our Lord Jesus Christ unto eternal life (Jude 20, 21).

This verse provides a fourfold prescription for spiritual vitality. The Greek participles serve as imperatives here, and they are to be understood as exhortations.

- *Build yourselves up on your most holy faith* (v. 20). This is a community responsibility, as individuals express mutual love and exercise their spiritual gifts.
- *Pray in the Holy Spirit* (v. 20). Individuals and the community are to pray as prompted by the Spirit and in assurance of His active participation.
- *Keep yourselves in the love of God* (v. 21). John's writings establish that we do this by obeying Christ's commands.
- *Look for the mercy of our Lord Jesus Christ* (v. 21). We are to keep our hope focused on the return of Jesus, rather than to set our hopes on anything in this present life.

Jude makes an important contribution to our understanding of prayer by setting it in a wider context. Christian mystics have tended to equate prayer and spirituality, even to the point of encouraging believers to withdraw from life to concentrate on prayer. Jude reminds us that prayer is one element in a balanced Christian life. This includes our investment in the lives of other Christians, daily obedience to Christ's commands, and an eagerness for Jesus' return.

SECRETS OF INTERCESSION

PRAYER PATTERNS IN THE EPISTLES
Romans—Jude

When Colette, a single mother with six young children, was told she might have ovarian cancer, our church knew what to pray. We prayed that if she had cancer it would be purged from her body. We prayed that the new job she had just found would be held for her for the month it would take her to recuperate. We prayed for peace of mind for her and her children.

God answered each of these prayers and others. We learned today that the operation was a success. Colette, whose mother died from cancer when she was her age, is cancer free. Her job is being held for her. Our church raised money to fly her sister from Utah to care for her and the kids. The church also arranged for a month of meals to be brought to the family. The whole experience has been enriching for Colette and her children, who started coming to our church just two months before her serious condition was diagnosed.

God clearly timed her coming to our church and to Him. And the Lord just as clearly timed the prayer support she needed. When needs like Colette's surface, there's no question about how we should pray. We should focus our prayers on very real and pressing needs.

But how are we to pray for others when they are not in crisis? How should we pray for our children, our loved ones? How should we pray to support the ministries of missionaries? Jesus responded to His disciples' request that He teach them how to pray by giving them the Lord's Prayer. Can we find instruction in Scripture on how to pray for others?

The answer to this important question is "Yes." Instruction on how to pray for others is provided in the model prayers of the apostle Paul, which are recorded in the New Testament epistles. For anyone who has wondered how to pray for others, these prayers provide clear guidance.

THE MOTIVATION OF PRAYERS RECORDED IN THE NEW TESTAMENT EPISTLES

All but one of the prayers recorded in the New Testament epistles are prayers of the apostle Paul. No less than eight times, the early church's preeminent missionary shared with believers the specific content of his prayers for them.

The apostle Paul cared deeply for the young believers he won to Christ in the new churches he planted. Paul, who was unmarried and had no family of his own, poured out all his love on the new believers, whom he viewed as his true family. Paul has been portrayed by some as harsh and unapproachable, but those who experienced his ministry knew better. The person who had nurtured them in their faith was a man whose relationship with young Christians is best portrayed in a beautiful passage in 1 Thessalonians 2. Paul recalled his relationship with members of this new congregation.

We were gentle among you, just as a nursing mother cherishes her own children. So, affectionately longing for you, we were well pleased to impart to you not only the gospel of God, but also our own lives, because you had become dear to us. For you remember, brethren, our labor and toil; for laboring night and day, that we might not be a burden to any of you, we preached to you the gospel of God. You are witnesses, and God also, how devoutly and justly and blamelessly we behaved ourselves among you who believe; as you know how we exhorted, and comforted, and charged every one of you, as a father does his own children, that you walk worthy of God who calls you into His own kingdom and glory (1 Thess. 2:7–12).

It is important to sense this love that Paul expressed here so beautifully. Each of Paul's prayers was motivated by his strong desire that believers might grow in Christ and experience the best that God had in mind for them.

THE PRAYERS

Paul's prayers serve as models that we can follow in praying for our own loved ones. What a wonderful gift these recorded prayers are. They provide a clear answer to the question, "How shall we pray for those *we* love?"

ROMANS 1:8–12:
A Prayer for Distant Brethren

One of the first things Paul mentioned in his letter to the Christians at Rome was his prayer that he might be allowed to spend time with them. These verses give the context and content of his prayer.

First, I thank my God through Jesus Christ for you all, that your faith is spoken of throughout the

In his letter to the believers in Rome, Paul told of his prayers for them and his longing to meet them in person.

whole world. For God is my witness, whom I serve with my spirit in the gospel of His Son, that without ceasing I make mention of you always in my prayers, making request if, by some means, now at last I may find a way in the will of God to come to you. For I long to see you, that I may impart to you some spiritual gift, so that you may be established—that is, that I may be encouraged together with you by the mutual faith both of you and me (Rom. 1:8–12).

The context of Paul's letter to the Romans. When Paul wrote this letter to the Christians at Rome, he had not yet visited them. Romans 16 makes it clear that Paul had a close relationship with many who lived in Rome. But he had not had the opportunity to spend time with the body of believers in that great city— the capital of the Roman Empire.

This passage reminds us that Paul not only prayed for believers in the churches he founded; he also prayed for believers he had not met personally. Paul's love for God's people was great enough to encompass all.

How often our prayers concern only members of our own family, or those in our local church whom we know well. Paul's concern for believers the world over challenges us to minister in prayer to believers everywhere.

"Without ceasing . . . always" (v. 8). Paul had a disciplined prayer life. He never mentioned maintaining a prayer list in any of his epistles. But Paul made it clear that he never neglected the believers in Rome when he prayed.

This same thought is expressed in his letters to other churches. He wrote to the Corinthians "I thank my God always concerning you" (1 Cor. 1:4). He assured the Ephesians that "I . . . do not cease to give thanks for you, making mention of you in my prayers" (Eph. 1:16). He reminded the Philippians, "I thank my God upon every remembrance of you, always in every prayer of mine making request for you all with joy" (Phil. 1:3, 4). Paul may not have made prayer lists, but he made it clear that each congregation was always on his mind and always in his prayers.

"Making request if . . . I may find a way in the will of God to come to you" (v. 10). Paul's contact with the Romans had been by word of mouth. He had heard about their faith, as had other Christians throughout the Roman Empire (Rom. 1:8). Paul had been praying for the opportunity to visit this church and to become personally involved in their lives.

One of the great values of praying for others is that it tends to forge a bond with them. The more we pray for others, the greater our concern for them. Most human beings are, if not selfish, self-centered. We tend to see things only from our own narrow point of view. Unlike God—who is aware of everything that happens in His universe and deeply concerned about every believer—we are concerned only with things which impact our lives and our loved ones. Learning to pray "without ceasing" and "always" for many others is a vital and practical way to grow in godliness.

"That I may impart to you some spiritual gift" (v. 11). Paul did not mean that he hoped to come to Rome in order to add to the spiritual gifts the Holy Spirit bestowed on Christians. What Paul wished for was the opportunity to use his own spiritual gifts among them. Paul was eager to do whatever he could to "establish" the believers in Rome. The word translated "establish" is *sterizo,* which means to strengthen or confirm. Paul was eager for God to work through him to help the believers in Rome become stronger Christians.

"That I may be encouraged together with you by the mutual faith both of you and me" (v. 12). This "afterthought" indicates how sensitive and caring Paul was. He was concerned that his desire to "impart to you some spiritual gift" might suggest to some that he saw himself as "superior" to the Roman Christians.

In fact, Paul, like Christ, was committed to servant ministry. He was convinced that all Christians are mutually interdependent. Each of us needs the gifts God has given to others. Each of us serves and is served, ministers and is ministered to. Paul wanted to make sure the Romans understand that he was eager to give of himself to them and just as eager to receive from them what they could contribute to his own growth in Christ.

Implications for our own prayer lives. This first of the recorded prayers in Paul's epistles teaches us several important things about prayer for others. (1) We need to be consistent in praying for Christians who live beyond the horizon of our own lives. (2) We need to develop a worldwide prayer ministry, built on learning all we can about Christians in other places. (3) As we pray for others, God will give us a deepening love for them.

2 CORINTHIANS 13:7–9:
A Prayer for the Obstinate

In this passage, Paul shared the content of his prayer for the Corinthians with that congregation. This content reflected a painful relationship that Paul had had with many of these believers.

Now I pray to God that you do no evil, not that we should appear approved, but that you should do what is honorable, though we may seem disqualified. For we can do nothing against the truth, but for the truth. For we are glad when we are weak and you are strong. And this also we pray, that you may be made complete (2 Cor. 13:7–9).

The context of Paul's letters to the Corinthians. In his first letter to the church at Corinth, Paul dealt with a number of problems in the congregation. Many in Corinth responded to his instruction. Others refused to submit, challenging Paul's authority.

In his second letter, Paul shared many new covenant principles of ministry that he had followed. The "weakness" which his critics despised was rooted in the realization that he must depend on God to work in the hearts of others. Behavior which seemed to the Corinthians to mark "strong" leaders was inappropriate for ministers of Christ. Yet as this second letter drew to a close, Paul warned the obstinate believers in Corinth who had refused to submit to the apostle's authority. If they insisted on proof of Paul's authority, he would not spare them on his return (2 Cor. 13:3). It was not that Paul would force their submission. Christ, "who is not weak toward you, but mighty in you" would deal with the obstinate.

Paul's prayer for the Corinthians is offered against this background.

"I pray to God that you do no evil" (v. 7). Paul's concern was not that the Corinthians should acknowledge his apostleship, but that they should do no wrong. The "wrong" Paul had in mind was their rejection of his God-given authority. Earlier Paul emphasized that God had given him his authority to build the Corinthians up, not to tear them down (cf. 2 Cor. 10:8). No matter how hostile the Corinthians had been toward Paul, Paul had only their best interests at heart.

"Not that we should appear approved, but that you should do what is honorable, though we may seem disqualified" (v. 7). If Paul should be forced to prove his authority, the Corinthians would be left with no doubt that he was an apostle. But Paul hoped that the Corinthians would respond to his letter and choose to "do no evil" long before he arrived. It was more important to Paul that the Corinthians do what was honorable and right than that his claim of apostleship be vindicated. He indicated he would rather they do what was right—and thus "seem to be disqualified" to the doubters in Corinth—than to be forced to demonstrate the authority that Christ had given him.

"And this also we pray, that you may be made complete" (v. 9). The word translated "made complete" is *katartisis*. This word is closer to the idea of "restored." It was used originally of the setting of dislocated bones, from which the meaning of being "put right" or "restored" was drawn. Paul's ultimate concern was that the Corinthians through doing no wrong might be restored to God, to the apostle, and to each other.

Implications for our prayer lives. Paul's prayer for the Corinthians was truly selfless. He was not concerned that he was being slandered. But Paul was concerned that the Corinthians were doing wrong—that their fellowship with him, with God, and with each other was hindered. Paul yearned to see right relationships reestablished as soon as possible.

He knew that if nothing happened to correct matters before his next visit, he had the authority to set things right. If he had to use this authority, the Corinthians would be forced to acknowledge him. But Paul desired that the Corinthians be restored before he could arrive, even if that left lingering doubts about him.

How unusual it is to find such a selfless person in the service of others. Yet prayer for others—the kind of constant, persistent prayer that characterized the apostle's life—will move us to put others first. When we pray regularly for others, even for our "enemies," God opens our heart to love them and to seek their welfare.

EPHESIANS 1:15–21:
A Prayer for Enlightenment

Paul recorded two lengthy prayers for the Christians at Ephesus. The first of these is found in chapter 1, with the specific content of the prayer indicated below in italics:

Therefore I also, after I heard of your faith in the Lord Jesus and your love for all the saints, I do not cease to give thanks for you, making mention of you in my prayers: that the God of our Lord Jesus Christ, the Father of glory, *may give to you the spirit of wisdom and revelation in the knowledge of Him, the eyes of your understanding being enlightened; that you may know what is the hope of His calling, what are the riches of the glory of His inheritance in the saints, and what is the exceeding greatness of His power toward us who believe,* according to the working of His mighty power which He worked in Christ when He raised Him from the dead and seated Him at His right hand in the heavenly places, far above all principality and power and might and dominion, and every name that is named not only in this age but also in that which is to come (Eph. 1:15–21).

The context of Paul's prayer for the Ephesians. The city of Ephesus was the center of the cult of Diana, the premier deity of Asia Minor. The temple of Diana drew hundreds of thousands of worshipers each year. The citizens of Ephesus were also devotees of sorcery and magic (see Acts 19:19). Paul's missionary team had a powerful impact on the city. So many became believers that the profits of those who made images of Diana and her temple were threatened. Yet those believers who had looked to dark powers had no clear idea of the matchless spiritual resources available to them now that they had become Christians.

In the first chapter of Ephesians, Paul encouraged these believers by reviewing the investment each person of the Trinity has made in their salvation (Eph. 1:3–14). He then recounted the content of this prayer that he offered for their enlightenment.

"I . . . do not cease to give thanks for you" (vv. 15, 16). Paul not only prayed for the Ephesians; he kept on praying for them. He thanked God for their salvation and the love they had for the saints. He was excited for

them as he thought about what God was doing in their lives.

"Making mention of you in my prayers" (v. 16). The phrase "making mention" (*mneian poioumenos*) implies that Paul was doing more than saying "thank you for the Ephesians." It implies that Paul prayed for individuals in Ephesus by name. It is one thing to pray "for the persecuted believers in Africa" and another thing to pray specifically for individuals about whom we read in Christian magazines or missionary newsletters.

"That . . . God . . . may give to you the spirit of wisdom and revelation in the knowledge of Him" (v. 17). In this prayer, Paul twice stated what he was praying. Then he used a purpose clause to explain why he was praying this way.

According to verse 17, *what* Paul was praying was that God might give them "the Spirit of wisdom and revelation" *in order that* the Ephesians might know God better.

It is best to understand the "spirit" here as the Holy Spirit. God had already made provision for the Ephesians to receive the Spirit. What Paul prayed was that the Ephesians might be fully endowed with the wisdom and the revelation that the Spirit alone could provide. Paul yearned to see the lives of these Christians flooded with the wisdom and the revelations which the Holy Spirit makes available to all believers.

Why was this a prayer priority of Paul's? The phrase "in the knowledge of Him" means simply "that you may know God better." To Paul, nothing was more important for believers that to know God.

It is important to make a distinction here. Paul was not praying that the Ephesians would gain knowledge *about* God. We want to know as much about God as we can. But Christians are never to settle for knowing *about* God. An individual can know a great deal about God without knowing Him personally or developing an intimate personal relationship with Him.

In his book *Knowing God,* J. I. Packer points out that knowing God is a matter of *personal dealing* and *personal involvement.* Knowing God is not intellectual but relational. The apostle Paul prayed that the Spirit might flood us with wisdom and revelation. As we respond to God's revelation of Himself to us, we come to a deeper knowledge of God.

"The eyes of your understanding being en- lightened" *(v. 18).* In verses 18 and 19, Paul used the same construction, indicating *what* he prayed, and then went on to explain the purpose underlying this prayer. What Paul prayed was that "the eyes of your understanding [might be] enlightened."

The best Greek manuscripts have "heart" in place of "understanding." In biblical thought, the heart was the seat of the intellect as well as feeling—the center of the human personality. Paul's second request was that the eyes of the Ephesians might be opened in such a way that their whole beings would be filled with awareness of the significance of their salvation.

Paul had a threefold reason for making this request. If the Ephesian believers grasped the full meaning of salvation in Christ, (1) they would "know the hope of His calling," (2) they would know "the riches of the glory of His inheritance in the saints," and (3) they would realize "what is the exceeding greatness of His power toward us who believe."

"The hope of His calling" *(v. 18).* In the New Testament, "hope" is a confidence that what God has promised will be ours. Those whom God has called to faith in Jesus Christ have an assured future. Paul had just written that believers have been chosen by God "that we should be holy and without blame before Him in love" (Eph. 1:4). We have been adopted as sons "to the praise of the glory of His grace" (Eph. 1:6). Through Jesus, "we have redemption through His blood, the forgiveness of sins, according to the riches of His grace" (Eph. 1:7). And in Christ, "We have obtained an inheritance" (Eph. 1:11) which is guaranteed by the Holy Spirit's presence in us "until the redemption" that awaits Christ's second coming (Eph. 1:14).

Salvation promises more than an eternity with God; it promises personal transformation here and now. What a hope we have in Christ Jesus!

"The riches of the glory of His inheritance in the saints" *(v. 18).* The Greek text makes it possible to read this verse as referring either to God's glorious inheritance in us, or to our glorious inheritance in Him. The content of Ephesians 1:11 and 14 make this second possibility the more likely meaning. Paul stated that "in Him we have obtained an inheritance" (1:11) and that the Holy Spirit "is the guarantee of our inheritance until the redemption" (1:14). Paul wanted the Corinthians to understand the full meaning of the salvation God had provided. That understanding would shift the focus of their lives from hopes of glory in this world to the glorious inheritance that awaits in heaven.

Some critics have charged that Christians are so heavenly minded that they are no earthly good. In fact, the opposite is true. The heavenly minded believer is freed to live a godly life here on earth, unmoved by the baubles that so often turn human beings away from the path of righteousness.

"The exceeding greatness of His power toward us who believe" *(v. 19).* In this verse, Paul struggled to express the vitality of a life lived in God's power. The best he could do was to collect synonyms for power and pile one upon another in this verse. The power that flows to us from God is *dunamis* (capability, potential), *energeia* (energy, effective power), *kratos* (exercised power), and *ischys* (vital, forceful power).

The premier example of God's power in operation is the resurrection of Jesus and His exaltation to God's right hand. This is the power God makes available to us "according to the working of His mighty power which He worked in Christ when He raised Him from the dead" (Eph. 1:19, 20).

Paul made this same point in Romans 8, describing the Holy Spirit as a source from which we draw power. Paul wrote, "If the Spirit of Him who raised Jesus from the dead dwells in you, He who raised Christ from the dead will also give life to your mortal bodies through His Spirit who dwells in you" (Rom. 8:11).

The important point here is that just as we are to know God experientially, we are to draw on the power God makes available to us in our daily lives. We may be weak in ourselves, but God's strength is available to us. There is no challenge too great for the believer—no mission too hard, no test too difficult. With the eyes of our hearts enlightened, we will glory in our salvation and in the future inheritance that God has set aside for the saved. We will live our lives by drawing on the strength God makes available to us in our times of need.

Implications for our prayer lives. We sometimes wonder how to pray for other Christians. Paul's first Ephesian prayer provides one possible prayer pattern. Remember that the structure of the Greek sentences makes it clear that Paul offered two specific prayers for Ephesian believers. And they explain just why he prayed as he did. Paul prayed:

1. *That*
   God might give the Spirit of wisdom and revelation
   in order that
   The Ephesians might know the Lord better
   and
2. *That*
   The eyes of their heart might be enlightened
   in order that they might:
   (1) know the hope of His calling,
   (2) know the riches of the glory of their inheritance, and
   (3) experience the exceeding greatness of the power God makes available to believers.

When we care about the spiritual well-being of other Christians, we cannot go wrong in praying this prayer for them.

EPHESIANS 3:14–19:
A Prayer that We Might Fully Experience Christ's Love

These verses contain a second prayer that the apostle Paul prayed for believers in Ephesus and quite possibly for believers in other churches as well. The content of the prayer appears below in italics:

For this reason I bow my knees to the Father of our Lord Jesus Christ, from whom the whole family in heaven and earth is named, *that He would grant you, according to the riches of His glory, to be strengthened with might through His Spirit in the inner man, that Christ may dwell in your hearts through faith; that you, being rooted and grounded in love, may be able to comprehend with all the saints what is the width and length and depth and height—to know the love of Christ which passes knowledge; that you may be filled with all the fullness of God* (Eph. 3:14–19).

The context of the prayer. See the discussion of the context of Ephesians 1:15–19 on page 234.

The structure of the prayer. The apostle Paul looked back on all that God had done for believers through Christ, and "for this reason" offered a special prayer to God the Father (3:14, 15). The prayer contains three requests, each introduced with the Greek word *hina,* "that." These cannot be easily distinguished in the English translation, but they are as follows:

(1) ***that*** *He would grant you, according to the riches of His glory, to be strengthened with might through His Spirit in the inner man, that Christ may dwell in your hearts through faith; that you, being rooted and grounded in love,*
(2) *[that you] may be able to comprehend with all the saints what is the width and length and depth and height—to know the love of Christ which passes knowledge;*
(3) ***that*** *you may be filled with all the fullness of God.*

These three petitions are closely linked, in something like a stairstep progression.

(3) and are filled with all
the fullness of God.
(2) so you experience the love of Christ
(1) That being rooted and grounded in love
Christ may dwell in your hearts through
faith.

Once we understand this structure and the relationship between the three requests, we can look more closely at each.

The introduction to the prayer (*Ephesians 3:1–14*). Paul indicated that he prayed to the Father of our Lord Jesus Christ from whom the whole family takes its name. We might wonder what "name" Paul had in mind for Christians. This is an important question, because in biblical times a "name" was considered to express the essence of the thing named. Whatever name Paul had in mind is central to our identity as a people of God and critical to our understanding of the content of his prayer.

Paul indicated that he prayed to the Father (*pater*) from whom the whole family (*patria*) takes its name. We can easily see the link between *pater* and *patria*. Because God truly is our Father, we who have a Father-child relationship with God are family. What is important here is not simply that we are His family, but that we are family to each other! Our relationship with our brothers and sisters in Christ is a family relationship, because each of us through Christ has become a child of God.

We must keep the essential nature of the Christian community as "family" in mind as we look at the content of Paul's prayer. What Paul prayed for depends on the existence of this family relationship.

Paul's first request (*Ephesians 3:16, 17*). Greek and English sentence structure differs in various ways. To understand what Paul was asking, it is helpful to restate the prayer as it would have been formed in English. What Paul asked was "that you may be rooted and grounded in love so that Christ may dwell in your hearts by faith, as the Holy Spirit encourages you within." To grasp the logic of Paul's complex request, we need to look at each element carefully.

1. "Being rooted and grounded in love" (*v. 17*)
The first question we must ask is, What "love" did the apostle have in mind? The New Testament speaks of three kinds of *agape* love. There is God's love for us, shown in Christ. There is our love for God, demonstrated by our obedience to Christ's commands. And there is the love of Christians for one another, which is modeled on Christ's love for us. The New Testament speaks more of the love Christians are to have for one another than of either of the other two loves.

The family identity of Christians is the key to understanding Paul's prayer. Thus, we conclude that the love Paul had in mind here is our love for one another. This is supported by the nature of the "rooted and grounded" analogy. Paul pictured a plant firmly rooted in rich soil, from which it draws nutrients. The soil in which God has rooted Christians is the church—the family of God—where we are nurtured and loved by one another.

2. "That Christ may dwell in your hearts through faith" (*v. 17*). At first this seems to be a strange request. We are taught in Scripture that Christ *does* dwell in the hearts of Christians! Why would Paul pray for something we already possess?

The answer is found in two Greek words for "dwell." One, *paoikeo,* means to dwell as a stranger or foreigner. The word used here, *katoikeo,* means to settle down and be at home. What Paul asked is that Christ might "be at home" in our hearts. And for this to happen, we are to be rooted and grounded in the family's love.

3. "Strengthened with might through His Spirit in the inner man" (*v. 16*). The word translated "strengthened" is *kataiothenai*. In Greek literature, this word was the opposite of "discouraged." Paul's phrase "the inner man" is a construction that seems to have been invented by Paul. In this context, it suggests the depth of the Spirit's penetration. We might paraphrase it like this: "Being encouraged through and through by the Spirit."

If we put all this together, Paul's first prayer for the Ephesians reads like this: "I pray that you might be firmly rooted and ground in family love, so that Christ will be at home in your hearts and you will experience the Spirit's encouragement through and through."

Paul's second request for the Ephesians (Ephesians 3:18–19a). We noted above that these three requests are linked in stairstep fashion. God's granting of the first requests is vital to His granting of the second. And Paul's second request for the Ephesians is "that you may be able to comprehend with all the saints" and so to "know the love of Christ which passes knowledge."

Paul made an important distinction here in speaking of the love of Christ. Christ's love is something Christians can *comprehend* and *know.* Yet at the same time, Christ's love is so great that it surpasses knowledge. There is simply no way that we can measure its width and length and depth and height.

While this may seem to be a paradox, Paul's careful choice of words makes his meaning clear. Christ's love is something we can *know*—in the sense of knowing by experience. This is because Christ's love is something that we "comprehend, with all the saints." The phrase "with all the saints" is critical. Christ's love is not something we can comprehend or experience alone. To comprehend—to perceive—and to experience Christ's love, we must be rooted and grounded in family love!

Paul reminds us here that Jesus loves us *through one another.* As we experience Christ's love expressed by our brothers and sisters, we sense the reality of this love, even though Jesus' love is too vast for us to begin to understand it.

So we see the first link between the prayers Paul offered for the Ephesians. Paul asked God to root and ground these believers in love for one another. Through love given and received by fellow believers, each person would experience the love of Christ.

Paul's third request for the Ephesians (Ephesians 3:19a). Paul's third and culminating request was the briefest: "That you may be filled with all the fullness of God." The phrase is best understood as rendered in an NEB footnote: "Filled with the fullness which God requires." Paul's final request—and the goal toward which his other requests were directed—was that the Ephesians might be mature or fulfilled Christians, transformed to reflect Jesus in all they did (cf. 2 Cor. 3:18).

Implications for our prayer lives. In this great prayer, Paul set out for us the path to Christian maturity. We are to take root in a church marked by family love. We are to sink our roots deep and to concentrate on loving others in the local body. As we love and are loved by our church family, we will sense the reality of Jesus' love for us. And as His love becomes more real to us, He will be increasingly at home in our lives. And we will grow, together with all the saints, into the persons God intends us to become in Christ.

How important it is that we pray for those we love, that they will find a loving church family where they can grow spiritually. And how important it is that we search out such a church, where we can also grow.

PHILIPPIANS 1:9–11:
A Prayer for Spiritual Progress

In this prayer, the apostle Paul was more concerned with the spiritual growth of believers than with their earthly needs.

And this I pray, that your love may abound still more and more in knowledge and all discernment, that you may approve the things that are excellent, that you may be sincere and without offense till the day of Christ, being filled with the fruits of righteousness which are by Jesus Christ, to the glory and praise of God (Phil. 1:9–11).

The context of the prayer. Philippi was a Roman colony city, populated primarily by discharged Roman soldiers and their families. It was one of the few cities Paul visited which did not have a synagogue. Paul was able to establish a small church here, even though the days he spent in Philippi were marked by controversy. His visit to the city ended with a brief imprisonment (see Acts 16).

When Paul wrote his letter to the Philippians, he was in Rome, awaiting trial. Paul encouraged his friends in Philippi not to be fearful for him, but to rejoice with him that his imprisonment actually was furthering the spread of the gospel. It is clear from this letter that Paul and the Philippian church had a warm relationship. In the prayer that Paul offered for them, we sense his priorities for these dearly loved believers.

The structure of the prayer. There are two parts to Paul's brief but significant prayer. Paul prayed that the Philippians might:

- be characterized by an ever-increasing and discriminating love, and
- become all they could be in Christ.

The first part of Paul's prayer (Philippians 1:9–10a). This part of the prayer reads, "That your love may abound still more and more in knowledge and all discernment, that you may approve the things that are excellent."

1. *Abounding love.* Paul used a word that means "overflowing" or "more than enough." This word is a favorite of Paul's, and is found 26 times in his writings. Paul acknowledged that the Philippians already loved each other. What he asked for them was that the love they had would keep on growing.

2. *Intelligent love.* Paul made it clear that he was not suggesting the kind of "love" that is a mere sentiment which embraces everyone and everything. These things marked the love that Paul wanted for these Philippian Christians:

- *Christian love is directed by knowledge* (epiginosis). Paul's use of this word is limited to religious and moral issues. Paul wanted the love the Philippians had to be guided by an awareness of what was appropriate in view of the gospel.
- *Christian love is directed by understanding* (aistheesei). The phrase "all understanding" is the ability to make a correct choice

from among many options. Once again, a moral dimension is implied.

3. *Effective love.* Love guided by knowledge and understanding would enable the Philippians to "approve the things which are excellent." The phrase *ta diasperonta,* "the things which are excellent," was frequently used by Greek philosophers to indicate the things that really matter. The word translated "approve" means to evaluate or distinguish between. Paul prayed that the Philippians might not merely distinguish between good and evil, but that their growing, regulated love would enable them to choose the *best* course in every situation.

The second part of Paul's prayer. Paul prayed that his friends in Philippi, through learning to love wisely, might become the best persons they could possibly be. He expressed this desire saying, "That you may be sincere and without offense till the day of Christ, being filled with the fruits of righteousness which are by Jesus Christ, to the praise and glory of God."

1. *"That you may be sincere"* (v. 10). To be the best we can be calls for *eilikrineis.* The word means pure or spotless. In the New Testament, this word always denotes moral purity.

2. *"And without offense"* (v. 10). The word here is *aproskopoi.* It describes a person who is careful never to do anything that might trip up another or cause him or her to stumble. We might call such a person "harmless."

3. *"Being filled with the fruits of righteousness"* (v. 11). The "fruits of righteousness" are moral qualities expressed in noble and good deeds.

What Paul prayed was that love guided by knowledge and understanding would enable the Philippians to make the very best possible moral choices. This would lead them to become pure, harmless, and principled persons whose lives would bring glory to God.

Implications for our prayer lives. Paul again focuses our attention on what is truly significant in life. It is important to pray for friends who are sick, out of work, or facing difficult times. But in the final analysis, the most important prayers we can offer for others are rooted in God's priorities for Christians. What a wonderful gift we offer when we ask for others a wise, overflowing love that will lead them to become all they can be in Christ.

COLOSSIANS 1:9–12:
A Pattern for Spiritual Growth

Most of Paul's prayers for believers focused on the transformation of Christians as a goal. This is also true of a unique petition that Paul made to God for the Colossians. The specific content of this prayer is shown below in italics.

For this reason we also, since the day we heard it, do not cease to pray for you, and to ask *that you may be filled with the knowledge of His will in all wisdom and spiritual understanding; that you may walk worthy of the Lord, fully pleasing Him, being fruitful in every good work and increasing in the knowledge of God;* strengthed with all might according to His glorious power, for all patience and longsuffering with joy; giving thanks to the Father who has qualified us to be partakers of the inheritance of the saints in the light (Col. 1:9–12).

The context of the prayer. Paul's letter to the Colossians was probably written as a corrective to the heresy of gnosticism. This system of belief came to full flower in the second century of the Christian era. It was rooted in a dualism which set the material and spiritual in opposition. According to the gnostics, the material world was evil and only the spiritual was good. Since God is good, He must be spiritual, and thus divorced from the material universe.

The gnostics believed that God did not create the material universe. It was created by an agent separated from God by a host of angelic ranks. In their view, Jesus must either be a low-ranking angelic being, or an apparition, for the good God could not take on evil flesh.

According to the gnostics, the human body and its passions were evil—a prison for the spark of the divine which was the true nature of human beings. Salvation was won by seeking hidden true knowledge of God, and it had nothing to do with the ordinary daily life which persons lived in the body.

In the same way, spirituality was divorced from bodily life. A gnostic might seek to become more spiritual by punishing his body (asceticism), or a gnostic might live for physical pleasure, convinced that nothing the evil body did could have any impact on the true, spiritual "self" trapped inside.

Paul's letter to the Colossians confronted gnosticism at every point. God did create the heavens and earth as well as the spiritual realm (Col.1:16). Jesus came to earth as God incarnate in a real human body (Col. 1:19). What's more, it was through the death of His body that Jesus won forgiveness for human beings (Col. 1:20, 22). The "spiritual" Christian is the person who does God's will daily, expressing his or her salvation by living in love and righteousness in obedience to God's will.

At every significant point, according to Paul, Christianity differed from what the gnostics believed and taught. It is against this background that we need to read Paul's prayer for the believers at Colosse.

The structure of the prayer. While most commentators take all of verses 9a through 12 as the content of Paul's prayer, it is best to take only 9a through 10 as its content. To do this, we need to read the verses as follows: "Since the day we heard it, [we] do not cease to pray for you ... [content of the prayer] ... strengthened with all might according to His glorious power, for all patience and longsuffering with joy, giving thanks to the Father who has qualified us to be partakers of the inheritance of the saints."

Verses 11 and 12, like 9a, *describe Paul praying.* Paul prayed without ceasing, and he was strengthened by God to pray with patience, longsuffering, and joy. As Paul prayed, he gave thanks to the Father who had chosen both Paul and the Philippians as his inheritance.

What we have left as the prayer itself, then, is verses 9b and 10:

That you may be filled with the knowledge of His will in all wisdom and spiritual understanding, that you may walk worthy of the Lord, fully pleasing Him, being fruitful in every good work and increasing in the knowledge of God (Col. 1:9b, 10).

The elements in this prayer are not separated from one another, but they describe a repeated cycle of Christian experience. This cycle begins with a knowledge of God's will, and it ends with knowing God better. This cycle is Paul's prescription for coming to know God better and better, in sharp contrast to the process suggested in gnosticism.

"That you may be filled with a knowledge of His will" (v. 9). The Greek language says, "be filled with a knowledge of *tou thelemata tou autou.*" The phrase would be better rendered a knowledge "of that which God has willed." We know what God has willed through the Scriptures. So Paul declared that coming to know God begins with His revelation to us in the Word of God.

"In all wisdom and spiritual understanding" (v. 9). The two Greek words here are *sophia* and *sunesin.* These words direct our attention to a specific way in which we are to know the Scripture. In both Old and New Testaments alike, *sophia* is knowledge applied to the making of righteous choices in daily life. The word *sunesin,* "insight," reinforces this emphasis.

Some people study the Bible as an intellectual pursuit—to learn about history, or as an adjunct to archaeology. Some study the Bible to build doctrinal systems and to refute error. What Paul encouraged is that we study the Bible in order to apply what Scripture says as a guide to righteous living day by day.

The gnostic looked in Scripture for hidden knowledge. To them, there was no need to apply Scripture to daily life. They believed that the daily life which human beings live in the flesh is irrelevant to God and has nothing to do with spirituality. Paul knew that just the opposite is true!

"That you may walk worthy of the Lord, fully pleasing Him" (v. 10). As Christians, we are eager to search out and apply God's revealed will to choices we make in our daily life. We do this because we want to be "worthy of the Lord." God has chosen us to bring Him glory, and we do so by living righteous lives in the here and now. Believers who are committed to such a lifestyle are "fully pleasing to Him."

Our daily lives are of vital concern to the Lord. Depending on the way we live them, we either reflect glory on the Lord, or we bring shame to His name. Only by adopting a lifestyle that is in full harmony with God's character can we hope to be pleasing to Him.

"Being fruitful in every good work" (v. 10). This phrase describes one outcome of seeking to apply God's revealed will as a guide to daily living. Such a commitment will lead to the production of "every good work." The Greek language has two words that are translated "good:" *kalos* and *agathos.* The first means beautiful or pleasing. The second, the word used here, means useful or beneficial.

As believers, we should seek to please God by applying His will to every situation in our daily lives. This will bring about results that are beneficial to us and useful to God. We will be living productive lives!

"And increasing in the knowledge of God" (v. 10). The cycle Paul described begins with a knowledge of what God has willed. It ends with the believer knowing God better. The knowledge of God that Paul had in view here is both personal and experiential. We do not simply know more about God; we know Him better. We experience a deepening personal relationship with the Lord.

The gnostics, like too many Christians today, assumed that knowing about God was the same as knowing God *personally.* They were wrong. It's one thing to read a book about a historical character like Napoleon. It's another thing entirely to be a member of Napoleon's household—to watch and listen and talk with him daily.

This is the distinction Paul made here. We can read the Bible and know a great deal about God. But to experience God—to live in

His presence daily—is far different and much more wonderful.

Implications for our prayer lives. Paul's prayer for the Colossians has implications for us as well as for our prayers. Paul teaches us that the way to experience God's presence is to study His Word and to apply its teachings as a guide to daily living. As we do, we will begin to live in ways which are worthy of the Lord and which are pleasing to Him.

Even more, our lives will become productive and beneficial to us and useful to God. And, most importantly, as we submit to God's Word as a guide for daily living, God Himself will become more and more real to us. We will truly come to know Him.

What a wonderful prayer to pray for others. And what a wonderful way of life to choose for ourselves.

COLOSSIANS 4:12:
A Prayer for Fulfillment

As Paul concluded his letter to the Colossians, he mentioned a Philippian brother who was with him in Rome. The apostle shared the content of this man's prayers for the little Christian community. The substance of this brother's prayers is a reflection of the prayer that Paul himself prayed for the Philippians, as recorded in 1:9b,10.

Epaphras, who is one of you, a bondservant of Christ, greets you, always laboring fervently for you in prayers, *that you may stand perfect and* complete in all the will of God (Col. 4:12).

The context of the prayer. See the discussion of context on page 240.

"That you may stand perfect." The word translated "perfect" is *teleioi.* We should not mistake standing perfect for sinlessness. The Greek word is to be understood as "fulfilled" or "mature." Like Paul, Epaphras had been praying that the Philippians might become all they could be in Christ.

"And complete in all the will of God." This second phrase further defines the maturity or

fulfillment for which Epaphras prayed. The mature Christian knows and does the will of God, finding fulfillment through living in the center of God's will.

Implications for our prayer lives. Again we are reminded that the most important thing in any believer's life is to grow into the person that Christ has made it possible for us to become. This should be our prayer for others as well as our goal for ourselves.

2 THESSALONIANS 1:11, 12:
A Prayer that Jesus Might Be Glorified

This final prayer of Paul for believers again reflected the apostle's concern for the spiritual growth of those whom he loved. The actual content of the prayer appears in italics in the fuller passage below.

Therefore we also pray always for you *that our God would count you worthy of this calling, and fulfill all the good pleasure of His goodness and the work of faith with power, that the name of our Lord Jesus Christ may be glorified in you, and you in Him, according to the grace of our God and the Lord Jesus Christ* (2 Thess. 1:11, 12).

The context of the prayer. Paul's second letter to the Thessalonians was written as a corrective. The Christians in that city were experiencing persecution, and they were eager for Christ's return. But some had misunderstood Paul's teachings about the future. Paul wrote this letter to correct these misunderstandings and to encourage these believers to live godly lives here and now. The hope we have of Christ's return in the future is an incentive to positive living in the present.

The structure of the prayer. Paul identified his motive for praying, the specific petition he made to God, and the outcome of God's answer of this prayer.

Paul's motive in praying for the Thessalonians. Paul's desire as he prayed for the Thessalonians was that "our God would count you worthy of this calling, and fulfill all the good pleasure of His goodness and the work of faith with power."

The Greek language says, "Lead a life worthy of the calling to which you have been called." God calls human beings to faith in Christ for His own good purposes. Our goal should be to be worthy of His calling. Our relationship with God is to set the direction and establish the purpose of our lives.

"And fulfill all the good pleasure of His goodness and the work of faith with power" (v. 11). If we are to lead a life worthy of God's calling, God Himself must be at work in our lives. Paul is referring to actions that are prompted by a desire for goodness and which are carried out in faith. We are to pursue what is right and beneficial for others, prompted by our faith.

"That the name of our Lord Jesus Christ may be glorified in you, and you in Him" (v. 12). When we do live in a way that is worthy of our calling, Christ is glorified. He is glorified now as His grace is reflected in us. But most importantly, when Jesus returns the lives we lived for Christ will bring glory to Him and to us.

"According to the grace of our God and the Lord Jesus Christ" (v. 12). Only God's grace makes it possible for saved sinners to please and glorify God. Paul directed his prayer to God, for God alone can give us the motive and the strength to live up to His calling.

Implications for our prayer lives. When we pray for others, we need to focus our prayers on eternal issues. What the Christian life is all about is, ultimately, the glory of God.

3 JOHN 2:
A Prayer That All Will Go Well

The apostle John revealed the content of one of his prayers for fellow Christians. John wrote,

Beloved, I pray that you may prosper in all things and be in health, just as your soul prospers (3 John 2).

At first, this prayer seems quite different from the reported prayers of the apostle Paul.

This is especially true if we intepret "prosper" as a reference to material wealth. Paul never asked for material blessings for believers, but he prayed for spiritual blessings. However, the difference is more apparent than real.

The custom in letter writing in the first century was to greet the recipient and then express as a prayer the wish that he was in good health. John followed this common approach, then added the wish that all things were going well for his reader's soul. The spiritual life has priority, and John knew that all was going well in Demetrius's relationship with God. He graciously wished the best for this Christian brother in all things, physical as well as spiritual.

Implications for our prayer lives. There is a difference between Paul's reports of the prayers he constantly offered for believers and the conventional greeting found in John's letter. John expressed best wishes; Paul opened his heart and showed his readers his deepest yearnings for their spiritual growth and well-being. Paul's letters tell us just what Paul said when praying for others. John did not share the same kind of information. We cannot compare the prayers of the two men, for we simply do not know what John prayed when he was interceding for others.

PRAYING FOR OTHERS: A SUMMARY

The prayers that the apostle Paul recorded in Scripture provide a unique insight into how Christians can minister to one another in prayer. They provide us with a list of prayer priorities.

These are prayers which pastors can pray for their congregations. They are prayers which husbands can pray for wives and wives for husbands. They are prayers that Christian parents can pray for their children.

The most significant prayer ministry we can have for others is to ask for them what Paul yearned to see in the lives of those whom he loved.

CHAPTER 17

ENDLESS PRAISE

PRAYER IN REVELATION

im, one of the men in a Bible study which I lead every Wednesday night, was in the military during World War II. He was married just a week before going overseas. For three years he communicated with his wife by letters. In his letters he poured out his love, sharing as much as he could of his experiences. How he longed to be home with her again.

Then, finally, the war was over. A few months later he walked down the gangplank of a troop ship and into his wife's arms.

That was over 50 years ago. For Jim and his bride the last five decades have been wonderful. They have known years of love and fulfillment as they have met life's challenges together and raised a family. Never in all that time have they been separated again.

The last book in the Bible, Revelation, reminds us that—like Jim—we live separated from the Lord we love. Our prayers are letters addressed to Him; Scripture and the Spirit's promptings are His communications to us. But one day soon the war between good and evil will be over. Satan, already defeated but still struggling, will be chained forever. And then, the final victory won, all of God's people

will go home. Then we will be with the Lord forever, with no need for petition. Our hearts and lives will be filled with endless praise.

THE BOOK OF REVELATION

The book of Revelation is closely linked with Old Testament predictive prophecy, but it remains unique. Prophets like Isaiah conveyed images of what God would do at history's end. The prophet Daniel provided many details of history's final battle. But only Revelation contains an eyewitness account of events that will take place in the end-time.

JOHN'S VISION OF THE FUTURE

When he was more than 90 years old, the apostle John was exiled to the little island of Patmos in the Mediterranean Sea off the coast of Asia Minor. One Lord's Day (Sunday) as John meditated, he was given a stunning vision of Jesus—not as John had known Him when He walked on earth but as He appeared in His essential glory as God the Son. Stunned, John "fell at His feet as dead" (Rev. 1:17). But Jesus encouraged John, giving the aged apostle messages to convey to seven churches in Asia Minor (Rev. 2; 3).

However, the bulk of the book of Revelation is not a report of what happened on Patmos. As chapter 4 of Revelation opens, John reports that he saw a door standing open into heaven. He heard a voice saying, "Come up here, and I will show you things which must take place after this" (Rev. 4:1).

This verse is the key to understanding the rest of the book of Revelation. It tells us three things about Revelation chapters 4—22. In these chapters,

- John describes what he is shown;
- John stands in heaven, observing not only what happens on earth but their heavenly causes; and
- John sees and describes events which "take place after this."

As John's report unfolds, we realize that what John describes are events which ancient prophets foretold would happen at history's end. John describes God's final victory over evil.

INTERPRETING THE BOOK OF REVELATION

As we read Revelation, we quickly find ourselves puzzled. What in the world is John talking about? For instance, early in Revelation John writes,

I looked when He opened the sixth seal, and behold, there was a great earthquake; and the sun became black as sackcloth of hair, and the moon became like blood. And the stars of heaven fell to the earth, as a fig tree drops its late figs when it is shaken by a mighty wind. Then the sky receded as a scroll when it is rolled up, and every mountain and island was moved out of its place (Rev. 6:12–14).

It is clear that John is describing something cataclysmic. But just what he portrays is far from clear.

Theologians have coined the phrase "apocalyptic language" to describe the images that dominate much of Revelation. They have also applied this term to many passages in the Old Testament. This phrase means "language used in descriptions of the end of the world."

Many assume that apocalyptic language is so different from other language that it cannot be taken literally. This view, however, ignores an important reality. Any person's ability to describe is limited by his or her experience and vocabulary.

For example, suppose you had lived in the United States in colonial times. Horses and wagons are the basic means of transportation. Roads are rutted tracks. Most villages have only a dozen or two cabins and perhaps a store. You cook your food and heat your cabin with wood fires in your fireplace. There are few books in your community and no newspapers or magazines.

Then suppose you were unexpectedly transported to the year 2000 and shown three scenes. The first takes place at night. From a vantage point a thousand feet in the air, you watch as cars stream along the Los Angeles highway system, looping from one five-lane road to another. A second vision takes place in the morning. You are transported to Chicago, where you look down on O'Hare Airport and watch the jets take off and land. Finally, you're taken into a modern home, where a family is watching a television interview beamed from a space station far above our planet. When the visions end, you find yourself back in your own time.

What will happen when you try to share your visions of the future with the people of your own time? Well, you will struggle! How will you possibly describe wonders so far beyond anything you and your neighbors have ever experienced? What words will you use, limited as you are to the vocabulary available in your own time? The best you can possibly do is to use similes, trying desperately to find something in your own time which is even slightly comparable to what you've seen.

In fact, your descriptions would most likely be filled with phrases very much like John's language in Revelation 6. You would use phrases such as,

- "black as sackcloth of hair"
- "became like blood"

John's vision of the end-times was marked by earthquakes and other cataclysmic events.

- "as a fig tree drops its late figs when it is shaken by a mighty wind"
- "as a scroll when it is rolled up"

The best you could do would be to suggest that what you saw was "like" or "similar to" something familiar to you and your friends.

What we have in Revelation is not "apocalyptic language" that has no correspondence to real events. What we have is the struggle of a person of the first century A.D. to describe actual events which neither he nor his contemporaries had the experience to understand or the vocabulary to communicate. When we read Revelation, we need to remember it is a description of "things which must take place after this."

While many of the details escape us, because of the language problem discussed above, the major events of that future are clear. According to Revelation, at history's end God will step into history to judge sin and put an end to evil. And afterward—when this universe is replaced by a new and perfect creation and when Satan and his followers have begun their sentence of eternal punishment in the lake of fire—the saved of all ages will begin an eternity of blessedness in the presence of our God.

REVELATION'S THEMES AND PRAYER

As we read the book of Revelation, we find frequent pauses for praise and prayer. The praise flows from the fact that now, at last, the victory of God is near, and His purposes in creation are about to be fulfilled. The references to prayer are also woven into the flow of the events that bring the history of this world to its dramatic close.

PRAISE IN THE BOOK OF REVELATION

John witnessed history's end from heaven. Throughout this great book, John reported what he observed in the realms of earth and heaven. Throughout the sequence of culminating events, praises echoed throughout heaven.

PRAISES OF THE ELDERS IN HEAVEN

In heaven John observed God's throne, and he saw various beings gathered around it. Among them were "living creatures," either cherubim or seraphim, who continually praised God. John also saw 24 elders, who wore golden crowns which they cast down before God as they worshiped Him.

The identity of the 24 elders is never stated. Some interpreters consider them to be representatives of Israel's 12 tribes and the 12 apostles, if not the patriarchs and the apostles themselves. Whoever the elders are, they are frequently shown offering praises to God.

Continual praise for God as Creator *(Revelation 4:10–11).* The first time we see the 24 elders, they are gathered around the throne of God praising Him as Creator. Such praise has been offered to God continually from the beginning of creation.

You are worthy, O Lord,
To receive glory and honor and
    power;
For You created all things;
And by Your will they
    exist and were created
    (Rev. 4:10, 11).

This same sense of wonder and praise is expressed in Psalm 104:24:

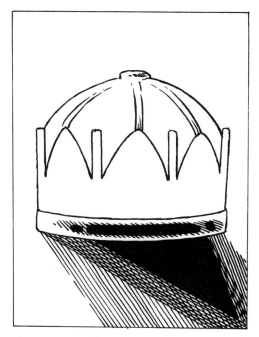

John saw twenty-four elders around God's throne wearing golden crowns, which they cast before Him in their worship.

O Lord, how manifold are
    Your works!
In wisdom You have made
    them all (Ps. 104:24).

The introduction of a new theme of praise *(Revelation 5:8–14).* As chapter 5 opens, John saw something that had not taken place in heaven before. God held out a scroll that had been sealed. The scroll contained God's plan for history's end; its opening will mark the beginning of the end. As John watched, Christ took the scroll from the Father's right hand.

At that moment, the 24 elders fell down before the Lord, to sing a new song of praise.

You are worthy to take the
    scroll,
And to open its seals,
For You were slain,
And have redeemed us to God
    by Your blood

Out of every tribe and tongue
    and people and nation,
And have made us kings
    and priests to our God;
And we shall reign on the
    earth (Rev. 5:9–10).

This song of the redeemed is filled with praise for redemption. Its content answers several questions.

1. Whoever the 24 elders are, they are human beings who have been redeemed by the blood of Christ. While angels have cause to praise God, we human beings have far greater reason to worship and adore Him. Angels were created pure, and those who refused to follow Satan in his rebellion have remained pure. We human beings were born in sin, have sinned willfully, and deserve God's condemnation. Yet rather than condemn us God chose to give His Son, and Jesus chose to die on the cross, that we might be forgiven and transformed. How much more we have to praise God for than any angel. And how heartfelt our praises should be!

2. The redeemed include human beings from "every tribe and tongue and people and nation." The best explanation for this is that God, who is rich in mercy, has taken infants who have died without committing personal sin. On the basis of Christ's death, He has chosen not to hold them responsible for the sin inherited from Adam. Not one tribe or tongue or people or nation has been overlooked, but individuals from all the world have been chosen to receive God's grace.

3. God not only forgives but transforms the saved, making us "kings and priests to our God." In Christ, we are lifted from guilt to glory. No wonder the elders, fully aware of the pit from which they and we have been lifted, joyfully sing the praises of the One who has redeemed them with His blood.

The angels and animal creation cannot fully grasp the wonder of the salvation that God has provided for us. They look on in wonder, then join in the song of praise. Myriads of angels sing,

Worthy is the Lamb who was
    slain
To receive power and riches
    and wisdom,
And strength and honor and
    glory and blessing! (Rev. 5:12).

And every living creature joins in, singing in its own way,

Blessing and honor and glory
    and power
Be to Him who sits on the
    throne,
And to the Lamb, forever and
    ever (Rev. 5:13).

God truly is to be praised as Creator. But it is as mankind's Redeemer that the fullness of God's grace and glory are displayed. And it is praise for redemption that moves us—and the whole creation—to offer the loudest, most joyous psalms.

Praise at God's triumph (*Revelation 11:16–18*). As angels announced that "the kingdoms of this world have become the kingdoms of our Lord and of His Christ, and He shall reign forever and ever," the 24 elders again praised and worshiped God. The theme of triumph is powerfully expressed in their words:

We give You thanks, O Lord
    God Almighty,
The One who is and who was
    and who is to come.
Because You have taken Your
    great power and reigned.
The nations were angry, and
    Your wrath has come,
And the time of the dead, that
    they should be judged,
And that You should reward
    Your servants the prophets
    and the saints,

And those who fear Your
    name, small and great,
And should destroy those who
    destroy the earth (Rev.
    11:17–18).

The ultimate triumph of God, with its blessings for the righteous and punishment of the wicked, is a cause for celebration. We who have endured and come to see the wreckage that sin causes truly welcome history's end and its devastating judgments. We know that after judgment God will create a new heaven and earth, and at last all will be set right.

THE PRAISE OF ANGELS IN HEAVEN

As John watched the events that unfolded in heaven, he witnessed the 24 elders praising God. John also saw angels praising the Lord. Their praise was also linked with specific events in heaven and on earth.

Praise as the scroll is handed to Jesus *(Revelation 5:12–13)*. Christ took the sealed scroll, and its opening initiated the sequence of events that brought history to a close. Then the angels joined in the praises. While angels do not experience redemption, they have from the creation of the world been witnesses of all that has transpired on earth. They have seen the tragedies which sin has imposed on humankind. They witnessed the Incarnation. They rejoiced when Jesus rose and shouted when He returned to heaven. Now they are about to witness the end of the great drama that has taken place on history's stage. Thrilled, they also praise Jesus the Redeemer.

    Worthy is the Lamb who was
        slain
    To receive power and riches
        and wisdom,
    And strength and honor and
        glory and blessing (Rev. 5:12).

The angels know the price Christ paid to redeem our lost race.

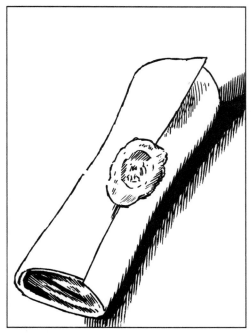

A sealed scroll describing the end of history could only be opened by Jesus.

Praise with the "song of Moses" *(Revelation 15:3–4)*. By the time the angels sing the "song of Moses," devastating judgments have already fallen on the earth. This song is raised when seven angels step forward, "having the seven last plagues, for in them the wrath of God is complete" (15:1).

This phrase helps us understand what the "song of Moses" is. When God gave the Law through Moses, He did more than spell out His expectations for Israel. He provided a standard against which individuals can be judged. While those who trusted God and sought to keep God's Law found it a source of blessing, it subjected those who disobeyed to judgment. As Paul wrote in Romans, "We know that whatever the law says, it says to those who are under the law, that every mouth may be stopped, and all the world may become guilty before God" (Rom. 3:19).

The "song of Moses" is praise to God as Judge, and it is offered as God finally pours

out His wrath on a sinful and sinning humanity.

> Great and marvelous are Your
>   works,
> Lord God Almighty!
> Just and true are Your ways,
> O King of the saints!
> Who shall not fear You,
>   O Lord, and glorify Your
>   name?
> For You alone are holy,
> For all nations shall come and
>   worship before You,
> For Your judgments have been
>   manifested (Rev. 15:3–4).

THE UNITED PRAISE OF ALL
CREATED BEINGS

As we scan Revelation, we see human beings and angels praising God, each from its
own perspective. Two passages are special in
that they unite all created beings in common
praise of the Lord.

United praise of Christ as Redeemer *(Revelation 5:13–14)*. Only human beings can praise
Christ as benefactors of His redemptive work.
But angels who have been witnesses of the
drama of salvation join in (see pp. 248–249):
"Every creature which is in heaven and on
earth and under the earth and such as are in
the sea, and all that are in them" praise Christ,
saying

> Blessing and honor and glory
>   and power
> Be to Him who sits on the
>   throne,
> And to the Lamb, forever and
>   ever! (Rev. 5:13).

Praise for salvation *(Revelation 7:9–12)*. Revelation 7 describes the commissioning of
144,000 Jews who will witness to Christ during the last months of the terrible tribulation
which will mark history's end. Those who ini-
tiate this praise are identified as "a great multitude . . . clothed with white robes" (Rev. 7:9).

When John asked who these persons were, he
was told that "these are the ones who come
out of the great tribulation, and washed their
robes and made them white in the blood of
the lamb" (Rev. 7:14). They are victims of
God's enemies—enemies whom He is judging
as history draws to its close.

In spite of the persecution these believers
have experienced, they are fully aware that
now is the moment toward which time itself
has rushed. They cry out joyfully, "Salvation
belongs to our God who sits on the throne,
and to the Lamb!" (Rev. 7:10). At this, all the
angels and elders join in, and united, all in
heaven cry,

> Amen! Blessing and glory and
>   wisdom,
> Thanksgiving and honor and
>   power and might,
> Be to our God forever and ever.
> Amen (Rev. 7:12).

No persecution here on earth, however intense, can alter God's firm commitment to accomplish His purposes in the world. And no
persecution can dampen the joy of those who
know that God's purposes for them will be fulfilled.

A final scene of united praise *(Revelation
19:1–7)*. When the last description of united
praise is given, Christ is about to return to
earth. His coming marks a final victory over
the forces of evil and, for believers, the "marriage supper of the lamb."

The image of the marriage supper is a
vivid one. In biblical times, a marriage took
place in two stages. In the first stage, two people were committed to each other and legally
binding papers were signed. Even though the
two had not yet lived together, they were
legally "married." Often, when a marriage involved two people who were very young,
there would be a lengthy delay between the
first stage of marriage and its consummation.

The marriage supper celebrated the actual
uniting of the couple. The bridegroom, ac-

companied by friends, came to the home of the bride. In a merry procession, she was taken to his home. Here family and friends gathered for a celebration that might last a week or ten days. During this time, the bride was honored as queen and the bridegroom as king. The marriage supper marked the beginning of the actual union of the two—a union which God intended to last throughout their lives.

What an image of the culminating event of history. Christ, the Bridegroom, will return to claim the church as His bride. Christ and the church have been truly and legally wed, bound together forever. Yet only at the end-time will this union be consummated. The marriage supper of the Lamb marks the beginning of the full and complete union of a redeemed humanity with the God who has so clearly expressed His love for us. This full and complete union will never end. God, and we with Him, will be together eternally.

No wonder John saw all unite in praise as the marriage supper of the Lamb took place at last.

After these things I heard a loud voice of a great multitude in heaven, saying, "Alleluia! Salvation and glory and honor and power belong to the Lord our God! For true and righteous are His judgments, because He has judged the great harlot who corrupted the earth with her fornications; and He has avenged on her the blood of His servants shed by her." Again they said, "Alleluia! Her smoke rises up forever and ever!" And the twenty-four elders and the four living creatures fell down and worshiped God who sat on the throne, saying, "Amen! Alleluia!"

Then a voice came from the throne, saying, "Praise our God, all you His servants and those who fear Him, both small and great!"

And I heard, as it were, the voice of a great multitude, as the sound of many waters and as the sound of mighty thunderings, saying, "Alleluia! For the Lord God Omnipotent reigns! Let us be glad and rejoice and give Him glory, for the marriage of the Lamb has come, and His wife has made herself ready" (Rev. 19:1–7).

And so all rejoice and praise God as His great victory over evil is confirmed.

PETITION IN THE BOOK OF REVELATION

Praise echoes throughout the book of Revelation. We can understand why this is true, for this wonderful book portrays the victory of God over evil, unveiling the significance of that victory for all who trust in Him.

The book of Revelation also records several petitions. These reflect the unique content of this final book in Scripture.

The futile petitions of the lost (Revelation 6:15–17). The terrible divine judgment which Revelation describes evokes a response from the unconverted. It is clear even to the lost that the events that mark history's end have a supernatural cause. This is reflected in a prayer reported in Revelation 6—a prayer uttered at the beginning of the period of judgment.

John first described the reaction of people everywhere to the cataclysms he described earlier in chapter 6. He wrote that "the kings of the earth, the great men, the rich men, the commanders, the mighty men, every slave and every free man, hid themselves in the caves and in the rocks of the mountains" (6:15). They fled in terror.

As they cowered in their hiding places, John described their prayer "to the mountains and rocks"—not to God.

Fall on us and hide us from the face of Him who sits on the throne and from the face of the Lamb! For the great day of His wrath has come, and who is able to stand? (Rev. 6:16, 17).

Those who were being judged realized what was happening. But the lost called on the rocks to hide them rather than turning to God! This strange reaction is also reflected in Revelation 9:20–21. As part of the final judgment, God caused devastating judgments that killed at least a third of earth's population. He then unleashed millions of demons, whose stings tormented those left. As John looked on in awe and wonder, he reported,

The rest of mankind, who were not killed by these plagues, did not repent of the works of their hands, that they should not worship demons, and idols of gold, silver, brass, stone, and wood, which can neither see nor hear nor walk. And they did not repent of their murders, or their sorceries or their sexual immorality or their thefts (Rev. 9:20, 21).

Under judgment, the lost called on inanimate nature to crush and hide them, but they would not repent and call on God to save them.

There are two explanations for this response to judgment. The first is that the more we persist in sin, the harder our hearts grow toward God. The second is that if we insist on persisting in sin, there will come a time when the opportunity to repent is removed. Those whose hearts are hard will grow even more stubborn as a judgment from God. This is what will happen when the day of judgment comes—when Christ opens the scroll that describes and initiates the events of history's end.

How we need to take this to heart. If anyone who reads this has hesitated to come to Christ, wait no longer! The end is drawing near, and one day soon the door of opportunity may be closed. How eager we should be to turn to Jesus while there is time—to join the throngs who will unite their voices with those of the angels in endless praise of God.

The prayers of persecuted saints (*Revelation 6:10*). In the same chapter in which we read of the futile prayers of the lost, we are given a glimpse of a prayer that is being answered. Revelation 6 describes John's vision of a great multitude "who had been slain for the word of God and for the testimony which they held" (6:9). These were martyrs, who held to their faith in Christ at the cost of their lives. Now they cried out to the Lord to act, saying

How long, O Lord, holy and true, until You judge and avenge our blood on those who dwell on the earth? (Rev. 6:10).

Those praying have no doubt that the holy God will judge their persecutors. They believed so firmly in Him that they were willing to surrender their earthly lives, looking to eternity. Their question is, "How long?" Their words express their request for God to hurry.

The smoke of incense mingled with the prayers of the saints before God's throne.

Here, in the context of Revelation, we realize that God *is* hurrying. Even now judgment has begun!

Prayers of the saints as incense (*Revelation 5:8; 8:3, 4*). Twice in Revelation the prayers of God's people are pictured as incense. The first use of this image occurs in Revelation 5:8. As the 24 elders began to sing redemption's "new song," they carried golden bowls filled with "incense, which represent the prayers of the saints" (Rev. 5:8). The other use of this image comes as a new series of judgments is about to be poured out on earth.

As a prelude to judgment, an angel took a golden bowl filled with incense which was to be burned on a golden altar with "the prayers of all the saints." John wrote, "The smoke of the incense, with the prayers of the saints, ascended before God from the angel's hand" (Rev. 8:4). As it ascended before the Lord, fire was cast on the earth, and angels announced new judgments with numerous blasts from their trumpets.

Incense played an important part in Old Testament worship. Exodus 30 gives a formula for mixing sweet-smelling spices to be burned as incense before the Lord (Ex. 30:34–37). This incense was to be burned only before the Lord, on a special altar placed within the Old Testament worship center, first the tabernacle and later the temple. Exodus required that the priest

shall burn on it sweet incense every morning; when he tends the lamps, he shall burn incense on it (Ex. 30:7).

The same obligation was laid on the priest when he lit the lamps at twilight.

He shall burn incense on it, a perpetual incense before the Lord throughout your generations (Ex. 30:8).

The sweet smell of the incense was to rise always to the Lord as an expression of praise and worship.

In the same way, our prayers are to be offered to God perpetually. What a wonder that God, who delights in our praise, should find our requests pleasing to Him.

SCRIPTURE'S LAST PRAYER (REVELATION 22:20, 21)

The final triumph of God over Satan and evil is described in Revelation 20. The last two chapters of this book are devoted to descriptions of the new heaven and earth that God will create. It is to be populated by the faithful angels and the saved of every age. The prospect that John held out is perhaps best summed up in Revelation 21:3, 4.

And I heard a loud voice from heaven saying, "Behold, the tabernacle of God is with men, and He will dwell with them, and they shall be His people. God Himself will be with them and be their God. And God will wipe away every tear from their eyes; there shall be no more death, nor sorrow, nor crying. There shall be no more pain, for the former things have passed away" (Rev. 21:3, 4).

What a wonderful prospect. As we have seen in our study of prayers in the Bible, even today we have a special relationship with God. We are privileged to look up to God as our loving Father to express our needs and share our joys. Such a privilege is wonderful in itself. But even this blessing is small in comparison as we consider what God has in store for us.

As John closed his book, he was filled with joy at the prospect of what lies ahead. God will triumph at history's end. Jesus will come and we will be united with Him forever. God will create a new and wonderful world, and He Himself will be present with us for endless ages to come.

No wonder John's prayer, the last prayer in Scripture, is "Amen. Even so, come, Lord Jesus!"

Come.

For we can hardly wait.

❖

HOW SHALL WE THEN PRAY?

APPLYING BIBLICAL LESSONS ON PRAYER

Jesus' disciples were impressed. It was apparent to them that Christ spent much time in prayer. Despite His dawn to dusk schedule of teaching and healing, despite the many weary miles He and His companions covered, Jesus often slipped away at night to spend time with His Father. The disciples must have talked about this practice of Christ's, and wondered. Finally they asked Him, "How shall *we* pray?"

In a sense the things we've discovered in our exploration of Bible prayers and petitions raise similar questions. We've observed Old and New Testament saints at prayer. We've listened to Jesus' own prayers, and heard what He had to say about prayer. We've seen the early church at prayer, and examined what the New Testament epistles say about prayer. It's appropriate as we come to the end of this study to ask the disciples' question. In view of all that Scripture shows us, "How shall we then pray?"

LESSONS FROM BIBLE WORDS FOR PRAYER

The Hebrew Old Testament uses a number of different words for prayer. Similarly a variety of words for prayer are found in the Greek New Testament. However, the meaning of the Greek words is best defined by the Hebrew words they were used to translate. Thus the biblical doctrine of prayer, as reflected in Bible words, is rooted in the Old Testament. Several things are striking about this biblical vocabulary.

The Bible's prayer vocabulary reflects a common vision of God. The words reflect the conviction that God exists, that God cares about human beings, and that God, who created the world, has unlimited power to affect the course of events. Bible people prayed to God because they were absolutely sure that God could answer prayer and that His answers would make a difference in their circumstances.

Moderns sometimes assume that the real value of prayer is in making us feel better. While prayer can and will lead to changes within us, Old and New Testament believers turned to God in prayer first of all because they were convinced that God could and would act to objectively change their circumstances. Hannah prayed to God for a son, not to feel better about her childlessness, but because she firmly believed God could cause her to become pregnant. Hezekiah prayed to God about an Assyrian invasion army, not to make him feel better about the impending doom, but because he firmly believed that God could throw back the enemy.

Everything the Bible reveals about prayer is rooted in the conviction that God exists and that He can and will act for us when we turn to Him.

The Bible's prayer vocabulary reflects a sense of personal relationship with God. Prayer in other ancient cultures was strikingly different from prayer in the Bible. The Sumerians and other Mesopotamian valley inhabitants assumed that the gods were dependent on human beings for offerings. While the gods didn't particularly care about people, they could be bribed to answer prayers. The Roman's assumed that the gods and goddesses were independent but self-interested. They could be bargained with, and prayer took on the character of bartering goods and honor in exchange for help. The Egyptians assumed that the gods and goddesses were either disinterested or hostile, but that they could be tricked and manipulated. Much in Egyptian "prayer" took the form of magical attempts to control the actions of a god or goddess who otherwise would not have helped a mere human being.

In utter contrast, biblical prayer is rooted in a sense of personal relationship with a loving, caring God. God does not have to be manipulated, tricked, or cajoled into helping. God wants to help those with whom He has established a covenant relationship and who have thus become His own. The most striking feature of biblical prayer is the childlike confidence so clearly displayed in a God who is known to be both willing and able to help.

We cannot begin to understand biblical prayer, or to pray as Scripture directs, unless we share these unimaginably powerful convictions that infuse Scripture's vocabulary of prayer. God is, and He has unlimited ability to act in our world. And God cares deeply for each one who has through faith established a personal relationship with Him.

LESSONS FROM OLD TESTAMENT PROSE PRAYERS

The Old Testament records nearly one hundred prose prayers. Most of them are brief; all of them occur in narrative passages. Over a third of these prayers report the words of ordinary men and women. Two features of these prose prayers are especially significant.

First, the prose prayers of the Old Testament are spontaneous. These are not formal prayers, intended to be repeated at set times. These are unique, singular expressions shaped by the life-experiences of believers. These prayers clearly indicate an awareness that God is involved in every circumstance of an individual's life, and that it is appropriate to speak to Him about anything at all.

Second, the prose prayers of the Old Testament are conversational. That is, they use the same words and patterns of speech a person would ordinarily use in speaking with other persons. There is no formal language, no "thee" or "thou," to mark these prose prayers as *religious*. The person praying simply talks to God, expressing thoughts and requests in ordinary, guileless ways. This feature of Old Testament prose prayers, perhaps more than any other, reminds us of how comfortable our relationship with God is to be. He is with us in everything, participating in our lives. How natural it is to speak to Him as we would to a familiar friend.

Our study of Old Testament prose prayers reminds us that prayer truly is "easy." This is true of each of the four basic kinds of Old Testament prose prayer: petition, complaint, confession, and blessing (thanksgiving). We can pray at any time. We can pray in any place. We can pray the moment we sense a need, with no special preparation. We can pray in any position that fits the occasion. Our prayers can be brief or long. And we can express ourselves to God spontaneously, conversationally, as to any concerned friend.

LESSONS FROM PERSONAL AND PUBLIC PRAYER PSALMS

The Old Testament also contains carefully crafted prayer poems. These prayer poems remind us that there is also a place for concentrated, thoughtful communication with God.

There is a place for deeper reflection on the conditions of our life and intensive meditation on the nature of God and our relationship with Him.

The contribution of personal prayer psalms. The psalms have long been recognized as the "prayer book" of the Old Testament and have served as models for concentrated, personal prayer. Three characteristics of the psalms are particularly significant for our prayer lives.

The psalms teach us to openly share all our thoughts and feelings with the Lord. It is impossible to read the psalms without being struck by the deeply emotional nature of their content. The psalmists display a total freedom to express to God every emotion they experience. While the psalms often reflect joy and thanksgiving, just as often they express frustration, anger, and bitterness. We get the clear impression that the psalmists spoke to God with utter honesty and transparency.

This freedom not only reflects the intensity of the emotions the psalmist felt, but also the fact that the psalmists were *comfortable* in God's presence. They were so confident of God's love, acceptance, and understanding that they were fearlessly honest with God, even when their frustration or anger were directed against Him!

The psalms teach us to focus our thoughts on those qualities of God which reassure us of His love and involvement. The spontaneous prose prayers of the Old Testament imply certain beliefs about God, but the crafted, thoughtful prayer poems of the psalms explicitly focus our attention on aspects of His nature and character. When troubled by injustice, the psalmists focus on God's nature as the Moral Judge of His universe. When endangered, the psalmists focus on the fact that God is One who acts to save the godly from the wicked, or the fact that God is a strong refuge in whom the godly are safe. When overcome by guilt, the psalmists focus on the fact that the Lord is a forgiving God. When feeling weak, the psalmists focus on God's strength. For every need there are

qualities of God on which believers can meditate, and to which we can appeal.

This characteristic of the psalms is of central importance. How often our thoughts are dominated by the circumstances in which we find ourselves. The psalms teach us to look away from circumstances to the Lord. We are not to ignore our circumstances, or to repress and deny our emotions, but we are to focus our attention on the Lord, and to let our awareness of His character and His presence reshape our perspective.

The psalms remind us that a focus on the God who can change our circumstances will also transform our emotions. Again and again we see psalmists who begin their prayers filled with anxiety but conclude them with refreshed confidence in the Lord. Psalmists who begin their prayers eaten up with envy and self pity end by thanking God for difficulties. While believers of every era are convinced that God does answer prayer and that God does change circumstances, the psalmists remind us that even when God chooses not to act for us, He does act in our hearts when we appeal to Him. In directing our thoughts and prayers to God we often gain a radically new perspective on our situation, a perspective which changes our emotions and brings unexpected peace and joy.

The personal prayer psalms encourage us to share all our thoughts and emotions with God, confident of His loving concern. We are encouraged to focus our thoughts on who He is rather than to let our thoughts and emotions be shaped by circumstances alone. And we are assured that prayer, which *can* change the world around us, most certainly *will* change us.

The contribution of public prayer psalms. Psalms used in public worship make the same contributions to our understanding of prayer as do private prayer psalms—with one very special addition. The public prayers, identified as such by superscriptions which direct their delivery to temple worship leaders, remind us that we are not isolated individuals but are participants in a community of faith. Everything that is true for us as individuals is true for us as members of the faith community. As we as individuals are to share freely with God, so we are to share corporately. As we as individuals are to focus on the character and nature of God, so is the community of which we are a part. And as our individual perspectives and emotions are to be shaped by a deepening understanding of who God is, so are our corporate perspectives and emotions.

We are called to live as members of a praying, praising community of faith.

LESSONS FROM JESUS' PRACTICE OF AND TEACHINGS ON PRAYER

While there is much that we can learn about prayer by examining the prayer lives of Old Testament saints, Jesus Christ is our ultimate authority on prayer. In His life on earth Jesus, God enfleshed, both offered prayers to the Father and received and answered prayers from His contemporaries.

Several themes recur in Jesus' teachings and comments on prayer which add significantly to Scripture's overall teaching.

Jesus emphasized the fatherliness of God. Without in any way challenging the deep convictions expressed in Scripture about the essential character and nature of God, Jesus stressed approaching God with utter confidence in His fatherly love.

A sense of God's fatherliness encourages us to come to Him frequently, eager to share our lives. Our conviction that God has a deep love for every child of His gives us a wonderful freedom in prayer. We know that He welcomes us and that He is completely committed to our good. The mystery of unanswered prayer is resolved for those who realize that God knows better than we what is truly good for us. While God considers what we want, as any loving father He chooses to give only what is best.

Jesus emphasized praying in His name. The full import of Jesus' instruction to pray in His name became clear only after His death and resurrection. In His death Jesus became both the ground of our salvation and the object of saving faith. It is through faith in Christ that we become God's children, objects of His fatherly love.

But those who heard Jesus tell them to pray in His name knew full well that even more was implied. In biblical times the "name" was understood to express something of the essential nature of the person or thing named. To pray in Jesus' name thus means to identify both the content and the motivation of our prayers with all that Jesus is. When our prayers are offered in Jesus' name, in full harmony with His purposes and with the intent of glorifying God, we can be sure that our prayers will be answered.

Yet there is nothing here to keep us from expressing *any* request to God. As Father, God cares about the little things that concern us as well as matters of cosmic concern. But in emphasizing prayer in His name Jesus reminds us that, as we mature in faith, our prayers will increasingly reflect God's purposes and His priorities. Understanding this, we see why we can be sure that "whatever we ask" in Jesus' name will be done.

Jesus emphasized willing submission to God's will. Again and again Jesus reminded His disciples of the priority of God's will. Jesus' own prayers were always effective, because all Jesus said and did was in total harmony with the Father's will. As we abide in Christ, ever responsive to His will for us, we will become more and more sensitive to what God's will is, and our prayers will be shaped by our deepening relationship with the Lord.

LESSONS FROM THE EARLY CHURCH'S EXPERIENCE WITH PRAYER

The book of Acts gives a brief narrative history of the spread of Christianity during the church's first three decades of existence. The many references to prayer in Acts reminds us how essential prayer was to the first Christians. Along with commitment to the apostles' doctrine and to mutual love and support, commitment to prayer was one of the identifying marks of the early church. Individuals and leaders made important decisions only after prayer. And whenever challenged by hostile forces, the church immediately turned to prayer.

The primary contribution of Acts to our understanding of prayer is to emphasize what an essential resource prayer is for the individual believer and for the church.

LESSONS FROM THE NEW TESTAMENT EPISTLES

While there are a number of references to prayer in the Epistles, three teachings stand out.

The Holy Spirit prays with and for us. For any who are frustrated by uncertainty about what or how to pray, the teaching of Romans 8:26 and 27 is especially important. We're told that when we pray the Holy Spirit prays with us and for us. The Spirit, who knows us intimately, and who is fully aware of God's will, is able to interpret our deepest desires to the Father and to harmonize what we want with what is best for us.

We are not left to struggle alone when we pray. We are joined by the Holy Spirit, who prays beside us. Through the Spirit's ministry our most hesitating prayers are made powerful and effective.

Prayer brings us the gift of God's peace. When we pray we place all those things which trouble us in God's hand. In prayer we reaffirm our conviction that God truly is sovereign. And when we pray God our Father lifts our burdens from our shoulders and takes responsibility for our welfare.

While prayer is always seen in Scripture as being effective objectively—in that God can and does act in this world in response to our prayers—the psalms and verses like Philippians 4:5, 6 also remind us that prayer has great

subjective benefits. When we submit our requests to God, our Heavenly Father replaces anxiety with a peace which passes all understanding.

Prayer gives us access to God's wisdom. God invites us to come to Him whenever we are uncertain about what to do and promises us the wisdom we need to make the right decision. This promise, recorded in the first chapter of James, contains an important caveat. When we look to God for direction, we must be willing to do as He directs. That ready submission to God's will is a precondition to receiving guidance from the Lord.

As oxygen is to the body, so prayer is to faith. Prayer is the very air which faith breathes, sustaining faith's life.

LESSONS FROM PRAYERS RECORDED IN THE EPISTLES

Found primarily in Paul's letters, these prayers are motivated by the great apostle's love for others, especially for those in the churches he himself founded. Strikingly, these recorded prayers all reveal a deep concern for spiritual growth and well-being. Paul's great desire is to see young Christians mature in their faith and experience all that life in Christ can provide.

These prayers in Scripture stand in rather stark contrast to the prayers most of us hear in church or offer for our own loved ones. Our prayers tend to focus on healing for the sick, jobs for the unemployed, protection for travelers, and salvation for friends. Surely we should pray such prayers. But the apostle's prayers remind us that what is truly important is the spiritual growth of our loved ones—that God's priority is for each believer to become all he or she can be in Christ.

Just as the psalms serve as a model for personal prayers, so the recorded prayers in the Epistles are a wonderful model for our intercessory prayers for others.

LESSONS FROM THE BOOK OF REVELATION

It may be difficult to interpret the details of the book of Revelation, but its theme is bold and clear. God is sovereign, and history is moving toward His intended end. The ultimate triumph of God and of good is sure, and heaven and earth will echo then with God's praises.

While notes of praise and thanksgiving are sounded throughout Scripture, they swell to a crescendo in this last book of the Bible. When the present heaven and earth pass away, to be replaced by God's new creation, we and all in glory will fill the renewed universe with endless praise.

Revelation reminds us that praise is the highest and the ultimate form of prayer. Whenever we approach God, it is appropriate to make our requests with thanksgiving, with our hearts filled with praise for the loving and glorious God to whom we come.

SO, HOW SHALL WE THEN PRAY?

We will pray as to an all-powerful Creator, on whose unlimited power we constantly depend. We will pray to a loving God, whose fatherliness moves Him to give only good gifts to His children.

We will pray freely, spontaneously, simply talking to God in ordinary language about our lives each day. And we will set aside time for concentrated, thoughtful communication with God, reflecting deeply on who He is and the full meaning of our relationship with His Son Jesus Christ.

In all, we will pray with full confidence in God's love, identifying the content and motivation of our prayers with Jesus, eager to ask in His name those things which will glorify Him. And we will pray thankfully, joyously submitting ourselves to His will, and praising Him that His will for us is perfect and good.

EXPOSITORY INDEX

An expository index organizes information by topic and guides the reader to Bible verses and book pages which are critical to understanding the subject. It does not list every verse referred to in the book, but seeks to identify key verses. It does not list every mention of a topic in the book, but directs the reader to pages where a topic is discussed in some depth. Thus an expository index helps the reader avoid the frustration of looking up verses in the Bible or the book, only to discover that they contribute in only a small way to one's understanding of the subject.

This expository index organizes references to prayers and petitions by topic. Topics and subtopics are identified in the left-hand column. Key Bible verses and passages are listed in the center column under "Scriptures." The far right column identifies pages in this book where the topic is covered.

In most instances, several of the key verses in the "Scriptures" column will be discussed on the book pages referred to. Very often additional verses will be referred to on the pages where the topic is covered. Our goal is to help you keep in focus the critical Bible verses and passages. Similarly, the book pages referred to are only those which make a significant contribution to understanding a topic, not every page on which a topic may be mentioned.

Please note that material under sub-topics is sometimes organized chronologically by the sequence of appearance in Scripture, and sometimes alphabetically, depending upon which organization will be most helpful in understanding and locating information.

OCCASIONS OF PERSONAL PRAYERS:

Psalms

TOPIC	SCRIPTURES	PAGE(S)
Obedience	Ps. 57	93–94
Praise	Ps. 9	85–86
Restoration	Ps. 80	97–98
Stress	Ps. 55	91–92
Suffering	Ps. 22	88
Suffering	Ps. 69	96–99
Testimony	Ps. 31	88–89
Thanksgiving	Ps. 18	86–87
Trust	Ps. 5	84
War	Ps. 20	87–88

PUZZLING ANSWERS TO PRAYER

A demon's prayer answered	Luke 8:32; Mark 5	173
Demonized man's refused	Luke 8:38–39; Mark 5	175

TEACHINGS ON PRAYER: EPISTLES

Anxiety and peace	Phil. 4:6, 7	219
Christ's prayer for us	Heb. 7:25	223
Commitment and prayer	Jude 20, 21	229
Confidence in prayer	1 John 5:14, 15	229
Constant prayer	1 Thess. 5:17	220
Constant prayer	Col. 4:2	220
Constant prayer	Eph. 6:18	218
Holy Spirit participation	Rom. 8:26, 27	215
Marriage and prayer	1 Cor. 7:5	215
Marriage and prayer	1 Pet. 3:7	228
Obedience and prayer	1 John 3:22	228
Oppressed, prayers of	James 5:3–8	226
Rulers, prayer for	1 Tim. 2:1, 2, 8	220
Sanctification and prayer	1 Tim. 4:4, 5	222
Sick, prayer for	James 5:13–18	226
Tongues and prayer	1 Cor. 14	217
Wisdom and prayer	James 1:5–7	223
Women and prayer	1 Cor. 11:4, 5, 13	216

TEMPTATION AND PRAYER | Matt. 6:13 | 140–41 |

TONGUES AND PRAYER | 1 Cor. 14 | 217 |

UNANSWERED PRAYERS

Of demonized man	Luke 8:38–39; Mark 5	175
Of distraught mother	Matt. 15:22–26; Mark 7:24–28	177
Of James and John	Matt. 20:22–23	178–79
Of Peter	Luke 5:4–10	176
Reasons for	James 4:2, 3	225

WEAKNESS AND PRAYER | Matt. 26:41; Mark 14:32–42 | 154 |

WOMEN AND PRAYER | 1 Cor. 11:4, 5, 13 | 216 |

❖ SCRIPTURE INDEX

(Bible references are in boldface type, followed by the pages on which they appear in this book.)

❖

THE "EVERYTHING IN THE BIBLE" REFERENCE SERIES

Every Covenant and Promise in the Bible. From the Old Testament covenants God made with Noah, Abraham, Moses, and David through the promises that still apply to our lives, this volume helps you develop a new appreciation for God's dependability and the power God's promises can afford to believers today. (Available)

Every Good and Evil Angel in the Bible. The Bible leaves no question about the reality of angels, even though humankind has not always been clear on their nature and function. This volume takes a thorough look at every mention of angels in the Bible—both those working for God and those working against Him. It also looks at the place of angels in the lives of contemporary believers. (Available)

Every Miracle and Wonder in the Bible. A God who created all that is certainly is capable of working miracles. Beginning with the miracle of Creation, this volume reviews God's wondrous works in dealing with His people. Major emphasis is given to the special evidences of God's activity in the Exodus, the ministries of Elijah and Elisha, and the ministry of Jesus. (Available)

Every Prayer and Petition in the Bible. The Bible is filled with evidences of prayers offered to God—some intensely private and others joyously public. Individuals are seen coming to Him with their requests and their complaints, their confessions and their praises. Three chapters look at the powerful prayers in the Psalms. Four chapters focus on Jesus' teachings about and practice of prayer. (Available)

Every Woman in the Bible (Available Spring 1999)

Coming soon

Every Man in the Bible

Every Name and Title of God in the Bible

Other titles are being planned.